EXPERIENCES IN MANAGEMENT AND ORGANIZATIONAL BEHAVIOR

WILEY SERIES IN ORGANIZATIONAL BEHAVIOR

EXPERIENCES IN MANAGEMENT AND ORGANIZATIONAL BEHAVIOR

THIRD EDITION

Roy J. Lewicki
The Ohio State University

Donald D. Bowen
The University of Tulsa

Douglas T. Hall
Boston University

Francine S. Hall
University of New Hampshire

WILEY

JOHN WILEY & SONS
New York   Chichester   Brisbane   Toronto   Singapore

Library of Congress Cataloging in Publication Data:

Experiences in management and organizational behavior

   (Wiley series in management, ISSN 0271-6046)
   Instructor's manual available.
   Includes bibliographies and index.
   1. Management—Problems, exercises, etc.
2. Organizational behavior—Problems, exercises, etc.
I. Lewicki, Roy J.   II. Series

HD30.413.E95 1988   658.4   87-25353
ISBN 0-471-83796-2 (pbk.)

Printed and bound in the United States of America by Braun-Brumfield, Inc.

10 9 8

PREFACE

Welcome to the third edition! Needless to say, as authors, we are delighted that this book has survived more than two editions and 12 years of heavy and consistent use by faculty and students. We believe it has truly become a "standard" resource book in the Organizational Behavior field, and we thank all of you who have helped to make it that way!

For those of you who are students, we hope that you enjoy and benefit from the questionnaires, role plays, simulations, games, and readings that make up this book. We have designed them to be easy to use and to understand, and yet to make strong and clear points about important principles in managerial psychology, organizational behavior, and human resource management. We hope that these resource materials make your course more interesting and relevant by bringing the academic issues to life in the classroom.

For faculty, we wish to thank you for your continued support of this book through consistent use and adoption. While there is persistent rumor that this book wins the award for the "most photocopied" (even *we* have done it at times), many of you have valued the materials sufficiently to adopt the book for courses, seminars, and educational programs. Without that support, we would not be into the third edition. We hope you find this new edition full of exciting and useful educational materials.

This third edition reflects a number of changes and improvements. We surveyed many previous users of the book, asking them what they liked, disliked, and wanted added or changed. We have tried to be responsive to those concerns while keeping the total number of exercises constant. Every exercise has been reviewed and updated. Eleven exercises are entirely new: Persuasive Interviewing (14), Creative Problem Solving (18), Campus Travel Agency (19), Third Party Conflict Resolution (21), My Best Boss (25), Delegation (26), Strategies for Taking Charge (27), Alien Invasion (31), The Power Game (32), Power in Management (34), and Model I and Model II Styles of Management (37). Many others have undergone extensive modification: Learning and Problem Solving (2), Expectancy Theory (3), What Do We Value in Work (5), Group Ranking Task (15), Competitive Escalation (17) and Managing Role Conflict

(48). *An accompanying Instructor's Manual, available from John Wiley, has also been totally revised.* However, even continuous revision and copy editing does not always produce a perfect collection of materials. If you have problems or concerns about any of the activities in this volume and wish to communicate with us, please write to us at our universities (listed on the title page) or to the editorial offices of John Wiley & Sons.

Any venture of this nature requires a number of "thank yous." First, we would like to thank the previous users of this book who responded to our questionnaires and told us which exercises should be dropped, added, or changed for this Third Edition.

We would like to acknowledge those colleagues who participated in this exercise:

Jeanne McGuire	University of Massachusetts
David Alexander	East Central University
Frederick Hauser, Ph.D.	Pace University
Sam Rabinowitz	Rutgers University
Magid Mazen	Illinois State University
Donald D. Bowen	University of Tulsa
Karyll Shaw	Illinois State University
Robert Eisenberger	University of Delaware
William Enslin	Glassboro State College
John Ogilvie	University of Delaware
Blake Ashforth	Wayne State University
J. M. Larsen, Jr.	University of Tennessee
Peter Allen	Ft. Lee, New Jersey

Second, we wish to thank again those colleagues who have permitted us to use or modify their classroom activities for this volume. While we have acknowledged each of them directly on the title page of each exercise, we want to thank them as a group for sharing their innovations so that we might all benefit.

We also wish to thank John Wiley and Sons for their continued support and assistance, particularly our editor, Cheryl Mehalik. Working with one author, no less four, is no easy business, and Cheryl has been extremely patient and helpful in translating this edition from concept to reality (particularly over lunch on Malibu Beach).

Finally, we want to thank Becky Gregory for her outstanding efforts in pulling these exercises together, keeping track of numerous revisions and corrections, tirelessly pasting, copying, and proofreading, and her most important ongoing task, humoring the whims of the first author. Without her perseverance, we would never have seen this project through to completion.

Roy J. Lewicki
Donald D. Bowen
Douglas T. Hall
Francine S. Hall

CONTENTS

PART IV **CHANGE**

SECTION 12 **PLANNED CHANGE**

SECTION 13 **LIFE, WORK, AND CAREER ROLES**

FOLIO OF RESOURCES
READINGS AND ASSESSMENT TECHNIQUES

APPENDIX
INDEX FOR ROLE PLAY POSITIONS

PART I
INDIVIDUALS

SECTION ONE
ICEBREAKERS

1
CONCERNS, EXPECTATIONS, AND RESOURCES

PURPOSE:
(1) To help a group of strangers get acquainted quickly.
(2) To assess the initial concerns, expectations, and resources of the group.

ADVANCE PREPARATION: None.
GROUP SIZE: Up to 60; 35 or fewer is probably optimal.
TIME REQUIRED: Varies, depending on the size of the group. The following are estimates: 18 to 25 participants: 55 minutes; 26 to 40 participants: 60 minutes; 41 to 65 participants: 70 minutes.
SPECIAL MATERIALS: Felt-tip pens, masking tape, sheets of newsprint.
SPECIAL PHYSICAL REQUIREMENTS: Movable furniture so that small groups can converse comfortably.

PROCEDURE

Step 1: 5 Minutes
Form groups of six to eight persons. Choose people you know *least well*.

Step 2: 20 Minutes
Obtain a felt-tip pen and newsprint. Meet and prepare a set of three lists as a group:

Expectations. What are your expectations for this course or program? What do you hope to get from it?

Concerns. Do you have any concerns or worries about this course or program?

This version of a widely used icebreaker was developed for this volume by Donald D. Bowen.

Resources. What talents, skills, background, or experiences do the members of your group have that could be used to enrich the learning of the people in this class or program?

It is not necessary for a concern or expectation be shared by everyone in the group. Put it on your list if it sounds important. Do *not* put names on the lists!

Appoint one person spokesperson for your group and tape your list to the wall of the room.

Step 3: 3 Minutes per Group
Each spokesperson presents her group's lists. Questions are permitted *for clarification, only* at this point.

Step 4: 20 Minutes
Group leader responds to the issues raised on the lists. Participants and leader discuss.

DISCUSSION QUESTIONS

1. Are your expectations for this course or program different now than they were before the exercise? How?
2. In what ways might participant expectations become "self-fulfilling prophecies"? (A "self-fulfilling prophecy" is when expectations that something will happen actually make it happen. For example, a person who is always looking for a fight can usually succeed in starting one.)
3. What must *you* do to ensure that your expectations are met?
4. What did you learn about yourself or others during the group meeting?
   a. Were people relatively open or closed? Why?
   b. Did some people dominate the conversation? How did the others feel about this (and how do you know that was what they were feeling)?
   c. Whose ideas got included or excluded from the list? Why did this happen?
   d. Do you feel that the list your group produced really represents the concerns and expectations of your group? Why?

Participant's Reactions

2
LEARNING AND PROBLEM SOLVING: YOU'RE NEVER TOO JUNG!

PURPOSE:
(1) To focus your attention on your own learning and problem-solving style.
(2) *Option one:* To explore the compatibility between your preferred learning style and the types of learning experience you will encounter in this course.
(3) *Option two:* To explore some implications of learning and problem-solving styles for organizational behavior.

ADVANCE PREPARATION:
(1) Read "Cognitive Style in Learning and Problem Solving" in the Folio of Resources in the back of this book.
(2) Read the Introduction to this book.
(3) Complete Step 1 in the procedure, below.

GROUP SIZE: *Option one:* Single, large discussion group. *Option two:* break the larger group into four learning/problem-solving "type" subgroups. If groups exceed eight or nine people, subdivide the groups to make more than one group for each type.

TIME REQUIRED: *Option one:* 30 minutes. *Option two:* 2 hours.

SPECIAL MATERIALS: None.

SPECIAL PHYSICAL REQUIREMENTS: Large room for entire group to meet. For Option two, subgroups need to meet for private discussions—small group meeting rooms or movable furniture and space enough to separate subgroups for private discussions will be helpful.

RELATED TOPICS: Planned change, Negotiation and conflict, Applied motivation and job design, Interpersonal communication, Managers as leaders.

PROCEDURE

BOTH OPTIONS

Step 1: 5 Minutes
The following brief descriptions of the types may help you to decide which pattern is most typical of you.

INFORMATION GATHERING DIMENSION

S (SENSING) TYPE	N (INTUITIVE) TYPE
>Attend to experience as it is.	>Interested in the meanings of facts and how they fit together.

Developed by Donald D. Bowen.

>Likes to use eyes and ears and other senses to find out what is happening.

>Dislikes new problems unless there are standard ways to solve them.

>Enjoys using skills already learned more than learning.

>Is patient with details, but impatient when the details get complicated.

>Often described as patient, precise, plodding, unimaginative, practical, systematic, shortsighted.

>Likes to use imagination to come up with new ways to do things, new possibilities.

>Welcomes new problems; dislikes routine.

>Likes using new skills more than practicing old ones.

>Is impatient with details, but doesn't mind complicated situations.

>Often described as impatient, creative, imaginative, erratic, inventive, one who jumps to conclusions.

INFORMATION PROCESSING DIMENSION

T (THINKING) TYPE

>Likes to decide things logically.

>Wants to be treated with justice and fair play.

>May neglect or hurt other people's feelings without knowing it.

>Gives more attention to ideas or things than to human relationships.

>Doesn't need harmony.

>Often described as analytical, impersonal, unemotional, objective, critical, "hard-nosed," rational.

F (FEELING) TYPE

>Likes to decide things with personal feelings and human values, even if they aren't logical.

>Likes praise, and likes to please people, even in unimportant things.

>Is aware of other people's feelings.

>Can predict how others will feel.

>Gets upset by arguments and conflicts; values harmony.

>Often described as sympathetic, people-oriented, unorganized, uncritical, understanding, ethical.

Obviously few of us are pure examples of a particular type, so it may help to think of each type as representing one end of a continuum divided into six equal steps (see Figure 1).

1. Rate *yourself* by putting an "X" on the locator that indicates how you see your learning/problem-solving style. Where would you place yourself on the *information-gathering* dimension? If you see yourself as primarily a "sensor," you will probably wish to place your "X" in column 1 or 2. If you are primarily an "intuitor," you might want to place your "X" in column 5 or 6. Columns 3 and 4 are for people who see themselves using both styles about equally. On the vertical or *information-processing* dimension, if you see yourself as essentially a "thinker," you probably fall in row 1 or 2, while "feeling" types are indicated in rows 5 and 6. (You may find this tough to do. "I'm a little of both poles," you might say. Jung foresaw this problem. He said that each of us has a "shadow self," a "weaker" style composed of the opposites to our predominant modes,

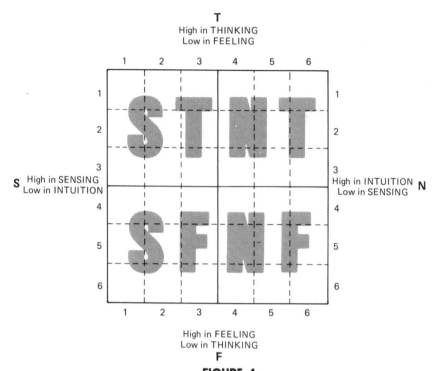

FIGURE 1

Learning and Problem Solving Type Locator

that may take over in times of stress, conflict, and the like. Rate yourself according to what you see your *predominant* style to be.)

2. Now think of the person you would *like to be*. Put a "B" in one of the cells of the Locator to indicate where your *ideal* self would be.

3. Now think of the *most effective manager* you have ever seen. Put an "M" on the Locator where you think this manager would fall. When you have finished your ratings, the group leader will instruct you to follow Option one or Option two.

OPTION ONE

25 minutes: Discuss the learning and problem-solving types in terms of the following questions:

1. Where would you guess most of the people in this program or class placed their "X" on the Locator? Their "B" (for the person they would like to become)? Why?

2. Survey the members of the class. How many are of each type? How many SFs? STs? and so on. Do students with different majors (e.g. accounting, engineering, liberal arts, marketing, etc.) tend to be similar to people with the same major? Different from those with different majors? Do the people with a particular major seem to be the "right" type for that major? Why?

3. Where do you think most people placed the "effective manager"? Why? Is an effective manager more likely to be of one type rather than another?
4. Do you think there would be any significant differences in how males and females would rate their present styles, their ideal styles, or their perceptions of an effective manager? Why?
5. What kind of person learns best from exercises such as those in this book? Why?
6. What can you do to learn to use your less preferred style of data gathering and information processing more effectively?

OPTION TWO

Step 2: 5 Minutes

Form learning/problem-solving "type" groups as directed by the group leader. This should create at least one group for each of the following types:

STs   NTs
SFs   NFs

Which group you belong to depends on your self-perception—where your "X" was placed on the locator.

Step 3: 40 Minutes

Each group now meets to perform one of two tasks (the group leader will indicate 1 or 2):

1. Design a management development program for the people in the "opposite" group, that is: STs design for NFs, and vice versa.
   SFs design for NTs, and vice versa.

2. Develop a statement about the leadership style that should be used with people in the group "opposite" to you to maximize their effectiveness. What kind of a leader would be most successful with them, given their problem-solving style?

Appoint one member of the group to act as *spokesperson* for the group. Prepare a presentation covering the following major points:

a. What is the *objective* of the suggested measures your group is proposing?
b. What *specific action* should be taken? (List four actions).
c. What is the *rationale,* the reasoning behind the proposed actions your group is suggesting?

Step 4: 20 Minutes

Meet with your "opposite" group. Take turns presenting your proposal (your management development program or proposed leadership approach) to the other group (5 minutes for your proposal and 5 minutes for answering questions—have someone keep time).

Step 5: 5 Minutes

Meet again with just the group of your own type (the people you met with in Step 3). Quickly decide whether you would recommend the proposal that has been made to you for adoption by management (*and* why).

Step 6: 3 Minutes per Group

When called upon by the group leader, the group spokesperson very briefly reports the group's proposal (objective, actions, and rationales). When the spokesperson has finished, the spokesperson for the "opposite" group reports the outcome of the group's decision to accept or reject the proposal, and why.

Step 7: 20 Minutes

Discuss the results of the exercise and their implications for organizational behavior in terms of the Discussion Questions.

DISCUSSION QUESTIONS

Discussion questions for Option one appear within the exercise. The following apply to Option two:

1. What did the different groups do when they designed for their "opposite" types? How did the opposite types feel about this?
2. Was there any evidence, in either the content or the style of the presentation, that people were properly classified?
3. How many people think they would *benefit* from the management development program or leadership style proposed by their opposite group? How many would *enjoy* the experience? Why?

GENERALIZATIONS AND CONCLUSIONS

Concluding Points

1. Is there a best learning/problem-solving style? Why?

2. How might the learning/problem-solving styles relate to problems that may arise in communication between people from different parts of the organization?

Participant's Reactions

READINGS AND REFERENCES

Kolb, D. A., "Four Styles of Managerial Learning." In D. A. Kolb, I. M. Rubin, and J. M. McIntyre (Eds.), *Organizational Psychology: A Book of Readings,* 2nd ed. (Englewood Cliffs, N.J.: Prentice-Hall, 1974), pp. 27–34.

Mann, H., Siegler, M., and Osmond, H. "Four Types of Personalities and Four Ways of Perceiving Time," *Psychology Today,* December (1972), 76–77, 79–80, 82, 84.

Mitroff, I. I., and Kilmann, R. H., "Stories Managers Tell: A New Tool for Organizational Problem Solving," *Management Review,* July (1975), 18–28.

SECTION TWO
MOTIVATION: BASIC CONCEPTS

3
EXPECTANCY THEORY: A PERSONAL APPLICATION

PURPOSE:
To demonstrate the application of expectancy theory to one's own decisions.

ADVANCE PREPARATION: Read text material or lecture notes on the expectancy theory of motivation.
GROUP SIZE: Any size.
TIME REQUIRED: 45 minutes.
SPECIAL MATERIALS: None.
SPECIAL PHYSICAL REQUIREMENTS: None.
RELATED TOPICS: Decision making, Life, work, and career roles.

INTRODUCTION

The expectancy theory of motivation is a theory of how people make choices between alternative courses of action. It is similar to rational economic theory in that it assumes people, when faced with the need to make a decision about how to behave, will be influenced by the possible costs and benefits of each course of action. Individuals will select the course of action with the greatest perceived expected net (positive minus negative) outcomes.

However, the attractiveness (valence) of the outcomes is not the only factor that affects the person's behavior. The perceived probability (expectancy) that a given outcome will in fact occur is also important. For example, if I buy a ticket for the

Developed by Douglas T. Hall. The helpful comments of Lloyd Baird and Max Bazerman on an earlier version are greatly appreciated.

state lottery, one possible outcome would be winning $1 million. This outcome has rather high valence for me. On the other hand, the probability of winning this amount is extremely low, so low that my overall motivation to buy a lottery ticket is near zero. And there would be negative outcomes associated with buying a ticket, such as spending money on the ticket or walking to the store. This explains why I have never bought a lottery ticket.

The strength of a person's motivation to choose a given course of action, then, is a function of the sum of both the valence of the outcomes that might result from that course of action, multiplied by the expectancies of these outcomes occurring.

$$\text{MF}_i = f_i \sum_{j=1}^{n} (E_{ij} V_j)$$

where

MF_i = motivational force to perform act i

Σ means summation

E_{ij} = the strength of the expectancy (a probability between 0 and 1) that act i will be followed by outcome j

V_i = the valence of outcome j

If you have taken a mathematics course, this equation may look familiar to you. Expectancy theory essentially says that people attempt to maximize subjective expected utility (which is the same as what mathematical decision theory tells us).

The following material (reprinted from *The Two Career Couple*[1]) may be of help in illustrating further how expectancy theory might be used in important decision making. It also shows how expectancies might be changed. The decision in question involves a job offer which would require geographic relocation.

> *Refusing an attractive job offer is a difficult step to take. It is also pretty permanent. Three months after you've turned a corporation down, you usually can't go back and tell them you've changed your mind (although it certainly has been done). So, it's important that you're as certain as you can be when you make that decision.*
>
> *We've prepared an "expectancy table" to help you consider all the possible consequences associated with a "yes" or a "no" decision. For each consequence, we assign a probability that it will actually happen. In other words, we try to guess the likelihood that a given choice will result in certain outcomes. We also assign a value to each outcome and multiply the probability by this value. After we have done this for each alternative, we compare the total expectancy values for the different alternatives or choices. Since there are usually "pluses" and "minuses" associated with each choice, we can compare how they add up. It is simply a way of systematically weighing the different costs and benefits associated with relocation. Let's look more closely at how it actually works.*

[1] F. S. Hall and D. T. Hall, *The Two Career Couple* (Reading, MA: Addison-Wesley, 1979), pp. 194–197. Reprinted by permission.

TABLE 1
Expectancy Tables for a Job-Transfer Decision

Choice 1: If I accept the transfer . . .

Outcome	Value	× Probability	= Expectancy
We will live in an urban area.	−3	1.0	−3.0
I will have a better job.	+5	1.0	+5.0
Poor neighborhood schools.	−4	0.5	−2.0
Spouse will have job.	+5	0.2	+1.0
Total:			+1.0

Choice 2: If I turn down the transfer . . .

Outcome	Value	× Probability	= Expectancy
We will live in a suburban area.	+3	1.0	+3.0
I will have a better job eventually.	+5	0.4	+2.0
Good schools for the kids.	+4	0.9	+3.6
Spouse will have guaranteed job.	+5	1.0	+5.0
Total:			+13.6

First, we identify all of the possible outcomes or factors that are important considerations in our decision. When we have these listed, we are in a position to assess the alternatives or choices in terms of the probability that a particular choice will, in fact, result in or lead to a particular outcome. The probability can range from 0 to +1.

When doing this, you should list as many considerations as possible. These should reflect all the issues that are important in your careers, your personal lives, and your family relationships. In addition to listing possible outcomes, it is also necessary to assign weights or values to each possible outcome. These may range from a high value of +5 to a low value of −5.

For example, three of your considerations may be: the job, the location, and schools for your children. While all three may be important to you, the possible outcomes associated with various choices on these three dimensions may be different and have different values for you. The job and schools, for examples, may carry more positive value under one choice than the location does. Thus, your expectancy table should include the value you attach to the potential outcomes for that alternative or choice. The basic format looks like Table 1.

While you aren't sure about the chances of your spouse getting a job, they look pretty low. Now let's look at the expectancy table for another choice—turning down the transfer (see the bottom half of Table 1).

When you compare the two choices in terms of possible outcomes, the second alternative (turning down the transfer) has a much higher total expectancy of resulting in positively valued outcomes. But what are the trade-offs? Clearly, accepting the transfer will result in a better job for you (which you value). To achieve 'this right now, however, means living with several negative outcomes. There is certainty that you will live in a negatively valued area, a fifty-fifty chance that schools for the kids will be poor (also a negatively valued outcome), and very little chance that your spouse will have a guaranteed job (also important to you). So, to gain a better job for yourself, your spouse and family will have to make some sacrifices.

The second alternative means that you forego the certainty of a better job now, with some probability of getting one eventually. At the same time, you increase the expectancy that you will have good schools, a good location, and a job for your spouse.

As you have probably realized by now, preparing an expectancy table is a bit of a guessing game. It is like betting, in a sense. One never knows for sure what the real probabilities are. It does raise an important question: Can you do anything to increase the probability that a positively valued outcome will result or to decrease the probability that a negatively valued choice will result? In other words, once you have an initial expectancy table, can you manipulate the likelihood of certain outcomes? The answer is yes—or at least you can try.

Look again, for example, at the two sample tables. Now ask yourself: What can I do (or what would I have to do) to increase the positive total expectancy associated with choice 1—the transfer? This is clearly the choice you want because it guarantees you the best job. To make it worthwhile for everyone else, however, you would have to manipulate location, schools, and your spouse's chances of getting a job. Is it possible to live in the suburbs, commute, and find a good school? Are private schools a possibility? Now try the expectancy table again, this time listing these different outcomes. What values do you attach to them and how do they work out? (Table 2 shows the revised values for choice #1.)

Clearly, the positive expectancy of this choice is now approaching the expectancy associated with staying where you are. And, there are really two unknowns. The probability you assign to your spouse having a job is questionable. If you could be sure that he or she would find a job, then the positively valued outcomes associated with the move would clearly indicate that it is a good choice. Of course, to have

TABLE 2
The Revised Job Transfer Decision

Choice 1 (Revised): If I accept the transfer ...

Outcome	Value	× Probability	= Expectancy
We can live in the suburbs.	$+3$	1.0	$+3.0$
I will have to commute.	$-2(?)$	1.0	-2.0 (need info)
I will have a better job.	$+5$	1.0	$+5.0$
Good schools for the kids.	$+4$	0.9	$+3.6$
Spouse will have a job.	$+5$	0.2	$+1.0$ (need info)
Total:			$+10.6$

the better job, you will have to commute if your family is going to continue to live in a suburban area. You are not sure how you value that (probably negatively).

At this point, it is usually helpful to get more information. The probability of getting a job for your spouse may be greater than you think. Commuting may be better or worse than you think. If there is a suburb with good train service into the city, it could turn out to be a plus factor—time to read and relax each day. If you have to battle traffic for two hours a day, it may be too high a price to pay for the job.

While the expectancy table doesn't make a decision for you, it is a good way to sort out all the issues associated with decision and to assess how important they are to you as a couple. It also helps you to zero in on those variable factors that you may be able to do something about. Often we accept certain outcomes as givens, when, in fact, they are things we can change. As our example shows, location and schools may be more flexible dimensions of a move than you initially assume. Similarly, your spouse's job may be something you can explore (and secure) before committing yourself.

Increasingly, employers are coming to terms with the special problems of the two-career couple. Companies are realizing that they have to help if they want to recruit or develop good people. Not long ago, while sitting in the J. Walter Thompson agency in Chicago, one of us overheard a conversation about job hunting for the wife of a new recruit. When asked about it, the person admitted that the way the agency people were able to recruit the man was by going out of their way to help his wife get a job. For the couple, this means that expectancies can often be increased by open negotiations with employers.

PROCEDURE

OPTION 1

Step 1: 15 Minutes

Think of a decision that you are in the process of making. You could be at any stage in the decision process. You could be just starting to think about it, as in the case of thinking about job choices when the recruiting season is still a couple of months away. You could be right in the middle of it; perhaps you have three job offers, and you have to decide by next week. Or, you could have just made a decision, but you're not totally comfortable that you have made the right choice, and you'd like to think it through a bit more. The decision could be about anything: what to major in, whether to get married, where to live, whether to change jobs, or what movie to see tonight.

The main thing is to think of a decision that is important and a "live issue" for you right now. However, don't pick one that is so personal that you would feel uncomfortable discussing it with someone in this course.

1. List all the possible courses of action that you are considering. Record them on Table 1. (Use additional paper if you need more space.)

TABLE 1
Expectancy Analysis for Decisions

Course of Action	Possible Outcomes	Valences (−10 to +10)	Expectancies (0 to 1.0)	E × V	Sum of E × V

Note: Use additional paper if more space is needed.

2. For each alternative course of action, try to think of the important things that could happen as a result of choosing that action. List them in the second column from the left, "Possible Outcomes." (Don't forget to include negative outcomes, as well as positive ones.)

3. Think of how attractive or unattractive each of these outcomes would be to you. Use a scale from -10 to $+10$ to rate the valence of each outcome. List the valences in the third column from the left. (A valence of -10 would be the most unpleasant, objectionable outcome you could think of; a valence of 0 would be for an outcome about which you are completely indifferent. A valence of $+10$ would describe an outcome that would be one of the best things that could ever happen to you.)

4. Think of what the probabilities or expectancies are that each of these outcomes might occur if you chose that particular course of action. Rate these probabilities from 0 (a probability indicating you are certain it will not happen) to 1.0 (which would indicate you are certain it would happen); use tenths (e.g., .2, .5, .7) to indicate values between 0 and 1.0. Enter these probabilities or expectancies in the fourth column from the left.

5. Multiply each valence score by the expectancy score next to it. Enter these products in the column labeled, $E \times V$.

6. For each course of action, add up all the products of $E \times V$. Enter each sum in the spaces in the far right-hand column of Table 1.

Step 2: Dyad Exercise, 20 Minutes

Get together with another person in the class whose opinion you respect. Spend 10 minutes discussing each person's expectancy table. When your partner's decision is being discussed, your objective is to be as helpful as possible to your partner as he or she describes the options being considered and the valences and expectancies involved. *How realistic* are the expectancies? What about the *"gut factor"* (what alternative does the person prefer in his or her "gut")?

At the end of your partner's 10 minutes, ask, "If you had to make a decision *right now*, what would it be?" This gives an idea of which way the person is "leaning." How does this choice compare with the alternative that has the highest expectancy analysis total? How does this choice compare with the "gut" preference? How does the "gut" preference compare with the expectancy total?

After spending 10 minutes on one partner's expectancy table, switch roles and discuss the other partner's table. Consider the same questions mentioned above.

Step 3: Class Discussion, 10 Minutes

Discuss the overall results of the various dyads' experiences. Use the Discussion Questions listed below.

PROCEDURE

OPTION 2

Step 1: Group Problem Solving, 15 Minutes
Read the following short passage describing two types of expectancy:

> *Expectancy 1* (*E 1*) is the likelihood that a given behavior or level of effort will result in a first-level outcome, such as task accomplishment or performance. When the first-level outcome sought is good performance, E 1 often involves a question of skill or training.
>
> *Expectancy 2* (*E 2*) is the likelihood that a given first-level outcome will lead to a second-level outcome, such as task accomplishment or performance resulting in a reward. E 2 is thus often a characteristic of the organization's reward system, a quality of the environment, whereas E 1 is a quality of the individual.

Next, meet in groups of five to seven people. Read the following short cases. For each case, based on expectancy theory, decide on the best alternative course of action from those given.

MOTIVATION: THREE CASES

For each of the following cases, determine whether the individuals will be motivated to behave as desired. Then select the appropriate managerial action from those listed.

Case One
Frank Edwards is head basketball coach at a small regional state university, a campus of the state's main university system. He has just had a visit with Walter Johnson, a local high school athlete who is clearly one of the state's blue-chip basketball prospects. Frank desperately needs a player of Walter's potential to turn his mediocre team around, but he realizes that it won't be easy to sign him. He is confident he made it clear to Walter that there is a scholarship available for Walter if he wants it. He also knows Walter needs a scholarship to be able to go to college. However, an article in the newspaper's Sunday sports section reports that two of the major state university coaches (larger schools upstate, with nationally-known basketball programs) intend to actively recruit Walter also. Coach Edwards should take which of the following actions:

a. Send Walter a written and notarized offer of the scholarship.
b. Write Walter's parents, stressing that the scholarship will cover all of his tuition, room and board, and book expenses.
c. Write a letter to Walter stressing to him the value of a college education.
d. Talk to Walter again, stressing the likelihood that he would make the starting five in his freshman year.
e. Do nothing. Walter will probably sign with him anyway.

Note: Option 2, including the following cases, was developed by Conrad Jackson and is used with his kind permission.

Case Two

Joyce, a recent College of Business graduate, has been working several months as a salesperson for a small manufacturer of computers and word processors. She is one of two salespeople working a large metropolitan area. Her sales manager, Eric Kurtz, is concerned about her performance, however. He is aware that Joyce wants very much to have high sales in order to participate in the company's generous incentive bonus plan. She has expressed her satisfaction with the way the plan operates and was clearly in agreement that there is a booming demand for computers and word processors in the market area. He is puzzled, therefore, by her poor performance. He should take which of the following actions.

    a. Post sales performance figures in the office so everyone can see how the salespersons are doing.
    b. Have a talk with Joyce, stressing the details of how she can benefit financially from increased sales.
    c. Tell Joyce that unless she begins to reach her quota within the next three months, she will be terminated from employment.
    d. Ask Joyce to accompany him on sales calls to several new customers.
    e. Do nothing. Her performance should soon be improving.

Case Three

Motumba is a small African nation with rich deposits of several rare metals. Tall, forbidding mountains to the north and west make it impossible to ship out ore in these directions. Kobutsu, the country bordering on their east has a modern deep-water port city, and an extensive rail network, which make it a logical alternative route for shipping out the ore. However, due to a long-running conflict between the heads of state of the two countries, Kobutsu has not allowed Motumban ore to be transported to and through it's port, and Motumba has been forced to settle for sending out small quantities through the neighboring country to the south via a long route of antiquated rail facilities. Recently, however, the government of Kobutsu changed, with a new head of state coming to power who had a reputation of being friendly toward Motumbans and cognizant of the potential benefits to Kobutsu of serving as a transportation route for their ore. As U.S. Department of State envoy to that area, your action should be:

    a. Meet with the Kobutsun head of State, stressing the potential benefits of being a transportation link for Motumban ore.
    b. Meet with the Motumban head of State and point out the opportunity present for a new constructive relationship with Kobutsu.
    c. Send a letter to the Kobutsun Minister of Commerce stressing the likelihood of being able to work out a trade agreement with Motumba.
    d. Invite both heads of state to the United States, and tell both of them the United States will cut off all economic aid to them if they do not begin to cooperate.
    e. Do nothing. They are likely to begin cooperating now anyway.

Step 2: Reporting Back, 20 Minutes

Have one spokesperson from each group report back to the total group. Give your answer for each case and the reasoning, (in expectancy theory terms). Does each case tend to center on one part of the expectancy model?

Step 3: Class Discussion, 15 Minutes

Discuss areas of agreement and disagreement between the groups' answers. In the discussion, try to clarify which part of the expectancy model you are focusing on.

DISCUSSION QUESTIONS

1. How difficult or easy was it to identify alternative courses of action, outcomes, valences, and expectancies? How rational do you think people are (or can be) in making personal decisions?
2. Based on your own experiences, how would you evaluate expectancy theory as a way of explaining motivation and decision making?
3. In what ways might a manager influence expectancies? Valences?

GENERALIZATIONS AND CONCLUSIONS

Concluding Points

1. Upon what assumptions does expectancy theory rest?

2. What is the status of expectancy theory, as indicated by research?

Participant's Reactions

READINGS AND REFERENCES

Lawler III, E. E., *Motivation in Work Organizations* (Monterey, Calif.: Brooks/Cole, 1973).

Lawler III, E. E., Nadler, D. A., and Cammann, C., *Organizational Assessment: Perspectives on the Measurement of Organizational Behavior and the Quality of Working Life* (New York: Wiley-Interscience, 1979).

Vroom, V., *Work and Motivation* (New York: Wiley, 1964).

Wanous, J. P., "Organizational Entry: Newcomers Moving from Outside to Inside." *Psychological Bulletin*, 84(1977), 601–618.

4
MONEY MOTIVATION DEBATE

PURPOSE:
(1) To examine the role of money in work motivation.
(2) To examine the importance of other factors in relation to money.
(3) To develop skills in using theory and research literature as a basis for successfully communicating a point of view (i.e., selling an opinion).
(4) To experience the dynamics of intergroup competition.

ADVANCE PREPARATION: Come to class prepared to discuss the role of money in motivation.
GROUP SIZE: Best for 10 to 30. Option for larger groups.
TIME REQUIRED: 55 minutes.
SPECIAL MATERIALS: None.
SPECIAL PHYSICAL REQUIREMENTS: None.
RELATED TOPICS: Organizational communication, Interpersonal communication, Intergroup issues and conflict, Group decision making and problem solving.

INTRODUCTION

The role of money as a motivator of work behavior has been widely debated in the literature on management and organizational behavior. Some theorists, such as Herzberg (1968), see money as a "dissatisfier," a factor whose absence can cause dissatisfaction but whose presence cannot cause high satisfaction or motivation. Other theorists, such as Lawler (1971), argue that money can provide both direct and symbolic gratification of human needs and can thus be a motivator if money rewards are linked to good performance. In this exercise you will be asked to think about motivation and to develop a convincing argument regarding the role of money in human work motivation.

PROCEDURE

Step 1: 20 Minutes

The class breaks into two halves, with three or four students withdrawing to act as judges. One-half of the class will prepare a debate, resolved that: *Money is a prime motivator of people in the workplace.* The other half prepares to argue that: *Money is not a prime motivator of people in the workplace.*

Each team appoints a discussion leader and spokesperson. They then prepare their

Originally developed by William H. Read. Adapted by Douglas T. Hall. Used with permission.

argument for *about 20 minutes*. During this time, the judging group decides on the criteria it will use.

Step 2: 15 Minutes

The class reassembles, and the arguments (point form) are presented. Post them in "shorthand" style on the board. Each group is allowed 5 minutes to make its presentation. Then the groups will have 5 minutes to prepare their rebuttals. Each group is given 1 minute for rebuttal. The judges act as timekeepers.

Step 3: 5 Minutes

The judges then meet in front of the rest of the participants and decide on the winner. In announcing their decision, they should state clearly why they decided as they did.

Step 4: 10 Minutes

Discussion and conclusion—summary of major points—see below.

DISCUSSION QUESTIONS

1. Without renewing the debate now that it is over, how many people think money *is* a key motivator of work behavior? How many think it is not?
2. Can a given study or theory support either side of this debate? If so, how? If not, why not?
3. How can management affect the *degree* to which money is a motivator?
4. If money is *not* available as a possible motivator (e.g., because of union contracts or seniority traditions), what could you do to motivate effective performance?
5. How many of you changed your minds as a result of the debate?

GENERALIZATIONS AND CONCLUSIONS

Concluding Points

1. In surveys of what people look for in work, does pay usually rank fairly high or fairly low?

2. According to March and Simon, employees make two kinds of decisions about an organization: the "decision to participate" (i.e., to join or remain in the organization) and the "decision to produce" (i.e., to perform well). Which of these two decisions is probably more strongly affected by pay?

3. Money is most likely to act as a motivator of good performance under what conditions?

Participant's Reactions

READINGS AND REFERENCES

Hammer, W. C., "How to Ruin Motivation with Pay," *Compensation Review* (1975).

Herzberg, F., "One More Time: How Do You Motivate Employees?" *Harvard Business Review,* 46 (1968), 53–62.

Lawler III, E. E., *Pay and Organizational Effectiveness: A Psychological View* (New York: McGraw-Hill, 1971).

5
WHAT DO WE VALUE IN WORK?

PURPOSE:
(1) To assess the priorities of work values for participants.
(2) To compare the work values of men and women.

ADVANCE PREPARATION: Fill out the questionnaire "What Do We Value in Work?" on page 25. Make a copy of your rankings to be turned in. Be sure to indicate whether you are female or male. You are not required to put your name on the copy you turn in; the data for the entire group will be tabulated anonymously.

GROUP SIZE: A single large group of up to 50 participants. Option two uses subgroups of 5 to 9 persons.

TIME REQUIRED: 45 minutes (add 5 minutes per group if Option two is followed).

SPECIAL MATERIALS: None.

SPECIAL PHYSICAL REQUIREMENTS: *Option one:* Single large room for all participants. *Option two:* Separate meeting rooms for discussion groups or a single large room where groups can hold discussions separately to the extent necessary to minimize disturbance.

RELATED TOPICS: Life, work, and career roles, Negotiation and conflict.

INTRODUCTION

What do people want to get out of their work? What values do they want to fulfill through work? In this exercise you will have an opportunity to think about your own priorities for what you want from work. You will also have a chance to look at data on the priorities of other people, and you will have an opportunity to compare your own reasons for continuing to work with the answers given by a survey of business students by Nicholas Beutell and O. C. Brenner (1986).

PROCEDURE

The group leader will designate Option one or Option two to be followed.

OPTION ONE

Step 1: 20 Minutes

The men in the group develop a consensual ranking of the items as they think the women in the sample ranked them. The women in the group *do not participate* in

Developed by Donald D. Bowen.

the ranking. (The women should take note of the primary issues raised while the men are making the rankings and comment on these in the discussion afterward.)

The instructor will lead the ranking process, tallying votes, suggestions, and so on, on a blackboard or easel. The ranking proceeds as follows:

1. The men nominate candidates from the list of nine work values for the value they believe women in general would rank first.
2. When all candidates have been identified, proponents of each candidate offer arguments as to why they think a particular value should be ranked first. When all arguments have been heard, a vote is taken by a show of hands. Items receiving the least votes are dropped from the list, and discussion is resumed. Votes are taken whenever the men indicate that they are ready. When one item finally receives a majority vote, it is ranked first.
3. Next, the group considers which item should be ranked *last*. The same procedure is followed until one of the remaining values receives a majority vote for last place. The group then works on the item to be ranked second, eighth, and so on, until all items have been ranked. When all items have been ranked, begin the discussion (see "Both Options," below).

OPTION TWO

Step 1: 20 Minutes

Form groups of five to nine persons. Each group should be composed entirely of men or women. Each group meets separately in a place designated by the instructor. Group meetings should last 15 minutes, and each group is to perform the following tasks:

1. Decide, as a group, which of the items was ranked number 1 by members of the opposite sex (from that of group members) in the Beutell and Brenner study.
2. Identify the main reasons why your group feels that each one of the other values was not the one ranked first.
3. Appoint a spokesperson to present the group's conclusions to the entire group. Rejoin the other members of the entire group at the end of the allotted 15 minutes for discussion.

Step 2: 5 Minutes per Group

Each group presents to the entire group its choice for number 1 and the reasons for rejecting the other values.

BOTH OPTIONS

20 Minutes

The instructor will provide the answers found by Beutell and Brenner. Discuss the issues raised by the exercise, using the discussion questions that follow.

WHAT DO WE VALUE IN WORK?

Instructions: Please *rank order* the nine items in terms of how important they would be to you in a job. Indicate the most important reason by putting the number "1" by that item in *column A* ("Myself"). Put a "2" by the second most important, and so on, until you have put a "9" by the least important (no ties, please). When you have finished ranking the items for yourself, rank them in *column B* as you think most male business students would rank them. (Think in terms of the "average person" rather than of individuals holding particular jobs.) Finally, rank order the items as you think most female business students would rank them in *column C*. EXP = experts
GRP = Group

How important is it to you to have a job which ...	A Myself	EXP	GRP	B Men	C Women	GRP	EXP
1. Is respected by other people.	5	1	8	3	4	1	1
2. Encourages continued development of knowledge and skills.	4	2.5	5	9	7	8	2
3. Provides job security.	3	2.5	2	7	1	3	5
4. Provides a feeling of accomplishment.	1	4.0	6	2	6	4	6.5
5. Provides the opportunity to earn a high income.	2	5.5	1	1	5	5	3.0
6. Is intellectually stimulating.	7	7.0	7	6	9	9	4.0
7. Rewards good performance with recognition.	8	5.5	4	4	3	6	8.5
8. Provides comfortable working conditions.	9	8.0	9	8	2	2	6.5
9. Permits advancement to high administrative responsibility.	6	9.0	3	5	8	7	8.5

My sex: ✓ Male
       _____ Female

DISCUSSION QUESTIONS

1. What do people in the group rank first for themselves? For men in general? For women in general? (Tabulate, separately by sex, the items ranked number 1 by each person for themselves.)
2. Do both groups generally assume that other men and women want something different from work than they themselves want? Why? (Tabulate, separately, men's estimates of the value ranked number 1 by other men and by women. Similarly, tabulate the women's estimates for men and other women.)
3. Do the Beutell and Brenner results seem consistent with theories of work motivation that you know about? Would any theories predict different results?
4. *For Option two, only:* Are women any more likely to rank the values accurately when they rank them for other women than men are? Did the men rank the values for other men more accurately than women? Why? What does this mean?
5. Compare the results obtained to those that have been reported for other groups.

GENERALIZATIONS AND CONCLUSIONS

Concluding Points

1. Most groups find it difficult to guess how the women in the Beutell and Brenner sample ranked the items. Moreover, their rankings for men and women in general do not resemble the rankings for themselves. Why does this happen?

2. Many theories of work motivation would predict the outcomes of the Beutell and Brenner study; "common sense" usually fails. What theories might be useful?

3. Are men and women similar or dissimilar in their statements of what they want from work? Why?

4. Why is it important for managers to know what people want from work?

Participant's Reactions

READINGS AND REFERENCES

Beutell, Nicholas J., and Brenner, O. C. Sex differences in work values. *Journal of Vocational Behavior, 28,* 1986, 29–41.

Terborg, J., "Women in Management: A Research Review," *Journal of Applied Psychology,* 62(1977), 647–664.

6
ASSIGNMENT: THE MEANING OF WORK

PURPOSE:
To develop an understanding of the meaning of work to people in different occupational categories.

ADVANCE PREPARATION: Read readings assigned by the instructor *before* starting the assignment.
GROUP SIZE: Groups of three to five.
TIME REQUIRED: Several days outside of class.
SPECIAL MATERIALS: None.
SPECIAL PHYSICAL REQUIREMENTS: None.
RELATED TOPICS: Applied motivation and job design, Life, work, and career roles.

INTRODUCTION

In this assignment, you will be asked to conduct interviews with a sample of people from different occupational walks of life. In a broad sense, you will be trying to find out what work means in their lives. Before you begin, be sure you understand the instructions, especially those defining the job categories to be sampled.

PROCEDURE

1. Form teams of three to five persons if participants are not already working in groups.
2. The assignment: Each team is to interview six people and write a short paper (length to be announced by instructor) summarizing the interviews. Each paper is to describe:
   a. Each person interviewed—occupation, marital status, age (approximately).
   b. The person's responses to the questions asked.
   c. A brief summary of the major points or issues of interest you have identified in the process of collecting and analyzing your data.
   Turn the paper in on the date designated by the instructor.
3. The sample: Each group is to seek out six people and ask them if they will talk to you about *what their job means to them, personally.* Choose two people each from the following occupational categories:
   a. Blue collar (unskilled or semiskilled workers).
   b. White collar (clerical workers, retail or door-to-door sales).
   c. Managerial or professional people.

Developed by Donald D. Bowen.

People sometimes have difficulty in determining into which category a job fits. The following examples are intended to help you differentiate between categories. The list is not exhaustive; it is merely intended to give you a general idea of where jobs fit.

Blue-Collar Occupations	White-Collar Occupations	Managerial or Professional Occupations
Service station attendant	File clerk	Lawyer
Steelworker	Secretary	Doctor
Custodian	Salesman (door-to-door	Engineer
Machine operator (but	or retail, but not	Foreman
not machinist or tool	industrial)	Manager
maker)	Receptionist	College professor
Bartender	Bank teller	Insurance broker
Security guard or	Insurance salesman	Accountant
policeman		

As a general rule, if you have difficulty classifying an occupation, include it with the highest possible category. Skilled tradesmen (machinists, tool makers, plumbers, etc.) will be difficult to categorize because, although we frequently think of them as blue-collar workers, their responses are more likely to sound like those of clerical or professional workers. Proprietors of small businesses are another group difficult to classify. Their attitudes toward work are likely to reflect their varied prior experience in working as employees before starting their own businesses. Don't interview part-time workers, such as college students, because their work is not a major component of their lives.

If you are female, find at least two women to talk to; if you are black, choose at least two blacks; and so on. In other words, try to find people you have something in common with.

4. Conducting the interview: *For each interview, try to have at least two members of the group present*. After the interview, you can check your impressions with the other person. Having at least two people present will also make it possible to take more comprehensive notes. During the interview, ask the following questons:

Required Questions
1. What are the major satisfactions you get in your work?
2. What are the major frustrations in your work?
3. If you had your life to live over again, would you go into the same line of work? Why?
4. What effect does your work have on your family life? How do you feel about this?

Optional Questions (follow group leader's direction on these)
5. How did you happen to get into this line of work?
6. Have you ever considered changing to another field or occupation?

7. Do you think most people are as satisfied (dissatisfied) with their work as you are? Why?
8. Do you have children? If you do, what advice do you give your children on preparing for a career? If you do not, what advice *should* people give to their children?

READINGS AND REFERENCES

Clark, J. V., "Motivation in Work Groups: A Tentative View," *Human Organization*, 19 (1960–61), 199–208.

Kanter, R. M., *Men and Women of the Corporation* (New York: Basic Books, 1977).

Maslow, A. H., "A Theory of Human Motivation," *Psychological Review*, 50 (1943), 370–71, 394–96.

McGregor, D. M., "The Human Side of Enterprise," *Management Review*, Nov. (1957), 22–28, 88–92.

Terkel, S., *Working* (New York: Pantheon, 1974).

SECTION THREE
APPLIED MOTIVATION AND JOB DESIGN

7
JOB REDESIGN

PURPOSE:
(1) To apply the theory of motivation to job design.
(2) To help participants learn to diagnose job characteristics.
(3) To provide practice in the techniques of brainstorming.

ADVANCE PREPARATION: Read the "Introduction."
GROUP SIZE: Any size. Will be split into groups of three to seven persons each.
TIME REQUIRED: 50 minutes.
SPECIAL MATERIALS: None.
SPECIAL PHYSICAL REQUIREMENTS: None.
RELATED TOPICS: Motivation: Basic concepts, Planned change, Managers as leaders.

INTRODUCTION

The Job Characteristics Model of Work Motivation

A method of analyzing the motivating potential of a job, developed by Hackman and Oldham (1980), and called the job characteristics model of work design, is summarized in Figure 1. The theory states that certain "core dimensions" of a job create critical

Concepts and model developed by J. Richard Hackman and Greg R. Oldham. Exercise adapted and written by D. T. Hall. The cooperation of Richard Hackman is gratefully acknowledged. Introduction adapted from J. R. Hackman and G. R. Oldham, *Work Redesign,* © 1980, Addison-Wesley, Reading, Massachusetts, pp. 71–94, 107–127, and 135–141. Reprinted with permission.

psychological states in the person. Job outcomes then result from these psychological states. The concepts in the model are defined as follows:

Job dimensions. The instrument provides a measure of the five core dimensions, which are as follows:

Skill Variety. The degree to which a job requires a variety of different activities in carrying out the work, which involve the use of a number of different skills and talents of the employee.

Task Identity. The degree to which the job requires completion of a "whole" and identifiable piece of work—that is, doing a job from beginning to end with a visible outcome.

Task Significance. The degree to which the job has a substantial impact on the lives or work of other people—whether in the immediate organization or in the external environment.

Autonomy. The degree to which the job provides substantial freedom, independence, and discretion of the employee in scheduling the work and in determining the procedures to be used in carrying it out.

Feedback from the Job. The degree to which carrying out the work activities required by the job results in the employee obtaining direct and clear information about the effectiveness of his or her performance.

The overall "motivating potential" of a job can be assessed either by simply adding up respondent scores on the five core dimensions, or by computing the following Motivating Potential Score (MPS), which derives from the theory of work design summarized in Figure 1.

Critical psychological states. There are three psychological states that are shown in Figure 1 as mediating between the core job dimensions and the outcomes of the work. These are:

Experienced Meaningfulness of the Work. The degree to which the employee experiences the job as one that is generally meaningful, valuable, and worthwhile.

Experienced Responsibility for Work Outcomes. The degree to which the employee feels personally accountable and responsible for the results of the work he or she does.

Knowledge of Results. The degree to which the employee knows and understands, on a continuous basis, how effectively he or she is performing the job.

Affective outcomes. Three important personal, affective reactions or feelings a person obtains from performing the job are:

General Satisfaction. An overall measure of the degree to which the employee is satisfied and happy with the job.

Internal Work Motivation. The degree to which the employee is self-motivated to perform well on the job—that is, the employee experiences positive internal

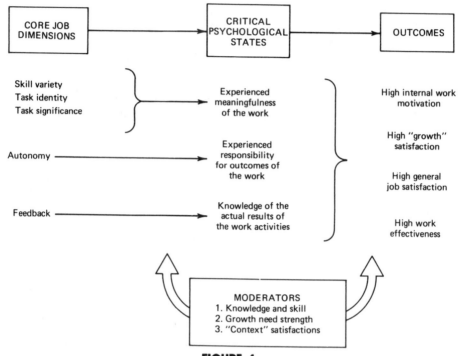

FIGURE 1

The Job Characteristics Model of Work Motivation (from Hackman and Oldham, 1980). Reprinted by Permission. R. Hackman and G. Oldham, *Work Redesign*, Copyright © 1980, Addison-Wesley, Reading, Mass., Figure 4.6. Reprinted with permission.

feelings when working effectively, and negative internal feelings when doing poorly.

Growth Satisfaction. The degree to which the employee is satisfied with opportunities for personal growth and development on the job.

Work Effectiveness. Obviously, from the organization's point of view, the critical test of any job redesign is the increase it produces in the quality and/or quantity of employee performance.

PLANNING, INSTALLING, AND SUPPORTING CHANGES IN JOBS

Implementing Concepts for Work Redesign

Five "implementing concepts" for enriching jobs are identified and discussed below. Each one is a specific action step aimed at improving both the quality of the work experience for the individual and his or her work productivity. They are:

1. Forming natural work units.
2. Combining tasks.

3. Establishing client relationships.
4. Vertical loading.
5. Opening feedback channels.

The links between the implementing concepts and the core job dimensions are shown in Figure 2. After completing a diagnosis of a job, a manager or change agent could turn to the implementing concepts to get ideas for how to improve the most problematic aspects of the job. How this might be done in practice is shown below, as each of the implementing concepts is discussed.

1. Forming Natural Work Units. The notion of distributing work in some logical way may seem to be an obvious part of the design of any job. In many cases, however, the logic is one imposed by just about any consideration except jobholder satisfaction and motivation. Such considerations include technological dictates; level of worker training or experience; "efficiency," as defined by industrial engineering; and current workload. In many cases, the cluster of tasks a worker faces during a typical day or week is natural to anyone *but* the worker.

For example, suppose that a typing pool (consisting of one supervisor and ten typists) handles all work for one division of a company. Jobs are delivered in rough draft or dictated form to the supervisor, who distributes them as evenly as possible among the typists. In such circumstances the individual letters, reports, and other tasks performed by a given typist in one day or week are randomly assigned. There is no basis for identifying with the work or the person or department for whom it is performed, or for placing any personal value upon it.

The principle underlying natural units of work, by contrast, is "ownership"—a worker's sense of continuing responsibility for an identifiable body of work.

There are two steps involved in creating natural work units. The first is to identify the basic work items. In the typing pool, for example, the items might be "pages to be typed." The second step is to group the items in natural categories. For example, each typist might be assigned continuing responsibility for all jobs requested by one or several specific departments. The assignments should be made, of course, in such

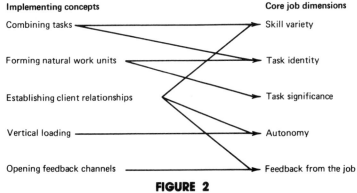

FIGURE 2
How the Implementing Concepts Relate to the Core Job Dimensions

a way that workloads are about equal in the long run. (For example, one typist might end up with all the work from one busy department, while another handles jobs from several smaller "accounts.")

At this point we can begin to see specifically how the implementing concepts relate to the core dimensions (see Figure 2). The "ownership" fostered by natural units of work can make the difference between the feeling that work is meaningful and rewarding and the feeling that it is irrelevant and boring. As the diagram shows, natural units of work are directly related to two of the core dimensions: Task Identity and Task Significance.

A typist whose work is assigned naturally rather than randomly—say, by departments—has a much greater chance of performing a whole job to completion. Instead of typing one section of a large report, the individual is likely to type the whole thing, with knowledge of exactly what the product of the work is (Task Identity). Furthermore, over time the typist will develop a growing sense of how the work affects coworkers in the department services (Task Significance).

2. Combining Tasks.   The very existence of a pool made up entirely of persons whose sole function is typing reflects a fractionalization of jobs that has been a basic precept of "scientific management." Most obvious in assembly line work, fractionalization has been applied to nonmanufacturing jobs as well. It is typically justified by "efficiency," which is usually defined in terms of either low costs or some time-and-motion type of criteria.

It is hard to find fault with measuring efficiency ultimately in terms of cost effectiveness. In doing so, however, a manager should be sure to consider *all* the costs involved. It is possible, for example, for highly fractionalized jobs to meet all the time-and-motion criteria of "efficiency," but if the resulting job is so unrewarding that performing it day after day leads to high turnover, absenteeism, drugs, alcohol, and strikes, then productivity is really lower (and costs higher) than data on "efficiency" might indicate.

The principle of combining tasks, then, suggests that whenever possible existing and fractionalized tasks should be put together to form new and larger modules of work. At the Medfield, Massachusetts plant of Corning Glass Works, a laboratory hotplate now is assembled from start to finish by one operator, instead of going through several separate operations performed by different people.

Some tasks, if combined into a meaningfully large module of work, would be more than an individual could do alone. In such cases, it is often useful to consider assigning the new, larger task to a small *team* of workers—who are given great autonomy for its completion. At the Racine, Wisconsin plant of Emerson Electric, the assembly process for trash disposal appliances was restructured in this way. Instead of a sequence of moving the appliance from station to station, the assembly is now done from start to finish by one team. Such teams include both men and women to permit switching off the heavier and more delicate aspects of the work. The team responsible is identified on the appliance. In case of customer complaints, the team often drafts the reply.

Task combination, like natural units of work, expands the Task Identity of the job.

For example, the hotplate assembler can see and identify with a finished product ready for shipment, rather than a nearly invisible junction of solder. Moreover, the more tasks that are combined into a single worker's job, the greater the variety of skills he or she must call on in performing the job. So, task combination also leads directly to greater Skill Variety—the third core dimension that contributes to the overall experienced meaningfulness of the work (Figure 1).

3. Establishing Client Relationships. One consequence of fractionalization is that the typical worker has little or no contact with (or even awareness of) the ultimate user of his or her product or service. By encouraging and enabling employees to establish direct relationships with the "clients" of their work, improvements can often be realized simultaneously on three of the core dimensions. Feedback increases, because of additional opportunities for the individual to receive *direct* praise or criticism of his or her work outputs. Skill Variety often increases, because of the necessity to develop and exercise one's interpersonal skills in maintaining the client relationship. And Autonomy can increase because the individual often is given personal responsibility for deciding how to manage relationships with the "clients" of the work.

Creating client relationships is a three-step process: first, identification of who the client actually is; second, establishing the most direct possible contact between the worker and the client; third, setting up some criteria by which the client can judge the quality of the product or service that is received. And, whenever possible, the client should have a means of relaying those judgments directly back to the worker.

The contact between worker and the client should be as great as possible and as frequent as necessary. Face-to-face contact is highly desirable, at least occasionally. Where that is impossible or impractical, telephone and mail can suffice. In any case, it is important that the performance criteria by which the worker will be rated by the client must be mutually understood and agreed.

4. Vertical Loading. Typically, the split between the "doing" of a job and the "planning" and "controlling" of the work has evolved along with horizontal fractionalization. Its rationale, once again, has been efficiency through specialization. And, once again, the excess of specialization that has emerged has resulted in unexpected but significant costs in motivation, morale, and work quality. In vertical loading, the intent is to partially close the gap between the doing and the controlling parts of the job—and thereby reap some important motivational advantages.

Of all the implementing concepts, vertical loading may be the single most crucial one. In some cases, where it has been impossible to implement any other changes, vertical loading alone has had significant motivational effects.

When a job is vertically loaded, responsibilities and controls that were formerly reserved for higher levels of management are added to the job. There are numerous means of carrying this out:

Return to the job holder greater discretion in setting schedules, deciding on work methods, checking on quality, and advising or helping to train less experienced workers.

Grant additional authority. The objective should be to advance workers from a
  position of no authority or highly restricted authority to positions of reviewed,
  and eventually, near-total authority for their own work.
Time management. The job holder should have the greatest possible freedom to
  decide when to start and stop work, when to break, and how to assign priorities.
Troubleshooting and crisis decisions. Workers should be encouraged to seek problem solutions on their own, rather than calling immediately for the supervisor.
Financial controls. Some degree of knowledge and control over budgets and other
  financial aspects of a job can often be highly motivating. However, access to this
  information frequently tends to be restricted. Workers can benefit from knowing
  something about the costs of their jobs, the potential effect upon profit, and
  various financial and budgetary alternatives.

When a job is vertically loaded it will inevitably increase in Autonomy. And, as
shown in Figure 1, this increase in objective personal control over the work should
also lead to an increased feeling of personal responsibility for the work—and ultimately to higher internal work motivation.

5. Opening Feedback Channels.   In virtually all jobs there are ways to open channels
of feedback to individuals or teams to help them learn whether their performance is
improving, deteriorating, or remaining at a constant level. Although there are numerous "channels" through which information about performance can be provided,
it is generally better for a worker to learn about his or her performance *directly as
the job is done*—rather than from management on an occasional basis.

Job-provided feedback usually is more immediate and private than supervisor-
supplied feedback, and increases the worker's feelings of personal control over his
or her work in the bargain. Moreover, it avoids many of the potentially disruptive
interpersonal problems that can develop when the only way workers have to find out
how they are doing is from direct messages or subtle cues from the boss.

Exactly what should be done to open channels for job-provided feedback varies
from job to job and organization to organization. Yet often the changes involve simply
removing existing blocks that isolate the individual from naturally occurring data
about performance—rather than generating entirely new feedback mechanisms. For
example:

Establishing direct client relationships (discussed above) often removes blocks
  between the worker and natural external sources of data about the work.
Quality control efforts in many organizations often eliminate a natural source of
  feedback. The quality check on a product or service is done by people other
  than the individuals responsible for the work. Feedback to the workers—if there
  is any—is belated and diluted. It often fosters a tendency to think of quality as
  "someone else's concern."
By placing quality control close to the workers (perhaps even in their own hands),
  the quantity and quality of data about performance that is available to them can
  dramatically increase.

Tradition and established procedure in many organizations dictate that records about performance are kept by a supervisor and transmitted up (not down) the organizational hierarchy. Sometimes supervisors even check the work and correct any errors themselves. The worker who made the error never knows it occurred—and is denied the very information that can enhance both the internal work motivation and the technical adequacy of work performance. In many cases, it is possible to provide standard summaries of performance records directly to the worker (as well as to the supervisor), thereby giving workers personally and regularly the data they need to improve performance.

Computers and other automated operations sometimes can be used to provide individuals with data now blocked from them. Many clerical operations, for example, are now performed on computer consoles. These consoles often can be programmed to provide the clerk with immediate feedback in the form of a CRT display or a printout indicating that an error has been made. Some systems have even been programmed to provide the operator with a positive feedback message when a period of error-free performance has been sustained.

Many organizations simply have not recognized the importance of feedback as a motivator. Data on quality and other aspects of performance are viewed as being of interest only to management. Worse, the *standards* for acceptable performance often are kept from workers as well. As a result, workers who would be interested in following the daily or weekly ups and downs of their performance, and in trying accordingly to improve, are deprived of the very guidelines they need to do so.

PROCEDURE

Step 1. 5 Minutes—Diagnosis of Need for Job Redesign—Identifying a Target Job

Ask for a member of the class to volunteer a job they now hold or held at one time as a candidate for job redesign. (If several people volunteer, the class and/or the instructor can select the job which seems most interesting. Another possibility is to select a job with which someone in the class is very familiar, but it is more interesting if someone in the class has actually held the target job.) Everyone should be *thoroughly familiar* with the job selected.

To help identify a job which will be a good candidate for job redesign, be sure that it meets the following criteria.

A. *Assessing the Need for Work Redesign*
   1. *Is there a specific problem or exploitable opportunity?*
      Sometimes work is redesigned for silly reasons. Unless a specific organizational problem can be identified for which work redesign *might* be helpful, the diagnosis should stop here.
   2. *Does the problem or opportunity centrally involve employee motivation, satisfaction, or work effectiveness?*
      If the issues are irrelevant to these matters, work redesign is unlikely to help.

If JDS data are available, check scores for internal work motivation, growth satisfaction, and general satisfaction.

3. *Might the design of the work be responsible for observed problems?*
There are many possible reasons for suboptimal performance effectiveness, motivation, and satisfaction. Is there reason to believe that the design of the work might be casual in this instance? Check the MPS score for the job.

4. *What aspects of the job most need improvement?*
If the work is not motivationally well-structured, what specific aspects of the jobs are most troublesome, and therefore deserving of special attention in any job changes?

B. *Determining the Feasibility of Work Redesign*

5. *How ready are the employees for change?*
Check the level of employee knowledge and skill, growth need strength, and context satisfaction. If one or more of these factors is low, the decision might be to proceed with work redesign very cautiously—if at all.

6. *How hospitable are intact organizational systems to needed changes?*
Sometimes work redesign is called for, but simply cannot be done because of immutable organizational constraints. Give particular attention to the technological system, to the personal system, and to the control system.

Careful attention to the six diagnostic questions summarized here often leads to a decision *not* to proceed with work redesign (or to delay changes until other features of the organization can be altered to create a more receptive climate for changes in the work itself). This conservation is well-warranted, given the number of work-redesign "failures" that occur because the work system was not a realistic candidate for change in the first place.

Step 2: 10 Minutes

Allow the class to interview the person who holds (or held, or knows) the target job, so that everyone understands the job activities.

Before you proceed, make sure the group is in agreement on the activities performed by a person holding this job. *Check to see if anyone has any questions about the job.*

Step 3: 20 Minutes

Form groups of three to seven people. *Brainstorm* as many possible changes in the job as your group can think of.

RULES FOR BRAINSTORMING

1. Write down all ideas that are produced.
2. Praise one another's ideas, help one another develop ideas, and add to others' ideas wherever possible.
3. Do *not* evaluate or criticize anyone's ideas. We all have a strong tendency to do this, but fight it. The creative process is a fragile one; don't be critical!

After you have finished brainstorming, then you can be critical. Go back over your brainstormed list and remove changes that (a) will not affect the core job characteristics in the model, (b) are technologically impossible or obviously cost-ineffective, or (c) are very abstract and general. Then pick a spokesperson to report your recommended changes to the rest of the class.

Step 4: 10 Minutes
Each group's representative will read off that group's list of recommended changes. (To save time, each group's list could be written on the board or on sheets of newsprint, and the class could spend a few minutes walking around and looking at each group's ideas.)

Step 5: Job Incumbent's Reactions, 5 Minutes
Ask the person who holds (or held, or knows) this job to comment on these redesign ideas. How realistic are they? What impact would they have? Have they ever been tried?

DISCUSSION QUESTIONS
1. What areas of agreement are found in most of the group's recommendations? Areas of disagreement?
2. Which recommendations would have the *strongest* impact on employee satisfaction and performance? The most *immediate* impact? Which would be the *least costly* or *least difficult* to implement?
3. Would there be any resistance to these changes? If so, from whom? How would you deal with it?

GENERALIZATIONS AND CONCLUSIONS

Concluding Points
1. Which of the core job dimensions seem easiest to change?

2. What may be the initial reactions of employees and supervisors to job enrichment?

3. What type of employee would be most likely to perform better in an enriched job?

Participant's Reactions

READINGS AND REFERENCES

Fein, M., "Job Enrichment: A Reevaluation," *Sloan Management Review*, Winter (1974), 69–88.

Hackman, J. R., "The Design of Self-Managing Work Groups," In B. King, S. Streufert, and F. E. Fiedler (Eds.), *Managerial Control and Organization Democracy* (Washington, D.C.: Winston, 1978).

Hackman, J. R., and Oldham, G. R., "Development of the Job Diagnostic Survey," *Journal of Applied Psychology*, 60 (1975), 159–170.

Hackman, J. R., and Oldham, G. R., *Work Redesign* (Reading, Mass.: Addison-Wesley, 1980).

Herzberg, F., "One More Time: How Do You Motivate Employees?" *Harvard Business Review*, January-February (1968), 53–62.

Herzberg, F., *The Managerial Choice* (Homewood, Ill.: Dow Jones-Irwin, 1976).

Walton, R. E., "The Diffusion of New Work Structures: Explaining Why Success Didn't Take," *Organizational Dynamics*, Winter (1975), 3–22.

8
DEVELOPING EFFECTIVE
MANAGERS: PERFORMANCE APPRAISAL

PURPOSE:
(1) To practice skills in performance appraisal and supervision of subordinates.
(2) To develop skills in communication and problem solving.

ADVANCE PREPARATION: Read the "Introduction," below.
GROUP SIZE: Any size.
TIME REQUIRED: 40 to 60 minutes.
SPECIAL MATERIALS: None.
SPECIAL PHYSICAL REQUIREMENTS: None.
RELATED TOPICS: Managers as leaders, Group decision making and problem solving, Power, Interpersonal communication, Organizational communication, Life, work, and career roles.

INTRODUCTION

Any kind of system, whether it be a person, organization, or a spacecraft, needs feedback from its environment to tell how close it is to being "on target" in achieving its objectives. One of the most important and useful sources of feedback to an employee is his supervisor. However, in the day-to-day course of our work experiences, we usually obtain little direct feedback on our performance from our supervisors—and we give an equal amount to our own subordinates.

One of the most common mechanisms for feedback between supervisors and subordinates is the *performance appraisal* discussion. In many organizations this is a formal process in which the supervisor fills out a standard form describing the employee's work, they discuss it, and the employee signs it. Then it is sent to higher-level managers, and is finally placed in the employee's personnel file.

Senior managers in most organizations will describe their performance appraisal system in detail, stressing the requirements, such as the employee's signature, that ensure the appraisal will, in fact, be conducted. However, when employees are asked about their performance appraisals, the response is often a blank stare. Many employees do not even know what a performance appraisal is. Others report that it is conducted in a cursory manner; many seem to be "conducted" in brief encounters in the hallway or by the coffee pot. Thus, there is a mysterious process whereby the performance appraisal is there when we talk to senior managers, but gone when we

Developed by Donald D. Bowen, inspired by a class demonstration used by Chris Argyris (who initially denied any memory of the exercise, whatsoever). This exercise is, therefore, dedicated to Chris Argyris, who has inspired all of us more than he knows (or at least more than he will admit). (Upon further reflection, however, his memory improved!) Adapted by Douglas T. Hall.

talk to employees. For this reason, the process has been dubbed the "vanishing performance appraisal" (Hall, 1976).

One of the reasons that performance appraisals disappear is that supervisors feel uncomfortable giving feedback in a one-to-one encounter. One reason they feel uncomfortable about it is that they have never developed the necessary skills. The purpose of this exercise is for you to begin to develop performance appraisal skills.

First, let us consider two different approaches to performance appraisal. Let us say you agree with Douglas McGregor (1967) on the following seven propositions:

Human Growth Potential

1. People are capable of growing in a social climate that permits and encourages growth.
2. People tend to grow when they can achieve their own goals by achieving those of the organization.

The Role of Communication and Feedback

3. Feedback is necessary for the survival and growth of any system.
4. Effective problem solving requires open exchange of information.
5. Transactional management (where power is shared) facilitates communication.

Effective Versus Ineffective Communication

6. People tend to become defensive when threatened; that is, hostile, protective behavior, overt compliance, and selective or distorted perception result.
7. People will use information if they find it helpful in achieving their goals.

What then, are the implications of these propositions for performance appraisal and the supervision of subordinates?

One important implication is that a *problem-solving approach* to performance appraisal is probably going to get more results than the *tell-and-sell* method. These two approaches are identified by Maier (1958), who describes the objectives, assumptions, employee reactions, and supervisor skills associated with each method.

The tell-and-sell method, which is the more commonly applied of the two, has two objectives: (1) to communicate evaluation, and (2) to persuade the employee to improve. It is based upon four assumptions: (1) the employee desires to correct weaknesses if he or she knows them, (2) any person can improve if she or he so chooses, (3) a superior is qualified to evaluate a subordinate, and (4) people profit from criticism and appreciate help.

The skills required on the part of the supervisor are salesmanship and patience. The employee usually reacts in three ways: (1) suppressed defensive behavior, (2) attempts to cover hostility, and (3) little change in performance.

The objective of the problem-solving method is to stimulate growth and development in the employee. It is based upon three assumptions: (1) growth can occur without correcting faults, (2) discussing job problems leads to improved performance and (3) discussion develops new ideas and mutual interests.

The skills required of the supervisor are: (1) listening and reflecting feelings, (2) reflecting ideas, (3) using exploratory questions, and (4) summarizing. The reaction is often problem-solving behavior and employee commitment to the changes or objectives discussed (because they are *his* or *her* ideas).

PROCEDURE

Two sets of roles are available for this exercise. One set (J. J. Stein and T. T. Burns) is for a partner and an audit manager, respectively, in a public accounting firm. The other set (D. P. Jones and C. J. Marshall) is for the president and production manager, respectively, of a manufacturing company.

Both sets of roles and a set of instructions for observers are in the Appendix at the end of this volume. See the Appendix Table of Contents for specific pages.

Step 1: 5 Minutes

The group leader will indicate which set of roles is to be used in this exercise. The class will be divided into groups of three people each. One person will play the role of the superior (D. P. Jones or J. J. Stein), one will be the subordinate (C. J. Marshall or T. T. Burns), and one will be an observer.

Read *only* the role description you have chosen or been assigned. Observers will read the "Instructions for Observers," as well as the role descriptions for both the superior and the subordinate.

Step 2: 20 Minutes

The superior conducts the appraisal interview with the subordinate. The observer is silent and takes notes on the process of the interviewer, using the "General Instructions" as a guide. At the conclusion of the interview, the observer gives feedback to the two participants. See Appendix Table of Contents.

Step 3: 15 Minutes

Discussion.

DISCUSSION QUESTIONS

1. *To observers:* Describe an interview that went very well. How did it start? Was there a "critical point" that turned things around? Describe an interview that did not work out well. What were the critical points here?
2. What evidence did you see of the tell-and-sell method? Of the problem-solving method?
3. How was the subordinate reacting to the method(s) that the boss used?
4. What could each person have done differently to help the discussion?

GENERALIZATIONS AND CONCLUSIONS

Concluding Points

1. Which method of performance appraisal is most likely to occur? Why?

2. What steps can the supervisor take to encourage a problem-solving discussion?

Participant's Reactions

READINGS AND REFERENCES

Hall, D. T. *Careers in Organizations* (Santa Monica, Calif.: Goodyear, 1976).

Levinson, H., "Management by Whose Objectives?" *Harvard Business Review*, July-Aug. (1970).

McGregor, D., *The Professional Manager* (New York: McGraw-Hill, 1967).

————, "An Uneasy Look at Performance Appraisal," *Harvard Business Review*, Sept.-Oct. (1972).

Maier, N. R. F., *The Appraisal Interview* (New York: Wiley, 1958).

Meyer, H. H., Kay, E., and French, J. R. P., Jr., "Split Roles in Performance Appraisal," *Harvard Business Review*, Jan.-Feb. (1965).

Oberg, W., "Make Performance Appraisal Relevant," *Harvard Business Review*, Jan.-Feb. (1972).

9
REDESIGNING ASSEMBLY-LINE JOBS: HOVEY AND BEARD COMPANY

PURPOSE:
(1) To evaluate a case of job redesign.
(2) To illustrate the systemwide, unanticipated consequences of planned change. _____

ADVANCE PREPARATION:
(1) For Option one: None.
(2) For Option two: Read Parts I and II of the Hovey and Beard Company case.
(3) For Option three: Read Parts I, II, and III of the Hovey and Beard Company case.

GROUP SIZE: Any size, split into subgroups of five to seven.

TIME REQUIRED: 50 to 105 minutes, depending upon option used. *Option one:* 105 minutes; *Option two:* 85 minutes; *Option three:* 50 minutes.

SPECIAL MATERIALS: None.

SPECIAL PHYSICAL REQUIREMENTS: Enough room for subgroup meetings.

RELATED TOPICS: Planned change, Power, Organizations, Motivation: Basic concepts.

INTRODUCTION

Much of the literature on planned change and job redesign describes the advantages of *participation* by employees in the change and job redesign process. Participation can increase the quality of the change, and the employees' acceptance of the change, although it can also increase the time required to plan and implement the change. On the other hand, there can be some unanticipated consequences of participation that are not always positive. Under what conditions is participation most effective?

PROCEDURE

OPTION ONE: START HERE

Step 1: 10 Minutes

Meet in groups of five to seven people. Read Part I of the Hovey and Beard Company case, below. Come to a group decision on the question at the end of Part I.

Adapted by D. T. Hall from "Group Dynamics and Intergroup Relations" by George Strauss and Alex Bavelas (under the title "The Hovey and Beard Case") from *Money and Motivation*, edited by William F. Whyte. Copyright © 1955 by Harper & Row, Publishers, Inc. Reprinted by permission of the publisher.

THE HOVEY AND BEARD COMPANY CASE[1]
Part I

The Hovey and Beard Company manufactured wooden toys of various kinds: wooden animals, pull toys, and the like. One part of the manufacturing process involved spraying paint on the partially assembled toys. This operation was staffed entirely by women.

The toys were cut, sanded, and partially assembled in the wood room. Then they were dipped into shellac, following which they were painted. The toys were predominantly two-colored; a few were made in more than two colors. Each color required an additional trip through the paint room.

For a number of years, production of these toys had been entirely handwork. However, to meet tremendously increased demand, the painting operation had recently been re-engineered so that the eight operators (all women) who did the painting sat in a line by an endless chain of hooks. These hooks were in continuous motion, past the line of operators and into a long horizontal oven. Each woman sat at her own painting booth so designed as to carry away fumes and to backstop excess paint. The operator would take a toy from the tray beside her, position it in a jig inside the painting cubicle, spray on the color according to a pattern, then release the toy and hang it on the hook passing by. The rate at which the hooks moved had been calculated by the engineers so that each woman, when fully trained, would be able to hang a painted toy on each hook before it passed beyond her reach.

The operators working in the paint room were on a group bonus plan. Since the operation was new to them, they were receiving a learning bonus that decreased by regular amounts each month. The learning bonus was scheduled to vanish in six months, by which time it was expected that they would be on their own—that is, able to meet the standard and to earn a group bonus when they exceeded it.

Discuss: What do you expect to happen over the next few months: Will production go up, down, or stay the same?

Step 2: 5 Minutes
Meet briefly as a total class group. Make a tally of how many groups think production will go up, how many think it will go down, and how many think it will stay the same.

Step 3: 5 Minutes
Now read Part II of the case. (Part II can be found in the Appendix at the end of this volume.)

OPTION TWO: START HERE
Make sure you have read Parts I and II of the case.

Step 4: 15 Minutes
Meet in subgroups. Discuss the question at the end of Part II.

---

[1]From Chapter 10 of *Money and Motivation* (New York: Harper & Row, 1955). The chapter was written by two coauthors of the book, Alex Bavelas and George Strauss, and was based on Dr. Bavelas's experience as a consultant. Reproduced by permission.

Step 5: 15 Minutes

Meet as a total class group. Each group then reports its recommendations. If there is time, briefly discuss the pros and cons of each recommendation.

Step 6: 5 Minutes

Now read part III of the case. (Part III can be found in the Appendix.)

OPTION THREE: START HERE

Make sure you have read Parts I, II, and III of the case.

Step 7: 15 Minutes

Meet again in subgroups. Discuss the question at the end of Part III.

Step 8: 5 Minutes

Meet briefly as a total class group. The group leader will count how many groups think production will go up, down, or stay the same. Make another tally for how many groups think satisfaction will go up, down, or stay the same.

Step 9: 10 Minutes

Meet in subgroups. Read Part IV (in the Appendix). Discuss the question at the end of Part IV.

Step 10: 10 Minutes

Meet as a total class group. In a general discussion, get brief predictions from each group on the question at the end of Part IV.

At this point, the group leader will read Part V to the group.

Step 11: 10 Minutes

Discuss the conclusions that can be drawn from this case.

DISCUSSION QUESTIONS

See discussion questions at the ends of Parts I through IV of the case.

GENERALIZATIONS AND CONCLUSIONS

Concluding Points

1. What often happens to motivation and satisfaction when employees participate in redesigning their own jobs?

2. What happens to production when employees participate in redesigning their own jobs?

3. What unintended consequences may occur when new procedures are introduced in one subsystem (e.g., work group or department) of a larger system (e.g., plant, organization)?

Participant's Reactions

READINGS AND REFERENCES

Bavelas, A., and Strauss, G., "Group Dynamics and Intergroup Relations." In Whyte, W. F., et al. (Eds.), *Money and Motivation* (New York: Harper & Row, 1955), pp. 90–96.

10
MOTIVATION THROUGH COMPENSATION

PURPOSE:
(1) To provide practice in making salary decisions.
(2) To evaluate and weigh different sources of information about employee performance.
(3) To develop skills in applying motivation theory to compensation decisions.

ADVANCE PREPARATION: Do Step 1.
GROUP SIZE: Any size group.
TIME REQUIRED: 35 Minutes.
SPECIAL MATERIALS: None.
SPECIAL PHYSICAL REQUIREMENTS: None.
RELATED TOPICS: Managers as leaders, Organizational communication, Organizational Structure and Design, Life, work, and career roles.

INTRODUCTION

For most people, their annual pay raise may be the most concrete information they have on how the organization evaluates their performance. Therefore, whether you as a manager intend it or not, the pay raise will be seen by the employee as either a reward or a punishment for last year's work performance. In Skinnerian terms, with the pay raise, you are either positively or negatively reinforcing last year's performance. Therefore, the pay raise can be either motivating or demotivating, depending upon how the employee views the connection between good performance and financial rewards. Issues of equity, expectancy, psychological needs, and social comparison are also involved in people's reactions to pay decisions.

PROCEDURE

Step 1: 20 Minutes

Read the instructions on the "Employee Profile Sheet," below, and then decide on a percentage pay increase for each of the eight employees.

EMPLOYEE PROFILE SHEET

You have to make salary increase recommendations for eight managers that you supervise. They have just completed their first year with the company and are now to be considered for their first annual raise. Keep in mind that you may be setting precedents and that you need to keep salary costs down. However, there are no formal company

Originally developed by Edward E. Lawler III. Adapted by D. T. Hall. Used by permission.

restrictions on the kind of raises you can give. Indicate the size of the raise that you would like to give each manager by writing a dollar amount next to their names. You have a total of $17,000 available in your salary budget to use for pay raises.

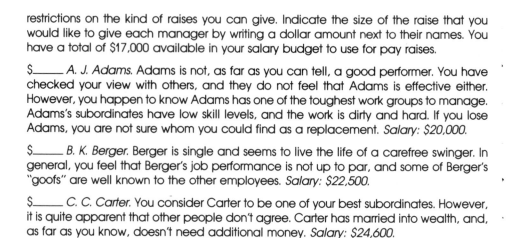

$_____ *A. J. Adams.* Adams is not, as far as you can tell, a good performer. You have checked your view with others, and they do not feel that Adams is effective either. However, you happen to know Adams has one of the toughest work groups to manage. Adams's subordinates have low skill levels, and the work is dirty and hard. If you lose Adams, you are not sure whom you could find as a replacement. *Salary: $20,000.*

$_____ *B. K. Berger.* Berger is single and seems to live the life of a carefree swinger. In general, you feel that Berger's job performance is not up to par, and some of Berger's "goofs" are well known to the other employees. *Salary: $22,500.*

$_____ *C. C. Carter.* You consider Carter to be one of your best subordinates. However, it is quite apparent that other people don't agree. Carter has married into wealth, and, as far as you know, doesn't need additional money. *Salary: $24,600.*

$_____ *D. Davis.* You happen to know from your personal relationship that Davis badly needs more money because of certain personal problems. As far as you are concerned, Davis also happens to be one of the best of your subordinates. For some reason, your enthusiasm is not shared by your other subordinates, and you have heard them make joking remarks about Davis's performance. *Salary: $22,700.*

$_____ *E. J. Ellis.* Ellis has been very successful so far. You are particularly impressed by this, since it is a hard job. Ellis needs money more than many of the other people and is respected for good performance. *Salary: $23,500.*

$_____ *F. M. Foster.* Foster has turned out to be a very pleasant surprise to you, has done an excellent job, and is seen by peers as one of the best people in your group. This surprises you because Foster is generally frivolous and doesn't seem to care very much about money and promotion. *Salary: $21,800.*

$_____ *G. K. Gomez.* Your opinion is that Gomez just isn't cutting the mustard. Surprisingly enough, however, when you check with others to see how they feel about Gomez, you discover that Gomez is very highly regarded. You also know that Gomez badly needs a raise. Gomez was just recently divorced and is finding it extremely difficult to support a house and a young family of four as a single parent. *Salary: $20,500.*

$_____ *H. A. Hunt.* You know Hunt personally. This employee seems to squander money continually. Hunt has a fairly easy job assignment, and your own view is that Hunt doesn't do it particularly well. You are, therefore, quite surprised to find that several of the other new managers think that Hunt is the best of the new group. *Salary: $21,000.*

Step 2: 10 Minutes

When everyone has completed the task (or when almost everyone is finished), one person posts on the board the raises he or she has decided upon. Then this person will explain the criteria for these choices.

Step 3: 10 Minutes

Then someone who has a quite *different* pattern of raises posts them, and explains the criteria for his choices.

Step 4: 15 Minutes

Briefly discuss the differences between the two sets of pay raises. Identify particular employees for whom there was strong disagreement. See what the other class members think the raises should be for these employees.

DISCUSSION QUESTIONS

1. What were the factors that affected your pay raise decisions?
2. What are the *reasons* for basing pay raises on each of these factors?
3. What are the *behavioral effects* of basing pay on each of these factors?

GENERALIZATIONS AND CONCLUSIONS

Concluding Points

1. For a pay plan to be effective, you need clear links (as perceived by employees) between employee behavior (effort, achievement) and what?

2. In view of concluding point 1 above, good performance appraisal and feedback become essential to the success of a pay plan. What conditions does a good performance appraisal system require?

3. These points suggest that an organization can use pay as a motivator, but it may not be worth the cost. What are some of the problems associated with using pay as a motivator?

Participant's Reactions

READINGS AND REFERENCES

Hammer, W. C. "How to Ruin Motivation with Pay," *Compensation Review* (1975).

Lawler III, E. E., "The Mythology of Management Compensation," *California Management Review* (1966), 11–22.

———— *Pay and Organizational Effectiveness* (New York: McGraw-Hill, 1971).

PART II
INTERPERSONAL AND GROUP RELATIONSHIPS

SECTION FOUR
INTERPERSONAL COMMUNICATION

11
INTERVIEWING TRIOS: INTERPERSONAL PROBLEM DIAGNOSIS AND RESOLUTION

PURPOSE:
(1) To provide practice in conducting an interview.
(2) To develop skills in observing interpersonal processes.
(3) To practice giving and receiving feedback.

ADVANCE PREPARATION:
(1) Read "Nondirective Interviewing" in the Folio of Resources at the back of this book.
(2) Read "Feedback: The Art of Giving and Receiving Help" in the Folio of Resources at the back of this book.

GROUP SIZE: Groups of three persons.

TIME REQUIRED: $1\frac{1}{4}$ hours plus discussion time (more if participants need lengthy introduction to concepts of feedback and nondirective interviewing).

SPECIAL MATERIALS: None.

SPECIAL PHYSICAL REQUIREMENTS: Several small rooms or a large area where each trio can conduct its interviews in reasonable privacy.

RELATED TOPICS: Icebreakers, Managers as leaders, Motivation, Basic concepts, Life, work and career roles, Negotiation and conflict.

Developed by Donald D. Bowen. Based on the "consulting trios" design.

INTRODUCTION

Managers frequently encounter situations where they need to help others solve problems—problems that cannot be solved simply by offering expert advice. Nondirective interviewing is a technique appropriate for these occasions. The nondirective interview is also extremely helpful in diagnosing organizational problems or conflicts (where each participant is likely to be operating from his own private perspective), and in interviewing prospective employees.

Nondirective interviewing is a difficult skill for most people to master, however. You should find that you get better at it as each member of your trio takes a turn and receives some feedback. A few tips may help you conduct the interview more effectively. For example:

You *must*

1. *Actively* listen.
2. Be receptive to the *feelings* the interviewee expresses.
3. *Reflect back* the feelings expressed (paraphrasing is particularly helpful here).

And you *must* not

4. Give *advice.*
5. *Probe* for information.
6. *Suggest* topics, ideas, or the like.
7. *Control* the interview (the interviewee should control it).

The interviewer's job is to create an atmosphere in which the interviewee can solve her own problem. Good interviewers probably do *less than 5 percent* of the talking!

This exercise will provide an opportunity for you to work on developing this difficult but useful skill.

PROCEDURE

Step 1: 5 Minutes

Participants choose two other persons with whom they can work comfortably. (If entire group does not divide evenly into groups of three, one or two groups of four can be formed; they will have two observers).

Step 2: 10 Minutes

Review the following instructions:

1. The instructor will indicate areas available to trios for their meetings.
2. Each trio is to meet by itself. Begin by having one member take the role of *interviewer,* one of the *interviewee,* and the third the role of *observer.* After the first interview, the interviewer becomes the interviewee, the observer the interviewer, and the interviewee the observer. Repeat the cycle until all persons have played each role.

Each interview is to take 15 minutes. The observer keeps time and ends the interview in exactly 15 minutes. Five minutes is then available for providing feedback to the interviewer on his interviewing technique.

The topic of the interview is to be chosen by the *interviewee*. The topic chosen should meet the following criteria:

1. It should be a problem that is very important to you right now. For example, you may decide you want to work on a problem related to your school work, your career, or a conflict that you have with someone. You may come up with an even better topic. That's okay, as long as it is an important issue for you. The interviewing approach being practiced here *only* works with important problems.
2. It should be an unresolved problem. Nondirective interviewing is not of much help if the problem is something you have pretty well worked out for yourself.

As the interviewer is interviewing the interviewee, *the observer is to take no part in the conversation*. The observer should sit to one side (but in a position with a good view of both parties) and take notes on the process of the interview. Observations may include observations of the interviewee's behavior, too, but the focus is to be on the interviewer's conduct of the interview.

Use the Interviewing Observation Form on page 91 to record your notes on the interview.

During the feedback session, the observer should check observations with both the interviewer and the interviewee to assess the accuracy of the feedback.

List behaviors that were particularly helpful or hindering to the process of the interview.

At the end of the exercise, reassemble at the location designated by the instructor.

Step 3: 60 Minutes
Conduct interviews.

DISCUSSION QUESTIONS
1. What differences in interviewing "style" did you observe within your trio?
2. Did you see any evidence during the interviews that the nondirective interviewing process helps the interviewee solve his or her problems? What occurred to lead you to this conclusion?
3. What behaviors helped or hindered the process of the interview?
4. What is your interpretation of the data collected for the questions asked? Do you see any evidence to indicate that the process of self-disclosure had a positive impact on the feelings of people for one another?
5. Did you find it hard or easy to maintain the nondirective stance as you conducted your interview? What parts were most difficult? Why are these difficult?

INTERVIEWING OBSERVATION FORM

Take notes on the interviewer's (*not* the interviewee's) behavior. The following suggestions may be helpful in deciding what to watch for.

Behaviors that facilitate the interview

Verbal behavior
1. Accepts feelings.
2. Reflects feelings.
3. Nonevaluative responses ("Uh-huh, I see," etc.).
4. Allows interviewee to end silent periods.

Nonverbal behavior
1. Eye contact (looks at interviewee without staring).
2. Posture (indicates interest, relaxation).
3. No distracting mannerisms.

Behaviors that inhibit the interview

Verbal behavior
1. Directs (gives advice, makes suggestions, etc.).
2. Cuts interviewee off.
3. Comments or questions that disrupt interviewee's train of thought.
4. Changes topic.
5. Speaks during a silence.

Nonverbal behavior
1. Eye contact (looks away from interviewee or stares at interviewee).
2. Posture (closed to or turned away from interviewee).
3. Nervous mannerisms or distracting behavior.

GENERALIZATIONS AND CONCLUSIONS

Concluding Points

1. Identify several situations in which a manager would want to use nondirective interviewing.

2. What is the most difficult problem in conducting an effective nondirective interview?

3. In what situations might a manager wish to use a more directive interviewing style?

Participant's Reactions

READINGS AND REFERENCES

Athos, A. G. and Gabarro, J. J. *Interpersonal behavior: Communication and Understanding in Relationships.* (Englewood Cliffs, NJ: Prentice-Hall, 1978). Especially Chapters 8–11.

Gibb, J. R., "Defensive Communication," *Journal of Communication* (1961), 141–48.

Maier, N. R. F., *Psychology in Industrial Organizations,* 4th ed. (Boston: Houghton-Mifflin, 1973), pp. 532–45.

Rogers, C. R., *Client Centered Therapy* (Boston: Houghton-Mifflin, 1951). See especially Chapter 2. "The Attitude and Orientation of the Counselor."

12
FEEDBACK

PURPOSE:
(1) To practice skills in providing and receiving feedback.
(2) To demonstrate the effect of feedback on working relationships in the group.
(3) To learn about one's own impact on other members of the group.

ADVANCE PREPARATION: Read, and be thoroughly familiar with, Mill's article "Feedback: The Art of Giving and Receiving Help," in the Folio of Resources at the back of this book.
GROUP SIZE: For small, ongoing groups of seven or less.
TIME REQUIRED: Option one: 95 to 120 minutes; Option two: 85 to 110 minutes. Both options may be adapted to two or three shorter periods.
SPECIAL MATERIALS: None.
SPECIAL PHYSICAL REQUIREMENTS: A large room or area where small groups can spread out to hold conversations (movable chairs preferable if a classroom is used), or individual small group meeting rooms.
RELATED TOPICS: Life, work, and career roles, Group decision making and problem solving, Planned change.

INTRODUCTION

We often observe that people should be willing to accept "constructive criticism," and we usually claim that *we* are open to candid, helpful evaluation, even if *other people* are not. Secretly, however, we know that we sometimes have difficulty listening to criticism without becoming defensive. And, surprisingly, sometimes it is also difficult to accept praise and compliments without feeling uncomfortable.

If we are to become effective in working with other people, we must acquire the skills of giving and receiving *feedback;* we must know what impact we have on others, and we need to be able to tell them how we perceive them. Giving and receiving feedback without creating defensiveness and distortion is a skill that can be developed.

PROCEDURE

Step 1: 10 Minutes
Review the criteria for effective feedback described in Mill's article. Be sure that you understand the criteria. Review the "Procedure," below, and ask any questions you may have.

Developed by Donald D. Bowen.

The instructor will indicate where each group is to meet and when the meetings are to end (at a particular time or after each member of the group has responded to a specified number of feedback questions).

OPTION ONE: FOR ONGOING GROUPS

Step 2: 60 Minutes (or More)

Sit in a circle and select one member of the group to be the first to receive feedback. Ask for volunteers, flip coins, or use any method you wish to select the first recipient of feedback. The person chosen is person A.

A asks any other person in the group to provide feedback on some aspect of A's behavior. A should ask for feedback on a specific point (see "Suggested Questions," below). The person to provide the feedback (B) is required to provide the feedback to A *as honestly and briefly as he can.*

When B has provided the feedback requested and A has asked whatever questions are necessary for clarification or verification, it becomes B's turn to ask a member of the group (A, C, or any other member) for feedback.

Continue the process for the remainder of the group meeting.

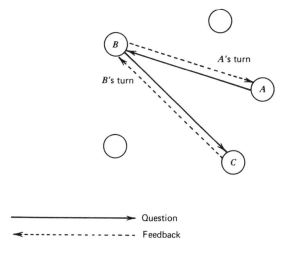

As you provide feedback to the others in your group, evaluate the feedback you, personally, provided on the set of scales, below. The first time you give some feedback, put the recipient's name and a "1" (e.g., "Joe 1") at the point on the scales that best reflects your assessment of the feedback you have just given. If you give feedback to another member next, put her name and a "1" on the scales. The second time you give feedback to a person, put the name and a "2" after it. As an example, at the end of the meeting, your first scale might look like this:

1	2	3	4	5
Descriptive nonevaluative				Evaluative, interpretive

Suggested Questions

Sometimes it is difficult to identify a good question. If you need help, the following list may be useful. Don't restrict yourself to these questions, however.

1. What puzzles you about me?
2. Do you think I can help you learn anything in this group?
3. What changes have you seen in me since you met me?
4. What was your first impression of me?
5. What am I doing that you like most?
6. What part do you think I am playing in this group?
7. What is my greatest strength in this group?
8. How do you perceive me?
9. What kind of a relationship do you want with me?
10. What do you think I'm up to?
11. Are you angry with me about something?
12. What is my greatest weakness in the group?
13. How do you think I would assess you?
14. What am I doing that creates difficulty for you?

FEEDBACK ASSESSMENT SCALES

A.

1	2	3	4	5
Descriptive, nonevaluative				Evaluative, interpretive

B.

1	2	3	4	5
Specific, concrete				General, vague

C.

1	2	3	4	5
Expressed my feelings				Did not express my feelings

D.

1	2	3	4	5
Directed toward controllable behavior				Not directed toward control- lable behavior

E.

1	2	3	4	5
Verified by others				Not verified by others

Step 3: 10 Minutes

Share the data from your Feedback Assessment Scales with the others in the group. Do they have feedback on your feedback? Do they agree with your self-assessments? Did you get better at giving feedback as the meeting progressed? Were there particular individuals to whom you found it easier (or harder) to give feedback? Are there particular aspects of giving feedback that you need to work on?

Step 4: 10 Minutes (Optional)

Each member of the group should now write a brief "Participant's Paper" covering the following points.

1. What did I learn about myself from the feedback process that I did not know before? If the answer is "nothing," what does this imply about how the other group members feel about me or about my defenses?
2. How do I *feel* right now about what I have learned from receiving this feedback?
3. What did I learn about myself as a provider of feedback? What do I need to learn to do better?

4. What seems to have been the general impact on the group as a result of sharing the feedback? Were any problems found? Resolved? Do group members feel closer or more distant than they did before?

OPTION TWO: FOR AD HOC GROUPS

Step 2: 5 Minutes
Select two members of the group from whom you would like to receive feedback. The procedure for forming the sub-groups is simply for everyone to get up and walk around the room until they find the other two people they want to work with. In selecting your partners, you will probably want to think about who the individuals are that you feel most comfortable with and who may be able to give you the most informative feedback on your behavior.

Step 3: 55 to 65 Minutes
Proceed in Steps 2 through 4 of Option one, except that you should finish Step 2 in 45 minutes.

DISCUSSION QUESTIONS
1. Did you find giving and receiving feedback hard or easy to do? Why?
2. In what respects did your feedback seem most effective? Ineffective? How does this relate to the "criteria for useful feedback"?
3. What do you think will be the effect of this session on your group if you continue to work together in the future? Will you be more cohesive? Effective?

GENERALIZATIONS AND CONCLUSIONS

Concluding Points
1. Suggest how an exercise like "Feedback" might be used to improve organizational effectiveness.

2. Under what conditions might an exercise like "Feedback" be counterproductive in its effect on organizational effectiveness?

Participant's Reactions

READINGS AND REFERENCES

Athos, A. G., and Gabarro, J. J., *Interpersonal Behavior: Communication and Understanding in Relationships* (Englewood Cliffs, N.J.: Prentice-Hall, 1978).

Gibb, J. R., "Defensive Communication," *Journal of Communication,* 11 (1961), 141–48.

Luft, J., *Group Process: An Introduction to Group Dynamics,* 2nd ed. (Palo Alto, Calif: National Press, 1974).

McCaskey, M. B., "The Hidden Messages Managers Send," *Harvard Business Review,* Nov./Dec. (1979), 135–48.

13
ASSERTIVENESS: AUTHENTIC INTERPERSONAL COMMUNICATION

PURPOSE:

(1) To demonstrate the concept of assertive communication.

(2) To provide an assessment of participants' interpersonal styles.

(3) To guide practice of assertiveness skills.

ADVANCE PREPARATION: Both options: Read "Toward a Viable Concept of Assertiveness," Unit 65 in the Folio of Resources. *Option one:* Complete Steps 1 through 3 before the class meeting. *Option two:* complete steps 1 through 3 of both options and Step 4 of Option two before the class meeting.

GROUP SIZE: Any size. Option two calls for subgroups of four to six participants.

TIME REQUIRED: *Both options:* 2 hours and 55 minutes; *Option one:* 50 minutes; *Option two:* 2 hours 10 minutes (or more) for option 2 (assuming subgroups of five persons each are used).

SPECIAL MATERIALS: None.

SPECIAL PHYSICAL REQUIREMENTS: Enough room for subgroup meetings in Option two.

RELATED TOPICS: Negotiation and conflict, Group decision making and problem solving, Managers as leaders, Power, Life, work and career roles.

PROCEDURE

ADVANCE PREPARATION FOR BOTH OPTIONS

Step 1: 5 Minutes

Complete the "Interpersonal Response Inventory" (IRI) page 000. (The group leader may ask you to turn in the questionnaire, but no names are required. You will be the only person who knows what your scores are, so feel free to be perfectly candid in your answers.)

INTERPERSONAL RESPONSE INVENTORY

Please check one:

__X__ Male

_____ Female

Developed by Donald D. Bowen.

How true are of the following statements as descriptions of your behavior? Enter the number that represents your answer in the space provided at the beginning of each statement.

4 = Always true   2 = Sometimes true

3 = Often true   1 = Never true

Please respond to *every* statement.

Your
response   Statement

_4_ 1. I respond with more modesty than I really feel when my work is complimented.
_1_ 2. If people are rude, I will be rude right back.
_2_ 3. Other people find me interesting.
_2_ 4. I find it difficult to speak up in a group of strangers.
_2_ 5. I don't mind using sarcasm if it helps me make a point.
_2_ 6. I ask for a raise when I feel I really deserve it.
_1_ 7. If others interrupt me when I am talking, I suffer in silence.
_1_ 8. If people criticize my work, I find a way to make them back down.
_4_ 9. I can express pride in my accomplishments without being boastful.
_3_ 10. People take advantage of me.
_2_ 11. I tell people what they want to hear if it helps me get what I want.
_4_ 12. I find it easy to ask for help.
_4_ 13. I lend things to others even when I don't really want to.
_1_ 14. I win arguments by dominating the discussion.
_3_ 15. I can express my true feelings to someone I really care for.
_4_ 16. When I feel angry with other people, I bottle it up rather than express it.
_1_ 17. When I criticize someone else's work, they get mad.
_3_ 18. I feel confident in my ability to stand up for my rights.

Step 2: 5 Minutes

When you have finished answering the IRI, score it as follows:

Pa: Sum your answers to items 1, 4, 7, 10, 13, 16.

Enter your *Pa* score here: 4   _____18_____
                             2   Pa (Passive)
                             1
                             3
                             4
                            ──18

Ag: Sum your answers to items 2, 5, 8, 11, 14, 17.

Enter your *Ag* score here. 1   _____8_____
                             2   Ag (Aggressive)
                             1
                             2
                             1
                             1
                            ──8

As: Sum your answers to items 3, 6, 9, 12, 15, 18

Enter your *As* score here: 18

                                           As (Assertive)

For each scale, you should have a score between 6 and 24.

Step 3: 10 Minutes

Read "Toward a Viable Concept of Assertiveness," Unit 60 in the Folio of Resources.

OPTION ONE

Step 4: 30 Minutes

The group leader will lead a group discussion to complete Figure 1. The group is to invent passive, aggressive, and assertive responses to each situation. Since this is an exercise in distinguishing between assertive and nonassertive behaviors, be sure to understand *why* a response is either assertive or nonassertive.

Step 5: 5 Minutes

Review your answers to the IRI. Do you see why the items are scored as they are? Do they make sense to you? If you have any questions, raise them in the next step for class discussion.

Step 6: 10 Minutes

Discuss the IRI items. Are there any clues in the IRI as to what behaviors you need to work on to be more effectively assertive? (If the group leader instructs you to do both options of the exercise, go to Step 5 of Option two when this step is finished.)

Step 7: 5 Minutes

Discuss this exercise in terms of the discussion questions and concluding points, below.

OPTION TWO

Step 4: Advance Preparation for Option Two, 20 minutes

Using the format shown in Figure 2, develop two dialogues that portray situations in which you have particular difficulty being assertive.

Step 5: 5 Minutes

If you are not already working in a group, the group leader will instruct you on formation of subgroups.

FIGURE 1

Some Common Assertiveness Situations

Instructions: Develop a passive, an aggressive, and an assertive response to each of the following situations.

Situation	Passive Response	Aggressive Response	Assertive Response
1. You have just completed a task you are very proud of. Your boss compliments you on it. You say....	It was nothing....	I deserved it. I did, didn't I.	Thank you
2. You have just completed a task where you felt you had done a very good job. Your boss says it is totally unacceptable. You say....	I'm sorry	Who are you to judge	Why wasn't it
3. Your subordinate worked overtime all week to get an important report ready for you. Having read it, you realize there are serious flaws in it. You say....	Can you e-mail me your report	A monkey could have written this - do it over	The content is good - need to restyle
4. A colleague who constantly borrows office supplies from your department (but never pays you back), asks to borrow some supplies your own people need. You say....	Sure	Absolutely not	No, but I need you to restock/reorder/replace the supplies you take.
5. Your boss takes you out to lunch and makes an unmistakable "pass" at you. You like your job and would like to keep it. You say...	Nothing	Back off. Don't even ask me again you pinhead	I'm flattered, but I feel this is inappropriate - I expect you as my boss.
6. You ask your boss for a raise you believe you deserve. You say....	I feel uneasy asking you, but can I have a raise?	I'm good and I deserve a raise	I've been working hard and would like you to consider me for a raise / earned a raise

FIGURE 2
Format for Describing Difficult Assertive Situations

Situation 1

State here what your goals are in the situation you describe. What is it you want to accomplish?

What Is Said	*What You Are Thinking But Not Saying*
(In play script form, duplicate the approximate dialogue as closely and in as much detail as you can. Indicate both what you say and what the other person(s) involved say.)	Indicate your thoughts here at various points during the dialogue.
Example:	
Me: Hello, Sue, this is Ed....	I hope she doesn't hang up.
Sue: (Impatiently) What do you want?	Oh, oh.
Me: ...	...

At the end, indicate how you feel about the interaction after it is *over*.

Prepare a second sheet in similar fashion for Situation 2.

Step 6: 10 Minutes per Person per Role Play (1 Hour and 40 Minutes for Five-Person Groups).

1. Person #1 shares one of her difficult assertiveness situations with the group.
2. Person #2 volunteers to role-play person #1 in a reenactment of the situation. Person #2 should play person #1 *behaving assertively* in one's situation. (If additional role players are needed, other members of the group should volunteer to play these parts.)
3. Person #1 role-plays *her antagonist,* or the person who represents the greatest problem for her in this situation.

Working from one's description of the situation, briefly role-play how it should go if person #1 were handling the situation assertively.

4. After each role play, provide feedback to each other on how you saw each other behaving.
5. Replay the scene until you feel that the group has developed an assertive solution. *NOTE:* If you are not sure whether a solution is assertive or not, compare it to the principles of assertiveness on pp. 415 to 416 of the Folio of Resources.

If person #2 is unable to discover an assertive solution, another group member should assume the role of person #1.

Work Quickly! You will need to move along very quickly to stay on schedule.

When the group has finished with one's situation, person #2 then presents one of his difficult assertiveness situations. Continue until all situations have been role-played and resolved.

Step 7: 15 Minutes

Working alone, review what you have learned in the role plays and look at your IRI scores. Did the IRI identify the types of problems you depicted in the difficult assertiveness situations? If not, does it suggest other areas where you may have problems with assertiveness?

Write a brief "contract" for yourself covering the following.

What are the most difficult assertiveness situations for you?

What would you like to accomplish in these situations? What are your objectives?

What things can you begin to do to build your ability to be assertive in these situations? (You may need to start with some elementary behaviors and gradually build up to the tough stuff.)

Set a target date for completing your plan.

Step 8: 10 Minutes or More

Discuss this exercise in terms of the discussion questions and concluding points, below.

DISCUSSION QUESTIONS

1. Can assertiveness help you with problems like being effective in managing your time, taking off weight, or acquiring new friends? How?
2. If assertiveness means expressing yourself in such a way as to make it easier for others to do the same, what are some examples of how you might do this?
3. What happens to people who are not assertive at work? Passive people? Aggressive people? Why?

GENERALIZATIONS AND CONCLUSIONS

Concluding Points

1. Many people report that they become very anxious in situations where they know they should be assertive. What should a person do if her anxiety keeps her from being assertive in a certain type of situation?

2. Popular assertiveness training books prescribe a number of "techniques" for dealing with certain situations. Do you regard the following (from Smith, 1975) as assertive? Why?

a. "Broken record." (When someone tries to talk you out of something, you simply repeat your position over and over again in a calm, controlled voice. For example, "I do not wish to buy any magazines today.")

b. "Fogging." (When someone criticizes you, you respond by agreeing, rather than becoming defensive or argumentative. You agree with the general principle of what they have to say, or you agree with any factual parts of their criticism. But you *don't* change your behavior. For example, *Boss:* "You'd better take it a little easy; no one can work and go to school at the same time." *Subordinate:* (Fogging) "It sure is a lot of work.")

Participant's Reactions

READINGS AND REFERENCES

See the readings listed at the end of "Toward a Viable Concept of Assertiveness" in the Folio of Resources.

Smith, M. J., *When I Say No I Feel Guilty* (New York: Dial Press, 1975).

14
PERSUASIVE INTERVIEWING

PURPOSE:
(1) To explore alternative approaches and techniques in persuasive interviewing.
(2) To practice conducting the persuasive interview.

ADVANCE PREPARATION:
(1) Read the Introduction
(2) If assigned, complete Steps 1 and 2.

GROUP SIZE: *Option I:* Entire class participates in demonstration and critique. *Option II:* Small groups of four to seven.

TIME REQUIRED: *Option I:* 65 minutes (or more, depending upon the number of role plays conducted). 45 minutes if Steps 1 and 2 are completed in advance. *Option II:* 60 minutes. 35 minutes if Steps 1 and 2 are completed in advance.

SPECIAL MATERIALS: None.

SPECIAL PHYSICAL REQUIREMENTS: *Option I:* Two chairs and a table set up to simulate an office. *Option II:* Room with moveable chairs.

RELATED TOPICS: Interpersonal communication, Organizational realities.

INTRODUCTION

In a persuasive interview, the objective is *to change the behavior and/or attitudes of another person.* In general, we expect resistance from the other person who usually has good reasons (although we may not know what they are) for thinking or behaving as they do—but our objective is to get him or her to see it our way. Common business examples include selling, asking the boss for a raise, getting a subordinate to follow a different procedure, convincing a colleague to change his or her way of doing things, and so forth.

In this exercise, you will prepare yourself for, and then conduct, a persuasive interview. The basic premise is that thorough preparation can help to make you more successful in achieving a mutually agreeable outcome. While no one can expect to hit a home run every time at bat, we believe this approach will improve your batting average considerably. Note that if you have already practiced nondirective or problem-solving interviewing (e.g. "Interviewing Trios"), the purpose here is quite different. In the persuasive interview, you are trying to satisfy your own needs, not those of the other person, although these are certainly relevant and need to be taken into account.

You should try to answer the following questions before you enter into the persuasive interview (for brevity, we have used the abbreviation TP—for target person).

Prepared for this volume by Donald D. Bowen.

GUIDELINES FOR PREPARING FOR THE INTERVIEW

1. What are my objectives? Be as specific as possible.
   What is the maximum value or outcome you hope to achieve?
   What is the minimum you are willing to settle for?
2. What needs or wants am I trying to satisfy in this situation?
3. Do I know what the TP's position is in this situation? If so, state it. If not, what do I need to know and how do I plan to find out?
4. If I know the TP's position, what needs or wants is he/she trying to satisfy in this situation?
5. What problems will TP have if I should achieve my objectives? Can these be resolved to TP's satisfaction? If so, how?
6. What are the reasons why TP should do or think as I propose? What am I willing to give up to get TP to comply?
7. What facts do I need to make the argument plausible to TP? Do I have these facts? If not, what do I need to do to get them before the interview?
8. What arguments will I raise to convince TP?
9. What counterarguments is TP likely to raise? How do I respond to these? Which ones does TP feel strongly about?
10. If my proposal is unacceptable to TP, what counterproposals am I willing to consider?

GUIDELINES FOR CONDUCTING THE INTERVIEW

11. How will I open the interview? Alternatives include:
    a. The direct approach: "Joe, I need to persuade you to do something for me."
    b. The indirect approach: "Joe, have you noticed the way the employees are avoiding us lately?"
    c. The very indirect approach: "Hi, Joe, how's the wife and kids? Getting in any golf nowadays?"
    Why did I decide to use this approach?
12. How will I conduct the main part of the interview? Alternatives include:
    a. Balanced approach: "The advantages to what I propose are. . . . The disadvantages are. . . ."
    b. One-sided: "Here's why I think we should take this course of action (with a list of advantages, but no disadvantages)."
    c. Anticipatory: "Joe, if I understand your position on the widget policy, it is (paraphrase Joe's position). Is that accurate?" When Joe agrees with the statement, then you might say: "I want to propose another approach that I think you might find acceptable."
    d. Coercion: "If you don't do as I say, you're fired!"
13. If TP should become highly emotional or unreasonable during the interview, what will I do?
14. Depending upon the outcome of the interview, do I want to do anything in particular by way of "closing." Do I need a signature on the dotted line? Do I need to summarize the discussion to make sure the agreement is clear in both

our minds? If things do not go as I wanted them to, is there something I should do in order to keep TP open for further discussion later?

HOW TO DEVELOP YOUR STRATEGY

We believe there are certain guidelines that can make you more effective in choosing among the alternatives for conducting the interview. While hard and fast rules are not possible, many people create barriers to their own effectiveness by making the wrong choice in many of these situations. Try the following guidelines and see if they work for you.

1. For openers:

The *direct approach* to opening the interview can be surprisingly effective in setting a tone of direct and honest interaction. Sharing your objective with the TP has the effect of reducing one source of tension and resistance from the beginning—that of the TP wondering what you are up to or why you are beating around the bush. As an alternative, particularly when you do not know whether the TP is aware of the situation or not, you might employ the *indirect approach*. The *very indirect approach,* on the other hand, is likely to leave the TP felling manipulated and used. "He came in here to tell me I was being transferred to Detroit, and he wasted half an hour beating around the bush before he got to the point."

2. The main part of the interview:

The *balanced approach* is probably best to use when the TP has strong feelings or needs involved in the situation. Similarly, when there are real alternative courses of action available, the balanced approach may signify you have given them careful consideration in arriving at the alternative you are proposing.

The *anticipatory approach* may be particularly useful if you are aware that the TP has strong feelings about the topic, or if you need to check to see if your understanding of those feelings is correct. When you have clarified the TP's feelings, then you may want to move to the balanced approach strategy.

The *one-sided approach* is probably best when the TP does not have strong feelings or opinions on the topic. Note that there is a risk in taking this approach, however, in that most people naturally resist one-sided presentations and are likely to tune out the entire message.

Although there are times when *coercion* may be the only effective alternative available, you should recognize that it has real limitations. At the very least, it engenders lingering resentment that is likely to backfire on you at some future time. At best, you can only count on a person changing his or her behavior during times when you can maintain surveillance over them. Coercion is notably unlikely to lead to commitment.

3. Explosions and other natural disasters

If strong feelings develop in the discussion, most of us have a tendency to try to deflect or avoid confronting the feelings. But strong feelings are an important aspect of the problem when they arise. Ignoring them or trying to get the other person to calm down and be more reasonable are strategies that are likely to make the problem worse, rather then better. As an alternative, try helping the TP to express the feelings. Paraphrase what TP says, with emphasis on what the TP seems to be feeling. Try to understand what is bothering the TP, then see if it is something you can deal with. Sometimes you will find that the TP has merely misunderstood what you proposed, and you can clarify your position. At other times, you may decide that TP's concerns have validity, and that you should consider withdrawing your proposal.

Okay, now you are ready to try some of these ideas out in an important simulated persuasive interview that confronts most people several times in their career. The instructor will indicate whether Option I or Option II is to be followed.

PROCEDURE

OPTION I

Step 1: 5 Minutes
The instructor will designate someone to role play S. W. Cartwright. When Cartwright has been assigned, the remaining members of the class will take turns playing the Vice President of Marketing in the Epitaph Insurance Company case. Read the role instructions for your role in the Appendix. *Read only your own role* at this time.

Step 2: 15 Minutes
Prepare a written plan for the interview from the point of view of the employee asking Cartwright for a raise. Answer all of the questions under Guidelines For Preparing the Interview as fully as possible. Decide on your strategies for conducting the interview following the Guidelines.

Step 3: 5 Minutes
Using available tables and chairs, set up an "office" for S. W. Cartwright where all of the class can see and hear the role plays to be conducted there.

Step 4: 5 Minutes/role play
Class members take turns role playing the Vice President. While playing the role, you will need to elaborate with details that are not shown in the description of Epitaph Insurance. This is acceptable, so long as the details you add are reasonable and realistic in light of the situation. As others play the roles, the rest of the class should take notes on the following:

  a. Was the Vice-President successful or making headway?
  b. What things did the Vice-President do that were particularly effective or inef-
     fective? How do these relate to the points in the guidelines?

Step 5: 5 Minutes/role play
After each role play, critique the Vice-President's performance. What went particularly well or particularly badly? In what ways did this illustrate any of the points in the guidelines?

Step 6: 15 Minutes
Discuss the role play using the Discussion Questions, below.

OPTION II

Step 1: 5 Minutes
If the class has not been previously organized into groups, the instructor will provide instructions for formation of small groups.

Step 2: 20 Minutes
One or more of the groups will be assigned to play the role of Cartwright in the role plays. The rest of the groups will take the role of the Vice-President. The group assigned the role of Cartwright should proceed in the same manner as the groups assigned to plan for the role of the Vice-President. Meet with the others in your assigned group, read the role instructions for your character (the instructor will tell you where to find these instructions in the appendix; *read only your own role* at this time). Prepare a written plan for the interview from the point of view of Cartwright or the Vice President who will ask Cartwright for a raise (depending upon the role that has been assigned to your group). Answer all of the questions under Guidelines For Preparing the Interview as fully as possible. Decide on your strategies for conducting the interview following the Guidelines. The Vice-President groups should appoint one of the group members to play the role of the Vice-President. The Instructor will select one or members of the "Cartwright" groups to play Cartwrights.

Step 3: 5 Minutes
The instructor will provide instructions for pairing up Cartwrights and Vice-Presidents. The remainder of the class should act as observers and take notes on the following during the role play:

a. Was the Vice-President successful or making headway?
b. What things did the Vice-President do that were particularly effective or ineffective? How do these relate to the points in the guidelines?

Step 4: 15 Minutes
Conduct role plays simultaneously with observers taking notes. Allot 10 minutes for role playing and 5 minutes for the observers to feed back their observations.

Step 5: 15 Minutes
(Entire class) discuss the role plays using the Discussion Questions below.

DISCUSSION QUESTIONS
1. How many of the Vice-Presidents succeeded in getting a raise? What elements of their arguments were critical in convincing Cartwright?
2. If Cartwright succeeded in talking the Vice-President out of a raise without having the Vice-President resign, what elements of Cartwright's argument were most effective?

3. If either Cartwright or the Vice-President did something to get the Vice-President fired, what happened?

GENERALIZATIONS AND CONCLUSIONS

Concluding Points

1. How many situations can you identify where a manager must use persuasion to get the job done?

2. What persuasive tactics are most likely to have a negative effect—either immediately or in the longer term?

3. In the instructions for drawing up your plan for the persuasive interview, you were told to identify your wants or needs in the situation. Why might this be an important step?

Participant's Reactions

READINGS AND REFERENCES

Karlins, M. and Abelson, H. I. (1970). *Persuasion: How Opinions and Attitudes are Changed* (2nd. ed.). New York: Springer.

Sincoff, M. Z. and Goyer, R. S. *Interviewing*. New York, Macmillan, 1984. See especially, Chapter 4.

SECTION FIVE
DECISION MAKING AND PROBLEM SOLVING

15
GROUP RANKING TASK: WINTER SURVIVAL

PURPOSE:
(1) To develop an understanding of group problem solving.
(2) To compare individual versus group decision making.

ADVANCE PREPARATION
(1) Read the "Introduction" below.
(2) Complete Steps 1 and 2 before session. *Do not discuss this exercise with anyone.*
GROUP SIZE: Any number of five- to nine-person groups.
TIME REQUIRED: Approximately 1½ hours. Allow more time for large groups.
SPECIAL MATERIALS: None.
SPECIAL PHYSICAL REQUIREMENTS: Movable chairs.
RELATED TOPICS: Interpersonal communication. Managers as leaders, Organizational communication.

INTRODUCTION

Research has shown that groups are frequently more effective than individuals in solving complex problems. This is especially true when the problem requires a quality decision. Groups may be more accurate and bring more knowledge to bear on the solution.

In this exercise you will have an opportunity to experiment and see whether this

Adapted by Roy J. Lewicki from "Winter Survival" in D. Johnson and F. Johnson, *Joining Together*, 3rd edition, Prentice Hall. Used with permission of D. Johnson.

is true. In Steps 1 and 2, you will be asked to try to solve a problem by yourself. Do not discuss this problem with anyone, either in your group or outside it. Work on the problem by yourself. When you come to your next session you will have an opportunity to solve the problem with a group. What do you expect to happen? Do you think your solution will be better than your group's?

PROCEDURE

Step 1: Read "The Situation," below:

Winter Survival Exercise: The Situation

You have just crash-landed in the woods of northern Minnesota and southern Manitoba. It is 11:32 A.M. in mid-January. The light plane in which you were traveling crashed on a lake. The pilot and copilot were killed. Shortly after the crash, the plane sank completely into the lake with the pilot's and copilot's bodies inside. None of you are seriously injured and you are all dry.

The crash came suddenly, before the pilot had time to radio for help or inform anyone of your position. Since your pilot was trying to avoid a storm, you know the plane was considerably off course. The pilot announced shortly before the crash that you were twenty miles northwest of a small town that is the nearest known habitation.

You are in a wilderness area made up of thick woods broken by many lakes and streams. The snow depth varies from above the ankles in windswept areas to knee-deep where it has drifted. The last weather report indicated that the temperature would reach minus twenty-five degrees Fahrenheit in the daytime and minus forty at night. There are plenty of dead wood and twigs in the immediate area. You are dressed in winter clothing appropriate for city wear—suits, pantsuits, street shoes, and overcoats.

While escaping from the plane, the several members of your group salvaged twelve items. Your task is to rank these items according to their importance to your survival, starting with 1 for the most important item and ending with 12 for the least important one.

You may assume that the number of passengers is the same as the number of persons in your group, and that the group has agreed to stick together.

Step 2: Winter Survival Decision Form (10 Minutes)

Rank the following items according to their importance to your survival, starting with 1 for the most important one and proceeding to 12 for the least important one.

_____ Ball of steel wool
_____ Newspapers (one per person)
_____ Compass
_____ Hand ax
_____ Cigarette lighter (without fluid)
_____ Loaded .45-caliber pistol
_____ Sectional air map made of plastic
_____ Twenty-by-twenty-foot piece of heavy-duty canvas
_____ Extra shirt and pants for each survivor

_____ Can of shortening
_____ Quart of 100-proof whiskey
_____ Family-size chocolate bar (one per person)

Step 3: Group Ranking (30 Minutes)

Copy your ratings from Step 2 onto the chart on the next page. Place them in the first column labeled "Individual Ranking." DO NOT LEAVE ANY RANKINGS BLANK. Rate all items, even if you are guessing. As a team, rank the 12 items according to the *group's consensus* on each item's importance to survival. Do not vote; try to reach true consensus. Base your decision on knowledge, logic, or the experiences of group members. Here are some guidelines to use in reaching consensus:

1. Avoid arguing *blindly* for your own opinions. Present your position as clearly and logically as possible, but listen to other members' reactions and consider them carefully before you press your point.
2. Avoid changing your mind just to reach agreement and avoid conflict. Support only solutions with which you are able to agree to at least some degree. Yield only to positions that have objective and logically sound foundations.
3. Avoid conflict-reducing procedures such as majority voting, tossing a coin, averaging, and bargaining.
4. Seek out differences of opinion. They are natural and expected. Try to involve everyone in the decision process. Disagreements can improve the group's decision because a wide range of information and opinions improves the chances of the group to hit upon more adequate solutions.
5. Do not assume that someone must win and someone must lose when discussion reaches a stalemate. Instead, look for the next most acceptable alternative for all members.
6. Discuss underlying assumptions, listen carefully to one another, and encourage the participation of *all* members—these are especially important factors in reaching decisions by consensus.

When the group is finished, every member should enter the group's decision in the second column labeled "Group Ranking."

Step 4: 5 Minutes

After all teams have finished, your group leader will read the rankings that were assigned to the items by an expert. As these are read, please enter the "correct" rank in the "Survival Expert's" ranking column on the Scoring Sheet.

Step 5: 10 Minutes

Compute the difference between your individual ranking and the group's ranking. Use the *absolute* difference—ignore plus and minus scores. Enter the difference for each item's ranking in the column on the "Scoring Sheet" labeled "Influence." Add these numbers to obtain a total of the differences.

This score might be called an "influence score." It may represent the extent that you influenced the group to "your way of thinking" about the correct way to rank the alternatives. Discuss for a few minutes the people who you feel were most influential in group discussion. Then share your "influence scores," and see how they compare—the smaller the score, the more the group's score parallels the private ranking of certain individuals.

SCORING SHEET

Items	Individual Ranking	Group Ranking	Survival Expert's Ranking	Influence	Individual Accuracy	Group Accuracy
Ball of steel wool						
Newspapers						
Compass						
Hand ax						
Cigarette lighter						
.45-caliber pistol						
Sectional air map						
Canvas						
Shirt and pants						
Shortening						
Whiskey						
Chocolate bars						
TOTALS						

Step 6: 10 Minutes

Compute the absolute difference between your individual ranking and the expert's ranking. Again, ignore the plus or minus scores. Enter the difference for each item's ranking in the column labeled "Individual Accuracy." Again, obtain a total score. This score might best be called your "accuracy" score.

Share your "accuracy" score with your group, and compare these to the "influence" scores from Step 5. The difference between these two scores might be called the "appropriateness of influence." If you had a very *low* accuracy score and a *low* influence score, you were really "right" and the group listened to you. If your accuracy score is high but your influence is low, you might try to explore why you had so much influence in spite of not being accurate; similarly, if you were accurate but had very little influence, you might try to find out why you didn't have a bigger impact on the group.

Step 7: 5 Minutes

Compute the absolute difference between your group's rankings and the expert's rankings. Enter these in the column labeled "Group Accuracy," and compute the total.

Step 8: 5 Minutes

Compute the average of the individual accuracy scores of group members, by adding up all of the individual accuracy scores and dividing by the number of members in the group. Enter this in the space for your group's Average Individual Score" on the "Composite Group Scoring Sheet."

COMPOSITE GROUP SCORING SHEET

	Team number					
	1	2	3	4	5	6
Average Individual Score: Add up all the individual accuracy scores in your group and divide by the number in the group						
Team Score						
Gain Score: The difference between the Team score and the Average Individual Score. If the Team score is lower than the Average individual Score, then gain is "+." If Team score is higher than Average Individual Score, then gain is "−."						
Number of group members scoring better than Team Score						
Lowest Individual Score ("Best" Individual Score)						

Step 9: 2 Minutes

Compute your "gain score" on the Composite Scoring Sheet. This is the difference between the average individual accuracy score and the group accuracy score. If the score is positive (+), this means the group's solution to the problem was better than what individuals could do by themselves without discussion. If the score is negative (−), this means the group discussion did not make good use of the best resources among members, and that the group product was worse than what individuals, on the average, could do by themselves without discussion.

Step 10: 3 Minutes

Enter the lowest individual score in your group. This is the "best" score obtained by an individual alone. Compare this against the average individual score (Step 8) and the team accuracy score. If your group worked extremely well in sharing information and making decisions, it is likely your team score was not only better than the average of individuals, but better than the best individual in the group. This shows that it is often possible for the group to excel even its best individual resource.

Step 11: 5 Minutes

When Steps 3 through 10 have been completed, the group leader will record the data from each group for the discussion. One member of your group should be prepared to provide these data.

Step 12: 15 Minutes

Discuss this experience as a total group with the group leader. Try to arrive at some conclusions about group problem solving and the relevance of the exercise to real-world problems in management.

DISCUSSION QUESTIONS

1. Based on the data generated in this exercise, does it appear that the groups solved the problem more accurately than individuals on the average? (Compare team scores with average individual scores for the groups.)
2. Did the groups do better than even the "best" individual?
3. Which people influenced your group the most? Was this influence based on perceived knowledge related to the solution or on other kinds of control?
4. Was the influence of various members reflected in your group's "accuracy" scores?
5. How was this task different from or similar to other tasks you have done as a group?
6. Do you think the nature of the task had any effect on how leadership needs were met in your group?
7. What were the characteristics of the decision-making process in the most accurate groups (those with the lowest team scores)?
8. What kinds of decision situations in organizations have elements in common with this exercise?

GENERALIZATIONS AND CONCLUSIONS

Concluding Points

1. Six factors to consider in managing decision making are:
   a.

   b.

   c.

   d.

e.

f.

2. Generally, group decision making or problem solving is more desirable and effective when:

   a.

   b.

   c.

   d.

   e.

3. Three advantages of group decision making are:

   a.

   b.

   c.

4. Four disadvantages of group decision making are:

   a.

b.

c.

d.

5. The advantage of groups composed of people from different parts of the organization is what? The disadvantage is what?

Participant's Reactions

READINGS AND REFERENCES

Cartwright, D., and Zander, A., *Group Dynamics: Research and Theory* (New York: Harper & Row, 1968).

Hall, J., "Decisions, Decisions, Decisions," *Psychology Today,* 5 (1971), 55ff.

Hinton, B. L., and Reitz, H. J., *Groups and Organizations* (Belmont, Calif.: Wadsworth Publishing Co., 1971).

Janis, I. L., *Victims of Groupthink* (Boston: Houghton Mifflin, 1972).

Napier, R. W., and Gershenfeld, M. K., *Groups: Theory and Experience* (Boston: Houghton Mifflin, 1973).

16
VALUES AND GROUP
DECISION MAKING: THE CITY COUNCIL

PURPOSE:
(1) To explore choices involving different value premises.
(2) To explore factors affecting group decision making.

ADVANCE PREPARATION: None.
GROUP SIZE: Any number of small groups.
TIME: 1 hour.
SPECIAL MATERIALS: None.
SPECIAL PHYSICAL REQUIREMENTS: Movable chairs.
RELATED TOPICS: Power, Managers as leaders, Interpersonal communication, Organizational communication.

INTRODUCTION

In this exercise you will be given a decision to make that is not uncommon in public service. As a group, you will have to make a decision that will affect the entire community. Unfortunately, there is no single "right" answer. Only your group can decide what the members feel is right. As you will see, your decision will involve a question of values. In this exercise you may also discover some of the ways that conflicts arise in decision situations and how these can be minimized.

PROCEDURE

Step 1: 5 Minutes
Form small groups, situated far apart if possible.

Step 2: 5 Minutes
Read the "Problem Description," below.

PROBLEM DESCRIPTION

On March 13, the City Council of New Bristol received notification that Stanley and Sophie Kuchinski had willed their property at 125 Ridge Road to the city. The letter stated that the Kuchinskis had attached the following stipulation:

1. The Council must accept the donation within 3 months or forego any claim to it;
2. The Council must also decide on its use by this date;

Developed by Francine S. Hall.

3. If the Council chooses to lease, sell, or donate the property, it may do so to either a nonprofit or profit organization as long as the use "contributes to the quality of life of the community."

It is now June 12, and the Council members are meeting to make their decision. Prior to the meeting, they solicited requests and suggestions for use of the property, a brick structure located on approximately 1 acre of prime land.

The following "bids" were received.

1. The Friendship House, a United Fund agency that runs programs for minority and disadvantaged youth, has requested that the city arrange a lease/purchase agreement. New Bristol is primarily an industrial town with a growing black and Puerto Rican population. There is clearly a need for programs for disadvantaged young people, but neighbors in the area have vocally come out against the Friendship House proposal, crying "We don't want 'them' over here."

2. Saint Stanislaus Church, whose property borders the Kuchinskis' on the east, has offered to buy the property at fair market value. The Church would convert it to additional parking facilities to accommodate their growing crowds on Bingo nights. Many senior citizens support this use, since Bingo is one of few recreational outlets for them, and "safe" off-street parking is at a premium.

3. A local builder has offered to buy the property and develop it into a moderately priced retirement condominium building. This would require special building permits, but would help the tax base and also be aesthetically pleasing.

4. A local women's group has proposed a three-year lease to set up a Women's Center. It would provide workshops, birth control and abortion counseling (and possibly a clinic), and also serve as a refuge for battered women. According to police, wife beating has increased drastically as inflation and layoffs increase stress in this working class community. The Rector of Saint Stanislaus' Church is strongly opposed to letting the women's group have the property.

5. One of the major oil companies has submitted a bid several times fair market value for the property if the Council will grant a zoning change to allow a gas station. These funds could be used to buy sorely needed playground equipment, but the gas station would be an eyesore on Ridge Road.

6. John Lateck has offered to buy the property for $200,000 and convert it to a "private club." He has assured the Council that it would not be an "ordinary" bar. Rumors are that John is a homosexual. Parents of children at Saint Stanislaus School have besieged the Council with letters smearing John and alleging that the property would turn into a gay bar.

7. Nafco, a statewide drug addiction service, has asked to lease the property to set up a drug rehabilitation center with residential facilities.

Assume that, as a group, you form the City Council. What will you do with the Kuchinski property? You must make a decision.

Step 3: 30 Minutes

After everyone is familiar with the problem, the group should discuss the alternatives until you reach consensus. You may *not* vote. All group members must agree to the final decision. Record the time it takes you to reach a decision. The group leader may give special instructions to some groups. Proceed according to any special instructions you receive.

Step 4: 10 Minutes

Each group will report on its decision-making process and outcome. The instructor will record the data on the board.

Step 5: 10 Minutes

Discussion and conclusion.

GENERALIZATIONS AND CONCLUSIONS

Concluding Points

1. What frequently happens when group members make decisions solely on the basis of individual values?

2. What are some of the ways that groups can facilitate decision making when value issues arise?

3. What are some of the techniques that groups resort to in resolving value conflicts?

4. How can an organization reduce value conflicts in decision making?

5. How do decisions involving values differ from decisions where there is an objective "right" answer?

Participant's Reactions

READINGS AND REFERENCES

Guth, W. D. and Tagiuri, R., "Personal Values and Corporate Strategy," *Harvard Business Review,* Sept./Oct. (1965), 123–32.

Powers, Charles W. and Vogel, David, *Ethics in the Education of Business Managers* (Hastings-on-the-Hudson, N.Y.: Institution of Society, Ethics, and Life Sciences, 1980).

Robbins, Stephen P., *Managing Organizational Conflict* (Englewood Cliffs, N.J.: Prentice-Hall, 1974).

17
COMPETITIVE ESCALATION: THE DOLLAR AUCTION

PURPOSE:
To understand processes of escalation of commitment.

ADVANCE PREPARATION: Bring money to class as specified by instructor.
GROUP SIZE: Entire class.
TIME REQUIRED: 25 minutes.
SPECIAL MATERIALS: Small change (nickels, dimes, and quarters), if specified by instructor.
SPECIAL PHYSICAL REQUIREMENTS: None.
RELATED TOPICS: Group decision making and problem solving, Organizational realities, Power, Organizational communication.

INTRODUCTION

In this activity, you will have the opportunity to explore the behavior of individuals in a competitive environment. The situation presented to you here is a simulation of a bidding exercise; the results demonstrate what usually occurs when individuals or groups are highly competitive with one another.

PROCEDURE

Step 1: 5 Minutes

The instructor will play the role of auctioneer. In this auction, the instructor will auction off $1 bills (the instructor will inform you whether this money is real or imaginary). All members of the class may participate in the auction at the same time.

The rules for this auction are slightly different from a normal auction. In this version, *both the highest bidder and the next highest bidder will pay their last bids* even though the dollar is only awarded to the highest bidder. For example, if Bidder A bids 15 cents for the dollar and Bidder B bids 10 cents, and there is no further bidding, then A pays 15 cents for the dollar and receives the dollar, while B pays 10 cents and receives nothing. The auctioneer would lose 75 cents on the dollar just sold.

Bids must be made in multiples of 5 cents. The dollar will be sold when there is no further bidding. If two individuals bid the same amount at the same time, ties are resolved in favor of the bidder located physically closest to the auctioneer. *During each round, there is to be no talking except for making bids.*

Adapted by Roy J. Lewicki from a research paradigm developed by Martin Shubik and Allan Teger.

Step 2: 15 Minutes

The instructor (auctioneer) will auction off five individual dollars to the class. Any student may bid in an effort to win the dollar. A record sheet of the bidding and winners can be kept in the table below.

	Amount Paid by Winning Bidder	Amount Paid by Second Bidder	Total Paid for This Dollar
First dollar			
Second dollar			
Third dollar			
Fourth dollar			
Fifth dollar			

DISCUSSION QUESTIONS

1. Who made the most money in this exercise—one of the bidders or the auctioneer? Why?
2. As the auction proceeded, did bidders become more competitive or cooperative? Why?
3. Did two bidders ever pay more for the money being auctioned than the value of the money itself? Explain how and why this happened?
4. Did you become involved in the bidding? Why?
   a. If you became involved, what were your motivations? Did you accomplish your objectives?
   b. If no, why didn't you become involved? What did you think were the goals and objectives of those who did become involved?
5. Did people say things to one another during the bidding to influence their actions? What was said, and how was it influential?

GENERALIZATIONS AND CONCLUSIONS

The psychology of the processes that occur in this exercise has been called "entrapment," and can occur when individuals invest more resources to justify or recover resources already spent. It can occur in severe conflict, when parties are so concerned about winning—or not losing—that they are willing to invest more resources than the victory itself is worth. Many critics of the Vietnam War would characterize American involvement there as a case of entrapment. Entrapment can also occur when individuals believe that further commitment of resources might "change their luck." Gamblers who have lost a great deal may continue to bet more, hoping they will soon "hit it big." Similarly, banks and financial lending officers continue to lend money to poorly managed companies hoping management will improve and the lenders will be able to recover their investment. Well-known examples of this process have occurred in recent years with the Penn-Central Railroad, Lockheed Corporation, and W. T. Grant Department Stores.

Competitive escalation and entrapment occur in a variety of settings—standing in a waiting line, being put on "hold" when telephoning for an airline reservation, deciding whether to repair an already dilapidated car, making a commitment of resources to a risky business venture, or the escalation of anger, threats, and destructive tactics that characterizes human conflict. Even when individuals are fully aware of the dynamics of entrapment, they nevertheless frequently become ensnared again. The following are several ways to avoid getting caught in this spiral.

1. *Set definite prior limits for how much of a commitment you will make.* A gambler who only takes $50 to the racetrack can only lose $50. If the gambler takes $100, even though he only intends to bet $50, he may be much more likely to bet the remainder.

2. *Get others to help you maintain these limits.* If you have to explain, justify, or defend the reasons why you exceeded your limits to someone else, you probably will expect to be embarrassed enough to want to avoid the situation. Inform others of your commitment or limits—make it public.

3. *Beware of your need to impress others.* Other people do not always help to prevent entrapment; there are times when the presence of others may encourage entrapment, particularly when we want to look good to these people. If people expect that maintaining or escalating a commitment will make them look good to others, even at cost to themselves, they are highly prone toward making entrapping commitments. While we all want to look good to others, we may be willing to make poor judgments as a consequence.

4. *Be pessimistic—keep costs in mind.* Evaluate your current situation in terms of *what you have already lost,* not what you are likely to gain if you win. Doing so will make current losses and future costs much more prominent in your decision to commit further resources, and make you more realistic about whether the risk of future gain is worth it.

Participant's Reactions

READINGS AND REFERENCES

Bazerman, Max H., *Judgment in Managerial Decision Making,* New York: John Wiley, 1986.
Rubin, Jeffrey Z., "Psychological Traps," *Psychology Today*, 15, March (1981), 52–63.
Teger, Allan I., *Too Much Invested to Quit* (New York: Pergammon Press, 1980).

18
CREATIVE PROBLEM SOLVING

PURPOSE

To introduce participants to the nature of creative thinking and its applications in the organizational world.

To begin developing both individual and group skills that use innovative and creative approaches to solving problems.

ADVANCE PREPARATION:

(1) Complete the questionnaire "How Creative Are You?" found in #55 in the Folio of Resources. Do this before reading ahead.

(2) Read Introduction A, "Creativity: What Is It?" and Introduction B, "Techniques To Increase Creative Thinking".

GROUP SIZE: Unlimited. Steps 1–4 are best accomplished in small task groups of five to nine people.

TIME REQUIRED: 50 minutes minimum

SPECIAL MATERIALS: Instructor will distribute or assign, if necessary.

SPECIAL PHYSICAL REQUIREMENTS: Moveable chairs. Room for several simultaneous discussion groups.

RELATED TOPICS: Communication, leadership, change

INTRODUCTION A

Creativity: What Is It?

What is creativity? Broadly defined, *creativity is the ability to discover or create solutions to problems.* We can do this alone or in groups. Most important, our ability to generate creative solutions can be applied in many contexts.

Most people think of creativity *just* as an artistic endeavor. Nonsense! Creative solutions are as important in managerial situations as they are in an artist's or a composer's studio, a chef's kitchen, or a designer's salon.

As a manager you will be seeking innovative approaches to a variety of problems. Think for a moment of the many problems for which there are no standard solutions— no set policies to guide you: contract and other negotiations, employee rewards, marketing campaigns, product development, interpersonal conflicts, and, especially, the budget process.

To be creative—to find an innovative solution, we the problem solvers need to be able to approach the problem with an *open mind, a willingness to hold off premature*

Developed by Francine S. Hall

judgment, and the *ability to look at the situation in new and different ways.* If you accept things the way they are, the way they have always been, or the way someone else says they should be, then it will probably be hard for you to come up with new or novel solutions. But, if you ask yourself, "Is there another way of looking at this situation?" then you are already on your way to creative results.

In Introduction B we look at specific techniques you can apply daily in your work and life to obtain more innovative results.

Before embarking on your creative development, however, think of some of the incredible accomplishments that have come from people who were willing to say, "We can," "Why not," "Let's try."

For example, we can look at science and technology and wonder where we would be without airplanes, telephones, TV, and lasers. Medicine is rampant with examples of artificial human parts and machines that keep us alive, not to mention the many drugs that have eradicated illnesses.

But what about the managerial contributions to our creative examples? Lee Iacocca has been hailed for his work in turning around Chrysler. It was not accomplished by continuing to move the organization in the "old" way. He did it by bringing new and different techniques to Chrysler. Or, look at People's Express and its early success. Both the services and personnel were designed in ways that set the company apart from others, made it price competitive, and encouraged growth and profitability. A random event? Hardly. Its founders were creative managers.

Finally, think of the examples we find in think tanks and consulting firms like Arthur D. Little of Cambridge, Massachusetts. ADL is credited with the invention of both a *lead balloon* and a *silk purse* made *from a sow's ear.* Any idea of how you would go about achieving those results? Ask your instructor after you have thought about it.

Meanwhile, read the next section to see, specifically, what you can do to enhance your own creativity.

INTRODUCTION B

Techniques to Enhance Creative Thinking

Roger Van Oech, author of the book *A Whack on the Side of the Head,* suggests that there are ten good ways to begin looking at problems more innovatively. While Van Oech's book presents a full discussion of each, it is helpful to alert you to his list at least briefly.

1. *Look for multiple "right answers."* Most of us have been trained to seek *the* right answer. By following this trend, we often fail to find other equally good (or sometimes better) ways to do things.
2. *Avoid excessive logic at first.* In order to germinate ideas, we can benefit from the kind of thinking that uses metaphors, fantasy, and diffuse and divergent viewpoints. Later, logic is most helpful when we get practical and evaluate ideas in terms of putting them into action or practice.

3. *Challenge Rules.* What this means is that flexibility enhances creativity. Inspect ideas, challenge the way things have always been, ask *why?* each time you are tempted to accept an idea *because* . . .

4. *Be Practical.* By this, Van Oech suggests that we ask *what if?* questions, seeking to think of the practical results that would be obtained *if* things were different. To do this, however, we each need to allow our imaginations to have free rein.

5. *Use Ambiguity.* When communicating, we all want to be as clear as possible. When looking for new ideas, however, a little ambiguity can be helpful. It makes us stop and look at things differently as we seek to "de-fuzz" the situation. Often, that is when we discover a new way to look at the problem.

6. *Foster the Creative Side of Errors.* While many people have been trained to avoid error (and seek one *right* answer), creativity comes from errors. Playing it safe often keeps us from trial-and-error behavior, from seeking a new (and better) way to do something, and finally, from using our failures to stimulate a new path to success. Don't be afraid of being wrong. Use the experience to look at your goal afresh.

7. *Use Play to Fertilize Your Thinking.* When we play, we put aside many of the blocks to creative thinking that have already been discussed. When we play, we tinker, we experiment, we are spontaneous, we just have fun. In the process, we may discover a new way to do something, a way we would not have discovered if we had approached the problem with a serious search for the quick right answer.

8. *Go Outside Your Area of Specialization.* Hunt for new ideas, new information, new models, and so forth. Use analogs and models from other disciplines.

9. *Use Foolish Thinking and Nonconformist Behavior* to generate new ideas. Most people are afraid to look foolish, so they act like everyone else, staying within established norms. Like the right-answer seekers they may miss the opportunity to try things in a new, different, or even innovative way.

10. *Believe You Are Creative and You Will Be.* Creative behavior *can* be your self-fulfilling prophecy. If you perceive yourself as capable of creative thinking you can become a creative problem solver. If you assume you are not, then you will act accordingly—and you won't be.

PROCEDURE

Step 1: Brainstorming Preparation (10 Minutes)

Each group will have an opportunity to develop some creative solutions to problems that typically arise during the life cycle of a new product.

Think of yourself as a young company that is learning to solve problems. Review the following steps in brainstorming and agree to follow the rules outlined below:

1. The first rule is that every idea—any and all ideas—are fair game. No idea cannot be expressed. No idea can be rejected initially.

Your first goal will be to *generate as many ideas as you possibly can.*
To do this, each member must refrain from discussing or evaluating ideas. Your task—individually and as a group—is to just throw out ideas and ideas and ideas.

2. The second rule is that no idea can be judged until after you have finished the generation of ideas—that is, exhausted your creative juices.

3. The third rule is that ideas can and should be used to spawn other ideas. Frequently one idea will cause someone to make an association and create a new connection that may, in fact, result in the ultimate solution. During brainstorming, the generative side of creative problem solving, ideas belong to the entire group. Don't be or feel possessive about your thoughts. They may cause someone else to be more creative. Share ideas!

Step 2: 10 Minutes total

Your instructor will hand out a copy of a picture that could be used in advertising copy. You will have 5 minutes after the words "BEGIN BRAINSTORMING" to *just* generate ideas. Remember, do not evaluate ideas.

Step 3: 10 Minutes

1. Each group will tally the total number of ideas generated. Divide by the number of group members to get an average.

2. Instructor will rotate among groups, asking for examples of ideas that came out of your brainstorming.

3. Discuss why your group did well or not. How did the process feel for the first time.

Step 4: 20 Minutes

Option A—Steps 2 and 3 can be repeated using a new stimulus provided by the instructor. Groups are able to see how their ability to brainstorm improves with practice.

Option B—Proceed with step 4, to develop a full product idea and complete the brainstorming cycle.

Step 4A: Your instructor will give you raw materials (or ask you to take out the ones you were instructed to bring) or give you a picture of your raw materials.

When the instructor announces: "Begin Brainstorming," you will have 5 minutes to *generate as many ideas as you can for a product or service you can produce* that utilizes your *company's raw materials. Make a list.*

Step 4B: Now take *10 minutes* to discuss and evaluate your ideas. Feel feel to combine, change, adapt, or even find a new solution from among those on your list.

Step 4C: You now have *5 minutes* to decide on the final product idea that you will present to the class.

Step 5: 10 Minutes

Discuss, as a total class, what happened in your groups. How did your ideas emerge? Were there frustrations that you experienced?

GENERALIZATIONS AND CONCLUSIONS

Concluding Points

1. What did you find most conducive to creativity in your group?

2. What got in the way?

3. What did you find most difficult about trying to be creative?

4. What would you like to work on as a personal goal regarding your creative behavior?

Participant's Reactions

READINGS AND REFERENCES

Oech, Roger von. *A Whack on the Side of the Head,* New York: Warner Books, 1983.
Oech, Roger, von. *A Kick in the Seat of the Pants,* New York: Harper & Row, 1986.
Smith, Emily. "Are You Creative?" *Business Week,* September, 1985.

SECTION SIX
NEGOTIATION AND CONFLICT

19
CAMPUS TRAVEL AGENCY: A NEGOTIATION ROLE PLAY

PURPOSE:

(1) To explore the dynamics of interpersonal bargaining.

(2) To experiment with negotiating strategy and tactics.

ADVANCE PREPARATION: Role positions may be read and prepared in advance.

GROUP SIZE: Subgroups of two or four (one or two role players for each side). Total group can be any size.

TIME REQUIRED: 45 minutes for the exercise, plus at least 30 minutes for discussion, depending on class size.

SPECIAL MATERIALS: None

SPECIAL PHYSICAL REQUIREMENTS: None

RELATED TOPICS: Group decision making and problem solving; Power; Interpersonal communication.

INTRODUCTION

A great deal of human activity in business situations is concerned with resolving conflicts. Individuals or groups have different needs, preferences and priorities; somehow, these conflicting preferences and priorities must be resolved if individuals or groups are going to work together. Negotiation is one major process parties use to resolve their conflicts and manage disputes.

Developed by Roy J. Lewicki.

The following scenario puts you in a negotiation situation. In this situation, you will either play the role of a travel agent or an airlines representative, trying to negotiate a price on tickets for a group charter. Your objective in this situation is to maximize your profits for the organization you represent.

PROCEDURE

OPTION 1

Step 1: 10 Minutes

Count off the class in groups of two, which will negotiate against one another. One person will play the representative of Campus Travel Agency, and the other will play the representative of Midwest Airlines. Each should read and prepare only his or her own role information (found in the Appendix). Each should become comfortable with the information and playing the role of a travel agent or an airline representative. Each should try to set a negotiating objective (the deal you would like to reach) and a "bottom line" (the minimally acceptable deal). Midwest Airlines should prepare to make the first offer on ticket price.

Step 2: 10 Minutes

Representatives of Campus Travel should meet together in groups of four to six people. Similarly, representatives of Midwest Airlines should meet together in groups of four to six people. The purpose of this group is simply to talk about the role they have been assigned to play, and to clarify any ambiguities in the role information or in their task. The group should NOT try to set collective goals or minimal deals to be achieved in the actual negotiation.

OPTION 2

Steps 1 and 2: 15-20 Minutes

Count off the class in groups of four. Two students will pair together to represent Campus Travel Agency, and two students will pair together to represent Midwest Airlines. Each pair should read it's own role information (found in the Appendix of this book). Once each has read the information, the two should work together to understand the information. They should try to set a negotiating goal (the deal they would like to achieve) and a "bottom line" (a minimally acceptable deal) as a team. Midwest Airlines should prepare to make the first offer on ticket price.

BOTH OPTIONS

Step 3: 15-20 Minutes

After individuals or pairs are prepared to negotiate, they should meet with their opponent(s). Each pair or foursome should attempt to negotiate an agreement that specifies:

- the number of tickets to be sold

- the percentage of commission that will be paid to Campus Travel Agency
- any other elements to the agreement.

You are *NOT REQUIRED* to agree. If you believe the other side is being unfair or unreasonable, you can take your business elsewhere.

The instructor will signal when time is finished. The Campus Travel representative(s) should be prepared to report to the class on the outcome and the process of their negotiations. If no deal was achieved, please report the last offers on the table before negotiations ended, and reasons why negotiations broke down.

Step 4: 30 Minutes

The instructor will ask for and record the results of the negotiations from each pair or foursome. The instructor will also ask for comments about the process of negotiation in each group, and the strategy and tactics used by various negotiators. Comparisons will be made, and the instructor will use this data to highlight the dynamics of the negotiation process.

DISCUSSION QUESTIONS

1. What was the outcome that you negotiated in in this situation? How did you feel about this outcome as you were agreeing to it?
2. How does your settlement compare to the other pairs or groups in the room? How do you feel about this settlement now that you have had a chance to compare it to what others did?
3. How does your outcome compare to the goal you set before negotiations began? Did you achieve your goal? Why or why not?
4. What strategy or tactics did you attempt to use to achieve your outcome? Did they work?
5. What strategy or tactics did your opponent(s) try? Did they work?

ADDITIONAL QUESTION FOR OPTION 2:

6. Did having a partner make this negotiation easier or more difficult? Why?

GENERALIZATIONS AND CONCLUSIONS

Concluding Points

1. What are the distinctive features of a competitive negotiation?

2. What impact does setting a goal and a "bottom line" have on negotiating behavior?

3. What are some of the most common strategies and tactics used in competitive negotiation?

4. What impact does sharing your agreement with others have on the way you feel about it?

5. What are some of the most common problems and dilemmas in competitive negotiation?

Participant's Reactions

READINGS AND REFERENCES

Brooks, E. and Odiorne, G. S. 1984. *Managing by Negotiations*. New York: Van Nostrand Reinhold.

Fisher, R. and Ury, W. 1981. *Getting to Yes*. New York: Houghton Mifflin.

Lewicki, R. J. and Litterer, J. 1985. *Negotiation*. Homewood, Il.: Richard D. Irwin.

20
TWO-PERSON BARGAINING: THE UGLI ORANGE CASE

PURPOSE:
(1) To explore the dynamics of two-person bargaining.
(2) To experiment with creative problem solving.

ADVANCE PREPARATION: None.
GROUP SIZE: Subgroups of two or three. Total group can be any size.
TIME REQUIRED: 30 minutes.
SPECIAL MATERIALS: None.
SPECIAL PHYSICAL REQUIREMENTS: None.
RELATED TOPICS: Group decision making and problem solving, Interpersonal communication.

INTRODUCTION

In many work settings, it is not possible for people to work independently as they pursue their work goals. Often we find ourselves in situations where we must obtain the cooperation of other people, even though the other people's ultimate objectives may be different from our own. This will be your task in the present exercise.

PROCEDURE

Divide the class into pairs. One student in each pair will read and prepare the role of Dr. Roland, and one will play the role of Dr. Jones. Students should read their respective role descriptions (from the Appendix) and prepare to negotiate (see Steps 2 and 3, below).

Step 2: 10 Minutes, Negotiation

At this point the group leader will read the following statement: "I am Mr. Cardoza, the owner of the remaining Ugli oranges. My fruit-exporting firm is based in South America. My country does not have diplomatic relations with your country, although we do have strong trade relations.

"After you have read about your roles, spend about 10 minutes meeting with the other firm's representative and decide on a course of action. Then pick a spokesperson who will tell me: (1) What do you plan to do? (2) If you want to buy the oranges, what price will you offer? (3) To whom and how will the oranges be delivered?

"After you have done this, you may negotiate with the other firm's representative."

Originally developed by Robert J. House. Adapted by D. T. Hall and R. J. Lewicki, with suggested modifications by H. Kolodny and T. Ruble. Used with permission.

Step 3: 15 Minutes

Following the negotiation, the spokesperson and the observer will report on the solution reached in each group and the process by which agreement was reached.

DISCUSSION QUESTIONS

1. Was there full disclosure by both sides in each group? How much information was shared?
2. Did the parties trust one another? Why or why not?
3. How creative and/or complex were the solutions? If solutions were very complex, why do you think this occurred?

Additional Question for Option 2

4. What was the impact of having an audience or constituency on the behavior of the negotiators? Did it make the problem harder or easier to solve?

GENERALIZATIONS AND CONCLUSIONS

Concluding Points

1. What is the relationship between trust and disclosure of information?

2. In a bargaining situation such as this, before competing or collaborating with the other person, what should you do first?

3. How does mistrust affect the creativity or complexity of bargaining agreements?

4. Do audiences to a negotiation increase competitiveness or cooperativeness? Why?

Participant's Reactions

READINGS AND REFERENCES

Fisher, R. and Ury, W. (1981) *Getting to Yes.* Boston: Houghton Mifflin.
Lewicki, R. J. and Litterer, J. (1985) *Negotiation.* Homewood, Il: Richard D. Irwin.

21
THIRD-PARTY CONFLICT RESOLUTION

PURPOSE:

(1) To understand the criteria that third parties use when they intervene and attempt to resolve others' conflicts.

(2) To practice mediation skills as a mechanism for resolving conflict between others.

ADVANCE PREPARATION: The instuctor will specify whether the case (Seatcor), "The Mediation Guide," and/or the role-playing materials are to be read and studied before class.

GROUP SIZE: Part 1 (Case): Any size group. Part 3 (Role Play): Subgroups of three, four if an observer is used.

SPECIAL MATERIALS: None

SPECIAL PHYSICAL REQUIREMENTS: None

RELATED TOPICS: Negotiation, Decision making and problem solving, Interpersonal communication.

INTRODUCTION

In addition to being involved in their own conflicts, managers are often called upon to intervene and to settle conflicts between other people. The two activities in this section are designed to explore how third parties may enter conflicts for the purpose of resolving them, and to practice one very effective approach to intervention. In the first activity, you will read about a manager who has a problem deciding how to intervene in a dispute, and you will discuss this case in class. Part 2 of this chapter contains a Mediation Guide, which will be useful to completing the role-playing activity in Part 3, in which some of you will actually attempt to resolve a managerial dispute.

PART 1

PROCEDURE

Step 1: 5 Minutes
Read "The Seatcor Company" case.

Developed by Roy J. Lewicki. The Mediation Guide developed by Larry Ray, American Bar Association, and Robert Helm, Oklahoma State University. "The Seatcor Manufacturing Company" and "The Summer Interns" developed by Blair Sheppard, Fuqua School of Business, Duke University. Used with permission.

THE SEATCOR MANUFACTURING COMPANY

You are Senior Vice-President of Operations and Chief Operating Officer of Seatcor, a major producer of office furniture. Joe Gibbons, your subordinate, is Vice-President and General Manager of your largest desk assembly plant. Joe has been with Seatcor for 38 years and is two years away from retirement. He worked his way up through the ranks to his present position and has successfully operated his division for five years with a marginally competent staff. You are a long-standing personal friend of Joe's and respect him a great deal. However, you have always had an uneasy feeling that Joe has surrounded himself with minimally competent people by his own choice. In some ways, you think he is threatened by talented assistants.

Last week you were having lunch with Charles Stewart, Assistant Vice-President and Joe's second in command. Upon your questioning, it became clear that he and Joe were engaged in a debilitating feud. Charles was hired last year, largely at your insistence. You had been concerned for some time about who was going to replace Joe when he retired, especially given the lack of really capable managerial talent on Joe's staff. Thus, you prodded Joe to hire your preferred candidate—Charles Stewart. Charles is relatively young, 39, extremely tenacious and bright, and a well-trained business school graduate. From all reports he is doing a good job in his new position.

Your concern centers around a topic that arose at the end of your lunch. Charles indicated Joe Gibbons is in the process of completing a five-year plan for his plant. This plan is to serve as the basis for several major plant reinvestment and reorganization decisions that would be proposed to senior management. According to Charles, Joe Gibbons has not included Charles in the planning process at all. You had to leave lunch quickly and were unable to get much more information from Charles. However, he did admit that he was extremely disturbed by this exclusion and that his distress was influencing his work and probably his relationship with Joe.

You consider this a very serious problem. Charles will probably have to live with the results of any major decisions about the plant. More important, Joe's support is essential if Charles is to properly grow into his present and/or future job. Joe, on the other hand, runs a good ship and you do not want to upset him or undermine his authority. Moreover, you know Joe has good judgment; thus, he may have good reason for what he is doing.

How would you proceed to handle this issue?

Step 2: 5 Minutes

Before discussing this case with anyone else, answer the following two questions:

1. Assume you were the Senior Vice President of Operations. Exactly what would you do in this situation regarding the conflict between Joe and Charles?
2. Why would you take this action—i.e. what are your primary objectives by intervening in this way?

Step 3: 20–30 Minutes

The instructor will discuss this case with the entire class.

Step 4: 10–15 Minutes

The instructor will summarize the case discussion and present a framework for understanding how participants analyzed the case and decided to intervene.

DISCUSSION QUESTIONS

1. How much agreement was there within the class about the way that the senior vice president should approach the problem? How did this compare with your own preferred strategy?

2. Which style of conflict intervention do you use most frequently? Which one do you use least frequently? Are there other styles that are commonly used which are not listed here?

3. Which one of the four criteria (efficiency, effectiveness, participant satisfaction and fairness) are typically most important to you when you intervene in someone else's dispute? Which one is most important when someone intervenes to settle a dispute you are having? If these are different, what are the implications of these differences for training managers in dispute resolution?

4. Do you use different styles in different situations? If so, what kind of situational factors affect which styles you use?

GENERALIZATIONS AND CONCLUSION

CONCLUDING POINTS

Compare your answers to the questions in Step 2 with the ways that others approached the problem. To practice your own comprehension of third party dynamics, answer the following questions:

1. What are the four different criteria that managers can have when they intervene in disputes?

2. What are the various styles that managers use to intervene in disputes?

3. Which of these styles is most effective given each of the four criteria?

PART 2

THE MEDIATION GUIDE

The Steps
Step 1: Stabilize the Setting
Step 2: Help the Parties Communicate

Step 3: Help the Parties Negotiate
Step 4: Clarify Their Agreement

Step 1: Stabilize the Setting

Parties often bring strong feelings of anger and frustration into mediation. These feelings can prevent them from talking productively about their dispute. You, as mediator, will try to gain their trust for you and for the mediation process. Stabilize the setting by being polite; show that you are in control and that you are neutral. This step helps the parties feel comfortable, so they can speak freely about their complaints, and safe, so they can air their feelings.

1. _____ Greet the parties.
2. _____ Indicate where each of them is to sit.
3. _____ Identify yourself and each party, by name.
4. _____ Offer water, paper and pencil, and patience.
5. _____ State the purpose of mediation.
6. _____ Confirm your neutrality.
7. _____ Get their commitment to proceed.
8. _____ Get their commitment that only one party at a time will speak.
9. _____ Get their commitment to speak directly to you.
10. _____ Use calming techniques as needed.

Step 2: Help The Parties Communicate

Once the setting is stable and the parties seem to trust you and the mediation process, you can begin to carefully build trust between them. Both must make statements about what has happened. Each will use these statements to air negative feelings. They may express anger, make accusations, and show frustration in other ways. But, with your help, this mutual ventilation lets them hear each other's side of the story, perhaps for the first time. It can help calm their emotions, and can build a basis for trust between them.

1. _____ Explain the rationale for who speaks first.
2. _____ Reassure them that both will speak without interruption, for as long as is needed.
3. _____ Ask the first speaker to tell what has happened.
   a. _____ Take notes.
   b. _____ Respond actively; restate and echo what is said.
   c. _____ Calm the parties as needed.
   d. _____ Clarify, with open or closed questions, or with restatements.
   e. _____ Focus the narration on the issues in the dispute.
   f. _____ Summarize, eliminating all disparaging references.
   g. _____ Check to see that you understand the story.
   h. _____ Thank this party for speaking, the other for listening quietly.
4. _____ Ask the second speaker to tell what has happened.
   a. _____ Take notes.
   b. _____ Respond actively, restate and echo what is said.

    c. _____ Calm the parties as needed.

    d. _____ Clarify, with open or closed questions, or with restatements.

    e. _____ Focus the narration on the issues in the dispute.

    f. _____ Summarize, eliminating all disparaging references.

    g. _____ Check to see that you understand the story.

    h. _____ Thank this party for speaking, the other for listening quietly.

5. _____ Ask each party, in turn, to help clarify the major issues to be resolved.

6. _____ Inquire into basic issues, probing to see if something instead may be at the root of the complaints.

7. _____ Define the problem by restating and summarizing.

8. _____ Conduct private meetings, if needed (explain what will happen during and after the private meetings).

9. _____ Summarize areas of agreement and disagreement.

10. _____ Help the parties set priorities on the issues and demands.

Step 3: Help The Parties Negotiate

Cooperativeness is needed for negotiations that lead to agreement. Cooperation requires a stable setting, to control disruptions, and exchanges of information, to develop mutual trust. With these conditions, the parties may be willing to cooperate, but still feel driven to compete. You can press for cooperative initiatives by patiently helping them to explore alternative solutions, and by directing attention to their progress.

1. _____ Ask each party to list alternative possibilities for a settlement.

2. _____ Restate and summarize each alternative.

3. _____ Check with each party on the workability of each alternative.

4. _____ Restate whether the alternative is workable.

5. _____ In an impasse, suggest the general form of other alternatives.

6. _____ Note the amount of progress already made, to show that success is likely.

7. _____ If the impasse continues, suggest a break or a second mediation session.

8. _____ Encourage them to select the alternative that appears to be workable.

9. _____ Increase their understanding by rephrasing the alternative.

10. _____ Help them plan a course of action to implement the alternative.

Step 4: Clarify Their Agreement

Mediation should change each party's attitude toward the other. When both have shown their commitment, through a joint declaration of agreement, each will support the agreement more strongly. For a settlement that lasts, each component of the attitudes toward each other—their thinking, feeling, and acting—will have changed. Not only will they now *act* differently toward each other, they are likely to *feel* differently, more positively, about each other, and *think* of their relationship in new ways.

1. _____ Summarize the agreement terms.

2. _____ Recheck with each party their understanding of the agreement.

3. _____ Ask whether other issues need to be discussed.

4. _____ Help them specify the terms of their agreement.
5. _____ State each person's role in the agreement.
6. _____ Recheck with each party *when* they are to do certain things, *where,* and *how.*
7. _____ Explain the process of follow-up.
8. _____ Establish a time for follow-up with each party.
9. _____ Emphasize that the agreement is theirs, not yours.
10. _____ Congratulate the parties on their reasonableness and on the workability of their resolution.

Steps in a Mediation Process

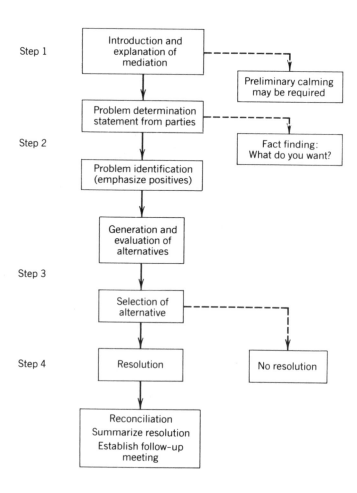

PART 3

PROCEDURE

Step 1: 15 Minutes

Read "The Mediation Guide" in this section, if it has not been previously assigned as advanced preparation.

Step 2: 5 Minutes

The instructor will divide the class into subgroups of three or four (the latter if an observer is to be used). One person should play the role of Samantha (Sam) Pinder, who will mediate the dispute. The other two parties will play the roles of Brenda Bennett (Director of Personnel) and Harold Stokes (Vice-President, Engineering), who are having a dispute over the hiring of summer interns.

Step 3: 10 Minutes

Each party should read his or her role information and prepare to play the role. Remember to:

1. Empathize with the role. Try to see the world as your assigned character sees it and behave accordingly.
2. Do not add facts that are not in the case.
3. Stay in your role. Do not jump out of the role to comment on the process.
4. Try to make it realistic.

The person playing the third party will try to defuse the conflict and seek a resolution. Do not make it unnecessarily difficult for this person; "play along" to observe how third-party dispute resolution can work. On the other hand, you are not required to settle if you believe that your character's needs are truly not being met by the proposed agreement.

Step 4: 20–30 Minutes

Sam Pinder will "lead" each small group in an effort to resolve the summer interns problem. When you have achieved a resolution, write it down so you can report it to the class later.

Step 5: 10–20 Minutes (optional)

Discuss how the mediation session went in each of the small groups. Use the Mediation Guide. If you had an observer assigned, the observer can comment on the strengths and weaknesses of the mediator's efforts.

Step 6: 20–30 Minutes

Be prepared to report to the class on the outcome of the mediation session, and particular problems that may have occurred with the mediation session in your small group.

DISCUSSION QUESTIONS

1. What were some of the different settlements arrived at by different groups?
2. How did your group's specific settlement emerge? How much influence did Pinder have in shaping the final settlement? How much influence did Stokes and Bennett have?
3. Was the mediation process fair? Was the achieved outcome fair? What made it fair or unfair?
4. What tactics did the mediator use that were most effective? Least effective?
5. When would it be most useful to use mediation in an organization? When would it be least useful to use mediation?
6. What are some of the major problems and obstacles to using mediation as a manager?

GENERALIZATIONS AND CONCLUSIONS

Concluding Points

1. Describe the major steps in mediation.

2. Under what conditions is mediation most and least effective?

READINGS AND REFERENCES

Folberg, J., & Taylor, A. (1984). *Mediation*. San Francisco: Jossey Bass.
Moore, C. (1986). *The Mediation Process*. San Francisco: Jossey Bass.

SECTION SEVEN
MANAGERS AS LEADERS

22
THE STORM WINDOWS: A ROLE PLAY

PURPOSE:
(1) To analyze a simulated case showing a difficult leadership problem.
(2) To experiment with and identify alternative ways of dealing with leadership problems.
(3) To give practice in diagnosing employee motivation and in responding flexibly.

ADVANCE PREPARATION: None. Participants are asked *not* to read the case materials *before* participating in the exercise.
GROUP SIZE: Any size.
TIME REQUIRED: 50 minutes.
SPECIAL MATERIALS: None.
SPECIAL PHYSICAL REQUIREMENTS: Table and four chairs at front of room.
RELATED TOPICS: Motivation: Basic concepts, Interpersonal communication, Organizational communication, Group decision making and problem solving, Negotiation and conflict, Power.

INTRODUCTION

Textbooks in management and organizational behavior stress the need for managers to be sensitive to the needs of different employees, and to be flexible in dealing with people. Yet textbooks also stress the need to recognize problems quickly and to take

From Maier, N. R. F., Solem, A. R., and Maier, A. A. *Supervisory and Executive Development: A Manual for Role Playing* (New York: Wiley, 1957). Adapted by D. T. Hall. Used with permission of A. A. Maier.

decisive action. It is often harder to apply concepts of leadership than it is to learn them. Here's a chance for you to apply what you know about leadership and motivation.

PROCEDURE

Step 1: 5 Minutes

1. Arrange a table and four chairs around it at the front of the room so that all occupants face the group as well as each other.
2. The group leader picks two people to play the role of Leigh Brown, the foreman. Both people playing the role of Brown are to leave the room and study "The Settling" and "Role Instructions." They are told that when they return they will be asked to read a script, after which they will be on their own. The people playing Brown should not return until instructed to do so.
3. The group leader selects four persons to occupy the seats at the table, each with a copy of the script. The other members of the class will act as observers.
4. Read "The Setting" and "Role Instructions," which follow.

THE SETTING

The National Telephone Company stationed a group of five telephone installers and repairmen, including the foreman-in-charge, in the community of Basking Ridge. The facility was an old two-story frame structure, which housed the four small trucks used by the workers. The second floor contained supplies, equipment, small tools and the like, which the workers required in their work. Of some significance to this case was the fact that the building had three windows on the first floor and three windows on the second floor on each of two sides of the building.

Because the flow of work was intermittent in character, depending upon the number of new telephones to be installed, weather conditions that might damage the lines, and similar variables, the workers did all the maintenance work required to keep the building in a clean and orderly condition. During those times when they were not otherwise occupied, they washed and greased their trucks, performed minor repairs on the building, and did a variety of "odd jobs."

The workers got along well with the working foreman and with each other. The informality of the situation gave the workers considerable freedom from "work rules" and other restraints that might be aggravating.

Many of their activities followed the lines of custom and practice that had developed through the years and were generally understood and accepted by all concerned. Among these was the practice of having the worker with the least seniority in the group assigned the "odd job" of washing the windows (inside and outside, using a ladder) and taking apart, cleaning and reassembling the aluminum combination screen/storm windows. This was done twice a year, in the spring and in the fall.

The day on which the incident we are about to witness occurred was a balmy spring day. The foreman had gone to the local bank on his lunch hour to transact some personal business. The four telephone installers had been sitting around the lunch table, where they were accustomed to heating some soup and making coffee, if they so desired, to go along with their lunches that they brought to work with them. They had been talking about current topics of local interest.

Cast of Characters

Leigh Brown .... Working foreman
Dale Jones .... Telephone installer—20 years' service
"Frenchy" Smith .... Telephone installer—18 years' service
C. J. Oswald..................... Telephone installer—14 years' service
Chris Bryan .... Telephone installer— 5 years' service

ROLE INSTRUCTIONS

The group is very close-knit and there is a great deal of respect for each member of the group by the other members. Because of this harmony within the group, members have a tendency to "kid" other members—sometimes to an excess. There is less "kidding" with Brown, the working foreman, than among the other members of the group. Brown is seen in a position of authority, even though this authority is seldom exercised. None of the members wants to put up the windows or see Chris fired.

Leigh Brown

Leigh Brown is 50 years old, married, with two children, both of whom are through school. Leigh gets along well with the group and has little difficulty in getting the work done that has been assigned from General Headquarters. At the present time. Leigh has the task of cleaning and changing the windows.

Dale Jones

Dale Jones is 52 years old, married, with four children, the youngest two of whom are still in high school. Dale is heavy-set and shows the years. Dale is "cutting" with some remarks—to such a degree that it sometimes makes people defensive. Dale is proud of having a long service record with the company.

"Frenchy" Smith

"Frenchy" Smith is 46 years old, married, with four children, all of whom are still in school. "Frenchy" has never worked for anyone else but the National Telephone Company and has the longest company-wide seniority, but has been in Basking Ridge two years less than Jones.

C. J. Oswald

C. J. Oswald is 34 years old and is single. Very popular with the opposite sex, Oswald has a good work record and keeps extracurricular activities confined to after hours. Oswald is usually the instigator of the kidding that goes on at work and has been known to have started more than one good argument among other members of the group. C. J. is a "needler," known for getting people in a corner and then not letting them work their way out. C. J. does get along with the other members of the group and would not want to see anyone get hurt. C. J. feels most strongly about Chris not working on the windows, for C. J. is next in line seniority-wise. C. J. also knows if Chris is fired, there will be a new hire before the windows have to go up in the fall, meaning C. J. would do the job only once. C. J. is a person who believes in principles.

Chris Bryan

Chris is 28, married, with five children, three preschool and two in grade school. Money is very tight at home. Chris is very defensive and hates to feel "taken advantage of." Chris is the slowest thinker in the group and is easily trapped by the kidding of the group, especially by Oswald. Chris finds it extremely difficult to back down and is vitally concerned with presenting an acceptable "face" and preserving the "face" once it is presented. Chris wants to feel an equal member of the group.

Step 2: 25 Minutes

1. The group leader reads "The Setting" aloud to the class and the actors. He or she then gives the signal for the reading of the script for scene 1, which can be found in the Appendix at the back of this book.
2. After scene 1 has been read, the two people playing the foreman, Leigh Brown, are asked to return to the room. One is asked to observe, and one is asked to read the script for scene 2, below. After this, Leigh and Chris make up their own lines, proceeding as they see fit.

SCRIPT FOR SCENE 2 OF "THE STORM WINDOWS"

(Enter Leigh Brown)

Brown: Hi, gang! Sure is a beautiful day. Say, Chris, I've got a nice light new aluminum ladder out there in the truck that I think ought to make your job of working on the windows quite a bit easier. Why don't you get started on it, if you're through with your lunch. Boy, I wish I had one of those aluminum ladders at home!

(Telephone installers, except for Chris, all exit hastily)

3. Role playing should continue to a point where the decision reached by the role players terminates the interview or where something else happens that requires an interruption.
4. If subsequent interviews are implied in the decision, such as having a discussion with the other employees as a group, role-play such meetings.
5. After the first "Leigh Brown" has finished his or her role play, stop for a brief discussion. The group leader will ask what Leigh and Chris were trying to accomplish, what needs they were feeling. The rest of the class may suggest what might be done differently.
6. With the second "Leigh Brown," repeat the role play (Step 2, parts 2 to 4 above).

Step 3: 20 Minutes

Discussion

DISCUSSION QUESTIONS

1. Use discussion to evaluate the process observed. How do the observers feel about the decision(s)?
2. List all the things Chris did in the role playing that indicated he or she had a

problem that was more than a dislike of working on windows. Distinctions should be made between (a) the status of the job; (b) the number of times Chris has done the job; (c) the influence of "kidding" on Chris; (d) Chris' statement to the others about refusing to work on the windows.

3. Analyze face-saving and insubordination as employee behaviors, and determine the extent of agreement in the class.
4. Evaluate face-saving problems of Foreman Brown and consider what can be done to avoid them.
5. Determine whether the group considers this a problem between the foreman and the crew or between the foreman and Chris.
6. See if the group can agree on some rule that will guide them as individuals in determining when a problem involves the group and when it does not.

GENERALIZATIONS AND CONCLUSIONS

Concluding Points

1. In handling a leadership problem, an extremely important first step is what?

2. To perform this activity (described in the answer to Question 1 above), what kind of skills must the manager develop?

3. Can the manager's needs affect the success of his or her leadership? If so, how?

Participant's Reactions

READINGS AND REFERENCES

Bennis, W. G., and Nanus, B. *Leaders* (New York: Harper & Row, 1985).

Fiedler, F. E., *A Theory of Leadership Effectiveness* (New York: McGraw-Hill, 1967).

Filley, A., House, R., and Kerr, S., *Managerial Process and Organizational Behavior* (Glenview, Ill.; Scott, Foresman 1976). See Chapters 11 and 12.

Maier, N. R. F., *Psychology in Industrial Organizations,* 4th ed. (Boston: Houghton-Mifflin, 1973). See Chapter 13, "Basic Principles in Motivation."

23
CHOOSING A LEADERSHIP STYLE: APPLYING THE VROOM AND YETTON MODEL

PURPOSE:

(1) To learn a method of diagnosing leadership situations.

(2) To learn how to choose managerial decision-making processes more effectively.

ADVANCE PREPARATION: Read "A New Look at Managerial Decision-Making" in the "Introduction" to this exercise, an article that describes the Vroom and Yetton model.

GROUP SIZE: Subgroups of three to five. Total group can be any size.

TIME REQUIRED: 50 Minutes.

SPECIAL MATERIALS: None.

SPECIAL PHYSICAL REQUIREMENTS: None.

RELATED TOPICS: Group decision making and problem solving, Applied motivation and job design, Organizational communication, Power, Planned change.

OPTION ONE[1]

1. Before doing any of the following reading by Vroom, read Cases I to IV, which appear later in this exercise (pp. 129–130). For each case, decide which of the following decision styles would be most appropriate, assuming you were the leader in each situation:

AI: You solve the problem or make the decision yourself, using information available to you at the time.

AII: You obtain the necessary information from your subordinate(s), then decide on the solution to the problem yourself.

CI: You share the problem with relevant subordinates individually, getting their ideas and suggestions without bringing them together as a group. Then *you* make the decision, which may or may not reflect your subordinates' influence.

CII: You share the problem with your subordinates as a group, collectively obtaining their ideas and suggestions. Then *you* make the decision, which may or may not reflect your subordinates' influence.

GII: You share a problem with your subordinates as a group. Together you generate and evaluate alternatives and attempt to reach agreement (consensus) on a solution, as a group.

[1]The authors are indebted to Professor David Boje for suggesting this option.

2. Now read the Vroom article. How do your recommendations compare with what Vroom might recommend?

3. Analyze each case with the decision tree in Figure 1. What decision style does the decision tree analysis lead to for each case?

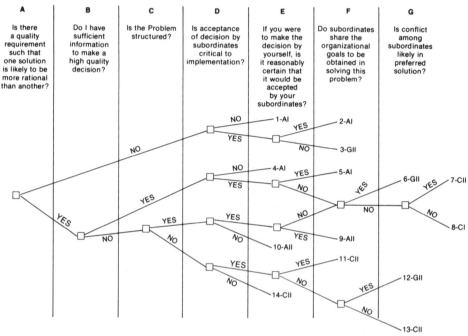

FIGURE 1:
Decision Process Flow Chart

OPTION TWO

INTRODUCTION: Read the following

A NEW LOOK AT MANAGERIAL DECISION-MAKING
Victor H. Vroom

While there are many differences in the roles that managers are called upon to play in organizations, all managers are decision-makers. Futhermore, there is little doubt that their effectiveness as managers is largely reflected in their "track record" in making the right decisions.

Several scholarly disciplines share an interest in the decision-making process. On one hand, we have the fields of operations research and management science, both concerned with how to improve the decisions which are made. Their models of decision-making, which are aimed at providing a rational basis for selecting among alternative courses of action, are termed normative or prescriptive models. On the other hand, we have, in the efforts of psychologists, sociologists, and political scientists, attempts to understand the decisions and choices that people do make. March and Simon were among the first to suggest that an understanding of the decision-making process could be central to an understanding of the behavior of organizations—a point of view that was later amplified by Cyert and March in their behavioral theory of the firm. In this tradition, the goal is understanding rather than improvement, and the models descriptive rather than normative.

Whether the models are normative or descriptive, the common ingredient is a conception of decision-making as an information-processing activity, frequently one which takes place within a single manager. Both sets of models focus on the set of alternative decisions or problem solutions from which the choice is, or should be, made. The normative models are based on the consequenses of choices among these alternatives; the descriptive models on the determinants of these choices. Alternatively, one could view the decision-making which occurs in organizations as a social or interpersonal process rather than a cognitive one. A major aspect of the manager's role in the decision-making process is to determine which person or persons should take part in the solution of the problem—or to put it more broadly—which social process should be engaged in the solution of the problem or the making of the decision.

. . . Underlying traditional approaches to leadership is the conviction that the manager is *the* problem-solver or decision-maker—that the task of translating problems into solutions is inevitably his task. In the alternative view of decision-making as a social process, we see the manager's task as determining how the problem is to be solved, not the solution to be adopted . . . .

Toward a Normative Model

[Let us begin] with [a] normative question. What would be a rational way of deciding on the form and amount of participation in decision-making that should be used in different situations? We [are] tired of debates over the relative merits of theory X and theory Y and of the truism that leadership depends upon the situation. We [feel] that it [is] time for the behavioral sciences to move beyond such generalities and to attempt to come to grips with the complexities of the phenomena with which they intended to deal.

Table 1 shows a set of alternative decision processes which we have employed in our research. Each process is represented by a symbol (e.g., AI, CI, GII) which will be used as a convenient method of referring to each process. The first letter in this symbol signifies the basic properties of the process (A stands for autocratic, C for consultative, and G for group). The roman numerals which follow the first letter constitute variants

TABLE 1:
Types of Management Decision Styles

AI: You solve the problem or make the decision yourself, using information available to you at that time.
AII: You obtain the necessary information from your subordinate(s), then decide on the solution to the problem yourself. You may or may not tell your subordinates what the problem is in getting the information from them. The role played by your subordinates in making the decision is clearly one of providing the necessary information to you, rather than generating or evaluating alternative solutions.
CI: You share the problem with relevant subordinates individually, getting their ideas and suggestions without bringing them together as a group. Then *you* make the decision which may or may not reflect your subordinates' influence.
CII: You share the problem with your subordinates as a group, collectively obtaining their ideas and suggestions. Then *you* make the decision which may or may not reflect your subordinates' influence.
GII: You share a problem with your subordinates as a group. Together you generate and evaluate alternatives and attempt to reach agreement (concensus) on a solution. Your role is much like that of chairman. You do not try to influence the group to adopt "your" solution and you are willing to accept and implement any solution which has the support of the entire group.

on that process. Thus, AI represents the first variant on an autocratic process, and AII the second variant, etc.[2]

Conceptual and Empirical Basis of the Model

A model designed to regulate, in some rational way, choices among the decision processes shown in Table 1 should be based on sound empirical evidence concerning the likely consequences of the styles. The more complete the empirical base of knowledge, the greater the certainty with which one can develop the model and the greater will be its usefulness. To aid in understanding the conceptual basis of the model, it is important to distinguish three classes of outcomes which bear on the ultimate effectiveness of decisions. These are:

1. The quality or rationality of the decision.
2. The acceptance of commitment on the part of subordinates to execute the decision effectively.
3. The amount of time required to make the decision.

The evidence regarding the effects of participation on each of these outcomes of consequences has been reviewed in a chapter written by the author for *The Handbook of Social Psychology*. It was concluded that:

[2]The absence of GI from the code is attributable to the fact that the list of decision processes used in this paper is a part of a larger set of such processes used in broader and more comprehensive models. A complete explication of the entire set of processes and of the models which use them may be found in Vroom and Yetton (1973).

The results suggest that allocating problem solving and decision-making tasks to entire groups requires a greater investment of man hours but produces higher acceptance of decisions and a higher probability that the decision will be executed efficiently. Differences between these two methods in quality of decisions and in elapsed time are inconclusive and probably highly variable . . . . It would be naive to think that group decision-making is always more "effective" than autocratic decision-making, or vice versa; the relative effectiveness of these two extreme methods depends both on the weights attached to quality, acceptance, and time variables, and on differences in amounts of these outcomes resulting from these methods, neither of which is invariant from one situation to another. The critics and proponents of participative management would do well to direct their efforts toward identifying the properties of situations in which different decision-making approaches are effective rather than wholesale condemnation or deification of one approach (Vroom, 1970, pp. 239–40).

Stemming from this review, an attempt has been made to identify these properties of the situation or problem which will be the basic elements in the model. These problem attributes are of two types: (1) those which specify the importance for a

TABLE 2
Problem Attributes Used in the Model

Problem Attributes	*Diagnostic Questions*
A. The importance of the quality of the decision.	Is there a quality requirement such that one solution is likely to be more rational than another?
B. The extent to which the leader possesses sufficient information/expertise to make a high-quality decision by himself.	Do I have sufficient information to make a high-quality decision?
C. The extent to which the problem is structured.	Is the problem structured?
D. The extent to which acceptance or commitment on the part of subordinates is critical to the effective implementation of the decision.	Is acceptance of decision by subordinates critical to effective implementation?
E. The prior probability that the leader's autocratic decision will receive acceptance by subordinates.	If you were to make the decision by yourself, is it reasonably certain that it would be accepted by your subordinates?
F. The extent to which the subordinates are motivated to attain the organizational goals as represented in the objectives explicit in the statement of the problem.	Do subordinates share the organizational goals to be obtained in solving this problem?
G. The extent to which subordinates are likely to be in conflict over preferred solutions.	Is conflict among subordinates likely in preferred solutions?

particular problem of quality and acceptance, and (2) those which, on the basis of available evidence, have a high probability of moderating the effects of participation on each of these outcomes. Table 2 shows the problem attributes used in the present form of the model. For each attribute, a question is provided which might be used by a leader in diagnosing a particular problem prior to choosing his leadership style.

In phrasing the questions, technical language has been held to a minimum. Furthermore, the questions have been phrased in Yes-No form, translating the continuous variables defined above into dichotomous variables. For example, instead of attempting to determine how important the decision quality is to the effectiveness of the decision (attribute A), the leader is asked in the first question to judge whether there is any quality component to the problem. Similarly, the difficult task of specifying exactly how much information the leader possesses that is relevant to the decision (attribute B) is reduced to a simple judgment by the leader concerning whether he has sufficient information to make a high-quality decision.

It has been found that managers can diagnose a situation quite quickly and accurately by answering this set of seven questions concerning it. But how can such responses generate a prescription concerning the most effective leadership style or decision process? What kind of normative model of participation in decision-making can be built from this set of problem attributes?

Figure 1 shows one such model expressed in the form of a decision tree. It is the seventh version of such a model which we have developed over the last three years. The problem attributes, expressed in question form, are arranged along the top of the figure. To use the model for a particular decision-making situation, one starts at the left-hand side and works toward the right, asking oneself the question immediately above any box that is encountered. When a terminal node is reached, a number will be found designating the problem type[3] and one of the decision-making processes appearing in Table 1. AI is prescribed for four problem types (1, 2, 4, and 5): AII is prescribed for two problem types (9 and 10); CI is prescribed for only one problem type (8); CII is prescribed for four problem types (7, 11, 13, and 14); and GII is prescribed for three problem types (3, 6, and 12). The relative frequency with which each of the five decision processes would be prescribed for any manager would, of course, be dependent on the distribution of problem types in his role.

Once all seven questions have been applied to a given problem, a feasible set of decision processes is given. The feasible set for each of the 14 problem types is shown in Table 3. It can be seen that there are some problem types for which only one method remains in the feasible set, others for which two methods remain feasible, and still others for which five methods remain feasible.

When more than one method remains in the feasible set, there are a number of alternative decision rules which might dictate the choice among them. One, which underlies the prescriptions of the model shown in Figure 1, utilizes the number of manhours used in solving the problem as the basis for choice. Given a set of methods

---

[3]Problem type is a nominal variable designating classes of problems generated by the paths which lead to the terminal nodes.

TABLE 3
Problem Types and the Feasible Set of Decision Processes

Problem type	Acceptable methods
1	AI, AII, CI, CII, GII
2	AI, AII, CI, CII, GII
3	GII
4	AI, AII, CI, CII, GII[a]
5	AI, AII, CI, CII, GII[a]
6	GII
7	CII
8	CI, CII
9	AII, CI, CII, GII[a]
10	AII, CI, CII, GII[a]
11	CII, GII[a]
12	GII
13	CII
14	CII, GII[a]

[a]Within the feasible set only when the answer to question F is Yes.

with equal likelihood of meeting both quality and acceptance requirements for the decision, it chooses that method which requires the least investment in manhours. On the basis of the empirical evidence summarized earlier, this is deemed to be the method furthest to the left within the feasible set. For example, since AI, AII, CI, CII, and GII are all feasible as in Problem Types 1 and 2, AI would be the method chosen. This decision rule acts to minimize manhours subject to quality and acceptance constraints.

Application of the Model

To illustrate how the model might be applied in actual administrative situations, a case will be presented and analyzed with the use of the model. Following the description of the case, the author's analysis will be given including a specification of problem type, feasible set, and solution indicated by the model. While an attempt has been made to describe (this) case as completely as is necessary to permit the reader to make the judgments required by the model, there may remain some room for subjectivity. The reader may wish, after reading the case, to analyze it himself using the model and then to compare his analysis with that of the authors.

... You are a manufacturing manager in a large electronics plant. The company's management has always been searching for ways of increasing efficiency. They have recently installed new machines and put in a new simplified work system, but to the surprise of everyone, including yourself, the expected increase in productivity was not realized. In fact, production has begun to drop, quality has fallen off, and the number of employee separations has risen.

You do not believe that there is anything wrong with the machines. You have had reports from other companies who are using them and they confirm this opinion. You have also had representatives from the firm that built the machines go over them and they report that they are operating at peak efficiency.

You suspect that some parts of the new work system may be responsible for the change, but this view is not widely shared among your immediate subordinates, who are four first-line supervisors, each in charge of a section, and your supply manager. The drop in production has been variously attributed to poor training of the operators, lack of an adequate system of financial incentives, and poor morale. Clearly, this is an issue about which there is considerable depth of feeling within individuals and potential disagreement between your subordinates.

This morning you received a phone call from your division manager. He had just received your production figures for the last six months and was calling to express his concern. He indicated that the problem was yours to solve in any way that you think best, but that he would like to know within a week what steps you plan to take.

You share your division manager's concern with the falling productivity and know that your men are also concerned. The problem is to decide what steps to take to rectify the situation.

Analysis

Questions A (Quality?) = Yes
          B (Manager's Information?) = No
          C (Structured?) = No
          D (Acceptance?) = Yes
          E (Prior Probability of Aceptance?) = No
          F (Goal Congruence?) = Yes
          [G (Conflict?) = Yes]
Problem Type: 12
Feasible Set: GII
Minimum Man-Hours Solution (from Figure 1): GII

Therefore, in the example, the appropriate decision process would be GII: you share the problem with your subordinates and arrive at a decision as a group.

PROCEDURE

Step 1: 10 Minutes
Review the "Decision Process Flow Chart" in Figure 1 of the Vroom article. Discuss any questions you may have about it. Run through the illustrative case at the end of the reading, and discuss the analysis at the end of the case. Be sure you understand the Vroom and Yetton model before proceeding to Step 2.

Step 2: 25 Minutes
In groups of three to five, analyze each of the four cases given below. Using the model in Figure 1 of the Vroom reading, decide upon the appropriate decision style to be used in each case. Try to achieve consensus, but if you reach an impasse, go on to

the next case and return to the disputed one later. Pick a spokesperson to report your group's solutions to the rest of the class.

CASE I

You are general foreman in charge of a large gang laying an oil pipeline. It is now necessary to estimate your expected rate of progress in order to schedule material deliveries to the next field site.

You know the nature of the terrain you will be traveling and have the historical data needed to compute the mean and variance in the rate of speed over that type of terrain. Given these two variables, it is a simple matter to calculate the earliest and latest times at which materials and support facilities will be needed at the next site. It is important that your estimate be reasonably accurate. Underestimates result in idle foremen and workers, and an overestimate results in tying up materials for a period of time before they are to be used.

Progress has been good, and your five foremen and other members of the gang stand to receive substantial bonuses if the project is completed ahead of schedule.

CASE II

You are supervising the work of 12 engineers. Their formal training and work experience are very similar, permitting you to use them interchangeably on projects. Yesterday your manager informed you that a request had been received from an overseas affiliate for four engineers to go abroad on extended loan for a period of six to eight months. For a number of reasons, he argued and you agreed that this request should be met from your group.

All your engineers are capable of handling this assignment, and from the standpoint of present and future projects there is no particular reason why any one should be retained over any other. The problem is somewhat complicated by the fact that the overseas assignment is in what is generally regarded in the company as an undesirable location.

CASE III

You are the head of a staff unit reporting to the vice-president of finance. He has asked you to provide a report on the firm's current portfolio, which will include recommendations for changes in the selection criteria currently employed. Doubts have been raised about the efficiency of the existing system in the current market conditions, and there is considerable dissatisfaction with prevailing rates of return.

You plan to write the report, but at the moment you are quite perplexed about the approach to take. Your own specialty is the bond market, and it is clear to you that a detailed knowledge of the equity market, which you lack, would greatly enhance the value of the report. Fortunately, four members of your staff are specialists in different segments of the equity market. Together, they possess a vast amount of knowledge about the intricacies of investment. However, they seldom agree on the best way to achieve anything when it comes to the stock market. Although they are obviously conscientious as well as knowledgeable, they have major differences when it comes to investment philosophy and strategy.

You have six weeks before the report is due. You have already begun to familiarize yourself with the firm's current portfolio and have been provided by management with a specific set of constraints that any portfolio must satisfy. Your immediate problem is to come up with some alternatives to the firm's present practices and select the most promising for detailed analysis in your report.

CASE IV

You are on the division manager's staff and work on a wide variety of problems of both an administrative and technical nature. You have been given the assignment of developing a universal method to be used in each of the five plants in the division for manually reading equipment registers, recording the readings, and transmitting the scorings to a centralized information system. All plants are located in a relatively small geographical region.

Until now, there has been a high error rate in the reading and/or transmittal of the data. Some locations have considerably higher error rates than others, and the methods used to record and transmit the data vary between plants. It is probable, therefore, that part of the error variance is a function of specific local conditions rather than anything else, and this will complicate the establishment of any system common to all plants. You have the information on error rates but no information on the local practices that generate these errors or on the local conditions that necessitate the different practices.

Everyone would benefit from an improvement in the quality of the data as they are used in a number of important decisions. Your contacts with the plants are through the quality-control supervisors who are responsible for collecting the data. They are a conscientious group committed to doing their jobs well, but are highly sensitive to interference on the part of higher management in their own operations. Any solution that does not receive the active support of the various plant supervisors is unlikely to reduce the error rate significantly.

Step 3: 15 Minutes

Meet again as a total class group. First, each group reports on the decision style it thought was appropriate for each case. (If there are more than three or four groups, take a vote to see how many groups chose which style for each case.) Next, the group leader will present Vroom's analysis of each case and the styles that are appropriate according to his analysis. Finally, discuss Vroom's and the class's analyses and the discrepancies (if any) between them.

DISCUSSION QUESTIONS

1. How much agreement was there within the class about the appropriate decision style for each case? Why?
2. How much agreement was there between the class's solutions and Vroom's analysis? Why? When in doubt between two styles, which one would you choose? Why?

GENERALIZATIONS AND CONCLUSIONS

Concluding Points

1. Before you choose the process that you will use to make a management decision, it is important first to do what?

2. Even though the Vroom and Yetton model seems clear-cut, people often differ on their answers to the diagnostic questions (A-G in Figure 1) about the situation. What factors may account for differences in the way people diagnose leadership situations?

3. To recapitulate, the appropriateness of a particular style of decision making depends upon the importance of what three factors?

Participant's Reactions

READINGS AND REFERENCES

Vroom, V., and Yetton, P., *Leadership and Decision-Making* (Pittsburgh: University of Pittsburgh Press, 1973).

24
ASSIGNMENT: WHAT DO MANAGERS DO?

PURPOSE:
To generate an analysis of the managerial job in terms of the roles performed by managers.

ADVANCE PREPARATION: Read readings assigned by the group leader before starting assignment.

RELATED TOPICS: Managers as leaders; Life, work, and career roles; Organizational communication; Interpersonal communication; Organizational structure and design, Planned change, Organizational realities.

INTRODUCTION

Students of management have attempted to develop a comprehensive description of the managerial job for many years. Fayol (1916) was one of the first to propose looking at managerial work in terms of the functions performed by a manager. Other approaches have been suggested as well, but the result has been a "jungle" of theoretical frameworks and empirical findings (Koontz, 1961), rather than a convergence toward a shared view of the managerial job.

Most recently, the work of Henry Mintzberg (1971, 1973a, 1973b) has attracted considerable attention and acclaim. Based on observations of managers at work, Mintzberg has developed a role model of the managerial job. Ten roles, falling into three broad categories or "families" of roles, were identified by Mintzberg. These ten roles form the basis of the interview you will conduct in this exercise.

PROCEDURE

After you have read the assignment, interview a manager, using the "What Do Managers Do?—Interviewing Questionnaire," below. Follow the instructions for the questionnaire carefully; be sure you have read them over and understand them before you begin the interview.

For purposes of this assignment, a manager is any person whose job primarily involves *supervising the work of other people*. The manager may work in a business, public or private agency, school, etc. The nature of the duties, not the type of organization, is the important criterion.

Developed by Donald D. Bowen. Based upon the theoretical framework proposed by Mintzberg (1971, 1973a, 1973b).

The Mintzberg roles are given—though not labeled—on the questionnaire in the following order:

Interpersonal roles	*Information roles*	*Decisional roles*
1. Figurehead	4. Monitor	7. Entrepreneur
2. Leader	("Nerve Center" in	8. Disturbance handler
3. Liaison	Mintzberg)	9. Resource allocator
	5. Disseminator	10. Negotiator
	6. Spokesman	

The role titles are left unlabeled on the questionnaire because managers tend to respond to the title rather than the content of the role. Bring the completed interview to the session specified by the group leader. The data will be summarized and discussed by the entire group.

WHAT DO MANAGERS DO?
—INTERVIEWING QUESTIONNAIRE

On the following pages, you will find a list of ten "roles"—that is, functions that have been found in studies of managerial work. Not every manager performs every role; not every role is equally important in each manager's job. And there may be things managers do that are not on the list. Note that there is an "Other" category for listing important things not already on the form.

The objective of this assignment is to provide an experience in which you can collect some information on what contributions managers make to achieving the organization's goals. Remember, for purposes of this study, *a manager is anyone whose job consists primarily of supervising other people.*

Instructions

1. Find a manager and conduct the interview, using the attached form as a guide. Obtain numerical answers, using the scale provided, for *all* of the questions in the first two columns:
   a. Which are the most important roles—*those which contribute to effective performance in the job?*
   b. Which are the most *time-consuming?*
   For the third column, ask the manager for an example of this role.
2. Discuss the results with the manager. Ask: Were there any roles that you had expected to be more (or less) important before the interview? Were there any roles where the time consumed seemed disproportionate to the importance of the role? Which are the most difficult roles? You may think of other questions you wish to ask, as well.
3. Take notes on the interview and bring them with you to refer to in the group discussion.
4. *You do not need to supply the name of the manager interviewed.* We are only interested in developing a sample of managerial views of their job. The responses

will be *anonymous,* and you should treat the interview as a *confidential* communication.

Ten roles and the typical activities involved in them are listed below, together with a space for you to list items that may be important but not provided for. For each role, enter the appropriate numbers based upon the following scale. In column 1, enter a number reflecting *how important the role is to effective* job performance for the manager.

Scale values for column 1:

1 = Of no importance; 2 = Of minimal importance; 3 = Of some importance; 4 = Of considerable importance; 5 = Of very high importance

Next, in column 2, enter a number from the scale to describe *how time-consuming the role is for the manager.*

Scale values for column 2:

1 = No time consumed; 2 = Minimal time consumed; 3 = Some time consumed; 4 = Considerable time consumed; 5 = A very high amount of time consumed

Finally, in the last column, briefly note *an example* of the job duties performed in fulfilling this role.

Fill in columns 1 and 2 for *every* job role, even if you have difficulty identifying an example for column 3.

ROLE ACTIVITIES AND EXAMPLES

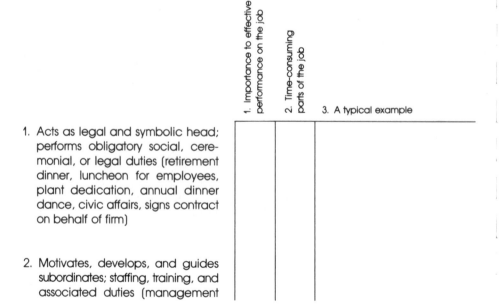

	1. Importance to effective performance on the job	2. Time-consuming parts of the job	3. A typical example
1. Acts as legal and symbolic head; performs obligatory social, ceremonial, or legal duties (retirement dinner, luncheon for employees, plant dedication, annual dinner dance, civic affairs, signs contract on behalf of firm)			
2. Motivates, develops, and guides subordinates; staffing, training, and associated duties (management			

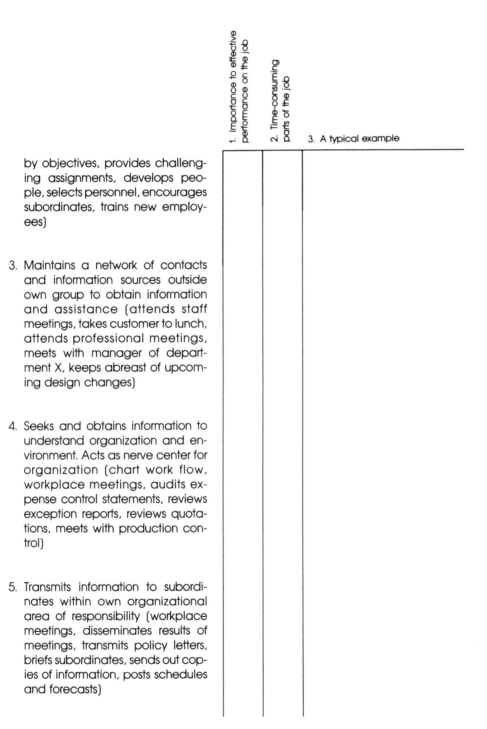

by objectives, provides challenging assignments, develops people, selects personnel, encourages subordinates, trains new employees)

3. Maintains a network of contacts and information sources outside own group to obtain information and assistance (attends staff meetings, takes customer to lunch, attends professional meetings, meets with manager of department X, keeps abreast of upcoming design changes)

4. Seeks and obtains information to understand organization and environment. Acts as nerve center for organization (chart work flow, workplace meetings, audits expense control statements, reviews exception reports, reviews quotations, meets with production control)

5. Transmits information to subordinates within own organizational area of responsibility (workplace meetings, disseminates results of meetings, transmits policy letters, briefs subordinates, sends out copies of information, posts schedules and forecasts)

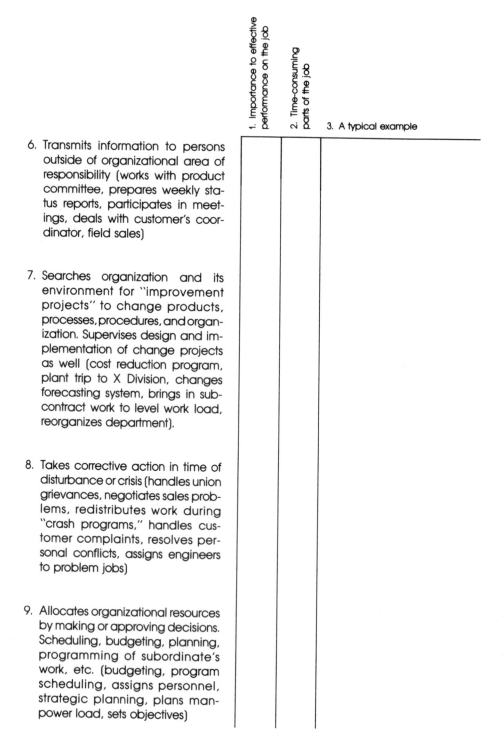

	1. Importance to effective performance on the job	2. Time-consuming parts of the job	3. A typical example
6. Transmits information to persons outside of organizational area of responsibility (works with product committee, prepares weekly status reports, participates in meetings, deals with customer's coordinator, field sales)			
7. Searches organization and its environment for "improvement projects" to change products, processes, procedures, and organization. Supervises design and implementation of change projects as well (cost reduction program, plant trip to X Division, changes forecasting system, brings in subcontract work to level work load, reorganizes department).			
8. Takes corrective action in time of disturbance or crisis (handles union grievances, negotiates sales problems, redistributes work during "crash programs," handles customer complaints, resolves personal conflicts, assigns engineers to problem jobs)			
9. Allocates organizational resources by making or approving decisions. Scheduling, budgeting, planning, programming of subordinate's work, etc. (budgeting, program scheduling, assigns personnel, strategic planning, plans manpower load, sets objectives)			

	1. Importance to effective performance on the job	2. Time-consuming parts of the job	3. A typical example
10. Represents organization in negotiating of sales, labor, or other agreements. Represents department or group negotiating with other functions within the organization (negotiates with suppliers, assists in quoting on new work, negotiates with union, hires, resolves jurisdictional dispute with department X, negotiates sales contract)			
Other:			

Participant's Reactions:

READINGS AND REFERENCES

Fayol, H., *Administration Industrielle et Generale* (Paris: Dunod, 1916). Available in English as *General and Industrial Management* (London: Pitman, 1949).

Knootz, H., "The Management Theory Jungle," *Journal of the Academy of Management,* 4 (1961), 174–88.

Knootz, H., "Retrospective Comment." In L. E. Boone and D. D. Bowen (Eds.) *The Great Writings in Management and Organizational Behavior* (Tulsa: PPC Books, 1980), pp. 271–276. Knootz's "The Management Theory Jungle" is also reprinted in this volume.

Mintzberg, H., "Managerial Work: Analysis from Observation," *Management Science,* Oct. (1971), B97–B110.

Mintzberg, H., *The Nature of Managerial Work* (New York: Harper & Row, 1973a).

Mintzberg, H., "A New Look at the Chief Executive's Job," *Organizational Dynamics,* 1 (1973b), 20–41.

25
MY BEST BOSS

PURPOSE:
(1) To help you reflect seriously on the motivational attributes of a manager who is a good leader.
(2) To allow you to share your views on leadership theory and practice with others and to compare their thoughts with yours.
(3) To provide an opportunity for you to get to know other participants in the course and learn about their work experiences.

ADVANCE PREPARATION: None. It can be helpful, however, if the class has read one or more theories of leadership before the class.
GROUP SIZE: Any size.
TIME REQUIRED: 50 minutes.
SPECIAL MATERIALS: None.
RELATED TOPICS: Motivation, power, interpersonal communication, organizational realities.

INTRODUCTION

Theories of leadership can be very dry and academic. The *practice* of leadership, on the other hand, is anything but dry and academic. Anyone who has worked with a dynamic, inspiring leader knows what a difference leadership qualities can make in a work setting.

It is important to distinguish between a manager and a leader! Some managers are leaders, but not all are. And some leaders are good managers, but not all are. A manager is a person who gets work done through the efforts of other people. This involves the traditional management functions of planning, organizing, motivating, and controlling. Managers also perform the various interpersonal, informational, and decisional roles described by Mintzberg. See the exercise "Assignment: What Do Managers Do?" for more detail on the manager's functions.

Leadership, on the other hand, involves the creation of organizational excitement and empowerment through the identification and communication of a common vision for a transformed organization. (See Chapter 27 "Strategies for Taking Charge" for more detail on the components of leadership.) Another distinction is that provided by Bennis and Nanus (1985): "Managers do things right. Leaders do the right thing."

This exercise will give you an opportunity to examine these qualities of leadership not by reading about them, but by studying your actual experiences with good leadership in a boss.

Adapted by D. T. Hall from Schermerhorn, J. R. Jr.; Hunt, J. G.; and Osborn, R. N. *Managing Organizational Behavior.* Second Edition. Copyright © 1985, John Wiley & Sons. Reprinted by permission of John Wiley & Sons.

PROCEDURE

Step 1: Individual analysis, 10 Minutes.

Working by yourself, think back over various bosses you have worked with. These could be people you worked with in a variety of settings: part-time jobs, full-time jobs, summer jobs, volunteer jobs, student organizations, and so forth. You might also consider athletic coaches or advisors to campus organizations with whom you have worked.

Identify the best boss you have ever worked for. Make a list of the *behavioral attributes* that describe that person. (If you have trouble identifying an actual manager or boss, make a list of the attributes you would like the manager in your next job to have).

Step 2: Group polling, 20 Minutes.

Convene in small groups of four to eight people. Go around the groups with everyone sharing his or her list of "best boss" qualities. Discuss any points of special interest, similarity, dissimilarity, disagreement, and so on.

As you go around the group, have one member write out a list that combines all the unique attributes of the best bosses represented in your group. Make sure that you have all the attributes listed, but list each only once. Place a checkmark next to any that were reported by two or more members. Have one of your members prepared to present the list in general class discussion.

Step 3: Total class discussion, 20 Minutes.

After all groups have finished constructing their lists, spokespersons should report to the total class. The instructor will make a running list of the "best boss" attributes as viewed by the class. Make a checkmark next to each attribute each time it is mentioned. In this way you will have an indication of the *frequency of mention* for each attribute.

Feel free to ask questions and discuss the results.

DISCUSSION QUESTIONS

1. Which attributes were mentioned most frequently? Why do you think these qualities are so important? In what ways do they affect your motivation and performance?
2. Which of these qualities would you say are *leadership* qualities (i.e. inspirational, transformational) and which seem to be *managerial* characteristics? (Put an "L" or an "M" next to each attribute to indicate which is which.) In what ways are you affected by leadership qualities? By managerial qualities? Is there a difference between the two in your experience?
3. How do these conclusions relate to any theories or models of leadership that you have read in the course so far? Based upon your observations of a best boss, what is *your* theory of leadership?

GENERALIZATIONS AND CONCLUSIONS:

1. Of all of the attributes that have been identified, what three qualities of a good boss do you think are most important?

2. What theory of leadership comes closest to your actual experience in working with a good boss?

Participant's Reactions:

READINGS AND REFERENCES:

Bennis, W. G., and Nanus, B. *Leaders: Strategies for Taking Charge*. New York: Harper & Row, 1985.

Tichy, N., and Devanna, M. A. *The Transformational Leader*. New York: John Wiley & Sons, 1986.

26
EFFECTIVE DELEGATION

PURPOSE:
(1) To understand the elements of effective delegation.
(2) To develop effective delegation *skills* as used by both managers and sub-ordinates.
(3) To practice feedback skills.

ADVANCE PREPARATION: Read "Introduction to Effective Delegation" and Step 1 below prior to completing exercise in class.
GROUP SIZE: Total group may be any size. Small trios (3 people) for individual role play.
TIME REQUIRED: Minimum 50 minutes
SPECIAL REQUIREMENTS: None
RELATED TOPICS: Applied motivation, Interpersonal communication, Managers as leaders, Power

INTRODUCTION

Effective Delegation: What and Why

Delegating can be defined as *handing over the responsibility and authority required to accomplish a task without relinquishing final accountability*. What this means for you, the manager, is that you have to give your subordinate(s) sufficient authority to match the responsibility it takes to get a job done. What it also means is that you, the boss, are ultimately responsible. Even though you delegated the work to someone else (a subordinate), you can't pass the buck. You are, in the end, accountable for your people as well as yourself.

There are a lot of reasons why a manager might need and want to delegate. Obviously, it makes for more efficient use of your time. Unfortunately, many managers mistakenly think that every task requires their constant attention from beginning to end. They have difficulty trusting younger, newer or lower-level people. Therefore, they have trouble entrusting work to other people. You can't do everything. You should do *the most important* things—the *tasks that only you can do*.

The inability to delegate—and delegate effectively—creates two negative consequences in the organization: (1) overloaded executives and (2) underutilized subordinates. Interestingly, each of these conditions is a factor associated with work-related stress and burnout. So, an organization in which delegation is ineffective or infrequent can expect productivity to be lower than it should be, primarily because of poor use of time, skills, and people.

Responsibility for tasks is one of the most valuable resources that any manager has

Developed by Francine S. Hall.

at his or her disposal. By delegating—giving responsibility to subordinates—*you give your subordinates the opportunity to do the following:*

- perform their jobs well
- demonstrate ability
- experience success
- be visible within the organization
- develop skills
- experience new challenges

These are all experiences that are an integral part of a person's career development. So, the effective delegator is above all an effective developer of people.

Delegation requires some knowledge about what produces good performance. You are, after all, not *just* giving responsibility to another, you are giving it because you believe the person can perform the task and free you to focus on even higher priority needs.

What produces performance? There are three factors:

Motivation ... the person has to *want* to
Ability ... the person has to be *able* to
Training ... the person needs to *learn* how

The three factors do not necessarily contribute equally to performance. The first two, motivation and ability, interact to produce the greatest contribution. The effects of training can be added to enhance performance.

Think of the handicapped persons you have known who were extremely motivated to succeed at a task. Even though their physical or mental limitations may have made tasks difficult, the interaction of limited ability and unbounded motivation can produce astonishing performance results. Doctors call these people overachievers. Obviously they are just highly motivated achievers. The counterpart is the gifted person with a brilliant intellect or talented body who could care less. No motivation, no performance.

So, what does all this have to do with delegation? Everything. To delegate, you need to know your people. Who has the know-how for the job. Who *can* do the task? Who *wants* to do it? Who is *enthusiastic*? Sometimes the most motivated person is the best person, even if he or she is *not* the most skilled. And that brings the discussion to training.

A large part of delegating *effectively* comes from the *support* (including training, if needed) that you provide for your subordinates. In fact, studies, like those done by Douglas Bray at AT&T and by Douglas T. Hall and Benjamin Schneider, have found that "supportive autonomy" on the part of the boss early in a person's career is highly correlated with the later career success of the person. Job challenge early in one's career is also highly correlated with career success as measured by promotions, salary, and responsibility.

What this means is that you, as a boss, have the opportunity to help your people get off on a positive career trajectory. You can do it by: (1) delegating challenging jobs; (2) providing the authority and resources necessary to carry out the responsibility; (3) trusting the subordinate so that he or she can act autonomously; and (4) providing back-up "support," but not meddling in the assignment.

How To Be An Effective Delegator

There are at least ten steps you can take to ensure that the handing over of task responsibility will be done effectively. Each of these is discussed briefly below. You will also find these reproduced separately later in this exercise as a checklist to be used with the role plays.

1. *Use delegation to develop, not dump.* As people become more concerned about time management, there has been a tendency to think that this means getting rid of unwanted tasks. Be sure you and your subordinate discuss the task in terms of what is in it for him or her. Don't just pass the buck. Pass on challenge, responsibility, and a chance to learn new skills or aspects of the organization.

2. *Set specific goals with the subordinate.* This includes a review of the task, especially the *results* expected, and a timetable for getting things done and reviewing progress. Don't assume that she or he understands what you expect and/or need. Be specific and *check for understanding*.

3. *Discuss the meaning of the assignment* in terms of its value within the larger organizational picture.

4. *Provide for autonomy.* Make it clear that the subordinate has the authority and resources and is free to "run with the ball," but, like a good coach, you will be there on the sidelines if he or she wants to take a time out to review the gameplan.

5. *Elicit questions* from the subordinate. Test for understanding of the talk.

6. *Get additional ideas* or other inputs from the subordinate.

7. *Provide feedback.* Your subordinate needs to know how he or she is doing. This is helpful for taking corrective action before a deadline. It is especially reinforcing after a goal is accomplished.

8. *Provide times for follow-up.* Don't just delegate and expect the results to just happen. Plan to meet, review preliminary results, discuss problems, and so forth.

9. *Select* the *most motivated* person.

10. *Delegate* only *once* and to only one person, group, or team. Nothing is more demoralizing for a subordinate than to find out that other people are working on a project that he or she thought had been delegated solely to him or her.

The backbone of the delegation relationship is, as has often been said, "the consent of the governed." A subordinate willing to take orders (and to follow through) is what it is all about. You, however, always retain control.

In the end, effective *delegation* is just another *example* of *effective leadership* and the design of enriched, motivating tasks. You set challenging goals, give people a chance to be self-directed and autonomous. You clarify how to achieve results as well as what's expected and when. You assign tasks that are meaningful as well as challenging. Finally, you provide support, feedback, and reinforcement.

PROCEDURE

Step 1: Role Play I (10 Minutes)

The instructor will ask for two volunteers. One will play the role of "Phyllis," the other "Bart."

The remainder of the group should read both roles while the volunteers prepare to play their individual role. The group should review the Checklist for Feedback on page 146. Be prepared to provide feedback to the role players after the scene has been played.

ROLE FOR PHYLLIS, DIVISION CHIEF

You are the division chief in charge of management services for the Department of Management and Finance in a large county of a southern state. You have held your job for two years, are highly respected by your subordinates, who are mostly male, and see yourself as a tough but fair boss.

Your subordinates perceive you about the same way, but they sometimes grumble that you are a stickler for details. You expect a job to be done correctly and on time and you will support your people in whatever way necessary to help them succeed.

Today you are meeting with Bart, your project manager, to discuss the construction of a new "Handicapped Ramp" at the county courthouse. Bart's responsibility is to *manage* the construction and ensure that federal standards are met. (These are listed in box below.) The public works department will choose a contractor for the actual construction.

You know that it is usually helpful in cases like this to prepare an architectural drawing and be very clear about standards with subcontractors.

The ramp must cover a rise of about 3 feet, so you expect a ramp about 30 feet long.

SPECIFICATIONS AND STANDARDS FOR CONSTRUCTION OF A HANDICAPPED RAMP

$\frac{1}{8}$ ratio slope is minimum
$\frac{1}{12}$ ratio slope is preferred

1. This means that each inch of rise (vertical) has to be sloped over 8 inches of horizontal space (or over 12 inches).
2. For either a $\frac{1}{8}$ or $\frac{1}{12}$ ratio slope, there must be a railing *and* a flat resting place every 30 feet.
3. If a $\frac{1}{20}$ ratio sloped sidewalk is built, then neither the railing nor the resting place is required.

CHECKLIST FOR FEEDBACK ON DELEGATION SKILLS:

Important: Be Sure Your Feedback Is:

_____ *Descriptive* (not evaluative)
_____ *Concrete* (cite specifics)
_____ *Behaviorally based* (not based on personality)
_____ *Focused on things* the person *can change*

Yes/No?

_____ 1. Oriented toward employee development?
        Example:

_____ 2. Defined specific task goals (results) for employer?
        Example:

_____ 3. Discussed task meaning and value?
        Example:

_____ 4. Spelled out degree of autonomy and authority?
        Example:

_____ 5. Elicited questions and checked for clarification with subordinate?
        Example:

_____ 6. Solicited subordinate's input and ideas regarding assignment?
        Example:

_____ 7. Provided feedback or created a chance to provide it later?
        Example:

_____ 8. Set plans for follow-up? Set time for progress reports and review?
        Example:

_____ 9. Showed concern for or appreciation of subordinate's motivation? Attempted to use delegation to motivate?
        Example:

_____ 10. Made it clear that task belongs to this subordinate (or group) only?
        Example:

ROLE FOR BART, PROJECT MANAGER

You are meeting with Phyllis about the ramp. She has sent you the specifications outlined in box above.

You have other jobs that are higher priority and just want to get this out of the way.

Step 2: (10 Minutes)

The instructor will ask the role players to play out the scene. The class will observe, using their checklist. Be prepared to provide feedback.

Step 3: (15 Minutes)

The instructor will stop the role play and ask the people playing Phyllis and Bart how *they* perceived the delegation process. The class will then provide feedback and discuss.

[At this point, additional volunteers may want to try this role play if time permits]

Step 4: (5 Minutes)

Entire class should now form trios. One member of each trio should take the role of boss and a second subordinate. A third will be an observer.

Step 5: (5 Minutes)

Read "The Delegation Problem" (below). Prepare to role-play the problem. The person playing the role of observer will provide feedback.

The Delegation Problem: Renovating The Station

The boss, Max, the division chief, is meeting with the subordinate, Joe, who is the maintenance manager for management services division of the county.

Their discussion will focus on Joe's latest assignment, overseeing the renovation of the fire station.

The desired result is getting the renovation completed according to the specifications with a minimum of disruption at the fire station. Included in the renovation are the kitchen and bathroom facilities used by the fire fighters.

The following facts may be helpful:

1. Joe may oversee the job or delegate it to one of *his* subordinates.
2. An architect was hired to produce the bidding specifications. The job was put out for bids. These were analyzed, references were checked, and, after all the responses were in, the contract was awarded to a local construction firm. The contractor has been messy on other jobs, but does quality work.
3. The signed contract specifies that the job will be completed in 90 days.
4. Historically, fire fighters have gotten involved to help with the renovation in their spare time.
5. The contractor is supposed to work with the building inspector regarding meeting specifications.
6. Payment is programmed to occur at specified times.
7. The architect of the renovation is also one of the fire fighters who has learned architecture in his spare time. He is supposed to make sure that the contractor and his subs understand the plans.

What Max needs most from Joe, the maintenance manager, is to oversee the job, make sure it moves along according to schedule, and is documented in case conflict should arise regarding the contractor's work or compliance with specifications.

Step 6: (5-10 Minutes)
Play out the problem, staying in your roles.

Step 7: (5 Minutes)
Observer provides feedback. Trio discusses.

Step 8, 9, and 10: (Optional depending on time, 10-15 Minutes per Iteration)
Rotate roles in the trio (or regroup trios in the class) and play out The Delegation Problem again. Each person should have an opportunity to play the role of boss, subordinate and observer.

GENERALIZATIONS AND CONCLUSIONS

1. Based on your *experience* today, what is/are the most difficult thing(s) for you to do when attempting to delegate?

2. Based on the feedback you received today, what are the skills you most need to develop?

3. What are some goals you might set to develop your delegation skills as a manager?

4. What can you do *as a subordinate* to facilitate effective delegation?

REFERENCES

Oncken, William, Jr., and Wass, Donald L. "Management Time: Whose Got the Monkey," *Harvard Business Review*, Nov/Dec 1974.

27
STRATEGIES FOR TAKING CHARGE

PURPOSE:
(1) To understand traditional and emerging models of effective leadership.
(2) To analyze the style of a real leader and to assess the effectiveness of that style

ADVANCE PREPARATION: Instructor must arrange for participants to read a case, book, or other material describing one or more leaders. An alternative is to obtain a videotape of a leader in action, which can be shown in class. (Strongly recommended: the Fred Henderson and Renn Zaphiropoulous tapes available from the Harvard Case Clearinghouse.)

GROUP SIZE: Any size. This activity works well in large classes.

TIME REQUIRED: 1-2 hours, depending upon whether videotape of a leader is used in class.

SPECIAL MATERIALS: Advance reading about a leader or a videotape of a leader.

SPECIAL REQUIREMENTS: None.

RELATED TOPICS: Motivation, Power, Organizational change, Decision making.

INTRODUCTION

A number of theories, as well, most probably, as your own experience, suggest that there is no one best way for a leader to behave. The contingency theories of Fiedler (1967), Hersey and Blanchard (1972), and Vroom and Yetton (1973), and others elsewhere in this volume, are some of the more popular models for diagnosing the conditions under which a particular leadership style is most likely to work. Those models tend to focus on two major facets of the leader's behavior:

1. How much *structure* or control the leader exerts vis-à-vis subordinates (as opposed to permitting the *participation* of subordinates in decision making), and
2. How much *interpersonal support* or *consideration* the leader provides: that is, how much concern for and skill in relationships the leader shows.

Subsequent approaches to leadership have gone beyond these two dimensions and probe the issue of the leader's ability to create *organizational excitement and empowerment*, to inspire employees to become committed to an organization's mission and sense of purpose. These abilities to create meaning and to communicate meaning and vision in a compelling way are critical in contemporary leaders.

David Bradford and Allen Cohen (1984) have described the "old" leader (the traditional leader, if you will) as being in the "heroic" vein (i.e., the leader was like

Developed by D. T. Hall.

the Lone Ranger and solved all problems single-handedly.) There were two models for the old heroic leader.

1. *The manager as technician.* Here the leader leads through breathtaking expertise. He or she is brighter, faster, and more skillful than anyone else and is able to solve all problems through close, direct supervision of each subordinate.
2. *The manager as conductor.* Here the leader is not the great solo performer but one who can orchestrate the work of great individuals. Or, even if this leader is a great technician, he or she realizes the futility of trying to be on top of every single problem personally. This leader's talent lies in the ability to recognize excellence in subordinates and to direct their efforts in the most productive ways.

In contrast, the current or "post-heroic" leader is the *manager-as-developer.* Bradford and Cohen see three critical components of the manager-as-developer model. First, the manager must build a *shared-responsibility team.* This means integrating talented people with diverse skills and often conflicting personal styles and goals. Second, the manager must facilitate *continuous development of individual skills.* Much of this is on-the-job development achieved through challenging, diverse tasks and daily interactions with other people from whom the employer can learn. The third component is *determining and building a common vision.* This requires achieving clarity in challenging common overarching goals, which is no mean feat.

In a recent study of 90 excellent leaders, Warren Bennis and Burt Nanus (1985) identified four critical competencies of leaders who were able to develop this sort of empowerment in their followers:

1. *Attention through vision.* This is the skill of creating focus on a *mission* and determining an agenda. It involves the development of an intense, compelling vision and a strong personal commitment.
2. *Meaning through communication.* Once the leader has a vision of his or her own, it is necessary to communicate that vision to followers so they can see it as clearly and intensely.
3. *Trust through positioning.* This is the quality of being clear, predictable, consistent, and persistent. It entails backing up the leader's stated ideals and values with behavior, showing commitment to the vision through action.
4. *Development of self through positive self-regard.* This is the skill of managing oneself in working on the people problems which take up 90% of a leader's time. This entails developing confidence in oneself and focusing intensely on the goal to be achieved, such that one does not even *think* about failure.

Noel Tichy and Mary Ann Devanna (1986) have dubbed the type of person who possesses these traits the *transformational leader.* This is the sort of person who has the vision and drive to lead the organization into a fundamental reshaping of its mission and structure. Jack Welch, the Chief Executive Officer of General Electric, has been cited as one example of the transformational leader. This form of leadership is closely related to the manager-as-developer described by Bradford and Cohen, in that the person has the vision (and the skills to communicate it) for a transformed organization, as well as the skills to develop that new organization out of its current membership.

PROCEDURE

Step 1: 10 Minutes

Review the "Introduction" above and think about other theories of leadership that you have read. Discuss with the instructor any questions you may have.

Step 2: Time variable.

Review material (book, case, reading, or tape) showing how a particular leader behaves (e.g., Chrysler's Lee Iacocca, Donald Burr of People's Express). Your instructor will tell you what method will be used here.

As you look at this leader (or leaders) in action, ask the following questions in Table 1.

TABLE 1
Profiles of two leaders.

	Leader A	Leader B
	Name: _____	Name: _____
1. In terms of the Bradford and Cohen models, was this person a: (check one or more)	____ Technician ____ Conductor ____ Developer	____ Technician ____ Conductor ____ Developer
2. Cite one or two specific examples of behavior to support your assessment in 1 above.	_____ _____ _____ _____	_____ _____ _____ _____
3. How would you assess these people in terms of the four competencies described by Bennis and Nanus? List *specific behaviors* you observed which lead you to your judgment for each leader. a. Creating a vision	____ Strong ____ Satisfactory ____ Deficient ____ Specific behaviors:	____ Strong ____ Satisfactory ____ Deficient ____ Specific behaviors:

TABLE 1 (*Continued*)
Profiles of two leaders.

	Leader A	Leader B
b. Communicating a vision	____ Strong ____ Satisfactory ____ Deficient ____ Specific behaviors:	____ Strong ____ Satisfactory ____ Deficient ____ Specific behaviors:
c. Developing trust	____ Strong ____ Satisfactory ____ Deficient ____ Specific behaviors:	____ Strong ____ Satisfactory ____ Deficient ____ Specific behaviors:
d. Managing self through positive self regard and focus on goals.	____ Strong ____ Satisfactory ____ Deficient ____ Specific behaviors:	____ Strong ____ Satisfactory ____ Deficient ____ Specific behaviors:
4. List *specific conditions under* which each leader would be *most* effective.	_____ _____ _____ _____ _____	_____ _____ _____ _____ _____
5. List *specific conditions under* which each leader would be *least* effective.	_____ _____ _____ _____ _____ _____ _____	_____ _____ _____ _____ _____ _____ _____
6. Overall, how would you guess the effectiveness of this leader?	____ Outstanding ____ Very Strong ____ Satisfactory ____ Marginal ____ Poor	____ Outstanding ____ Very Strong ____ Satisfactory ____ Marginal ____ Poor
7. Would you personally like to work for this person?	____ Yes ____ No Why? _____ _____ _____ _____	____ Yes ____ No Why? _____ _____ _____ _____
8. Would you like to have this person working for you?	____ Yes ____ No Why? _____ _____ _____	____ Yes ____ No Why? _____ _____ _____

Step 3: 10 Minutes. *Your* style.
Complete the following questionnaire and score it on the scoring sheet that follows.

LEADERSHIP QUESTIONNAIRE

For each of the following 10 pairs of statements, divide 5 points between the two according to your beliefs, perceptions of yourself, or according to which of the two statements characterizes you better. The 5 points may be divided between the A and B statements in any one of the following ways: 5 for A, 0 for B; 4 for A, 1 for B; 3 for A, 2 for B; 1 for A, 4 for B; 0 for A, 5 for B, but not equally $2\frac{1}{2}$ between the two. Weigh your choices between the two according to the one that characterizes you or your beliefs better.

1. _____ A As leader I have a primary mission of maintaining stability.
   _____ B As leader I have a primary mission of change.
2. _____ A As leader I must cause events.
   _____ B As leader I must facilitate events.
3. _____ A I am concerned that my followers are rewarded equitably for their work.
   _____ B I am concerned about what my followers want in life.
4. _____ A My preference is to think long range: What might be.
   _____ B My preference is to think short range: What is realistic.
5. _____ A As a leader I spend considerable energy in managing separate but related goals.
   _____ B As a leader I spend considerable energy in arousing hopes, expectations, and aspirations among my followers.
6. _____ A While not in a formal classroom sense, I believe that a significant part of my leadership is that of teacher.
   _____ B I believe that a significant part of my leadership is that of facilitator.
7. _____ A As leader I must engage with followers at an equal level of morality.
   _____ B As leader I must represent a higher morality.
8. _____ A I enjoy stimulating followers to want to do more.
   _____ B I enjoy rewarding followers for a job well done.
9. _____ A Leadership should be practical.
   _____ B Leadership should be inspirational.
10. _____ A What power I have to influence others comes primarily from my ability to get people to identify with me and my ideas.
    _____ B What power I have to influence others comes primarily from my status and position.

SCORING SHEET FOR LEADERSHIP QUESTIONNAIRE

Transformational *Your Point(s)*	*Transactional* *Your Point(s)*
1. B _____	1. A _____
2. A _____	2. B _____
3. B _____	3. A _____
4. A _____	4. B _____
5. B _____	5. A _____
6. A _____	6. B _____
7. B _____	7. A _____
8. A _____	8. B _____
9. B _____	9. A _____
10. A _____	10. B _____

Column totals: _____   _____

NOTE: The higher column total indicates that you agree more with, and see yourself as more like, either a transformational leader or a transactional leader.

Step 4. Discussion. 30 Minutes.

Discuss your answers to the questions in Step 2.

For question 1, take a vote to see how many class members see the leader as technician, how many see him or her as a conductor, and how many as a developer.

Similarly, take a vote on the answer to question 3 to see how many people think he or she possesses each of the four competencies identified by Bennis and Nanus.

If you have studied two effective leaders (such as Renn Zaphiropoulos or Fred Henderson), take the above votes on each one. Treat the results as *competency profiles* on each leader.

The leadership questionnaire assesses *transformational leadership* (in the sense discussed by Bennis and Nanus) and *transactional leadership*. Transformational leadership is similar to the Bradford and Cohen manager-as-developer model, while transactional leadership is more like the manager-as-conductor style.

Divide the class into people who scored highest on transformational leadership and those who were highest in transactional leadership. Is there any relationship between your own leadership score and your evaluation(s) of the leader(s) you have studied?

DISCUSSION QUESTIONS

1. How can two people who are so different both be such effective leaders?
2. Under what conditions or for what type of organization would each leader be most effective?

3. What is the relationship (if any) between your own leadership style and your assessment of the leader(s) you have studied in this exercise?
4. If you were a subordinate, how would you behave with each boss?
5. If you were the boss of each how would you manage them?

GENERALIZATIONS AND CONCLUSIONS

Concluding points:

1. What is the most effective style of leadership?

2. What are some of the contingencies that influence the effectiveness of a particular leadership style?

3. What is the relationship between management and leadership?

Participant's Reactions

READINGS AND REFERENCES

Bennis, W., and B. Nanus. *Leaders: The Strategies for Taking Charge* (New York: Harper & Row, 1985).

Bradford, D. L., and Cohen, A. R. *Managing for Execellence* (New York: John Wiley & Sons, Inc., 1984).

Hersey, P., and Blanchard, K. H. *Management of Organizational Behavior* (Second Edition). Englewood Cliffs, NJ: Prentice-Hall, 1972).

Ticky, N., and Devanna, M. A. *The Transformational Leader.* (New York: John Wiley & Sons, Inc., 1986.)

PART III
ORGANIZATIONS

SECTION EIGHT
ORGANIZATIONAL REALITIES

28
LARRY ROSS: A CASE FOR DISCUSSION

PURPOSE:
To provide a basis for discussion of organizational power and politics and their relationships to our own careers.

ADVANCE PREPARATION: Read "Larry Ross" and prepare your answers to the questions provided.

GROUP SIZE: Any size that permits case discussion. For large groups (over 50) see the Instructor's Manual for alternative procedures.

TIME REQUIRED: 50 minutes or more.

SPECIAL MATERIALS: None.

SPECIAL PHYSICAL REQUIREMENTS: None.

RELATED TOPICS: Managers as leaders; Motivation: basic concepts; Power; Organizational communication; Life, work, and career roles; Negotiation and conflict.

LARRY ROSS[1]

The corporation is a jungle. It's exciting. You're thrown in on your own and you're constantly battling to survive. When you learn to survive, the game is to become the conqueror, the leader.

Adapted by Donald D. Bowen. Originally used as a case in A. R. Cohen, S. L. Fink, H. Gadon, and R. D. Willits in *Effective Behavior in Organizations* (Homewood, Ill.: Irwin, 1976).

[1]"Larry Ross" is from S. Terkel, *Working: People Talk About What They Do All Day and How They Feel About What They Do.* Copyright © 1972, 1974 by Studs Terkel. Reprinted by permission of Pantheon Books, a division of Random House, Inc. Abridged by permission of the author and publisher.

"I've been called a business consultant. Some say I'm a business psychiatrist. You can describe me as an advisor to top management in a corporation." He's been at it since 1968.

I started in the corporate world, oh gosh—'42. After kicking around in the Depression, having all kinds of jobs and no formal education, I wasn't equipped to become an engineer, lawyer, or a doctor. I gravitated to selling. Now they call it marketing. I grew up in various corporations. I became the executive vice president of a large corporation and then of an even larger one. Before I quit I became president and chief executive officer of another. All nationally known companies.

Sixy-eight, we sold out our corporation. There was enough money in the transaction where I didn't have to go back in business. I decided that I wasn't going to get involved in the corporate battle any more. It lost its excitement, its appeal. People often ask me, "Why weren't you in your own business? You'd probably have made a lot of money." I often ask it myself, I can't explain it, except. . . .

Most corporations I've been in, they were on the New York Stock Exchange with thousands and thousands of stockholders. The last one—whereas, I was the president and chief executive, I was always subject to the board of directors, who had pressure from the stockholders. I owned a portion of the business, but I wasn't in control. I don't know of any situation in the corporate world where an executive is completely free and sure of his job from moment to moment.

Corporations always have to be right. That's their face to the public. When things go bad, they have to protect themselves and fire somebody. "We had nothing to do with it. We had an executive that just screwed everything up." He's never really ever been his own boss.

The danger starts as soon as you become a district manager. You have men working for you and you have a boss above. You're caught in a squeeze. The squeeze progresses from station to station. I'll tell you what a squeeze is. You have the guys working for you that are shooting for your job. The guy you're working for is scared stiff you're gonna shove him out of his job. Everybody goes around and says, "The test of the true executive is that you have men working for you that can replace you, so you can move up." That's a lot of baloney. The manager is afraid of the bright young guy coming up.

Fear is always prevalent in the corporate structure. Even if you're a top man, even if you're hard, even if you do your job—by the slight flick of a finger, your boss can fire you. There's always the insecurity. You bungle a job. You're fearful of losing a big customer. You're fearful so many things will appear on your record, stand against you. You're always fearful of the big mistake. You've got to be careful when you go to corporation parties. Your wife, your children have to behave properly. You've go to fit in the mold. You've go to be on guard.

When I was president of this big corporation, we lived in a small Ohio town, where the main plant was located. The corporation specified who you could socialize with, and on what level. (His wife interjects: "Who were the wives you could play bridge with.") The president's wife could do what she wants, as long as it's with dignity and grace. In a small town they didn't have to keep check on you. Everybody knew. There are certain sets of rules.

Not every corporation has that. The older the corporation, the longer it's been in a powerful position, the more rigid, the more conservative they are in their approach. Your swinging corporations are generally the new ones, the upstarts, the *nouveau riche*. But as they get older, like duPont, General Motors, General Electric, they become more rigid. I'd compare them to the old, old rich—the Rockefellers and the Mellons—that train their children how to handle money, how to conserve their money, and how to grow with their money. That's what happened to the older corporations. It's only when they get in trouble that they'll have a young upstart of a president come in and try to shake things up.

The executive is a lonely animal in the jungle who doesn't have a friend. Business is related to life. I think in our everyday living we're lonely. I have only a wife to talk to, but beyond that. . . . When I talked business to her, I don't know whether she understood me. But that was unimportant. What's important is that I was able to talk out loud and hear myself—which is the function I serve as a consultant.

The executive who calls me usually knows the answer to his problem. He just has to have somebody to talk to and hear his decision out loud. If it sounds good when he speaks it out loud, then it's pretty good. As he's talking, he may suddenly realize his errors and he corrects them out loud. That's a great benefit wives provide for executives. She's listening and you know she's on your side. She's not gonna hurt you.

Gossip and rumor are always prevalent in a corporation. There's absolutely no secrets. I have always felt every office was wired. You come out of the board meeting and people in the office already know what's happened. I've tried many times to track down a rumor, but never could. I think people have been there so many years and have developed an ability to read reactions. From these reactions they make a good, educated guess. Gossip actually develops into fact.

It used to be a ploy for many minor executives to gain some information. "I heard that the district manager of California is being transferred to Seattle." He knows there's been talk going on about changing district managers. By using this ploy—"I know something"—he's making it clear to the person he's talking to that he's been in on it all along. So it's all right to tell him. Gossip is another way of building up importance within a person who starts the rumor. He's in, he's part of the inner circle. Again, we're back in the jungle. Every ploy, every trick is used to survive.

When you're gonna merge with a company or acquire another company, it's supposed to be top secret. You have to do something to stem the rumors because it might screw up the deal. Talk of the merger, the whole place is in a turmoil. It's like somebody saying there's a bomb in the building and we don't know where it is and when it's going to go off. There've been so many mergers where top executives are laid off, the accounting department is cut by sixty percent, the manufacturing is cut by twenty percent. I have yet to find anybody in a corporation who was so secure to honestly believe it couldn't happen to him.

They put on a front: "Oh, it can't happen to me. I'm too important." But deep down, they're scared stiff. The fear is there. You can smell it. You can see it on their faces. I'm not so sure you couldn't see it on my face many, many times during my climb up.

I always used to say—rough, tough Larry—I always said, "If you do a good job, I'll give you a great reward. You'll keep your job." I'll have a sales contest and the men who make their quota will win a prize—they'll keep their jobs. I'm not saying there aren't executives who instill fear in their people. He's no different than anybody walking down the street. We're all subject to the same damn insecurities and neuroses—at every level. Competitiveness, that's the basis of it.

Why didn't I stay in the corporate structure? As a kid, living through the Depression, you always heard about the tycoons, the men of power, the men of industry. And you kind of dream that. Gee, these are supermen. These are the guys that have no feeling, aren't subject to human emotions, the insecurities that everybody else has. You get in the corporate structure, you find they all button their pants the same way everybody else does. They all get the same fears.

The corporation is made up of many, many people. I call 'em the gray people and the black—or white—people. Blacks and whites are definite colors, solid. Gray isn't. The gray people come there from nine to five, do their job, aren't particularly ambitious. There's no fear there, sure. But they're not subject to great demands. They're only subject to dismissal when business goes bad and they cut off people. They go from corporation to corporation and get jobs. Then you have the black—or white—people. The ambitious people, the leaders, the ones who want to get ahead.

When the individual reaches the vice presidency or he's general manager, you know he's an ambitious, dedicated guy who wants to get to the top. He isn't one of the gray people. He's one of the black-or-white vicious people—the leaders, the ones who stick out in the crowd.

As he struggles in this jungle, every position he's in, he's terribly lonely. He can't confide and talk with the guy working under him. He can't confide and talk to the man he's working for. To give vent to his feeling, his fears, and his insecurities, he'd expose himself. This goes all the way up the line until he gets to be president. The president *really* doesn't have anybody to talk to, because the vice presidents are waiting for him to die or make a mistake and get knocked off so they can get his job.

He can't talk to the board of directors, because to them he has to appear as a tower of strength, knowledge, and wisdom, and have the ability to walk on water. The board of directors, they're cold, they're hard. They don't have any direct-line responsibilities. They sit in a staff capacity and they really play God. They're interested in profits. They're interested in progress. They're interested in keeping a good face in the community—if it's profitable. You have the tremendous infighting of man against man for survival and clawing to the top. Progress.

We always saw signs of physical afflictions because of the stress and strain. Ulcers, violent headaches. I remember one of the giant corporations I was in, the chief executive officer ate Gelusil by the minute. That's for ulcers. Had a private dining room with his private chef. All he ever ate was well-done steak and well-done hamburgers.

There's one corporation chief I had who worked, conservatively, nineteen, twenty hours a day. His whole life was his business. And he demanded the same of his executives. There was nothing sacred in life except the business. Meetings might be called on Christmas Eve or New Year's Eve, Saturdays, Sundays. He was lonesome when he wasn't involved with his business. He was always creating situations where he could be surrounded by his flunkies, regardless of what level they were, presidential, vice presidential. . . . It was his life.

In the corporate structure, the buck keeps passing up until it comes to the chief executive. Then there ain't nobody to pass the buck to. You sit there in your lonely office and finally you have to make a decision. It could involve a million dollars or hundreds of jobs or moving people from Los Angeles, which they love, to Detroit or Winnipeg. So you're sitting at the desk, playing God.

You say, "Money isn't important. You can make some bad decisions about money, that's not important. What is important is the decisions you make about people working for you, their livelihood, their lives." It isn't true.

To the board of directors, the dollars are as important as human lives. There's only yourself sitting there making the decision, and you hope it's right. You're always on guard. Did you ever see a jungle animal that wasn't on guard? You're always looking over your shoulder. You don't know who's following you.

The most stupid phrase anybody can use in business is loyalty. If a person is working for a corporation, he's supposed to be loyal. This corporation is paying him less than he could get somewhere else at a comparable job. It's stupid of him to hang around and say he's loyal. The only loyal people are the people who can't get a job anyplace else. Working in a corporation, in a business, isn't a game. It isn't a collegiate event. It's a question of living or dying. It's a question of eating or not eating. Who is he loyal to? It isn't his country. It isn't his religion. It isn't his political party. He's working for some company that's paying him a salary for what he's doing. The corporation is out to make money. The ambitious guy will say, "I'm doing my job. I'm not embarassed taking my money. I've got to progress and when I won't progress, I won't be here." The schnook is the loyal guy, because he can't get a job anyplace else.

Many corporations will hang on to a guy or promote him to a place where he doesn't belong. Suddenly, after the man's been there twenty-five years, he's outlived his usefulness. And he's too old to start all over again. That's part of the cruelty. You can't only condemn the corporation for that. The man himself should be smart enough and intuitive enough to know he isn't getting anyplace, to get the hell out and start all over. It was much more difficult at first to lay off a guy. But if you live in a jungle, you become hard, unfortunately.

When a top executive is let go, the king is dead, long live the king. Suddenly he's a *persona non grata*. When it happens, the shock is tremendous. Overnight. He doesn't know what hit him. Suddenly everybody in the organization walks away and shuns him because they don't want to be associated with him. In corporations, if you back the wrong guy, you're in his corner, and he's fired, you're guilty by association. So what a lot of corporations have done is, when they call a guy in—sometimes they'll call him in on a Friday night and say, "Go home now and come in tomorrow morning and clean out your desk and leave. We don't want any farewells or anything. Just get up and get the hell out." It's done in nice language. We say, "Look, why cause any trouble? Why cause any unrest in the organization? It's best that you just fade away." Immediately his Cadillac is taken away from him. His phone extension on the WATS line is taken away from him.* All these things are done quietly and—bingo! he's dead. His phone at home stops ringing because the fear of association continues after the severance. The smell of death is there.

We hired a vice president. He came highly recommended. He was with us about six months and he was completely inadequate. A complete misfit. Called him in the office, told him he was gonna go, gave him a nice severance pay. He broke down and cried. "What did I do wrong? I've done a marvelous job. Please don't do this to me. My daughter's getting married next month. How am I going to face the people?" He cried and cried and cried. But we couldn't keep him around. We just had to let him go.

I was just involved with a gigantic corporation. They had a shake-up two Thursdays ago. It's now known as Black Thursday. Fifteen of twenty guys were let go overnight. The intelligent corporations say, "Clear out, leave tonight, even if it's midweek. Come in Saturday morning and clean your desk. That's all. No good-bys or anything." They could be guys that have been there anywhere from a year to thirty years. If it's a successful

---

*Wide area telecommunications service. A prerogative granted important executives by some corporations: unlimited use of the telephone to make a call anywhere in the world.

operation, they're very generous. But then again, the human element creeps in. The boss might be vindictive and cut him off without anything. It may depend what the corporation wants to maintain as its image.

And what it does to the ego! A guy in a key position, everybody wants to talk to him. All his subordinates are trying to get an audience with him to build up their own positions. Customers are calling him, everybody is calling him. Now his phone's dead. He's sitting at home and nobody calls him. He goes out and starts visiting his friends, who are busy with their own business, who haven't got time for him. Suddenly he's a failure. Regardless what the reason was—regardless of the press release that said he resigned—he was fired.

The only time the guy isn't considered a failure is when he resigns and announces his new job. That's the tipoff. "John Smith resigned, future plans unknown" means he was fired. "John Smith resigned to accept the position of President of X Company"—then you know he resigned. This little nuance you recognize immediately when you're in corporate life.

DISCUSSION QUESTIONS

1. Does Larry Ross provide an accurate and realistic picture of how organizations operate? If you think so, is it true of all, most, some or only a few organizations? Why did you answer as you did?
2. Is the organization better (or worse) off if managers behave like Larry Ross? Why?
3. Assuming that you would like to become an executive in a large organization, would you be willing to do the things Ross does to achieve your goal? Why?
4. Do you see Larry Ross as a person who has largely contributed to his own problems, or as a person who simply goes along with a world he did not create? Why?

GENERALIZATIONS AND CONCLUSIONS

Concluding Points

1. Are people like Larry Ross usually successful in getting themselves promoted into top executive positions? Once there, are they effective leaders?

2. Is there any reason to suspect that Ross contributes to his own problems?

Participant's Reactions

READINGS AND REFERENCES

Argyris, C. "Interpersonal Barriers to Decision Making," *Harvard Business Review,* March–April, 44 (1966), 84–97.

Frost, P. J., Mitchell, V. F., and Nord, W. R. (Eds.), *Organizational Reality: Reports From the Firing Line* (Santa Monica, Calif.: Goodyear, 1978).

Hamner, W. C. (Ed.), *Organizational Shock* (New York: Wiley, 1980).

Livingston, J. S., "Pygmalion in Management," *Harvard Business Review,* July-August, 47 (1969), 81–89.

Maccoby, M., *The Gamesman* (New York: Simon & Schuster, 1976).

Ritti, R. R., and Funkhouser, G. R., *The Ropes to Skip and the Ropes to Know: Studies in Organizational Behavior* (Columbus, Ohio: Grid Publishing, 1977).

Rotter, J. B., "Interpersonal Trust, Trustworthiness, and Gullibility," *American Psychologist,* 35 (1980), 1–7.

29
CAREER STYLE INVENTORY: AN ASSESSMENT EXERCISE

PURPOSE:

(1) To assess the personal style that one currently expresses, or intends to express, in organizational life.

(2) To explore the dynamics of that style with others of similar disposition, and understand how individuals of different styles perceive one another in organizations.

ADVANCE PREPARATION: The questionnaire may be completed as a homework assignment, if specified by the instructor.

GROUP SIZE: *Option one:* Break larger group into subgroups, based on responses to the questionnaire. If subgroup exceeds eight to nine members, subdivide into more than one group for each "style." *Option two:* Single large discussion group.

TIME REQUIRED: *Option one:* 2 hours. *Option two:* 30 minutes.

SPECIAL MATERIALS: None.

SPECIAL PHYSICAL REQUIREMENTS: For Option one, additional small meeting rooms for subgroup meetings, or movable chairs and space sufficient to separate subgroups for private discussion.

RELATED TOPICS: Larry Ross (Exercise 28); Motivation: basic concepts; Managers as leaders; Power; Life, work and career roles.

INTRODUCTION

There have been a number of efforts by behavioral scientists to describe, categorize, and classify different personal styles in organizations. Many of these efforts have concentrated on describing different styles of leaders (e.g., Blake and Mouton, 1964; Tannenbaum and Schmidt, 1958; Hersey and Blanchard, 1977), while other works have focused on the basic characteristics of those who work for organizations (e.g., Whyte, 1956; Jay, 1968, 1971).

The following questionnaire was developed to measure individual dispositions toward another set of personal styles in organizations, proposed by Michael Macoby (1976). After completing the questionnaire below, you will have the opportunity to read about these styles, and to evaluate your own responses to the questionnaire.

BOTH OPTIONS

Step 1: 20 Minutes

Complete the questionnaire that begins on page 166.

Developed by Roy J. Lewicki.

CAREER STYLE INVENTORY

Below are a number of descriptive paragraphs. They describe a set of beliefs or perceptions that may be held by different individuals who work for large organizations. The paragraphs are divided into four sections: Life Goals, Motivation, Self-Image, and Relations with Others. For each section, there are four paragraphs. Please evaluate these paragraphs as follows:

1. Read the paragraph. Treating the paragraph as an entity—that is, using *all* of the information in the paragraph, not just one or two sentences—*rate* the paragraph on a scale from "not at all characteristic of me" (1) to "highly characteristic of me" (7).
2. Rate each paragraph in terms of the way you would *like* to be. Regardless of how you are now, rate each description as it represents an "ideal" managerial style. Rate each on a scale from "not like to be like this at all" (1) to "very much like to be like this" (7).

Please be as honest, realistic and candid in your self-evaluations as possible. Try to accurately describe yourself, not represent what you think others might want you to say or believe.

Scales:

1	2	3	4	5	6	7
Not at all characteristic of me		Somewhat characteristic of me		Generally characteristic of me		Highly characteristic of me

1	2	3	4	5	6	7
I would not like to be like this at all		I would somewhat like to be like this		I would generally like to be like this		I would very strongly like to be like this

A. Life Goals

1. I equate my personal success in life with the long-term development and success of the organization that I work for. I enjoy a sense of belonging, responsibility, and loyalty to an organization. I believe I will benefit most if my organization prospers. I would be satisfied with my career if I progressed no higher than a middle management level.

   How characteristic is this of you (1–7) _____ ?

   How much would you like to be like this (1–7) _____ ?

2. I have two major goals in life: to do my job well, and to be committed to my family. I believe strongly in the work ethic, and want to succeed by skillfully and creatively accomplishing goals and tasks. I also want to be a good parent and provider for my family. Work and family are equally important.

How characteristic is this of you (1–7) _____ ?
How much would you like to be like this (1–7) _____ ?

3. My goal in life is to acquire power; success for me means being involved in a number of successful, diverse enterprises. I generally experience life and work as a jungle; like it or not, it's a dog-eat-dog world, and there will always be winners and losers. I want to be one of the winners.
How characteristic is this of you (1–7) _____ ?
How much would you like to be like this (1–7) _____ ?

4. I tend to view life and work as a game. I see my work, my relations with others, and my career in terms of options and possibilities as if they were part of a strategic game that I was playing. My main goal in life is to be a winner at this game.
How characteristic is this of you (1–7) _____ ?
How much would you like to be like this (1–7) _____ ?

B. Motivation

1. My interest in work is in the process of building something. I am motivated by problems that need to be solved; the challenge of work itself or the creation of a quality product gets me excited. I would prefer to miss a deadline rather than do something halfway—quality is more important to me than quantity.
How characteristic is this of you (1–7) _____ ?
How much would you like to be like this (1–7) _____ ?

2. I like to take risks, and am fascinated by new methods, techniques, and approaches. I want to motivate myself and others by pushing everyone to their limits, beyond their normal pace. My interest is in challenge, or competitive activity, where I can prove myself to be a winner. The greatest sense of exhiliration for me comes from managing a team of people and gaining victories. When work is no longer challenging, I fell bored and slightly depressed.
How characteristic is this of you (1–7) _____ ?
How much would you like to be like this (1–7) _____ ?

3. I like to control other people and to acquire power. I want to succeed by climbing the corporate ladder, acquiring greater positions of power and responsibility. I want to use this power to gain prestige, visibility, financial success, and to be able to make decisions that affect many other people. Being good at "politics" is essential to this success.
How characteristic is this of you (1–7) _____ ?
How much would you like to be like this (1–7) _____ ?

4. My interest in work is to derive a sense of security from organizational membership, and to have good relations with others. I am concerned with the feelings of people who I work with, and am committed to maintaining the integrity of my organization. As long as the organization rewards my efforts, I am willing to let my commitment to my organization take precedence over my own self-interest.
How characteristic is this of you (1–7) _____ ?
How much would you like to be like this (1–7) _____ ?

C. Self-Image

1. I am competitive and innovative. My speech and my thinking are dynamic, and come in quick flashes. I like to emphasize my strengths, and I like to be in control. I have a lot of trouble realizing and living within my limitations. I pride myself on

being fair with others; I have very few prejudices. I like to have limitless options to succeed; my biggest fears are being trapped, or being labeled as a loser.

How characteristic is this of you (1–7) _____ ?

How much would you like to be like this (1–7) _____ ?

2. My identity depends upon being part of a prestigious, protective organization. I see myself as trustworthy, responsible, a "nice guy" who can get along with almost everyone. I'm concerned with making a good impression on others, and representing the company well. I'm not sure that I have as much confidence, toughness, aggressiveness, and risk-taking skill as I would like. I am aware of these weaknesses, but I also think I should receive credit for the contributions I have made to my organization.

How characteristic is this of you (1–7) _____ ?

How much would you like to be like this (1–7) _____ ?

3. My sense of self-worth is based on my assessment of my skills, abilities, self-discipline, and self-reliance. I tend to be quiet, sincere, modest, and practical. I like to stay with a project from conception to completion.

How characteristic is this of you (1–7) _____ ?

How much would you like to be like this (1–7) _____ ?

4. I tend to be brighter, more courageous, and stronger than most of the people I work with. I see myself as bold, innovative, and an entrepreneur. I can be exceptionally creative at times, particularly in seeing entrepreneurial possibilities and opportunities. I am willing to take major risks in order to succeed, and willing to be secretive or manipulative with others if it will further my own goals.

How characteristic is this of you (1–7) _____ ?

How much would you like to be like this (1–7) _____ ?

D. Relations with Others

1. I tend to dominate other people because my ideas are better, and/or I am willing to take risks and withstand a lot of criticism. I generally don't like to work closely and cooperate with others. I would rather have other people working for me, following my directions. I don't think anyone has ever really freely helped me; either I controlled and directed them, or they were expecting me to do something for them in return.

How characteristic is this of you (1–7) _____ ?

How much would you like to be like this (1–7) _____ ?

2. My relations with others are generally good. I value highly those people who are trustworthy, committed to this organization, and act with integrity in the things that they do. In my workgroup, I attempt to sustain an atmosphere of cooperation, mild excitement, and mutuality. I get "turned off" by others in the organization who are out for themselves, who show no respect for others, or who get so involved with their own little problems that they lose sight of the "big picture."

How characteristic is this of you (1–7) _____ ?

How much would you like to be like this (1–7) _____ ?

3. I like to be in control; I am tough and dominating, but I don't think I am destructive. I tend to classify other people as winners and losers. I evaluate almost everyone in terms of what they can do for the team. I encourage people to share their knowledge with others, trying to get a work atmosphere that is both exciting and

productive. I am impatient with those who are slower and more cautious, and don't like to see weakness in others.

How characteristic is this of you (1–7) _____ ?

How much would you like to be like this (1–7) _____ ?

4. My relations with others are generally determined by the work that we do. I feel more comfortable working in a small group, or on a project with a defined and understandable structure. I tend to evaluate others (my co-workers and superiors) in terms of whether they can help or hinder me in doing a craftsmanlike job. I do not compete against other people as much as I do against my own standards of quality. On the other hand, I often find myself on the defensive, trying to preserve my integrity from the exploitative demands of the more aggressive managerial types around me.

How characteristic is this of you (1–7) _____ ?

How much would you like to be like this (1–7) _____ ?

Step 2: 10 Minutes

When you have evaluated each paragraph, turn to page 170 and "score" the questionnaire by entering your ratings for each paragraph. Then obtain a Total Score for each of the four orientations.

Step 3: 10 Minutes

Read the following description of the four orientations.

THE CORPORATE CLIMBER HAS TO FIND HIS HEART[1]

A new type of man is taking over the leadership of the most technically advanced large companies in America. In contrast to the jungle-fighter industralists commonly associated with the turn of the century, the new leader is driven not to build or preside over empires, but to organize winning teams. Unlike the security-seeking organization man who became the stereotype of the Fifties, he is excited by the chance to cut deals and to gamble.

The new industrial leader is not as hardhearted as the autocratic empire builder, nor is he as dependent on the company as the organization man. But he is more detached and emotionally inaccessible than either. And he is troubled by that fact: he recognizes that his work develops his head but not his heart.

As a practicing psychoanalyst, I reached these conclusions on the basis of interviews with 250 managers, ranging from chief executives down to lower-level professional employees in twelve well-known corporations. The study was sponsored by the Harvard Seminar on Science, Technology, and Public Policy and supported by the Andrew W. Mellon Foundation. With the help of Douglass Carmichael, Rolando Weissmann, Dennis M. Greene, Cynthia Elliott, and Katherine A. Terzi, I conducted the interviews over six years.

In some cases we returned to particular managers several times to talk about how

[1]Excerpt from article by Michael Maccoby in *Fortune* (December 1976). Reprinted by permission of Dr. Maccoby.

CAREER STYLE INVENTORY SCORING KEY

For *each* orientation, refer to the respective sections and paragraphs listed below. *Add* the rating scale values for the "characteristic of me" scales, and for the "would like to be" scales, in each grouping.

	Characteristic of me	Would like to be like this
Craftsman Orientation		
Life Goals—Paragraph 2		
Motivation—Paragraph 1		
Self-Image—Paragraph 3		
Relations with Others—Paragraph 4		
TOTAL score for Craftsman		
Company Orientation		
Life Goals—Paragraph 1		
Motivation—Paragraph 4		
Self-Image—Paragraph 2		
Relations with Others—Paragraph 2		
TOTAL score for Company Man		
Jungle Fighter Orientation		
Life Goals—Paragraph 3		
Motivation—Paragraph 3		
Self-Image—Paragraph 4		
Relations with Others—Paragraph 3		
TOTAL score for Jungle Fighter		
Gamesman Orientation		
Life Goals—Paragraph 4		
Motivation—Paragraph 2		
Self-Image—Paragraph 1		
Relations with Others—Paragraph 1		
TOTAL score for Gamesman		

their work was influencing the development of their characters. All together, we spent at least three hours with most, as long as twenty hours with some. In a few cases we also interviewed their wives and children, and seventy five executives took Rorschach tests.

In contrast to psychoanalysts who study the emotionally disturbed, we concentrated on healthy people in healthy companies. Most of the companies have sales exceeding $1 billion a year and all are highly technological, creators of some of the most advanced products of our age. They practice, and some invented, managerial techniques and business strategies that others admire and copy. Their top managers tend to speak out on major public issues, and a few have held high govenment positions. No one has accused these companies of trying to overthrow governments, bribe officials, or beg Washington to bail them out of their mistakes.

Creatures In a Corporate Culture

I wanted to find out what motivates the managers of these corporations—what mix of ambition, greed, scientific interest, security seeking, or idealism. How are managers molded by their work? What is the quality of their lives? What type of person reaches the top (and what type falls by the wayside)? Once we had studied the interviews and Rorschach tests, it became clear that the corporation is populated by four basically different character types. These are "ideal" types in the sense that few people fit any one of them exactly. Most executives are mixtures of two or more, but in practically every case, we were able to agree on which type best described a person. And the individual and his colleagues almost always agreed with our assessment.

The types:

The Craftsman, as the name implies, holds traditional values, including the work ethic, respect for people, concern for quality, and thrift. When he talks about his work, he shows an interest in the *process* of making something; he enjoys building. He sees others, co-workers as well as superiors, in terms of whether they help or hinder him in doing a craftsmanlike job.

Many of the managers in the great corporate laboratories, such as Du Pont and Bell Labs, are craftsmen by character. Their virtues are admired by almost everyone. Yet they are so absorbed in perfecting their own creations—even to the exclusion of broader corporate goals—that they are unable to lead complex and changing organizations.

The Jungle Fighter lusts for power. He experiences life and work as a jungle where it is eat or be eaten, and the winners destroy the losers. A major part of his psychic resources are budgeted for his internal department of defense. Jungle fighters tend to see their peers as either accomplices or enemies, and their subordinates as objects to be used.

There are two types of jungle fighters, lions and foxes. The lions are the conquerors who, when successful, may build an empire. In large industry, the day of the lions—the Carnegies and Fords—seems virtually ended. The foxes make their nests in the corporate hierarchy and move ahead by stealth and politicking. The most gifted foxes we encountered rose rapidly, by making use of their entrepreneurial skills. But in each case they were eventually destroyed by those they had used or betrayed.

The Company Man bases his sense of identity on being part of the protective organization. At his weakest, he is fearful and submissive, seeking security even more than success. At his strongest, he is concerned with the human side of the company, interested in the feelings of the people around him, and committed to maintaining corporate integrity. The most creative company men sustain an atmosphere of cooperation and stimulation, but they tend to lack the daring to lead highly competitive and innovative organizations.

The Gamesman sees business life in general, and his career in particular, in terms of options and possibilities, as if he were playing a game. He likes to take calculated risks and is fascinated by techniques and new methods. The contest hypes him up and he communicates his enthusiasm, energizing his peers and subordinates like the quarter-back on a football team. Unlike the jungle fighter, the gamesman competes not to build an empire or to pile up riches, but to gain fame, glory, the exhilaration of victory. His main goal is to be known as a winner, his deepest fear to be labeled a loser.

Molded by the Psychostructure

The higher our interviews took us in the corporation, the more frequently we encountered the gamesman—he is the new corporate leader. Again, it must be emphasized that the top-level executive is not a pure type, but rather a mixture. He most often combines many of the traits of the gamesman with some attributes of the company man. He is a team player who identifies closely with the corporation.

The gamesman reaches the top in a process of social (in contrast to natural) selection. The companies that excel tend to be run by people who are well adapted to fulfill the requirements of the market and the technology, and who create an atmosphere that encourages productive work. These executives in turn stimulate traits in their subordinates that are useful to the work, while discouraging those that are unnecessary or impede it. As an executive moves to the top, therefore, his character is refined.

Any organization of work—industrial, service, blue or white collar—can be described as a "psychostructure" that selects and molds character. One difference between the psychostructure of the modern corporate hierarchy and that of the factory is the fineness of fit required between work and character. Managers must have characters closely attuned to the "brain work" they perform. Only a minimal fit is required to perform simplified, repetitive tasks in a factory.

The gamesman's character, which might seem a collection of near paradoxes, can best be understood in terms of its adaptation to the requirements of the organization. The gamesman is cooperative but competitive, detached and playful but compulsively driven to succeed, a team player but a would-be superstar, a team leader but often a rebel against bureaucratic hierarchy, fair and unprejudiced but contemptuous of weakness, tough and dominating but not destructive. Competition and innovation in modern business require these gamelike attitudes, and of all the character types, only the gamesman is emotionally attuned to the environment.

OPTION ONE

Step 4: 5 Minutes

Form "career style" groups as directed by the group leader. There should be at least one group for each of the four types.

Step 5: 40 Minutes

Each group will meet to perform one or more of the following tasks (the instructor will indicate which ones):

1. Evaluate whether you think the description of the people in your group is generally accurate, based on (a) the questionnaire paragraphs that describe this style, and (b) the overall description in the reading. If inaccurate, what modifications or changes would you make?
2. Evaluate the advantages and disadvantages of this style. Think about this style in an organization. What would be the strong points, and the weak points of having this style? What kind of problems would a person with your type of style encounter in his/her first job.
3. Evaluate the kind of organization in which your style would function well. In what kind of organization would your style function poorly?
4. What would you expect the career path of people with your style to look like? What types of things would you have to do in your career in order to maximize success, and feelings of personal satisfaction? What things would you do well? What kind of problems would you create for yourself?

5. Examine each of the groups with styles *different* from yours. What kind of leadership or supervisory style should be used with people from each of these groups, in order to maximize their effectiveness?

Appoint one member of the group to act as a spokesperson for the group. Prepare a presentation to be made to the class, covering the topics of your discussion.

Step 6: 20 Minutes

After the groups reconvene, each group makes a presentation of the discussion topics covered in your small group. Take careful note of the comments made about your group by the other groups. Evaluate whether you agree or disagree with these views.

OPTION TWO

Step 4: Discussion Questions

Discuss the different career styles in terms of the following questions:

1. In this program or class, what would be your guess as to the style most people use to describe themselves? What is the least frequently used style? Why?
2. In this program or class, what is your guess as to the style most people would like to be? What is the style they would least like to be? Why?
3. Survey the members of the class. How many are there of each type? How many are there of each "desired" (would like to be) type? Do you think these numbers would be characteristic of other student groups completing this questionnaire?
4. How many people wanted to be styles different from the ones they are now? What were their reasons for wanting to be different?
5. Do you think there are any significant differences in how males and females would rate their present styles or their ideal styles? Why?
6. What would be the best type of job, managerial role, or organization for each style? Why?
7. What would be the advantages, or assets, for individuals possessing each style, in an organizational setting? What would be the disadvantages or weaknesses of each style?
8. What can people in each style learn to do, in order to function more effectively in a variety of organizational roles and responsibilities?

DISCUSSION QUESTIONS

Discussion questions for Option Two appear in the exercise. The following apply to Option One:
1. How effective were the members of each style group at identifyin their strong points and weak points? What kind of problems would each have on the first job, or progressing in a management career?
2. How did the various groups evaluate styles different from their own? Do you agree with their analysis?

3. Was there any evidence, in either the content or the style of the presentation, that people were properly classified? How or Why?

GENERALIZATIONS AND CONCLUSIONS

1. How easy or difficult is it to classify individuals according to corporate styles? Is this a useful classification to make, and to know about oneself?

2. Is there a "best" corporate style, in terms of what people are, or what they would like to be? Why?

3. How might the differences in corporate style reflect differences in the kinds of jobs people enjoy, the career paths they follow, and the ways they are rewarded by their organizations?

Participant's Reactions

READINGS AND REFERENCES

Blake, R. R., and Mouton, J. S., *The Managerial Grid* (Houston, Tx.: Gulf Publishing Co., 1964).

Hersey, P., and Blanchard, K., *Management of Organizational Behavior: Utilizing Human Resources* (Englewood Cliffs, N.J.: Prentice Hall, 1977).

Jay, A., *Management and Machiavelli* (New York: Holt, Rinehart and Winston, 1968).

Jay, A., *Corporation Man* (New York: Random House, 1971).

Maccoby, M., *The Gamesman* (New York: Simon and Schuster, 1976).

Maccoby, M., "The Corporate Climber Has to Find His Heart," *Fortune*, December (1976), 98–108.

Tannenbaum, R., and Schmidt, W., "How to Choose a Leadership Pattern," *Harvard Business Review*, March–April (1958), 95–102.

Whyte, W. F., *The Organization Man* (New York: Simon and Schuster, 1956).

30
VANATIN: GROUP DECISION MAKING AND ETHICS

PURPOSE:

(1) To understand factors that contribute to decision making regarding ethical practices and moral values.

(2) To explore the aspects of group dynamics that affect ethical decisions.

ADVANCE PREPARATION: None. Roles may be prepared in advance if time is a problem, but this is not encouraged.

GROUP SIZE: Seven-person groups. If there are less than seven members in a group, individuals may be assigned to observe, or roles may be deleted (see Instructor's Manual).

TIME REQUIRED: 1½ hours. Exercise may be divided into two class periods— see Instructor's Manual.

SPECIAL MATERIALS: Scenario Instructions, role-play forms for each class member, decision recording form. File cards or self-stick labels that can be used as nametags for role players to identify their roles.

SPECIAL REQUIREMENTS: Movable furniture arranged in a circle of seven chairs, and/or extra space for groups to spread out.

RELATED TOPICS: Negotiation and conflict; Group decision making and conflict.

INTRODUCTION

The Vanatin case provides an opportunity for group members to struggle with questions of social responsibility and ethics in decision making. The case is constructed around a medical product, considered by experts to be injurious to the health of consumers—even to the point of possibly causing death. These consequences must be evaluated against the potential economic losses to the company, which would be substantial if sale of the drug were discontinued. The decision is not an easy one, but nevertheless the problem is common to many corporate and governmental groups that must consider both their own interest and the overall interests of society and public welfare.

Step 1: 10 Minutes

The instructor will divide the class into groups and assign you one of the seven roles (see the Appendix). Read the scenario below. Then read *only* your own role. Make notes on the points you want to emphasize in the group discussion.

Adapted by Roy J. Lewicki from an exercise developed by J. Scott Armstrong, University of Pennsylvania. Used by permission.

BACKGROUND INFORMATION FOR THE VANATIN CASE

Assume that it is August 1969 and that you are a member of the Booth Pharmaceutical Corporation Board of Directors. You have been called to a Special Board Meeting to discuss what should be done with the product known as "Vanatin."

Vanatin is a "fixed-ratio" antibiotic sold by prescription. "Fixed-ratio" means that it contains a combination of drugs. It has been on the market for more than 13 years and has been highly successful. It now accounts for about 18 million dollars per year, which is 12 percent of Booth Company's gross income in the United States (and a greater percentage of net profits). Profits from foreign markets, where Booth is marketed under a different name, is roughly comparable to that in the United States.

Over the past 20 years, there have been numerous medical scientists (e.g., the AMA's Council on Drugs) who have objected to the sale of most fixed-ratio drugs. The argument has been that (1) there is no evidence that these fixed-ratio drugs have improved benefits over single-drugs, and (2) the possibility of detrimental side effects, including death, has *at least* doubled. For example, these scientists have estimated that Vanatin is causing about 30 to 40 unnecessary deaths per year (i.e., deaths that could be prevented if the patients had used a substitute made by a competitor of Booth). Despite these recommendations to remove fixed-ratio drugs from the market, doctors have continued to use them. They offer a shotgun approach for the doctor who is unsure of his diagnosis.

Recently a group of impartial scientists appointed by the National Academy of Science and the National Research Council panel, carried out extensive research studies on the drug and recommended unanimously that the Food and Drug Administration (FDA) ban the sale of Vanatin. One of the members of the panel, Dr. Alphonse Peterson of the University of Texas, was quoted by the press as saying, "There are few instances in medicine when so many experts have agreed unanimously and without reservation [about banning Vanatin]." This view was typical of comments made by other members of the panel. In fact, it was typical of comments that had been made about fixed-ratio drugs over the past 20 years. These impartial experts, then, believe that while all drugs have some possibility of side effects, the costs associated with Vanatin far exceed the possible effects.

The special Board Meeting has arisen out of an emergency situation. The FDA has told you that it plans to ban Vanatin in the United States and wants to give Booth time for a final appeal to them. Should the ban become effective, Booth would have to stop all sales of Vanatin and attempt to remove inventories from the market. Booth has no close substitutes for Vanatin, so that consumers will be switched to close substitutes currently marketed by rival firms. (Some of these substitutes apparently have no serious side effects.) It is extremely unlikely that bad publicity from this case would have any significant effect upon the long-term profits of other products made by Booth.

The Board is meeting to review and make decisions on two issues:

1. What should be done with Vanatin in the U.S. market (the immediate problem)?
2. Assuming that Vanatin is banned from the U.S. market, what should Booth do in the foreign markets? (No government action is anticipated in any of the foreign markets.)

Decisions on each of these issues must be reached at today's meeting. The Chairman of the Board has sent out this background information. He also wanted you to give some thought as to which of the following alternatives you would prefer for the domestic market:

a. Recall Vanatin immediately and destroy.
b. Stop production of Vanatin immediately, but allow what's been made to be sold.
c. Stop all advertising and promotion of Vanatin, but provide it for those doctors that request it.
d. Continue efforts to most effectively market Vanatin until sale is actually banned.
e. Continued efforts to most effectively market Vanatin and take legal, political, and other necessary actions to prevent the authorities from banning Vanatin.

A similar decision must also be made for the foreign market *under the assumption that the sale was banned in the United States.*

Step 2: 45 Minutes

The Chairman of the Board will conduct the discussion of the Vanatin problem. By the end of 45 minutes, the groups should reach a decision on what to do about *both* the domestic and international distribution of Vanatin.

At the end of the 45 minutes, each Chairman should record the group decisions below.

RECORDING FORM

Group Decision on Vanatin

1. Check the option that most closely approximates your position with regard to the U.S. market (circle one letter only):
   a. Recall Vanatin immediately and destroy.
   b. Stop production of Vanatin immediately, but allow what's been made to be sold.
   c. Stop all advertising and promotion of Vanatin, but provide it for those doctors that request it.
   d. Continued efforts to most effectively market Vanatin until sale is actually banned by the FDA.
   e. Continue efforts to most effectively market Vanatin and take legal, political, and other necessary action to prevent the FDA from banning Vanatin.
2. Assume that the FDA did succeed in banning Vanatin but that it was still legal to sell Vanatin in foreign countries. Which option most closely approximates your position with regard to foreign markets (circle one letter only)?
   a. Recall Vanatin immediately and destroy.
   b. Stop production of Vanatin immediately, but allow what's been made to be sold.
   c. Stop all advertising and promotion of Vanatin, but provide it for those doctors that request it.
   d. Continue efforts to most effectively market Vanatin until sale is banned in each particular country.
   e. Continue efforts to most effectively market Vanatin and take legal, political, and other necessary actions to prevent the FDA from banning Vanatin.

Step 3: 20 to 35 Minutes, Discussion

The instructor will review the decision forms and tabulate the type of decisions made by each group for the U.S. and foreign markets. You may record the decisions on the table below.

1. *Record* in columns 1 and 2 the actual decisions made by the discussion groups.
2. *Privately* note to yourself what you think Booth actually did in this case. The instructor will tally the predictions, and you may record these predictions in Columns 3 and 4.
3. *Record* in columns 5 and 6 what Booth actually did.

	Decisions Made by Groups[a]		What Do You Think Happened?		What Actually Happened	
Decision	U.S.	Foreign	U.S.	Foreign[b]	U.S.	Foreign
a. Recall Immediately b. Stop Production c. Stop Advertising and Promotion d. Continue to Market e. Block FDA						
	(1)	(2)	(3)	(4)	(5)	(6)

[a]Record the decision of the various groups in the proper place.

[b]You can skip this column temporarily until you discuss what actually happened in the U.S. market (see next column).

DISCUSSION QUESTIONS

1. What factors in your own group's discussion affected the way the decision was arrived at? For example,
   a. How much control did the Chairman of the Board exercise over the *type* of decisions arrived at?
   b. Which group members had the most influence, in terms of the *persuasiveness* of their arguments on the group's final decision?
   c. Which group members had the most influence, in terms of *persuasion techniques* they used to get other people to agree with them?
   d. How were group members viewed and treated when they made strongly *ethical* arguments for banning Vanatin?
   e. How were group members viewed and treated when they made strongly *pragmatic* arguments for the effects of the ban on corporate profits and sales?
2. How similar or different is this decision from other decisions you have made as a group?
3. What kinds of decision situations in organizations have elements in common with this exercise?

GENERALIZATIONS AND CONCLUSIONS

The basic model for this case is this: what would happen if one constructed an extreme case where there were obvious and direct tradeoffs between profits and the quality of life? Under what conditions would people continue to make decisions to maximize profits in such a case?

There have been a number of variations in the construction of this case. Each variation seems to result in the same conclusion. While these conclusions are not pleasant, they reflect the dynamics of groups and the behavior of individuals who may not have to "live with" or directly experience the pain and suffering that particular policies or practices may be causing.

Participant's Reactions

READINGS AND REFERENCES:

Cavanagh, Gerald I., *American Business Values* (2nd Ed.) (Englewood Cliffs, N.J.: Prentice-Hall, 1976).

DeGeorge, Richard T., *Business Ethics* (2nd Ed.) (New York: MacMillan, 1986).

Heilbroner, Robert, *In the Name of Profit* (Garden City, N.Y.: Doubleday, 1972).

Janis, I., *Victims of Groupthink* (Boston: Houghton-Mifflin, 1972).

Latane, B., and Darley, J., *The Unresponsive Bystander* (New York: Appleton Century Crofts, 1970).

Longnecker, Justin G., "Management Priorities and Management Ethics," *Journal of Business Ethics,* 4(1), 1985, 1–80.

Milgram, Stanley, *Obedience to Authority* (New York: Harper and Row, 1974).

Mintz, Morton, "FDA and Panalba: A Conflict of Commercial and Therapeutic Goals," *Science,* 165, (August 1969), 875–881.

31
ALIEN INVASION:
AN ORGANIZATIONAL CULTURE ASSIGNMENT

PURPOSE:
(1) To introduce the concept of organizational culture.
(2) To provide an opportunity for applying the culture concept to an actual organization.
(3) To practice observing indicators of culture.

ADVANCE PREPARATION: Read the Introduction.
GROUP SIZE: Teams of three to seven members.
TIME REQUIRED: In class: 10 minutes to introduce exercise and prepare for company visits. 20 minutes per team for team reports.

Out of class: Approximately 4 hours for site visit plus time to prepare report.

SPECIAL MATERIALS: None.
SPECIAL PHYSICAL REQUIREMENTS: None.
RELATED TOPICS: Organizational climate, Leadership, Organizational realities.

INTRODUCTION

In 1980, Terrence Deal and Allan A. Kennedy wrote, *Corporate Cultures: The Rites and Rituals of Corporate Life*. Deal and Kennedy's book quickly became a best seller because it helped to define an aspect of organizational life that was unquestionably critical, an aspect that had largely been ignored in the management literature. Borrowing from anthropology, they suggested that *culture* was the element that explained why companies differed so greatly, even those in the same industry. Differences in the culture of a company could largely explain why some organizations were much more successful than others. They also observed that some companies have "strong" cultures, but others have "weak" cultures.

THE CULTURE CONCEPT

While culture is a major analytical concept in anthropology, anthropologists have had difficulty defining it. (Kroeber and Kluckhohn, 1952) The problems of defining "culture" seem akin to the problem of defining pornography; as one Supreme Court justice observed, "I can't define it, but I know it when I see it." Managers are likely to define culture as: "the way we do things around here." (Deal and Kennedy, p. 4)

One way of defining culture is: " ... *the set of important assumptions (often un-*

Prepared for this volume by Donald D. Bowen

stated) that members of a community share in common." (Sathe, 1985, p. 10) Schein (1983) observes that cultures tend to emerge as an organization discovers, invents, or develops solutions to the problems that it faces. Successful approaches to solving problems tend to become a part of the culture and are used whenever similar conditions are faced.

Trice and Beyer (1984, p. 654) define culture as: " . . . *the system of . . . publicly and collectively accepted meanings operating for a given group at a given time."* In this definition, we see emphasis on the role that culture plays in helping people to decipher their world. We also note that the contents are "publicly" accepted. Individuals within the culture may have their private reservations, but they are likely to pay at least public lip service to the tenets of the culture.

Trice and Beyer note that there are two basic components to culture: (1) the meanings contained in its ideologies, values, and norms, and (2) the forms or practices that constitute the culture. They then provide us with a useful listing of the types of cultural forms that anthropologists study. (Trice and Beyer, p. 655)

First, there are a number of cultural forms that tend to constitute the substance of public functions and events staged by the group.

1. A *rite* is a relatively elaborate, dramatic, planned set of activities that consolidates various forms of cultural expressions into a single event, which is usually carried out through social interaction and usually for the benefit of an audience. A wedding ceremony might be a good example. Another might be the awarding of the "Salesperson of the Year" award at the annual company banquet.
2. *Ceremonials* are "systems of several rites connected with a single occasion or event." An example of a ceremonial might be a company banquet where several awards were made to recognize performance.
3. *Rituals,* on the other hand, are "a standardized, detailed set of techniques and behaviors that manage anxieties, but seldom produce intended, technical consequences of practical importance." Wright (1979, p. 35) has described two rituals at General Motors. The first involves meeting traveling executives at the airport (the more important the executive, the larger the reception party). The second is an eating ritual—headquarters executives are expected to eat lunch together in the executive dining room when they are in Detroit.

The second category of cultural forms consists of the ways that members of a group or organization typically communicate and express themselves.

1. *Stories* are accounts based on true events, but often contain both truth and fiction. In many organizations, the members have a collection of stories that they tell repeatedly.
2. *Myths* can be either a type of story ("a dramatic narrative of imagined events, usually used to explain origins or transformations of something") or a type of belief ("an unquestioned belief about the practical benefits of certain techniques and behaviors that is not supported by facts"). Myths differ from stories in that

they lack a factual basis. Old-timers' stories about how things were "in the good old days" are frequently myths.

3. *Sagas* are one of the most important categories of stories for organizations. The *saga* is: "an historical narrative describing the unique accomplishments of a group and its leaders." According to Peters and Waterman (1982) members of "strong culture" companies are likely to have an enormous fund of stories to tell about the exploits of the founder or other strong leader. At Hewlett Packard, the sagas feature the legendary accomplishments of the founders, Bill (Hewlett) and Dave (Packard) and are used to communicate the unique way of doing things at HP to outsiders or newcomers.

4. *Legends* are stories about some wonderful event that has actually occurred, but has subsequently been embellished with fictional details (e.g. tales of the Battle of the Alamo)

5. *Folktales* are a purely fictional stories.

6. *Symbols* are central to understanding cultures. A symbol is "any object, act, event, quality, or relation that serves as a vehicle for conveying meaning." We are all familiar with such common symbols as the Coca-Cola or IBM logos. But symbols can include symbolic gestures or symbolic events (which are likely to be recounted in the organization's myths, sagas, and legends).

In order to communicate, members of a particular culture also need both:

1. A common *language*.
2. Accompanying *gestures* to convey their meaning.

One of the most commonly recognized examples of the emergence of unique forms of expression within an organization is the development of specialized jargon (often almost unintelligible to an outsider) among people who work together.

A third category of cultural forms involves material goods and the physical environment. This category includes:

1. *Artifacts* or manufactured items such as tools, attire, art work, furniture, books, appliances, and the like.
2. *Physical settings,* including buildings, open spaces, office furnishings, shop layouts, and so forth.

Consider, now, the following description of Wal-Mart, the extremely successful chain of discount stores as described by Peters and Waterman (pp. 246–248):

WAL-MART

Wal-Mart, with over 26,000 employees, is now the number four retailer in the United States. During the 1970s, growth took the company from $45 million in sales to $1.6 billion, from 18 stores to 330. Sam Walton, or "Mr. Sam," as he is called in the company, is the driving force behind this success, and Walton, quite simply, cares about his employees. In fact, almost all his managers, at his insistence, wear buttons that say, "We Care About Our People."

Walton learned the people business at J. C. Penney. Like Penney's, his people are referred to as "associates," not employees. And he listens to them. "The key is to get out into the store and listen to what the associates have to say," he says. "It's terribly important for everyone to get involved. Our best ideas come from clerks and stock-boys." Walton stories have become legends. According to *The Wall Street Journal:* "Mr. Walton couldn't sleep a few weeks back. He got up and bought four dozen donuts at an all night bakery. At 2:30 A.M., he took them to a distribution center and chatted for a while with workers from the shipping docks. As a result he discovered that two more shower stalls were needed at that location." Again, the astonishing point is not the story per se: any small business person could relate a host of similar tales. The surprising news is that a top executive still exhibits such a bone-deep form of concern for his people in a *$2 billion enterprise.*

The message that down-the-line people count is mirrored in every activity. The executive offices are virtually empty. Headquarters resemble a warehouse. The reason is that Walton's managers spend most of their time out in the field in Wal-Mart's eleven state service areas. And what are they doing? "Leading local cheerleading squads at new store openings, scouting out competing K mart stores, and conducting soul-searching sessions with the employees." Walton himself visits every store every year (330 now, remember) as he has done since 1962.

Everyone at Wal-Mart feels like a winner. The regular management meetings start at 7:30 A.M. on Saturday. The buyer of the month receives a plaque. There are "honor roll" stores, every *week.* And every week the "SWAT" team that swoops down to remodel stores testifies to jobs well done. Mr. Sam stands up and yells, "Who's number one?" And everyone, of course, yells back "Wal-Mart!"

So, it's intense rah-rah, and, yes, it's hocum, and—like so many other situations we see—it's fun. As *The Wall Street Journal* reports: "Mr. Walton seems to have the most fun. Not long ago he flew his aircraft to Mt. Pleasant, Texas, and parked the plane with instructions to the co-pilot to meet him 100 or so miles down the road. He then flagged a Wal-Mart truck and rode the rest of the way to 'Chat with the driver—it seemed like so much fun.' "

The theme of fun in business runs through a great deal of the excellent companies research. The leaders and managers like what they do and they get enthusiastic about it. Or, as Howard Head said in a recent speech, "It seems to me you have to be personally associated with what you do. I just love design. If it weren't fun, I wouldn't do it."

How many examples of the cultural forms in this company culture can you spot?

Clearly Wal-Mart has its share of *stories,* accounts that collectively add up to the *saga* of "Mr. Sam." Some of the stories may be *folktales,* but it doesn't really matter whether they are true or not. Wal-Mart people will tell the stories because they symbolize the Wal-Mart way of doing business. *Rites* and *ceremonials* also abound in the rousing new store openings, the sessions with employees, and the management meetings. An example of the special *language* Wal-Mart uses to convey its ideology about the importance of employees ("associates") is provided. Several *symbols,* including Mr. Sam himself, the slogans of the company, and, again, the term "associate" all help the company convey its unique ideas about what is important in managing an efficient growing enterprise. *Artifacts,* too, tell us something about the company—from the eloquent buttons declaring how management cares about the people to the plaques awarded to the honor stores. The message is that through caring about their people, Wal-Mart encourages productive team efforts. The urgency of the entire operation is evident from the fact that the CEO flies around the country in an airplane. The airplane is an artifact and an important symbol of his status—except when he is hitching a ride in one of the company trucks. Hitching a ride is an important symbolic gesture affirming his democratic attitudes.

From this brief analysis, you might conclude a number of things about organizational culture. First, the company's culture is a major vehicle through which the company communicates and reaffirms its basic values and ideology. In Wal-Mart's case, the strong value-orientation for both employees and performance are clear in this brief vignette. Second, culture imbues almost everything the organization does, says, or owns. Because culture surrounds us so pervasively, individuals in an organization may have a problem recognizing what it is, much like the fish who is unaware of water because he lives in it. To outside observers, however, unique aspects of a company culture often seem obvious simply because they contrast so sharply with the culture in their own organization.

Another point about the forms of culture is that a single item or event may serve several symbolic purposes simultaneously. For example, the buttons reassure employees that management really cares, but these same buttons remind management that they are *expected* to care. The awarding of plaques to honor stores serves not only to reward and reinforce the desirable behavior that won the plaque, but also reminds non-winners of what is expected of them. Because of the multi-faceted purposes that any symbolic gesture or artifact serves, culture becomes a complex web that can only be deciphered completely after extensive study.

Moreover, not all elements of the organization's culture will make positive contributions to the organization's welfare. Anthropologists have concluded that much of our behavior has both "functional" and "dysfunctional" (damaging) consequences. The functional consequences are usually *intended* results; the dysfunctional outcomes are *unintended* or unforeseen. As an example, in order to improve its service to customers, a bank in a Midwestern city instituted strict rules about coffee breaks for its tellers. The tellers, who had grown accustomed to taking a break whenever they felt like it (providing there were no customers in line) resented the new rule. Enforcement of the new rule led to the intended functional consequence (more tellers available to service customers) and to an unforeseen dysfunctional outcome (grouchy tellers who were rude to the customers).

One problem in dealing with the dysfunctional features of a culture is that the organization members (including management) are so immersed in the culture that they are often unaware of how their actions create the problems. The entrepreneurial founder of an organization may be a person who dislikes and avoids paperwork. As long as the business remains small, it can frequently get away with all but a minimum of paperwork. But if the firm grows in size and sales, it becomes more complex and can no longer rely on the memories of key individuals to keep transactions straight. But at the same time, the organization has grown up with a cultural norm of keeping minimal records. The firm may have great difficulty in changing to a more systematic mode of operation because the founder instilled a way of doing things that worked with great success in the past. That way of doing things may now be regarded as one of the secrets of the firm's success.

On the other hand, because the organization's culture is so omnipresent, much of it (sometimes more than the organization wants to reveal) is readily evident to the observant visitor. The trick is in learning to "read" the clues to decipher a culture. What does the building style and layout say about this company? What symbols does it use in its dealing with the public and what do those symbols say about how the company wants to be seen? What can we interpret from the activities of employees? Are certain physical settings reserved for certain types of behavior (for example, sales clerks are likely to behave quite differently in the back room of the store as compared to when they are on the sales floor)? Are they energetic or apathetic? Are they friendly or hostile? What stories do they tell about the organization and the major executives of the firm? What is the moral of these stories? What are the norms of dress? How formal are relationships between people, particularly people of different status levels such as the boss and the secretary? Are there some members of the organization who are "stigmatized" and others who are heroes or heroines? If so, what is it about them that earns them this special treatment? It is surprising how often one can pick up a real "feel" for an organization by simply looking and listening carefully.

ASSIGNMENT

You will be assigned to a team (if you are not already in one) and instructed to visit an organization by your instructor.

1. Visit the site assigned as a team.
2. Take detailed notes on the cultural forms that you observe.
3. Prepare a presentation for the class that describes these forms and draw any inferences you can about the nature of the culture of the organization—its ideologies, values, and norms of behavior.
4. Be sure to explain the basis of your inferences in terms of the cultural forms observed.

You will have twenty minutes to report your findings, so plan your presentation carefully. Use visual aids to help your audience understand what you have found.

You are Martians who have just arrived on Earth in the first spaceship from your planet. Your superiors have ordered you to learn as much about Earthlings and the way they behave as you can without doing anything to make them aware that you are Martians. It is vital for the future plans of your superiors that you do nothing to disturb the Earthlings. Unfortunately, Martians communicate by emitting electromagnetic waves and are incapable of speech, so you cannot talk to the natives. Even if you did, it is reported by the usually reliable Bureau of Interplanetary Intelligence that Earthlings may become cannibalisitic if annoyed. However, the crash course in Earth languages taught by the Bureau has enabled you to read the language.

These instructions limit your data collection to observation and request that you *not* talk to the "natives." There are two reasons for this instruction. First, your objective is to learn what the organization does when it is simply going about its normal business and not responding to a group of students asking questions. Second, you are likely to be surprised at how much you can learn by simply observing if you put your mind to it. Many skilled managers employ this ability in sensing what is going on as they walk through their plant or office area.

Since you cannot talk to people, some of the cultural forms (legends, sagas, etc.) will be difficult to spot unless you are able to pick up copies of the organization's promotional literature (brochures, company reports, advertisements) during your visit. Do not be discouraged, because the visible forms such as artifacts, setting, symbols, and (sometimes) rituals can convey a great deal about the culture. Just keep your eyes, ears, and antennae open!

REFERENCES AND READINGS:

Deal, T. E. & Kennedy, A. A., *Corporate Cultures: The Rites and Rituals of Corporate Life.* (Reading, MA: Addison-Wesley, 1982)

Ford's idea machine. *Newsweek,* November 24 (1986), pp. 64–68.

Kilmann, R. H., Corporate Culture. *Psychology Today,* April (1985) 63–68.

Kroeber, A. L., and Kluckhohn, C., *Culture: A Critical Review of Concepts and Definitions.* Cambridge. Papers of the Peabody Museum, 1952 47(1).

Peters, T. J., and Waterman, R. H., Jr., *In Search of Excellence.* (New York: Harper & Row, 1982)

Sathe, V., *Culture and Related Corporate Realities.* (Homewood, IL: Irwin, 1985)

Schein, E. H., The Role of the Founder in Creating Organizational Culture. *Organizational Dynamics,* Summer (1983) 13–28.

Trice, H. M., and Beyer, J. M. Studying Organizational Cultures through Rites and Rituals. *Academy of Management Review, 9,* (A84), 653–669.

SECTION NINE
POWER

32
THE POWER GAME

PURPOSE:

(1) To explore the dynamics of power at the individual, interpersonal, group, and system levels.

(2) To create the opportunity for students to examine their personal beliefs about power, power strategies, and reactions to power.

ADVANCE PREPARATION: See Instructor's Manual.

GROUP SIZE: 15–40 students

TIME REQUIRED: 80–90 minutes for the exercise, 60 minutes for discussion.

SPECIAL MATERIALS: Role instructions in Instructor's Manual.

SPECIAL PHYSICAL REQUIREMENTS: Three separate rooms or gathering spaces for groups.

RELATED TOPICS: Negotiation and Conflict, Organizational Communication, Organizational Realities, Organizational Structure and Design

INTRODUCTION

The concept of "power" is a complete, elusive, and almost paradoxical one. It is complex because there is a wide variety of definitions of what constitutes power, and how it is effectively accumulated and used. It is elusive because there seems to be very little consensus about the definitions, or the best way to describe power and

Adapted from an exercise developed by Lee Bolman and Terrence Deal, Harvard Graduate School of Education. Previously published in *Negotiation: Readings, Exercises and Cases,* Roy J. Lewicki and Joseph Litterer, Richard D. Irwin, 1985. Used with permission of authors and Richard D. Irwin.

talk about it in action. Finally, power is paradoxical because it doesn't always work the way it is "expected" to; sometimes those who seem to have the most power really have the least, while those who may appear to have the least power are most in control.

This simulation offers an opportunity to experience power in a wide variety of forms and styles. During the activity, you will become aware of your own power, and the power of others. Your objective will be to determine who has power, how power is being used, and how other's power may be effectively counteracted with your own power in order for you to achieve your goals. This type of analysis is essential to effective negotiations in power-laden situations.

PROCEDURE

Step 1: 5 Minutes
Your instructor will ask you for a monetary contribution. This money is to be given to the instructor. He will then announce what he will do with it.

Step 2: 5 Minutes
Your instructor will assign you to a group. You will become acquainted with the group that you are assigned to. You will be given a place to meet.

Step 3: 60 Minutes
Your instructor will give you descriptions of the duties and responsibilities of the group that you are assigned to. Please read this information closely. You will have exactly one hour to conduct the exercise, unless your instructor gives you different instructions.

DISCUSSION QUESTIONS
1. What did you learn about power from this experience?
2. Did this experience remind you of events you have experienced in other organizations? If so, what were the similarities?
3. What did you learn about yourself personally, and the way that you react to power or use?
4. What events occurred in your own subgroup? Did you feel satisfied with the amount of power you had? With the way you used it? Why?
5. What did you or your group do to exercise power, or to gain more power? How did it work out?

READINGS AND REFERENCES
Block, P., *The Empowered Manager*. (San Francisco: Jossey Bass, 1987)
Yates, D., *The Politics of Management*. (San Francisco: Jossey Bass, 1985)

33
ANALYSIS OF PERSONAL POWER

PURPOSE:
(1) To help you explore the typical ways that you interact with people.
(2) To help you think about the meaning of power to you, in terms of your relations with other people.
(3) To identify those individuals in the learning environment who have more or less power, and to understand how this power is derived.

ADVANCE PREPARATION: At discretion of group leader.
GROUP SIZE: Unlimited group size; three-to four-person groups may be used to discuss the results.
TIME REQUIRED: Part I, 1 hour; Part II, 1 hour.
SPECIAL MATERIALS: None.
SPECIAL PHYSICAL REQUIREMENTS: None.
RELATED TOPICS: Motivation: basic concepts, Managers as leaders.

INTRODUCTION

The first part of this exercise is designed to help you explore some aspects of your relations with other people. You will do this by responding to a questionnaire. That questionnaire will be scored in class, and the group leader will explain the concepts needed to help you interpret your scores. The second part of this exercise will help you to explore the different ways that power can be used, and the impact of that approach on behavior.

PROCEDURE

Step 1: 10 Minutes
Read the following description.

The questionnaire in this section is based on a theory called FIRO. FIRO was developed by Dr. William Schutz as a measure of an individual's basic interpersonal needs. Schutz proposed that individuals differed in the strength of their interpersonal needs along three major dimensions: inclusion, control, and affection. For each of these three needs, individuals also differed in the degree to which an individual was comfortable expressing each need toward others, and the degree to which individuals wanted others to express that need toward him. His theory led him to develop a

Adapted by Roy J. Lewicki from *FIRO: A Three Dimensional Theory of Interpersonal Behavior* by William C. Schutz (New York: Rinehart & Co., 1958). Part II is adapted from "An Exercise in Social Power" by Gib Akin, *Exchange,* Vol. 3, No. 4 (1979).

questionnaire that measured individual differences on the three major dimensions (inclusion, control, and affection), and the strength of each need on both expressed (toward others) and wanted (from others).

Inclusion refers to your need to establish and maintain contact with other people. Some people have high needs for inclusion—that is, they like to be with other people, to be part of a group, to be included in a lot of formal and informal social groups and events, and to be around people a great deal. Some other people have low needs for inclusion—that is, they prefer to be alone, to do things by themselves, to have only a few friends, or to avoid groups and social gatherings. Finally, still other people have moderate needs for inclusion. Individuals can differ in the degree to which they express this need for inclusion to others, *and* to the degree that they want others to express inclusion to them. These two orientations can vary independently. For example, it is not uncommon for a somewhat shy person to express very little inclusion toward others, but want others to express a lot of inclusion toward her.

Control refers to the need to have influence or control other people, or have them influence and control you. Some people have high needs for control—that is, they like to have influence over others, to be in charge, to tell other people what to do. Other people have low needs for control—that is, they have little or no interest in whether they have influence or not, or whether they are in charge, or whether someone is giving direction and orders. Finally, still other people have moderate needs for control. Individuals can also differ in the degree to which they express this need for control over others, and the degree to which they want others to express control to them. These two dimensions can also vary independently. For example, it is not uncommon for an individual to want someone else to make the decisions and control him, but have little or no interest in controlling others.

Affection refers to the need to have a close, personal relationship with other people, to be comfortable in expressing affection, and in having it expressed to you. Some people have high needs for affection—that is, they like to have close and personal relationships with other people. Other people have low needs for affection—that is, they prefer to have rather cool and distant relationships with people. Finally, still other people have moderate needs for affection. Individuals can also differ in the degree to which they express this need for affection to others, and the degree to which they want others to express affection toward them. These two orientations can also vary independently. For example, it is not uncommon for an individual to be very comfortable in expressing affection, but very uncomfortable in receiving it.

The questionnaire below is designed to have you estimate the strength of your own needs along two scales for each of six dimensions: expressed inclusion, want inclusion, expressed control, want control, expressed affection, and want affection. You are to select one number from 0 (very low) to 9 (very high) for each of the 12 scales. Several descriptive statements and phrases are placed along each dimension to help you pick the number that best identifies the strength of your need.

Before you make your ratings, we want to offer two statements of caution:

1. Please be as candid as you can. Do not try to answer this questionnaire as you think you "should". *There are no right answers! No one set of answers makes*

*you appear healthier or unhealthier, better or worse than somebody else! You
will not be required to share your answers with anyone, so please try to describe
yourself as you really think you are!*

2. As you read this description of the major needs, you may recognize that your
   needs vary. For example, sometimes you may want to be around people and
   sometimes you don't. Or there are some people you want to be around a lot,
   and some you don't. That's true! You will note that there are two scales for each
   dimension. One asks you to rate yourself on the strength of your need in terms
   of how often it occurs, while the other asks you to rate yourself on the number
   of other people with whom you feel this need.

Step 2: 10 Minutes

Below you will find two scales for each of the six dimensions. Rate yourself along
each of the scales. Circle *one* number, from 0 to 9, indicating your best guess as to
the strength of your need on that particular scale. Then find the *average* of your two
scale scores for each of the six dimensions.

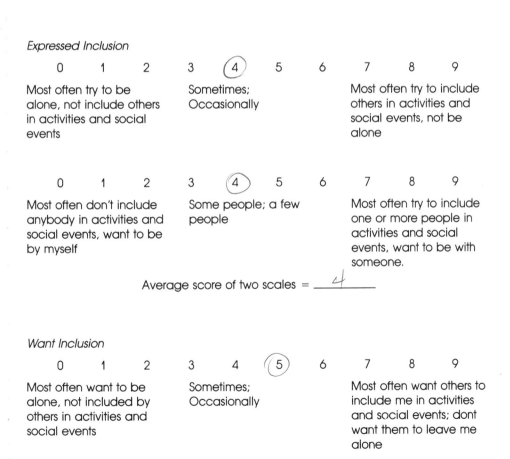

Expressed Inclusion

0   1   2   3   (4)   5   6   7   8   9

Most often try to be
alone, not include others
in activities and social
events

Sometimes;
Occasionally

Most often try to include
others in activities and
social events, not be
alone

0   1   2   3   (4)   5   6   7   8   9

Most often don't include
anybody in activities and
social events, want to be
by myself

Some people; a few
people

Most often try to include
one or more people in
activities and social
events, want to be with
someone.

Average score of two scales = ____4____

Want Inclusion

0   1   2   3   4   (5)   6   7   8   9

Most often want to be
alone, not included by
others in activities and
social events

Sometimes;
Occasionally

Most often want others to
include me in activities
and social events; dont
want them to leave me
alone

0	1	2	3	4	5	(6)	7	8	9

Dont want anybody to include me in activities and social events, want to be alone

Some people; a few people

Want most people to include me in their activities and social events; want to be included by a lot of people

Average score of two scales = ___5.5___

Expressed Control

0	1	2	3	(4)	5	6	7	8	9

Most often avoid influencing others, avoid trying to be dominant, avoid taking charge

Sometimes; Occasionally

Most often try to influence others, try to be dominant, try to take charge

0	1	2	3	4	(5)	6	7	8	9

Don't try to influence anybody, don't try to be dominant or take charge over most people

Some people; A few people

Try to influence most people, try to be dominant of or take charge over most people

Average of two scale scores = ___4.5___

Want Control

0	1	2	(3)	4	5	6	7	8	9

Usually don't want to be influenced by others, don't want to be dominated, usually avoid others taking charge of me

Sometimes; Occasionally

Usually want to be influenced by others, want to be dominated, want others to take charge of me.

0	1	2	3	(4)	5	6	7	8	9

Usually don't want anyone to influence me, don't want anyone to dominate me, don't want anyone to take charge of me

Some people; A few people

Want lots of other people to influence me, dominate me, take charge of my activities

Average of the two scales = ___3.5___

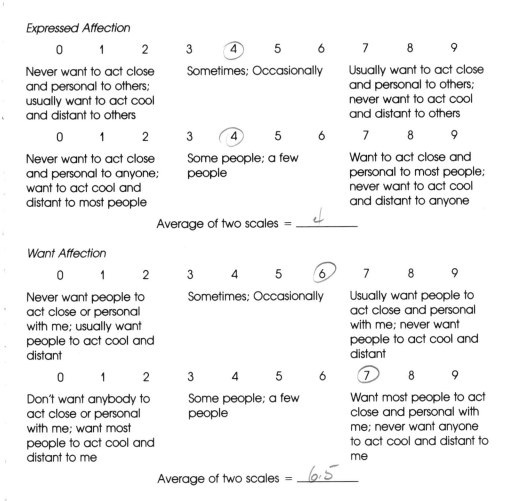

Expressed Affection

| 0 | 1 | 2 | 3 | ④ | 5 | 6 | 7 | 8 | 9 |

Never want to act close and personal to others; usually want to act cool and distant to others

Sometimes; Occasionally

Usually want to act close and personal to others; never want to act cool and distant to others

| 0 | 1 | 2 | 3 | ④ | 5 | 6 | 7 | 8 | 9 |

Never want to act close and personal to anyone; want to act cool and distant to most people

Some people; a few people

Want to act close and personal to most people; never want to act cool and distant to anyone

Average of two scales = ___4___

Want Affection

| 0 | 1 | 2 | 3 | 4 | 5 | ⑥ | 7 | 8 | 9 |

Never want people to act close or personal with me; usually want people to act cool and distant

Sometimes; Occasionally

Usually want people to act close and personal with me; never want people to act cool and distant

| 0 | 1 | 2 | 3 | 4 | 5 | 6 | ⑦ | 8 | 9 |

Don't want anybody to act close or personal with me; want most people to act cool and distant to me

Some people; a few people

Want most people to act close and personal with me; never want anyone to act cool and distant to me

Average of two scales = ___6.5___

Step 3: 5 Minutes

Enter the averages from the six scales in the appropriate spaces below. In each box, you should have a number between 0 and 9:

	Inclusion	Control	Affection
You give (express to others)	$e^i = 4$	$e^c = 4.5$	$e^a = 4$
You get (want from others)	$w^i = 5.5$	$w^c = 3.5$	$w^a = 6.5$

Each of these scores, individually and together with the others, can tell you something about yourself and your relations with others. As you read the brief description below, and think about your scores, compare that against your own feelings and beliefs about yourself. When you have read the description you may want to share your scores with others who know you well, to verify their accuracy.

Remember that each individual, if he makes his ratings honestly, will probably have a different profile of scores. There is no "right" answer to this questionnaire, except that it is "right" for your impressions about yourself.

Step 4: Interpreting the Questionnaire, 10 Minutes

The *inclusion* scales are designed to measure your needs to establish and maintain contact with other people. How might some people behave, based on their scores? A person who has a high score on *expressed* inclusion, and a low score on *wanted* inclusion (e.g. 9,0) will be very outgoing toward others. He will be continually making gestures toward others to include them in group activities—sports, parties, work activities, going out to lunch, and so on. However, he probably has no strong needs for others to include him in their groupings. On the other hand, a person who has a high score (e.g. 0,9) on *expressed* inclusion and a low score on *wanted* inclusion (e.g. 0,9) will seldom make invitation gestures toward others, but desperately wants others to include him. People who have strong scores in both categories will both want and express a lot of inclusion, and a person with two low scores on inclusion will be more of a "private" person, who neither wants to include a lot of people in his activities or be included in theirs.

More interesting problems occur when you explore the needs of two people and their "compatibility" based on inclusion scores. Two people who are strong on both *expressed* and *wanted* will probably see a lot of one another, since each wants to involve the other and get satisfaction from being involved. Similarly, people with "complementary needs" may also find their relationship satisfactory, since one is always initiating inclusion and the other wants to receive it. (The 9,0 says, "Hey, let's go to the movies," and the 0,9 says, "I thought you'd never ask.") Difficulties arise where both people are high in *expressed* inclusion, but low in *wanted* inclusion ("Hey, let's go to the movies." "No I really don't want to, but would you like to go to the ball game tomorrow?") or when both are high in *wanted* but low in *expressed*. (Each thinks, "I wish he would invite me to go to the movies.") People low on both inclusion scales will probably be very comfortable spending a lot of time by themselves, rather than in group situations.

The *control* scales are designed to measure your needs to control or be controlled by other people.

A person with a high *expressed* power score (e.g. 9,0) will like to be in charge. When he encounters another 9,0 person, there is likely to be a strong battle for leadership in the group. The high want control person likes to be controlled, and will make an excellent subordinate for any 9,0. (In addition, he probably will not understand the conflict between the two 9,0s—"How could anyone get that concerned about wanting to run things?") However, when the 0,9 person meets another 0,9 person, there is a "power gap" in which each waits for the other to take over and run things—there is usually no action, and no productivity. The 0,0 person withdraws from power, having no strong needs either to be controlled or to control others.

The 9,9 individual may seem "enigmatic"—how can a person both like to be controlled and control others at the same time? However, when we explore the role of middle management in most organizations, we find that the 9,9 thrives on his dual responsibilities of (1) taking orders and direction from above, and (2) at the same time managing and controlling those below him. The 9,9 is really the "perfect second lieutenant" in the military, completely willing and able to be a good subordinate to his superiors and a good superior to his subordinates.

Comparing inclusion to control, we can say that individuals with strong inclusion needs want to be on the team, regardless of what it is doing and how it is performing. The person with strong control needs wants to be a winner, regardless of what team he is on or who the people on it are.

The *affection* scales are designed to measure your needs to express love and affection to others, or have it expressed to you. A person with a high *expressed* affection score (9,0) will be likely to show others how much he cares for them. He has strong needs for (and will be very comfortable) being warm, caring, and demonstrating his liking. The person with the high *wanted* affection score (0,9) will be drawn to this expression, and so we can expect that a 9,0 and an 0,9 could form a very strong relationship, but in which the affection goes all one way. Similarly, two 9,9 individuals, high on both *expressed* and *wanted* affection, will constantly be preoccupied with showing their liking for one another, and receiving those gestures. Obviously, two 0,0 people will neither show much affection for the other, nor really need it for themselves.

Again, problems may occur when two individuals have mutually strong *expressed* scores without want (9,0s), or mutually strong *wanted* scores without expression (0,9). In the first case, the two individuals probably offer the other individual a lot of liking and attraction, yet they are uncomfortable about receiving it. Each may come to see the other as "gushy" and overly affectionate because they can't manage the receiving end of the affection. Similarly, two 0,9s will be attracted to one another but very seldom express it, and draw away from one another *not* because of their feelings but because of their low need to or ability to express their feelings for the other person.

Overall Pattern of Scores

We may look at the six overall scores, and also make the following inferences:

1. Obtain the *total* for each column (inclusion, control and affection); this should indicate how much inclusion, power or affection are important to you and the ways you spend your time.
2. Obtain the *discrepancy* for the scores in each column (inclusion, control and affection); this should indicate how much more you express things toward others than they express them toward you (or the reverse).
3. Obtain the *total* of all six scores. This will be a number from 0 to 54, and should give you some strong indication of the relative importance of people in your life. The higher the total score, the more important your relations with people are.

Step 5: Discussion, 15 to 30 Minutes

The previous steps asked you to rate yourself on the "magnitude" of your concern for personal power in relation to interpersonal needs for inclusion in social groupings and affection with others. As you review these scores, consider the following:

1. Think about examples or situations from your experience that reflect your scores—for example, instances where you wanted to be included or wanted to include others, wanted to be in charge, and so on. Which examples confirm your scores, and which ones disconfirm them?
2. Think about a situation in which you had a problem relating to other people in a group—deciding who was a "member" of the group, who was in "charge" or making decisions for the group, or who belonged to subgroups that were very close to one another. Do the ideas of "compatibility" between two or more people's styles help you to understand how people behaved?
3. Try completing this questionnaire several times, each time with respect to a particular social group. That is, try responding to the questionnaire in terms of your family, work group, student friends, fraternity or sorority, and so on. Do the responses differ? What does this say about how your needs vary from group to group?

PART II

Step 1: 5 Minutes

The instructor will divide the class into three equal-size groups. These groups may be subdivided if there are more than six people per group.

Step 2: 5 Minutes

Read the following scenario:

You are the manager of a group of research scientists and laboratory technicians in a chemical research laboratory. The scientists and technicians receive a monthly salary, and are expected to work from 8:30 to 4:30, 5 days a week. In fact, many of the scientists work late or come into the laboratory on weekends in order to complete their experiments.

Recently, you have become aware that one of your best laboratory technicians is repeatedly late for work, and sometimes goes out for too long a coffee break soon after getting to work. The technician seems to be satisfied with his salary and his overall performance is good, but you would like to see him come in on time, work harder in the morning, and thus do even better in his job performance. You even feel that the technician might get turned on to starting research experiments of his own, and perhaps be promoted to a project leader position.

As a manager, you are respected and liked by the others in the lab, and it irritates you that this person treats your dedicated management with such a cavalier attitude. You want to influence the technician to start work on time.

Step 3: 15 Minutes

Each group has the task of preparing an *actual influence strategy* to be used by the manager in correcting the technician's behavior. This strategy will be role-played in class; therefore, you must:

1. Specify exactly what the manager will do with the technician.
2. Select one member of your group to role-play the manager.
3. Select one member of your group to role-play the technician with a manager from another group.
4. Decide on the "environment" in which the role play will take place (the manager's office, coffee shop, chemistry laboratory, etc.).

Step 4: 15 to 20 Minutes

The instructor will select several groups. Each group will role-play the strategy developed.

Step 5: Discussion

1. As each group role-plays each influence attempt, think of yourself on the receiving end of the influence (i.e., as the technician). Record your own reaction:

	Group 1	Group 2	Group 3	Group 4
a. As a result of the influence attempt, I will . . . 1　2　3　4　5 definitely comply　　definitely not comply	___	___	___	___
b. Any change that does come about will be . . . 1　2　3　4　5 temporary　　permanent	___	___	___	___
c. My own personal reaction is . . . 1　2　3　4　5 resistant　　acceptant	___	___	___	___
d. As a result of this influence attempt, my relationship with the manager of the laboratory will probably be . . . 1　2　3　4　5 worse　　better	___	___	___	___

2. Look at your reactions to these questions for each influence attempt. Compare them to the reactions of others when the instructor asks for the information.

a. Which group designed the influence attempt that would most likely result in im-mediate change of the technician's behavior
b. Which group's strategy will have the most long-lasting effects?
c. Which strategy do people find the most acceptable?
3. By now, your instructor will have told you how the groups were composed at the beginning of the activity. What difference did you observe in the ways that the groups worked together to plan their role play? What implications does this have for con-sidering individual member "styles" in the formation of the task groups?

GENERALIZATIONS AND CONCLUSIONS

Concluding points:

1. FIRO-B is an instrument with three scales (inclusion, control and affection) and two subscales for each scale (expressed and wanted). Describe the behavior pat-terns of a person scoring high on each of the six scales.
2. Which scales on the FIRO-B would be most related to the ability to:
   a. Work with others on a team project?
   b. Follow the direction of a leader?
   c. Reorganize a department in a company?
   d. Develop good relationships in a marriage?
3. (For Part II) Identify the types of influence strategies that are developed when people of a similar style work together, as well as the problems that may occur in these groups as a result of all members having similar styles.

Participant's Reactions

READINGS AND REFERENCES

Jacobsen, W., *Power and Interpersonal Relations* (Belmont, Calif.: Wadsworth Publishing Co., 1972).
French, J. R. P., and Raven, B. H., "The Bases of Social Power," in D. Cartwright (Ed.), *Studies in Social Power* (Ann Arbor, Michigan: Institute for Social Research, 1959).
Schutz, W., *The Interpersonal Underworld* (Palo Alto, Calif.: Science and Behavior Books, 1966).
Winter, D., *The Power Motive* (New York: The Free Press, 1973).

34
POWER IN MANAGEMENT: CORRECTING PERFORMANCE

PURPOSE:
(1) To demonstrate the use of power in superior-subordinate relations
(2) To explore techniques for improving performance

ADVANCE PREPARATION: Role scenarios may be assigned and prepared in advance.

GROUP SIZE: Any number of dyads or trios (observers may be assigned to each pair).

TIME REQUIRED: 90 minutes total for preparation, role playing, and debriefing.

SPECIAL MATERIALS: None.

SPECIAL PHYSICAL REQUIREMENTS: None.

RELATED TOPICS: Applied Motivation, Interpersonal Communication, Negotiation and Conflict, Managers as Leaders

INTRODUCTION

The performance appraisal process in superior-subordinate interaction and managerial strategies for performance improvement have typically been treated by organizational behavior as problems of motivation and goal setting. Yet motivation and goal-setting perspectives on this process typically ignore the power differences and power dynamics between managers and their subordinates. Managers have the formal authority and power to critique and correct a subordinate's performance; the way they exercise this power and authority can have a significant impact on the willingness of the subordinate to change his or her behavior and the future relationship between them. Subordinates have power, too, and can exercise it in different ways. The purpose of this exercise is to examine power dynamics in superior-subordinate interaction.

PROCEDURE

Step 1: 15 Minutes

The instructor will give an introductory lecture on types of power and their use in organizations.

The original "Joe Summers/John Nolan" role play was created by Prof. Henry P. Sims, The Pennsylvania State University. Used with permission of the author. Adapted and developed in this context by Roy. J. Lewicki.

Step 2: 5 Minutes

The instructor will divide the class in half. All students in one group will be designated to play the role of the superior, Jan Summers. The other group will play the role of the subordinate, Lee Nolan.

Step 3: 10–20 Minutes

Each student should read his or her role and prepare for the meeting between Nolan and Summers. Instructors may also assign all Nolans to meet together (as a group) and all Summers to meet together (as a group) to prepare. Each Nolan and Summers should prepare individual goals that they want to attain from the meeting.

Step 4: 20–30 Minutes

Each Nolan and Summers will pair up as instructed. Conduct the role play. Be prepared to report to the class on the specific outcome of your meeting and how the outcomes were achieved.

Step 5: 20–30 Minutes

Discussion of role-play results and procedures.

DISCUSSION QUESTIONS

1. What were the actual outcomes of the meetings?
2. How did the actual outcomes match what each party wanted to achieve?
3. What kinds of power were used by each party?
4. Which power tactics were likely to be most effective in getting the other to change his or her behavior? Which power tactics were least effective? Why?

READINGS AND REFERENCES

Bell, C. R., *Influencing: Marking the Ideas that Matter*. (Austin, TX: Learning Concepts, 1982)

Lewicki, R. J., and Litterer, J., *Negotiation* Chapter 11. (Homewood, IL: Richard D. Irwin, 1985)

SECTION TEN
ORGANIZATIONAL COMMUNICATION

35
ONE-WAY VERSUS TWO-WAY COMMUNICATION

PURPOSE:
To demonstrate the differences between one-way and two-way communication.

ADVANCE PREPARATION: None.
GROUP SIZE: Six or more.
TIME REQUIRED: 40 minutes (including discussion).
SPECIAL MATERIALS: None.
SPECIAL PHYSICAL REQUIREMENTS: None.
RELATED TOPICS: Applied motivation and job design, Managers as leaders, Organizational Structure and Design, Group decision making and problem solving.

INTRODUCTION

Most communication in organizations can be described as either *one-way* or *two-way*. In two-way communication, information can flow back and forth between the original communicator of a message and the receiver. The receiver can ask questions, receive clarifications, and in other ways give the communicator *feedback* on what has been heard. Through this feedback, mutual understanding is increased. In one-way communication there is no feedback from the receiver back to the original com-

---

This exercise is based upon H. Leavitt and R. Mueller, "Some Effects of Feedback on Communication." *Human Relations,* 4 (1951), 401–10. The exercise has been used in numerous publications in various forms. The present version was written by D. T. Hall and D. D. Bowen.

municator; the sender tells the receiver something, and this message ends the communication.

The following are examples of one-way communication: memos, lectures, written instructions on a test, and mass media (television, radio, newspapers, and magazines). Examples of two-way communication are telephone conversations, question-and-answer sessions, and discussions. (Of course, if one party monopolizes conversations or discussions, they can possibly become in effect more one-way than two-way.)

In this exercise we will examine both one-way and two-way communication and see which takes more time, which is more accurate, and which is more satisfying. Before we start, which do you think is more accurate? Takes more time? Is more satisfying?

PROCEDURE

Step 1: 5 Minutes
The group leader will ask class members to select one person who is an especially good communicator, capable of giving directions clearly. This person will be the communicator in this exercise. The remainder of the group will be the receivers. You should be ready with paper and pencil to follow the communicator's instructions.

On one sheet of paper, you are to reproduce the geometric figure described to you by the communicator. The communicator will attempt to explain it so well that each participant will be able to make one exactly like it. The communicator will have her back turned to you while describing the figure to be copied. During this time *you may not speak to the communicator,* and *the communicator will not answer any questions.* Do not look at anyone else's drawing—base your drawing entirely upon the instructions provided by the communicator. At this point, the group leader will answer any questions you may have.

Step 2: 5 Minutes—One-Way Communication
When questions have been answered, the communicator will stand, *back* to audience, and direct you in drawing Figure 1.

Step 3: 10 Minutes—Two-Way Communication
After everyone has completed the first drawing, the communicator will face you and give instructions for drawing Figure 2. You may ask questions at any time to clarify the instructions, but the communicator may not use gestures in giving her answers.

Step 4: 10 Minutes—Scoring
When both figures have been drawn, the group leader will ask you to estimate how many objects in the first figure you think you have drawn correctly under the one-way condition (five, four, three, two, or one), and will record your estimates on the board. Then the group leader will ask for the same estimates for the second figure, under two-way communication.

To examine *attitudes* under both conditions, the group leader will ask the communicator how she felt under the one-way condition. Under the two-way condition? Then the group leader will ask how the rest of the participants felt under one-way communication, and under two-way communication.

Next, the group leader will draw the correct figures on the board. Count the number of figures you had correct under one-way communication. Then count how many you had correct under two-way communication. (*To be correct,* an object must be the *right shape* and *in proper relation to the other objects.*)

Next, the group leader will ask how many people had all five figures correct for the *one*-way communication. How many? Four? Three? Two? One? He will record these answers on the board, and then ask how many people had five figures correct for the *two*-way communication. How many? Four? Three? Two? One? He will record these responses on the board.

DISCUSSION QUESTIONS

1. What do the accuracy scores tell us about the relative efficiency of the two communication tactics?
2. What do the elapsed time scores suggest in regard to the relative efficiency of the two communication tactics?
3. Would you say that time or accuracy is the more important consideration in most organizational situations?
4. Which of the two conditions was most satisfying to the communicator? To the receivers?
5. How do these communication styles relate to the leadership style of a manager?
6. Give an example of one-way organizational communication. Give an example of two-way organizational communication.

GENERALIZATIONS AND CONCLUSIONS

Concluding Points

1. Two-way communication, compared to one-way, usually takes much (more/less) time.

2. Two-way communication, compared to one-way, results in (greater/less) accuracy.

3. In one-way communication, the communicator usually feels what? The receiver feels what?

4. In two-way communication, the communicator usually feels what? The receiver usually feels what?

Participant's Reactions

READINGS AND REFERENCES

Leavitt, H., *Managerial Psychology,* 3rd ed. (Chicago: University of Chicago Press, 1972), esp. pp. 114–24.

Leavitt, H., and Mueller, R., "Some Effects of Feedback on Communication," *Human Relations,* 4 (1951), 401–10.

36
UPWARD COMMUNICATION:
YOUNG MANUFACTURING COMPANY

PURPOSE:

To explore organizational communication and decision-making processes.

ADVANCE PREPARATION: Read the "Introduction," below.

GROUP SIZE: *Option one* (multiple role play): Requires groups of five. Ten or more groups can do the exercise simultaneously. *Option two* (demonstration role play): unlimited group size.

TIME REQUIRED: Both options: 1 hour.

SPECIAL MATERIALS: None.

SPECIAL PHYSICAL REQUIREMENTS: *Option one:* Small group meeting rooms or large room with movable chairs to accommodate each group. *Option two:* Table and five chairs at front of or in middle of room.

RELATED TOPICS: Managers as leaders, Power, Organizational structure and design, Motivation: basic concepts, Group decision making and problem solving, Interpersonal communication, Organizational realities.

INTRODUCTION

The Young Manufacturing Company is a role-play exercise of a meeting between the President of a small company and four of his subordinates. Each character's role is designed to re-create the reality of a business meeting. Each character comes to the meeting with a unique perspective on a major problem facing the company as well as some personal impressions of the other characters, developed over several years of business and social associations.

THE CAST OF CHARACTERS

Bob Young, the President, is the principal owner of Young Manufacturing, a small fabricator of automotive replacement parts. The firm employs 500 people, and during its nine years of operations has enjoyed better profits than its competitors because of a reputation for high-quality products at a modest cost. Recently, however, competitors have begun to overtake Young Manufacturing, resulting in declining profits for it. Bob Young is expending every possible effort to keep his company comfortably at the top.

Roy Conti, Manager of Quality Control, reports directly to Young. He has held this position since he helped Young establish the company nine years ago.

Donna Kelly, Production Manager, also reports to Young. She has been with the firm seven years, having worked before that for one of the "big three" auto firms in production management.

Developed by Donald D. Bowen. Helpful suggestions for this version were supplied by David Bradford.

Mike Cohen, Supervisor of Final Assembly, reports to Donna Kelly. He came to Young Manufacturing at Kelly's request, having worked with Kelly previously at the same large auto firm.

Fran Kurowski, Supervisor of Subassembly, also works for Donna Kelly. Kurowski was promoted to this position two years ago. Prior to that time, Fran had gone through a year's management training program after receiving an MBA from a large urban university.

The company organization chart is shown in Figure 1.

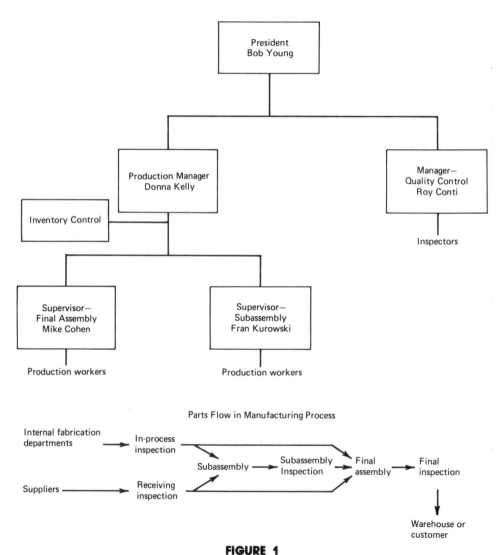

FIGURE 1
Organization Chart and Parts Flow: Young Manufacturing Company

Today's Meeting

Bob Young has called a meeting with these four managers (the Operations Committee), in order to attempt to solve some problems that have developed in meeting production schedules. Young must catch a plane to Detroit in half an hour; he has an appointment to negotiate a key contract that means a great deal to the future of Young Manufacturing. He has only 20 minutes to meet with his managers and still catch the plane. Young feels that swinging the Detroit deal is absolutely crucial to the future of the company. The meeting will begin when you receive instructions from your instructor. It will last for *exactly 20 minutes.*

PROCEDURE

BOTH OPTIONS

Step 1: 10 Minutes

The group leader will divide the total group into five equal-sized groups. The members of each of these first groups will all prepare to play the same character later in the roleplay. That is, the members of one of these preliminary groups will all be preparing for the part of Bob Young; another group will concentrate on Donna Kelly, a third on Roy Conti, and so on—one group for each character.

Go to the meeting place designated by the group leader to meet with the other persons who will also be playing the role you have been assigned. When you have all assembled, the group leader will tell you where to find the role instructions for the role you are to play.

From this point on, until you receive instructions from the group leader to the contrary, you are not to share any details of your role with people playing other characters. Stay *in role* until you are explicitly instructed to stop role-playing. Do not let the other managers hear your planning or see your role instructions. Share your thoughts about how your character will feel or behave only with people who have been assigned the same role.

Step 2: 15 Minutes

Prepare, with the assistance of others assigned the same role, to play the part of your character. Ask yourselves questions such as the following: What does it feel like to be this person? What does it feel like to be in the situation of this character? How would your character react to the other characters in the role play? What are the implications of your position in the organization for your behavior? What will you try to get out of the meeting? What outcomes will you try to avoid?

Talk about these questions, and develop perspectives on the role with others assigned to the same role.

It is not necessary that everyone should play the role in exactly the same way. The point is, given the role, how would *you* play it? What do others assigned to this role think of your approach?

OPTION ONE

20 minutes: Following the instructor's directions, meet in a five-person group with the four others assigned to play the roles of the other managers. Start the meeting only when told to proceed by the instructor. Remember: *Stay in role,* even if you should happen to finish before 20 minutes have elapsed. At the end of the meeting, go to Step 3, "Both Options," below.

OPTION TWO

20 minutes: During the preliminary meeting, members of the group select one person to play the role. The role players meet in an "office" set up in the front or middle of the room. Remember: *Stay in the role,* even if you are not chosen to play the part. Remain in the role even after the end of the role play. The designated role players hold the meeting, ending in exactly 20 minutes.

BOTH OPTIONS

Step 3: 15 Minutes

Discuss the exercise, following the Discussion Questions suggested below. Stay in role until after Bob Young has responded to Question 1.

DISCUSSION QUESTIONS

1. Bob Young, how did you see the situation at the end of the meeting? In particular:
   a. How would you define the problem?
   b. Is there any evidence that any of your subordinates have made serious mistakes or goofs?
   c. Did you find any of your subordinates particularly *helpful* in solving the problem? Who? Were any of them a hindrance? Who?
   d. Did you feel that it was relatively easy or relatively difficult to get the information you wanted from the group?
   What do these data mean? (Discuss.)
2. What factors operated to create the kind of communication you saw in the Young Manufacturing Company? Can anything be done to improve these communications?

GENERALIZATIONS AND CONCLUSIONS

Concluding Points

1. What are the central variables operating to affect communications at Young Manufacturing Company, and what effect do they have?

2. What might Bob Young do, by way of a long-term solution, if he begins to experience the typical difficulties so often found in the Young Manufacturing Company?

Participant's Reactions

READINGS AND REFERENCES

Argyris, C., *Interpersonal Competence and Organizational Effectiveness* (Homewood, Ill.: Irwin-Dorsey, 1962).

Gibb, Jack R., "Defensive Communication," *Journal of Communication,* 11 (1961), 141–148.

Porter, L. W.; Allen, R. W.; and Angle, H. L; The Politics of Upward Influence in Organizations. In J. R. Hackman, E. E. Lawler, III, and L. W. Porter (Eds.), *Perspectives on Behavior in Organizations.* New York: McGraw-Hill, 1983. Pp. 358–368.

Read, W. H., "Upward Communication in Industrial Hierarchies," *Human Relations,* 15 (1963), 3–15.

Roethlisberger, F., "The Foreman: Master and Victim of Double-Talk," *Harvard Business Review,* 45 (1965), 23ff.

37
MODEL I AND MODEL II
STYLES OF MANAGEMENT

PURPOSE:

(1) To introduce and explore the concepts of "espoused theory" versus "theory-in-use" and Model I versus Model II.

(2) To explore one of the most difficult problems in managerial communication—criticizing a subordinate.

ADVANCE PREPARATION: 1. Read the Introduction.

2. If assigned, complete Step 1 before class.

3. If assigned, complete Step 2 of Option II before class.

GROUP SIZE: Option I: Groups not used.

Option II: Dyads.

TIME REQUIRED: Option I: 70 minutes (50 minutes if Step 1 is assigned as advance preparation).

Option II: Two hours and 15 minutes (one hour and 25 minutes if Steps 1 and 2 are assigned as advance preparation).

SPECIAL MATERIALS: None.

SPECIAL PHYSICAL REQUIREMENTS: None.

RELATED TOPICS: Managers as Leaders, Planned Change, Organizational Realities, Power, Negotiation and Conflict.

INTRODUCTION

Read the following:

Since 1974, Professor Chris Argyris of the Graduate School of Education at Harvard and his collaborator, Donald Schon of M.I.T., have been working on a new approach to improve the ability of managers and organizations to learn from their experience. Argyris, one of the founding fathers of modern organizational behavior, has consulted with many top management teams in government and industry on their decision-making practices and relationships. He noted early in this work that ineffective interpersonal skills tended to become a barrier to productive decision making for executives in almost all organizations. The problem, in highly over-simplified form, might be stated as follows:

Executives tend to be programmed to communicate interpersonally with a style that emphasizes *evaluating* others, *avoiding expression of feelings* (especially neg-

Prepared for this volume by Donald D. Bowen.

ative feelings), and insisting upon *rationality* and *conformity* from others. As a result of this style, the executives censor their communication—they don't say what they are really thinking and feeling. Sensing this in their colleagues (while remaining largely blind to it in their own behavior), the executives begin to distrust each other and therefore to distort and withhold even further information from each other. As they withhold information from each other, the decision-making capability of the organization and, ultimately, organizational performance and productivity begin to decline because an organization needs valid information to make effective decisions. The organization becomes caught up in a vicious circle of declining effectiveness because the executives know only one style, the one that created the problem in the first place. Despite the best of intentions, they can only make the problem worse (Argyris, 1962).

Argyris noted that the problem was not just in the interpersonal style of executives of large organizations, but in the interpersonal strategies employed by people at all levels of the organization. Available concepts and training programs did not seem to address the issues, so Argyris and Schon (1974) began to develop their own ideas. The following paragraphs will provide a brief overview of major elements of these ideas that have appeared over the years in a series of books and articles (see the references at the end of this exercise).

Espoused Theory versus Theory in Use

If I were to ask you to tell me what you think a good manager should do, you would undoubtedly enumerate a number of behaviors. Your list might include such things as: gives clear directions to subordinates, provides support to employees who are trying to improve their performance, and gets input of subordinates in formulating departmental goals. If we listed all the behaviors you could think of, we would have a statement of your *espoused theory* of management. Your espoused theory is something you are consciously aware of, and which you can articulate if I ask you to do so. Your espoused theory describes *the kind of manager you try to be,* and it is based on a number of values (supportiveness, participation, etc.) that are important to you.

If I followed you around for a day on the job, taking notes on what you actually do, it would come as no surprise to either of us that what you actually do does not always exactly match what you say you would like to do.

If your actual behavior is not determined entirely by your espoused theory, why not? Why can't you do what you want to do? And why is it that we see you doing some things over and over again in spite of your stated intentions to do just the opposite? Perhaps your behavior is based on some theory other than your espoused theory. Argyris believes you will be unaware of this second theory (and therefore unaware of how large a gap there is between what you tell people you want to do and what others see you doing). You will frequently experience frustrations in your relationships with others, but you will be blind to your own contribution to your ineffectiveness. You will be like the executives already described who cannot counter the organization's slide into declining effectiveness, but who are also unaware of how they are causing the problem.

The "theory" that you are unaware of, but which really shapes your behavior, is your *theory in use*.

Model I

Argyris has mapped out the theory in use that he believes most of us use almost universally. He calls this theory *Model I*. The top part of Figure 1 portrays Model I schematically. The model begins with the *governing values,* the underlying values upon which the theory is based. For Model I, these are the values of unilaterally controlling the situation, maximizing the probability that we will win, minimizing the expression of negative feelings, and emphasizing rationality (the same values that underlie the ineffective interpersonal communication of the executives described earlier). If one attempts to achieve these values, the "action strategies" one will employ will be those of arguing for one's own position while unilaterally saving face—one's

FIGURE 1
Model I and Model II

Model I:

Governing Values ------→	*Action Strategies* ----------	*Consequences*
Control the purpose of the meeting or encounter.	Advocate your position in order to be in control and win.	Miscommunication
		Mistrust
		Protectiveness
Maximize winning and minimize losing.	Unilaterally save face (your own and others').	Self-fulfilling prophecies
Minimize negative feelings.		Self-sealing processes
Maximize rationality.		Escalating error

Model II:

Governing Values ------→	*Action Strategies* ---------→	*Consequences*
Valid (confirmable) information.	Advocate your position and combine with public testing.	Reduction of self-fulfilling, self-sealing, error-escalating processes.
Free and informed choice.	Minimize unilateral face saving.	
Internal commitment to the choice.		Effective problem solving.

From Argyris (1985), Figures 3.1 and 9.1.

own and others'. "Unilateral face saving" involves not only trying to look good oneself, but also not confronting others when saying what we are really thinking might cause them embarrassment. We often do this in a way that we become overly protective— protecting the other person even when they don't want to be protected and not giving them a voice in the matter. A negative aspect of this protectiveness is that we "protect" people from learning-and-development opportunities that they may need and want.

There are several negative consequences for both ourselves and others that arise when we apply Model I. When we withhold or distort our messages, *miscommunication* results. As the other person senses this, *mistrust* builds. However, our *protectiveness* prevents us from discussing what bothers us about the other person's behavior. Consequently, we begin to build *self-fulfilling prophecies.* For example, as the other person senses our unspoken distrust, he or she becomes suspicious and distrusting in turn, and becomes hostile and competitive toward us. My expectations have now created the very behavior that I cannot trust in the other person.

However, I cannot discuss the problem of the declining trust between myself and the other person because of my commitment to the strategy of unilateral saving of face. Thus the process becomes "self-sealing"—something we cannot examine and learn from. As more and more self-fulfilling prophecies and self-sealing processes build up in my relations with my colleagues, our communication efficiency declines and our decisions are marked by *escalating error.*

What are the signs that a person is operating from Model I? Argyris mentions several characteristics of the Model I communication. One is that the person tends to avoid presenting the "data" for their perceptions and assumptions. They might tell you that you are a "lousy listener," but they won't tell you what you do that leads them to that inference. In general, Argyris emphasizes the use of:

1. *Unillustrated attributions*—statements about a person's motives, intentions, or beliefs, which do not include specific descriptions of the behavior of the person that led the speaker to the conclusion
2. *Unillustrated evaluations*—statements about the value of a person's behavior, which are made without explanation of why the speaker judges the person that way
3. *Unillustrated inferences*—judgments or assumptions about how events are related, which are made without any explanation of how one arrived at the conclusion

When a person deliberately avoids saying many of the things he or she is thinking and when there are frequent inconsistencies between the messages one gets from a person, it is likely that Model I characteristics are present. When a person tells you they believe in "giving it to you straight, even when the truth hurts" and then the same person withholds negative information out of "concern for your feelings," you have an example of Model I communication.

While Argyris feels that almost all of us are programmed by society to operate from Model I, he observes that Model I *is* an appropriate strategy for dealing with the relatively routine and trivial affairs of daily living. It is only when we must make important decisions of a nonroutine nature that we need an alternative to Model I. Moreover, he notes that the alternative is not the opposite of Model I, but a model (Model II) that begins with an entirely different set of governing values.

Model II

Referring again to Figure 1, we note that the governing values of Model II are valid (confirmable) information, free and informed choice, and internal commitment. In order for information to qualify as valid and confirmable, we must be able to test the information to determine whether it is really true and accurate. Moreover, the test must be a public testing—one that, if performed for the benefit of several people, will lead all of them to the same assessment of the data. For instance, suppose you go to your doctor with complaints of feeling run-down and tired. Your doctor draws a sample of blood and from tests run on the sample, presents you with the not very welcome news that you have mononucleosis. The test performed on the blood sample is "public," not because it was done in public (which it wasn't), but because the same test done by a different technician on your blood would yield the same readings, the ones that led your doctor (and, presumably, any other doctor) to conclude that you have mono. In other words, Argyris is suggesting that we should submit the evidence we use in our interactions to the same basic procedures that scientists use in establishing the validity of data and observations.

If people make decisions and choices that are based on evidence and data that all concerned accept as valid, the choices made are likely to be relatively free and well-informed; people who allow themselves to be guided by the logic of the facts cannot and need not be coerced, cajoled, or manipulated into making the right decision. Hence the second governing variable.

People will feel internal commitment to decisions freely made on the basis of full and complete data. Internal commitment is staying with a course of action because you believe it is right or intrinsically satisfying. (External commitment is doing something to achieve a promised reward or to avoid a punishment that someone else will administer.

Model II, then, is designed to help us make decisions by altering the conditions Argyris found in his early research on management groups. Valid, rather than partial and distorted information, enables managers to pursue issues in an atmosphere of trust and openness, rather than distrust and competitiveness. This approach improves the quality of the decisions made. The commitment to accomplishing the objectives and programs that the managers decide upon is heightened by the knowledge that the decisions are based on valid data rather than office politics.

It is a much simpler task to describe Model II than it is to apply it in our managerial and interpersonal relationships, however. Most managers find learning the new model a difficult and stressful experience of becoming aware of and overcoming ingrained habits of long standing. Perhaps an illustration will help to appreciate how difficult it is to overcome our habits in relating to others.

PROCEDURE

BOTH OPTIONS

Step 1: 20 Minutes

Read the case of Lou and Sandy, which follows, and select the strategy you would recommend to Lou. Note your reasons for why your strategy is superior and what your criticisms of the alternative strategies would be. Use Models I and II in your analysis, and select a strategy that comes as close to Model II as possible.

THE CASE OF LOU AND SANDY

Lou's superior, the Vice President, told Lou to talk to Sandy about Sandy's performance and attitude. Lou was to make it absolutely clear that this was a last warning. Sandy would be fired if dramatic changes were not noted in the very near future. The Vice President and Lou agreed that Sandy had extraordinary talent and would be an excellent candidate for promotion if the present performance-and-attitude problems could be resolved. Both of them would like to save Sandy if they could.

When Sandy entered Lou's office, Lou laid it on the line. "Your department's performance is below par again this month, Sandy. Moreover, you seem to have a negative attitude toward everything and everyone. This has got to stop immediately.

"I want you to know that I have your best interests at heart, Sandy, but I can't help you if you won't help yourself. I hear too many stories from people you work with to ignore this any longer. They say you are negative, uncommitted, and apathetic. Our managers must have positive attitudes and real commitment. We have to be role models for our employees.

"I know you think that several of these folks have done you wrong in the past, but I don't think it would be very productive to talk about past history. We can't do anything about that. We have to work on today and take it from there. I want to talk to you about your future around here from now on."

Assume that Lou came to you and asked for some help. Lou reports that Sandy did not seem to respond constructively to the message. Sandy's reaction was to become sullen and very closed. Sandy's only comment was when Lou said, with growing irritation, "Look, Sandy, I'm only doing this for your own good!" Sandy, with elaborate sarcasm, retorted, "Yeah, sure you are."

Assume, also, that there are no further relevant facts that you do not know about.

There are several approaches that Lou might have used with Sandy. Which would you recommend to Lou? What are your reasons for this approach?

Strategy 1

Lou, your general approach is basically right, except that you were not forceful enough. Sandy is a tough cookie and the only way to get Sandy's attention is to be even more

---

[1]Lou and Sandy is based upon the case of X and Y (Argyris, 1982).

blunt and forceful than you were. Don't let Sandy get control of the conversation because all you are going to get is an argument.

Strategy 2

Lou, if you criticize people's performance, you are just going to make them defensive. It is doubly traumatic to have some one jump right into it like you did. It would be more effective if you would ease in a bit. Start with a little small talk ("How's the family? How's your golf game coming?"). Then tell Sandy some of the things that you have liked about Sandy's performance in the past to balance off the negative message. End with the criticism, but invite Sandy to talk about any feelings or thoughts that Sandy may have. Finish by assuring Sandy that you are there to provide help and invite Sandy back to talk at any time.

Strategy 3

In this strategy, Lou should avoid directly evaluating the work and attitudes of Sandy in order to avoid triggering Sandy's defensiveness. Lou asks Sandy to prepare a self-evaluation of personal and departmental performance and sets a meeting for Sandy to present the information to Lou. As Sandy goes through the presentation, Lou looks for points where Sandy rates performance as below expectations. Lou uses these as opportunities to encourage Sandy to develop plans for overcoming the shortcomings.

Strategy 4

You may feel that some other strategy would be most productive. Design your own and explain why you think it would be superior.

OPTION I

Step 2: 10 Minutes

Share your solutions and rationales with the class as directed by the instructor.

Step 3: 15 Minutes

Discuss which of the solutions comes closest to Model II. Why do you see it that way?

Step 4: 10 Minutes

The instructor will read Argyris's analysis of the situation.

Step 5: 15 Minutes

Discuss the situation, using the Discussion Questions at the end of the exercise.

OPTION II

Step 2: 30 Minutes

Using the format shown in Figure 2, prepare a two-page script of how you think the discussion would go between Lou and Sandy if Lou followed your advice. On the

FIGURE 2

Example of the Lou and Sandy Dialogue in Script Format

What they think or feel, but don't say	What they say
Oh, boy, I hope this works!	Lou: C'mon in, Sandy. Have a seat. How's the wife and kids?
I wonder what she has on her mind today.	Sandy: Thanks, Lou. They are all just fine.
I'll feel him out a little before I hit him with the problems with his performance.	Lou: How is everything going? Is the Acme job coming along the way we had hoped?
What is she up to? She knows good and well that I wouldn't let that project get behind schedule.	Sandy: You don't need to worry about that one, Lou. I'm right on top of it. Nothing has popped up since I reported to you yesterday.
Oops! I think he is getting suspicious.	Lou: Well, that is an important project, as you know. I want to stay right on top of it.
Etc.	Etc.

right hand side, write out what Lou and Sandy would say. On the left hand side, write out what you think Lou and Sandy would be feeling but not saying as the dialogue progresses.

Step 3: 30 Minutes

Pair up with another student and share your scripts. Take turns critiquing each other's scripts on the basis of the concepts in the introduction. Does either script produce a Model II solution? Why or why not?

Step 4: 15 Minutes

The instructor will ask class members who believe they have a Model II solution to share their solutions with the class. If your solution is one of those selected, indicate which of the four choices you made, what the nature of your solution is if you chose number four, and why you have concluded this is a Model II solution.

Step 5: 15 Minutes

As a class, discuss the solutions that were presented in Step 4. Are these truly Model II solutions? Why or why not?

Step 6: 10 Minutes

The instructor will present the analysis of the solutions as Argyris would see them.

Step 7: 10 Minutes

Discuss in terms of the Discussion Questions below.

DISCUSSION QUESTIONS

1. If Argyris is correct in believing that almost everyone is programmed with Model I strategies, isn't it unrealistic to expect that managers can be reprogrammed to Model II?
2. What are the essential elements of implementing a Model II strategy in a situation like the Lou and Sandy case?

READINGS AND REFERENCES

Argyris, C., *Interpersonal Competence and Organizational Effectiveness*. (Homewood, Ill.: Irwin-Dorsey, 1962)

Argyris, C. & Schon, D., *Theory in Practice: Increasing Professional Effectiveness*. (Reading, Mass.: Addison-Wesley, 1974)

Argyris, C., Theories of Action That Inhibit Individual Learning, *American Psychologist, 31,* 1976a, 638–654.

Argyris, C., *Increasing Leadership Effectiveness*. (New York: Wiley-Interscience, 1976b)

Argyris, C. & Schon, D., *Organizational Learning*. Reading, Mass.: Addison-Wesley, 1978)

Argyris, C., *Reasoning, Learning and Action: Individual and Organizational*. (San Francisco: Jossey-Bass, 1982)

Argyris, C. *Strategy, Change and Defensive Routines*. (Boston: Pitman, 1985)

SECTION ELEVEN
ORGANIZATIONAL STRUCTURE AND DESIGN

38
WORDS-IN-SENTENCES COMPANY

PURPOSE:

(1) To experiment with designing and operating an organization.

(2) To compare production and quality outputs under different organization structures and/or leadership styles.

ADVANCE PREPARATION: None.

GROUP SIZE: Any number of 5 to 15-person groups.

TIME REQUIRED: 1 ½ hours.

SPECIAL MATERIALS: None.

SPECIAL PHYSICAL REQUIREMENTS: Movable chairs, or separate rooms if groups are large; table helpful but not essential.

RELATED TOPICS: Applied motivation and job design, Group decision making and problem solving, Negotiation and conflict, Managers as leaders, Organizational communication.

INTRODUCTION

In this exercise, you will form a "mini-organization" with several other people. You will also compete with other companies in your industry. The success of your company will depend on your (1) objectives, (2) planning, (3) organization structure, and (4)

Adapted by Francine S. Hall. After contacting several persons thought to have developed this task, the editors were unable to identify its originator. We regret we cannot acknowledge the source of this contribution to experiential learning.

quality control. It may also depend on leadership style. It is important, therefore, that you spend some time thinking about the best design for your organization.

PROCEDURE

Step 1: 5 Minutes
Form companies and assign workplaces. The total group should be subdivided into small groups of comparable size. Since the success of any one group will not be dependent on size alone, do not be concerned if some groups are larger than others. *Each group should consider itself a company.* Your instructor may designate a manager and give him/her special directions.

Step 2: 10 Minutes
Read the "Directions" below and ask the group leader about any points that need clarification. Everyone should be familiar with the task before beginning Step 3.

DIRECTIONS

You are a small company that manufactures words and then packages them in meaningful (English language) sentences. Market research has established that sentences of at least three words but not more than six words each are in demand. Therefore, packaging, distribution, and sales should be set up for three-to-six-word sentences.

The "words-in-sentences" (WIS) industry is highly competitive; several new firms have recently entered what appears to be an expanding market. Since raw materials, technology, and pricing are all standard for the industry, your ability to compete depends on two factors: (1) volume and (2) quality.

Group Task
Your group must design and participate in running a WIS company. You should design your organization to be as efficient as possible during each 10-minute production run. After the first production run, you will have an opportunity to reorganize your company if you want to.

Raw Materials
For each production run, you will be given a "raw material word or phrase." The letters found in the word or phrase serve as the raw materials available to produce new words in sentences. For example, if the raw material word is "organization," you could produce the following words and sentence: "Nat ran to a zoo."

Production Standards
There are several rules that have to be followed in producing "words-in-sentences." If these rules are not followed, your output will not meet production specifications and will not pass quality-control inspection.

1. The same letter may appear only as often in a manufactured word as it appears in the raw-material word or phrase; for example, "organization" has two o's. Thus "zoo" is legitimate, but zoology is not. It has too many o's.

2. Raw-material letters can be used again in different manufactured words.
3. A manufactured word may be used only once in a sentence and in only one sentence during a production run; if a word—for example, *a*—is used once in a sentence, it is out of stock.
4. A new word may not be made by adding *s* to form the plural of an already used manufactured word.
5. A word is defined by its spelling, not its meaning.
6. Nonsense words or nonsense sentences are unacceptable.
7. All words must be in the English language.
8. Names and places are acceptable.
9. Slang is not acceptable.

Measuring Performance

The output of your WIS company is measured by the *total number of acceptable words* that are packaged in sentences. The sentences must be legible, listed on no more than two sheets of paper, and handed to the Quality Control Review Board at the completion of each production run.

Delivery

Delivery must be made to the Quality Control Review Board 30 seconds after the end of each production run.

Quality Control

If any word in a sentence does not meet the standards set forth above, *all* the words in the sentence will be rejected. The Quality Control Review Board (composed of one member from each company) is the final arbiter of acceptability. In the event of a tie vote on the Review Board, a coin toss will determine the outcome.

Step 3: 15 Minutes

Design your organization using as many group members as you see fit to produce your "words-in-sentences." There are many potential ways of organizing. Since some are more efficient than others, you may want to consider the following:

1. What is your company's objective?
2. How will you achieve your objective? How should you plan your work, given the time allowed?
3. What division of labor, authority, and responsibility is most appropriate, given your objective, your task, and the technology?
4. Which group members are most qualified to perform certain tasks?

Assign one member of your group to serve on the Quality Review Board. This person may also participate in production runs.

Step 4: 10 Minutes—Production Run 1

1. The group leader will hand each WIS company a sheet with a raw material word or phrase.
2. When the Instructor announces "Begin production," you are to manufacture as

many words as possible and package them in sentences for delivery to the Quality Control Review Board. You will have 10 minutes.

3. When the group leader announces "Stop production," you will have 30 seconds to deliver your output to the Quality Control Review Board. Output received after 30 seconds does not meet the delivery schedule and will not be counted.

Step 5: 10 Minutes

1. The designated members from the companies of the Quality Control Review Board review output from each company. The total output should be recorded (after quality control approval) on the board or easel.
2. While the Board is completing its task, each WIS company should discuss what happened during Production Run 1.

Step 6: 10 Minutes

Each company should evaluate its performance and organization. Companies may reorganize for Run 2.

Step 7: 10 Minutes—Production Run 2

1. The group leader will hand each WIS company a sheet with a raw material word or phrase.
2. Proceed as in Step 4 (Production Run 1). You will have 10 minutes for production.

Step 8: 10 Minutes

1. The Quality Control Review Board will review each company's output and record it on the board or easel. The total for Runs 1 and 2 should be tallied.
2. While the Board is completing its task, each WIS company should prepare an organization chart depicting its structure for both production runs. If the group had a "manager," what effect did the manager's leadership style have on the group's motivation and production?

Step 9: 10 Minutes

Discuss this exercise as a total group. The group leader will provide discussion questions. Each company should share the organization charts it prepared in Step 8.

GENERALIZATIONS AND CONCLUSIONS

Concluding Points

1. How do classical and contemporary theories of organization differ in their treatment of organization structure and design?

2. How would you classify the technology of a WIS company? Why?

3. What would theory predict to be the best or most appropriate structure for a WIS company? Why?

4. How did leadership style affect the groups? Were all styles equally effective?

Participant's Reactions

1. What did you learn about the relationship between the design of an organization and its effectiveness?

READINGS AND REFERENCES

Brown, W. B. and Moberg, D. J., *Organization and Management: A Macro Approach* (New York: Wiley, 1980).

Galbraith, J., *Designing Complex Organizations* (Reading, Mass.: Addison-Wesley, 1973).

Miles, R. H., *Macro Organization Behavior* (Santa Monica, Calif.: Goodyear Publishing Co., 1980).

Robbins, Stephen P., *Organization Theory: The Structure and Designs of Organizations* (Englewood Cliffs, N.J.: Prentice-Hall, 1983).

Robbins, Stephen P., *Organization Theory: Structure, Design, and Applications* (Englewood Cliffs, N.J.: Prentice-Hall, 1987).

39
ORGANIZATIONAL DIAGNOSIS: FAST FOOD TECHNOLOGY

PURPOSE:

(1) To diagnose an organization in terms of goals, policies, procedures, structure, climate, technology, environment, job design, communication, and leadership.

(2) To compare and contrast two organizations on these variables.

ADVANCE PREPARATION: Form groups and do Steps 1 and 2 in advance. Be prepared to report your diagnosis and recommendations to management to the rest of the group on the assigned day.

GROUP SIZE: Subgroups of four or six.

TIME REQUIRED: Several days out of class for preparation; 50 minutes or 1 hour in class, depending on size of total group.

SPECIAL MATERIALS: None.

SPECIAL PHYSICAL REQUIREMENTS: None.

RELATED TOPICS: Applied motivation and job design, Managers as leaders, Organizational communication, Planned change.

INTRODUCTION

A critical first step in improving or changing any organization is *diagnosing* or analyzing its present functioning. Many change and organization development efforts fall short of their objectives because this important step was not taken, or was conducted superficially. To illustrate this, imagine how you would feel if you went to your doctor complaining of stomach pains, and he recommended surgery without conducting any tests, without obtaining any further information, and without a careful physical examination. You would probably switch doctors! Yet, managers often attempt major changes with correspondingly little diagnostic work in advance. (It could be said that they undertake vast projects with half-vast ideas.)

In this exercise, you will be asked to conduct a group diagnosis of two different organizations in the fast food business. The exercise will provide an opportunity to integrate much of the knowledge you have gained in other exercises and in studying other topics. Your task will be to describe the organizations as carefully as you can in terms of several key organizational concepts. Although the organizations are probably very familiar to you, try to step back and look at them as though you were seeing them for the first time.

Originally developed by D. T. Hall and F. S. Hall.

PROCEDURE

Step 1: 10 Minutes

The group will be formed into subgroups of four or six people. Your assignment is described below.

YOUR ASSIGNMENT

One experience most people in this country have shared is that of dining in the hamburger establishment known as McDonald's. In fact, someone has claimed that 25th-century archeologists may dig into the ruins of our present civilization and conclude that 20-century religion was devoted to the worship of golden arches.

Your group, Fastalk Consultants, is known as the shrewdest, most insightful, and most overpaid management consulting firm in the country. You have been hired by the president of McDonald's to make recommendations for improving the motivation and performance of personnel in their franchise operations. Let us assume that the key job activities in franchise operations are food preparation, order-taking and dealing with customers, and routine clean-up operations.

Recently the president of McDonald's has come to suspect that his company's competitors such as Burger King, Wendy's, Jack in the Box, various pizza establishments, and others are making heavy inroads into McDonald's market. He has also hired a market research firm to investigate and compare the relative merits of the sandwiches, french fries, and drinks served in McDonald's and the competitor, and has asked the market research firm to assess the advertising campaigns of the two organizations. Hence, you will not need to be concerned with marketing issues, except as they may have an impact on employee behavior. The president wants *you* to look into the *organization* of the franchises to determine the strengths and weaknesses of each. Select a competitor who gives McDonald's a good "run for its money" in your area.

The president has established an unusual contract with you. *He wants you to make your recommendations based upon your observations as a customer.* He does not want you to do a complete diagnosis with interviews, surveys, or behind-the-scenes observations. He wants your report in two parts.

1. Given his organization's goals of profitability, sales volume, fast and courteous service, and cleanliness, he wants an analysis that will *compare and contrast McDonald's and the competitor* in terms of the following concepts:

   Organizational goals
   Organizational structure
   Technology
   Environment
   Employee motivation
   Communication
   Leadership style
   Policies/procedures/rules/standards
   Job design
   Organizational climate

2. Given the corporate goals listed under point 1 above, what specific actions might McDonald's management and franchise owners take in the following areas to achieve these goals (profitability, sales volume, fast and courteous service, and cleanliness)?

Job design and workflow
Organization structure (at the individual restaurant level)
Employee incentives
Leadership
Employee selection

How do McDonald's and the competitor differ in these aspects? Which company has the best approach?

Some guidelines
Substantiate your recommendations by reference to one or more theories of motivation, leadership, small groups, or job design.

The president wants concrete, specific, and practical recommendations. Avoid vague generalizations such as "improve communications" or "increase trust." Say very clearly *how* management can improve organizational performance.

As you make your group presentation, the rest of the group will play the role of the top management executive committee. They may be a bit skeptical. They will ask tough questions. They will have to be sold on your ideas.

You will have *10 minutes* in which to present your ideas to the executive committee and to respond to their questions.

Step 2: Approximately 3 Hours outside of Class
Complete the assignment by going as a group to one McDonald's and one competitor's restaurant. If possible, have a meal in each place. To get a more valid comparison, visit a McDonald's and a competitor located in the same area. After observing each restaurant, meet with your group and prepare your 10-minute report to the executive committee.

Step 3: 50 Minutes
In class, each subgroup will present its report to the rest of the group, who will act as the executive committee. The group leader will appoint a timekeeper to be sure that each subgroup sticks to its 10-minute time limit.

DISCUSSION QUESTIONS
1. What similarities are there between the two organizations?
2. What differences are there between the organizations?
3. Do you have any "hunches" about the reasons for the particular organizational characteristics you found? For example, can you try to explain why one organization might have a particular type of structure? Incentive system? Climate?
4. Can you try to explain one set of characteristics in terms of some other characteristics you found? For example, do the goals account for structure? Does the environment explain the structure? Is leadership or communication in the orga-

nization a function of the tasks to be performed or the people working in the organization?

5. To what extent do you think the structures of the organizations "fit" with the technology in each organization?

6. To what extent do the organizations' structures "fit" with their environment?

7. What are the major strengths of each organization? What are the major weaknesses? What changes would you recommend to improve the effectiveness of the organization?

GENERALIZATIONS AND CONCLUSIONS

Concluding Points

1. The factors that had the strongest direct influence on employee behavior were:

2. The technology employed in cooking the food in both places was what? Which technology calls for what kind of supervision [according to Woodward]?

3. Overall, the structure of the two organizations [in Burns and Stalker's terms] is what? This type of structure fits best with what kind of environment?

Participant's Reactions

READINGS AND REFERENCES

Duncan, Robert. "What is the Right Organization Structure?" *Organizational Dynamics*, Winter, 1979, 59–79.

Hodge, B. J. and William P. Anthony. *Organization Theory: An Environmental Approach* (2nd Ed.) (Rockleigh, N.J.: Allyn & Bacon, 1984).

Pfeffer, J., *Organizational Design* (Arlington Heights, Ill.: AHM Publishing, 1978).

Robbins, Stephen, P. *Organization Theory: Structure, Design and Applications* (Englewood Cliffs, N.J.: Prentice-Hall, 1987).

40
PLANNING AND PRODUCTION TASK: REAL ESTATE PROBLEM

PURPOSE
(1) To explore the effects of objectives, planning, and organizing on group productivity and output.
(2) To examine different factors that may affect profitability in a production company.

ADVANCE PREPARATION: (1) Read "introduction" below. (2) Form teams. (3) Complete steps 1 and 2 of the exercise.
GROUP SIZE: Any number of five- to ten-person groups.
TIME REQUIRED: 1 hour in class.
SPECIAL MATERIALS: Construction cards, staplers and staples, tape, scissors, rulers, 3 × 5 cards.
SPECIAL PHYSICAL REQUIREMENTS: Tables or movable desks, easel, separate rooms if large number of groups.
RELATED TOPICS: Managers as leaders, Organizational communication, Organizational structure and design.

INTRODUCTION

Most textbooks describe the management process as one that involves four functions: planning, organizing, directing, and controlling. How each of these functions is performed will determine to a great extent whether a company is successful or not in meeting its objectives.

Like larger systems, small groups must also consider these functions if they are to be successful. Frequently, group task accomplishment involves interdependencies among members and requires a high degree of coordination.

In both cases, tasks to be accomplished must be analyzed and objectives must be established in advance. Once these objectives are clear, the company or group can plan how it will organize its members and utilize resources to achieve these objectives. In many companies, one of the objectives will involve profitability. Just as companies must plan and organize for production, they also need to plan and organize to ensure that profit objectives are met.

In this exercise you will have an opportunity to compete with other groups in constructing a building. The success of your group will be measured by the profit you make in your project. Profit is determined by subtracting costs from the total appraised value of the finished structure. As you will see, several factors are involved in determining the appraised value. Therefore, it is essential that your group analyze this task carefully, set some objectives, and plan the best possible organization that will allow you to meet them.

PROCEDURE

Step 1

Each team should allow itself sufficient time to become familiar with the "Task Directions" given below. Discuss these until everyone understands them, then proceed to Step 2.

TASK DIRECTIONS

Each group will be required to construct a building out of construction cards (provided by the instructor) and to "sell" it at the end of the exercise. The sale price will be the total appraised value as determined by the real estate board valuation standards outlined below. The winning group will be the group with the greatest profit, regardless of the appraised value of the building.

Materials and Tools

Every group will have the same raw materials and tools available. These are construction cards, one ruler, one scissors, one stapler, and one roll of tape. Extra staples and tape will be available, upon request, without extra charge. The cost of construction cards (raw materials) is described below.

Cost of Cards

Cards cost $70 each. At the beginning of the exercise, each group will receive a package of 100 cards and be charged $7,000, as an initial, startup investment. Additional cards may be purchased from the supplier at the regular price. At the end of the exercise, you may redeem any unused cards for $50 each. If you need to purchase or redeem cards, one person and only one person from your group must go to the supply depot to carry out the transaction. The group leader will designate the supply depot at the beginning of the exercise.

Construction and Delivery Time

At the beginning of the exercise, the group leader will announce the amount of time you will be allotted to construct your building. No team is allowed to build until the group leader announces "Begin production." When the time is up, the group leader will announce "Stop production." No construction is allowed after this point. You will have *30 seconds* in which to deliver your completed structure to the real estate board for appraisal. Buildings received after 30 seconds will not be appraised. They will also be disqualified. No team members are allowed to remain with the building after it is delivered, except for the board members.

Real Estate Board

Each group should designate one member to serve on the board. The board member may help plan your building, but he or she will not be able to actually help during the construction phase. The board is responsible for appraising each building and assuring that building codes are met. The board will convene during the construction period to decide on criteria for the "drop-shock" test and quality and aesthetic values. The board must appraise one building before going on to the next. Once a building is appraised, it cannot be reappraised later.

Building Code
All buildings must be fully enclosed (floors and roofs). They must also have ceilings and be capable of withstanding a "drop-shock" test. The "drop-shock" test may consist of dropping the building or dropping an object (e.g., heavy book) on the building. It will be the real estate board's responsibility to decide on the test.

Appraisal Values
Buildings are appraised on the basis of quality and aesthetics. The *total* of the quality and aesthetic values is then multiplied by the total square inches of floor space in the building to obtain the total appraised value.

Quality Valuation
Quality is determined by subjecting the building to the "drop-shock" test. Various qualities are assigned values as follows:

Minimal quality: $12.00 per square inch of floor space

Good quality: $14.00 per square inch of floor space

Better quality: $16.00 per square inch of floor space

Top quality: $18.00 per square inch of floor space

Aesthetic Valuation
The real estate board can set this value anywhere from zero to $3.00 per square inch, depending on their appraisal of aesthetic value.

Other Instructions
Once construction begins (Step 4), you will not be allowed to ask the group leader to clarify any game rules or resolve any group difficulties. You are on your own. Five minutes before construction is to stop, the group leader will notify you of the time remaining. While the real estate board is appraising buildings, each group will be expected to clean up left-over raw materials and return them to the supply depot. All unused cards should be redeemed.

Step 2
Your group should discuss the task and then establish the following:

1. What are your objectives in this project?
2. What plan will you use to achieve your objectives?
3. How will group members be organized and coordinated to accomplish the group's tasks?
4. How will you utilize resources?

5. Who will serve on the real estate board?
6. How will you deal with the uncertainties, that is, unknown time allocation and "drop-shock" test?

One member of the group should be designated to report on your objectives, plan, and organization structure during the discussion at the end of the exercise.

Step 3 (Beginning of Session)
Each group should assemble together at one work place (table or cluster of desks). The group leader will designate the following: (1) supply depot and supply person(s); (2) delivery station for real estate board; and (3) construction time. In addition, the group leader will distribute all materials and tools to the groups. Finally, the people designated to serve on the real estate board will be asked to convene. No one is to use any materials or tools at this point.

Step 4
When the group leader announces "Begin production," you may build. When group leader announces "Stop production," you must deliver your building to the real estate board *within 30 seconds.*

Step 5: 10 Minutes
The real estate board appraises the buildings. The groups clean up and return the raw materials. The group leader and supply person(s) compute total cost and enter figures on board or easel. The real estate board enters total value of buildings on board or easel.

Step 6
Compute the profit for each group. The total costs are subtracted from the total appraised value for each building. Determine the winning group (most profitable).

Step 7
The total group and the group leader should discuss the results in terms of the objectives, plan, and organization of each group to determine how these factors affected output and profits. Group members should respond to discussion questions for their own groups.

DISCUSSION QUESTIONS
1. What was the primary objective in this task?
2. Given this objective, what other objectives did your group set? Did you try to minimize/maximize floor space? Quality? Resources used? Aesthetic value? Costs?
3. Did your group's plan allow for the uncertainty associated with construction time? Did you establish any contingency plans or alternatives for long or short construction periods? Different shock tests?

4. Did your group members attempt to influence the real estate board either before or during the appraisal?
5. What factors in your group's efforts do you think account for its success or failure in this task?
6. How did your group's division of labor and coordination of efforts affect your performance?
7. What effect has your group's success or failure experience had on: (a) you? (b) group cohesion/identity? (c) attitudes toward other groups and/or individuals?

GENERALIZATIONS AND CONCLUSIONS

Concluding Points

1. What does this exercise demonstrate about the role of group objectives?

2. What is the value of planning as demonstrated in this exercise?

Participant's Reactions

READINGS AND REFERENCES

Bennis, W. G., Benne, K. D., Chin, R., and Corey, K. E., *The Planning of Change*. Third Edition (New York: Rinehart and Winston, 1976).

Goodman, P. S. and Associates, *Designing Effective Work Groups* (San Francisco: Jossey Bass, 1986).

Hellriegel, D., Slocum, J. W. and Woodman, R. W., *Organizational Behavior*. Third Edition, Chapters 17 and 18 (St. Paul, MN: West Publishing Company, 1983).

Szilagyi, A. D., *Management and Performance*. Second Edition (Glenview, IL: Scott Foresman, 1984).

41
PEOPLE'S NATIONAL BANK, UNIVERSITY BRANCH

PURPOSE:
(1) To analyze the structure and design of an organization.
(2) To develop action steps to improve organizational effectiveness.

ADVANCE PREPARATION: Read the case. Come to class prepared to discuss the two questions at the end of the case.
GROUP SIZE: Any Size. Can be discussed in small groups or in the total class.
TIME REQUIRED: 50 minutes to 2 hours, depending on number of issues covered.
SPECIAL MATERIALS: None.
SPECIAL PHYSICAL REQUIREMENTS: None.
RELATED TOPICS: Motivation: basic concepts, Applied motivation and job design, Managers as leaders, Group decision making and problem solving.

INTRODUCTION

The topic of organization design is often difficult for people to comprehend because of the size and complexity of many organizations. This is a case study of a branch bank, which has the twin benefits of being small enough to really study in detail, yet being large enough to have a fairly full set of organizational functions and problems. This case will put you in the role of a young new branch manager, a recent graduate. You may find yourself in a similar situation in a few years!

PROCEDURE

Read the following case. Discuss the two questions at the end of the case.

PNP UNIVERSITY BRANCH

People's National Bank (PNB) is the lead bank of a moderate-sized bank holding company located in a large midwestern state. As the major bank in the company, located in the state's capital city, PNB accounts for $600 million of the company's $2 billion in assets. At the core of PNB is its branch banking system. Unlike many East Coast banks, branch banking accounts for a large percentage of PNB's income, and many of the top managers of the bank have come up through the branch system.

The senior vice-president for branch operations, John B. Green, directly supervises the operations of 21 branch banks. Approximately 10 more branches are planned for the next three years. Each branch is headed up by a branch manager, who runs the branch with a relatively high degree of freedom. A typical branch includes a group of tellers,

Case written by David Nadler. Adapted by D. T. Hall. Used by permission.

directed by a teller supervisor, and a "desk" staff of financial consultants, loan officers, and some clerical personnel. Some of the larger branches have assistant managers who may supervise either operations or the loan activity. Although the actual work technology is extremely standardized (i.e., procedures for opening accounts, processing loans, etc.), the branch manager is free to manage the branch as he desires, and different branches have greatly varying structures, procedures, and climates.

Each branch is a profit center within the larger bank. Branch revenue is figured by adding income from loan volume together with a figure representing income derived from the funds that the branch has brought in (based on deposit figures). From the revenue figure actual branch expenses, building expenses, and allocated overhead are subtracted to yield a monthly branch profit figure. Each year, the branch manager and John B. Green develop a profit plan for the coming year, and managers are paid a sizable bonus depending upon the performance of their branch against the profit plan.

A Change at the University Branch
Two weeks ago, the branch manager of the University Branch of PNB informed John B. Green that he would be leaving the bank at the end of the following week to "join the ministry of God." Faced with an unanticipated managerial vacancy in a large and critical branch, Green met with his staff and decided to appoint Gary Herline, an up-and-coming young man in the commercial lending department, as manager of the University Branch. Herline was notified on Wednesday and was told to report to the University Branch on the following Monday to take up his duties as branch manager.

Herline's Background
Herline had been with the bank for a few years when he received the sudden notice of his appointment as branch manager. He received his MBA from a well-known business school four years ago and, upon graduation, was faced with several offers from financial institutions. He chose PNB, rather than one of the large New York banks, because he felt that there would be greater opportunities to move up in the organization quickly at PNB. He started out his first year in the bank's training program, and was rotated through a wide variety of assignments, including a brief assignment as a financial consultant at a branch. During this period, Gary learned that he had been identified by management as a "hot prospect" and that his performance was being watched closely. After the training rotation period, he spent two years in the trust department and had worked in the commercial lending department for a year when he heard about his move to the University Branch.

Information about University Branch
Having heard about his move late on Wednesday, Gary spent most of Thursday and Friday talking to some of his contacts within the bank about the University Branch, while he tried to conclude his work in commercial lending. The University Branch, one of the largest in the system, had been a problem branch for some time, with quite a bit of turnover among the employees and the managerial staff. Located adjacent to the state university campus, it faced a market area different from almost any other branch in the system. By Friday afternoon, Gary had listed the important things that he had learned

about the branch (see Exhibit 1). As he prepared to start at University Branch on Monday morning, he asked himself the following questions:

1. "From what I know about the branch, what are the critical issues I am going to have to deal with during the next 6 months at University Branch?"
2. "When I get to the branch on Monday, what are the first things I should do—what should my first day look like?"

EXHIBIT 1: PNB UNIVERSITY BRANCH

Herline's summary of important information about University Branch:

It's a large branch. 8 desk people, 18 tellers, fairly good physical plant, high volume.

Loan volume has been very poor during the past three years, but there has been a recent increase over the past two or three months. Some people feel that this reflects an absence of any management and that the loans are not "good" ones (that delinquency will go up in the coming months).

Very young staff, particularly the tellers. All except two of the tellers are women and many have Bachelor of Arts degrees; some even have Masters degrees.

Branch has the highest number of accounts and highest volume of transactions of any branch in the system; however, many accounts are very small, and many transactions are for small amounts of money (i.e. checks for less than $10).

There is no official assistant manager, but one of the loan officers seems to function as an assistant manager. He is resented by the tellers, however, and seems to get into disagreements with the teller supervisor, who has been at the branch for 17 years.

Desk staff seem to be of uneven quality. There are some real winners, but some dead wood also.

Turnover among tellers is very high. It has run at about 75 percent per year for the last five years. Recently the tellers submitted an informal group grievance to the manager complaining about working hours and low pay.

Competition for the university area business is keen. The other two major commercial banks in town have branches on the same block as PNB. Both branches are newer and better laid out than the PNB branch. Also, several S&Ls are close by.

Some of the key commercial accounts in the University Branch area have been taken by aggressive loan officers and branch managers of other nearby PNB branches as well as by competing banks.

For the last year, the branch has consistently failed to meet the profit plan, and has even shown losses in several months.

GENERALIZATIONS AND CONCLUSIONS

Concluding Points

1. In what ways are the financial performance of this organization affected strongly by employee motivation and behavior?

2. Why is it difficult for Herline to be too specific at this point about what immediate actions he will take?

Participant's Reactions

READINGS AND REFERENCES

Frost, Peter J., *Organizational Culture* (Sage Publications, 1985).

Mirvis, P. H., and Lawler III, E. E., "Measuring the Financial Impact of Employee Attitudes," *Journal of Applied Psychology,* 62 (1977), 1–8.

Schein, Edgar H., *Organizational Culture and Leadership: A Dynamic View* (Jossey-Bass, 1985).

Schneider, B., "The Perception of Organizational Climate: The Customer's View," *Journal of Applied Psychology,* 57 (1973), 248–256.

42
EXPERIENCING ORGANIZATIONAL CLIMATES

PURPOSE:
To assess the relationship between specific organizational experiences and the climate perceptions they produce.

ADVANCE PREPARATION: None.
GROUP SIZE: Any number of five-to-ten-person groups.
TIME REQUIRED: 30 to 50 minutes.
SPECIAL MATERIALS: None.
SPECIAL PHYSICAL REQUIREMENTS: None.
RELATED TOPICS: Managers as leaders, Organizational culture, Motivation: basic concepts.

INTRODUCTION

Organization climate has become an increasingly popular concept for describing the generalized perceptions that people employ in thinking about and describing the organizations in which they work. Climate is an "umbrella concept" in that it is a way of summarizing numerous specific, detailed perceptions in a small number of general dimensions.

When new people enter a work setting, one of the first things they need to figure out is exactly how they should behave. Are people friendly with their bosses? Do people get along really well with each other? Do people really "put out" with effort? Is "shoddy" work tolerated? Are customers and clients all treated courteously? Is safety important? These are the kinds of impressions new employees pick up as they perceive what happens around them and to them.

New employees probably form an impression about *each* of the issues noted and many others. Each impression is based on the perception of numerous events, practices and procedures, that is, on the basis of the kinds of behaviors that new employees note are rewarded and supported by supervisors, co-workers, and organizational policy. The more *particular* kinds of events, practices, and procedures happen to, and around, employees the more they begin to sense that a particular atmosphere or climate exists.

New employees sense particular climates, then, as a function of the ebb and flow of everyday activities, events, practices, and procedures in a work place. Because no one can remember each and every little thing that happens to them and around them, people tend to group or "chunk" perceptions into meaningful clusters. These clusters are made up of the perceptions of activities, events, practices, and procedures that tend to connote a common theme.

Exercise developed by Benjamin Schneider. Adapted by D. T. Hall. Used by permission of Dr. Schneider.

How do we detect the climate of an organization? One of the best ways to determine climate is to identify *norms* in the environment—the (mostly) unwritten rules that people seem to follow about how to behave in an environment. One way to help people identify these factors is to identify the "dos and don'ts" or "OKs and no-nos" that characterize life in a particular culture. For example, "It's not OK to come to work without your hard hat" or "Although you're supposed to wear your hard hat all the time, it's OK to take it off when you're in the office."

This exercise will ask you to think about the climate of an organization in terms of the "dos and don'ts" that govern people's behavior in a particular environment.

OPTION ONE

Step 1: 15 Minutes

Meet in small groups. Think of yourselves as new employees in a work setting. The setting is a paint factory. Think about the climate for physical safety in the plant. When you report for work, you are told that "you should try to be careful, to follow the safety rules here; otherwise you're liable to get hurt."

What are the "dos and don'ts" around you that would create a *climate for safe behavior?* Brainstorm as many norms and characteristics of the work environment as you think of that would indicate a climate for safe behavior. Pick a spokesperson to present your list to the rest of the class.

Step 2: 15 to 35 Minutes

Report each group's list to the rest of the class. Examine the ways in which very specific experiences and features of the work organization combine to produce global perceptions of the climate of the organization.

GENERALIZATIONS AND CONCLUSIONS

Concluding Points

1. How are perceptions of organizational climate formed?

2. What effect do climate perceptions have on an employee's behavior? On a client or customer's behavior?

3. In this exercise we have focused on the climate for safety. What other aspects of climate can you think of, say, in a bank (a service organization)?

4. Based on what we have concluded about how climate perceptions are formed, what can you say about how climates are changed?

OPTION TWO

Consider an organization with which you are all familiar, such as the institution in which you are presently attending this class. (Another possibility would be to consider the organization in which you are currently employed, if you are now employed.)

Step 1: Completing and Scoring the Questionnaire

First complete the questionnaire below, describing first the ideal and then the actual state of the organization, as you see it. (The "organization" can be this class, a work group, your employer, or any other organization.) Then compute your ideal and actual scores on the six dimensions of climate given at the end of the questionnaire. Compute the gap between ideal and actual states on each dimension.

ORGANIZATION CLIMATE QUESTIONNAIRE

Using the spaces in the left-hand column, first describe the ideal practices and procedures you would like to see in this organization. Next, using the spaces in the right-hand column, describe what you believe actually happens now in this organization.

Developed by Benjamin Schneider and C. J. Bartlett. Used by permission. This version of the questionnaire is not presented for research purposes. Those interested in the total set of items should contact Benjamin Schneider, Department of Psychology, Michigan State University, East Lansing, MI 48824.

Put a number in the space beside each statement according to the following key: 1 = almost never; 2 = infrequently; 3 = sometimes; 4 = frequently; 5 = very frequently.

Ideal   *Actual*

_____ 1. This organization takes care of the people who work for it.   _____

_____ 2. Members enjoy keeping up with national and international   _____
current events.

_____ 3. People in this organization ask each other how they are   _____
doing in reaching their goals.

_____ 4. Management effectively balances people problems and   _____
production problems.

_____ 5. There are definite "in" and "out" groups within the organi-   _____
zation.

_____ 6. This organization encourages employees to exercise their   _____
own initiative.

_____ 7. This organization takes an active interest in the progress of   _____
its members.

_____ 8. Members of this organization have a wide range of interests.   _____

_____ 9. More experienced members of this organization take time   _____
to help newer members.

_____ 10. The management runs a people-oriented organization.   _____

_____ 11. Members of this organization always have grievances no   _____
matter what is done to correct them.

_____ 12. This organization willingly accepts the ideas of its members   _____
for change.

_____ 13. This organization recognizes that its life depends upon its   _____
members.

_____ 14. Members keep themselves informed on many topics besides   _____
their immediate job-related activities.

_____ 15. People in this organization speak openly about each others'   _____
shortcomings.

_____ 16. There is a sense of purpose and direction in this organization.   _____

_____ 17. Members are prone to overstate and exaggerate their ac- _____
complishments.

_____ 18. Management does not exercise authoritarian control over _____
members' activities.

Scoring:

Scale	Add Items	Ideal Total	Actual Total	Gap (Ideal-Actual)
Organizational Support	1, 7, 13	_____	_____	_____
Member Quality	2, 8, 14	_____	_____	_____
Openness	3, 9, 15	_____	_____	_____
Supervisory Style	4, 10, 16	_____	_____	_____
Member Conflict	5, 11, 17	_____	_____	_____
Member Autonomy	6, 12, 18	_____	_____	_____

Step 2: Computing Group Averages and Discrepancies

If other members of your organization or group have also completed the Organization Climate Questionnaire, get together with them and compute group means for the ideal and actual organization climate. Then compute the gap between ideal and actual climate scores on each of these group means.

Discuss where the greatest gaps occurred and the reasons for this state of affairs. What could be done to reduce this gap?

Discuss where the smallest gaps occurred. What accounts for this state of affairs?

Participant's Reaction

READINGS AND REFERENCES

Hall, D. T., and Schneider, B., *Organizational Climates and Careers: The Work Lives of Priests* (New York: Seminar Press, 1973).

Schneider, B., "Organizational Climate: Individual Preferences and Organizational Realities," *Journal of Applied Psychology,* 56 (1972), 211–17.

Schneider, B., "The Perception of Organizational Climate: The Customer's View," *Journal of Applied Psychology,* 57 (1973), 248–256.

Schneider, B., "Organizational Climates: An Essay," *Personnel Psychology,* 28 (1975), 447–479.

Schneider, B., Parkington, J. J., and Buxton, V. M., "Employee and Customer Perceptions of Service in Banks," *Administrative Science Quarterly* (1981), in press.

Zohar, D., "Safety Climate in Industrial Organizations: Theoretical and Applied Implications," *Journal of Applied Psychology,* 65 (1980), 96–102.

SECTION TWELVE
PLANNED CHANGE

43
CHANGE OF WORK PROCEDURES

PURPOSE:
(1) To diagnose and practice overcoming resistance to change.
(2) To illustrate the distinction between the quality of a decision and its acceptability.
(3) To provide practice in participative decision making.

ADVANCE PREPARATION: None.
GROUP SIZE: Subgroups of five. Total class can be any size. Works best with groups of from four to six.
TIME REQUIRED: 50 minutes.
SPECIAL MATERIALS: None.
SPECIAL PHYSICAL REQUIREMENTS: None.
RELATED TOPICS: Applied motivation and job design, Group decision making and problem solving, Managers as leaders, Power, Interpersonal communication.

INTRODUCTION

Most changes in organizations are seldom confined to the technical aspects of production; they may also require alterations in the *work* and *social* satisfactions of the employees. New methods must be not only of high *quality* (i.e. workable and efficient from an objective standpoint), but they must also be *acceptable* to the employees who will be using them.

Developed by N. R. F. Maier. Adapted for the present volume by D. T. Hall. Used by permission.

This added factor of **acceptance** makes the problem of introducing changes different from purely technical problems of evaluating new equipment or procedures. For one thing, the **quality** of a solution and its **acceptability** are different characteristics and do not necessarily go together. A second complication is that, although management can control solution quality by reserving decision making to itself, acceptance is inherently voluntary with the employees and is not subject to the will of management. At the same time, failure to obtain employee acceptance of changes that affect them aggravates many of the problems of management. In some instances, resistance is expressed directly in the form of grievances about rates and earnings, quits, work stoppages and open hostility toward management. In other instances, the resistance may be shown in such indirect ways as restriction of output, waste, low-quality workmanship, slow learning of the new methods, excessive absenteeism, and the like.

One might think of two general approaches to introducing change: *selling* and *mutual problem solving*. In selling, facts and arguments are presented to employees showing the advantages of change. In mutual problem solving, the manager and subordinates discuss the need for change and arrive jointly at a plan for change. In between these two approaches is *consultation,* in which the manager discusses the need for change with subordinates, solicits their ideas, and then makes the decision alone.

In order to deal with problems of change, the first step is to learn the nature of the resistance to change. In the present case there are a variety of forces operating. Some of these are in the direction of change, some opposed or resisting. The supervisor in charge will want to identify the resistance forces and try to reduce them, while trying to constructively use the positive forces.

The kind of discussion the new supervisor stimulates may introduce new negative or new positive forces so that the outcome may, in part, be determined by the discussion which is initiated.

PROCEDURE

Step 1: 5 Minutes
The group is divided into subgroups of five. If the total group size is not a multiple of five, some subgroups of four or six can be used. All groups are to select one of their members to act as the supervisor, "Thompson." After the supervisors have been chosen, they should raise their hands to indicate that the group has a leader.

The other members in each group will be crew members and observer(s). Beginning with the supervisor and going in clockwise order, their names will be "Jackson," "Stevenson," and "Walters." The fifth members (and sixth, if present) will be observers.

Step 2: 5 Minutes
When all members have received their roles, the group leader will read aloud the section entitled "General Information," below.

GENERAL INFORMATION

This role play takes place in a company that manufactures small hand-held electronic calculators and components for computer systems. In this company, the assembly work is done by small groups of employees. Several of these employees work under a supervisor, Thompson. In one of these groups, Jackson, Stevenson, and Walters work together assembling components for hand-held calculators. Because of the constant change in model, style, and capability of hand-held calculators, and the popular demand for them, the workers usually have a fairly constant backlog of two to three weeks in work orders.

This operation is divided into three jobs or positions, called position 1, position 2, and position 3. Supplies for each position are located next to the bench where the work takes place. Employees work side by side and can help each other out if they wish. Since all the jobs are simple and fairly similar, these three employees exchange positions on the line every now and then. This trading of positions was developed by the employees themselves. It creates no financial problem because the crew is paid by a group-piece rate. In this way, the three members share the production pay equally.

Presently each of you will be asked to be one of the following: Thompson, Jackson, Walters, or Stevenson. Today, Thompson, the supervisor, has asked Jackson, Walters, and Stevenson to meet in the office to talk about "something".

Next, the role players should study (only) their individual roles in preparation for the small group discussions. The roles for Thompson, Jackson, Stevenson, and Walters are found in the Appendix to this book, as are the instructions for observers.

The Thompsons should stand up beside their groups when they have finished studying their roles, thus giving the group leader a signal that they are ready to begin.

When all supervisors are standing, the group leader will set the stage for the role playing by commenting that the supervisor has asked the crew members to meet to discuss a problem before starting work. The group leader will explain that when the supervisor is asked to sit down, this will be the signal that Thompson had entered the office and hopes that the employees will speak upon entering.

Step 3: 25 Minutes

The leader will ask if anyone has any questions. When everyone understands their function, the leader will ask the supervisors to sit down. All groups should role-play simultaneously. Approximately 25 minutes is needed by the average group to reach a decision.

Step 4: 15 Minutes

Collect results.

DISCUSSION QUESTIONS

1. What conclusions can be drawn from the table of results? Is there any relationship between the method used and the degree of acceptance or resistance? What method was used most often?
2. Construct a problem analysis diagram of this situation. What were the *resistance*

forces (i.e. the members' objections to the change)? What were the *change* forces (i.e. possible gains or advantages to the crew under the new method)?
3. Which of the forces in the diagram are based on emotions (fear, hostility, etc.)? Which are based on actual information about the changes?

GENERALIZATIONS AND CONCLUSIONS

Concluding Points

1. As a strategy for change, is it generally better to try to reduce the resistance forces or to increase the change forces?

2. What three factors primarily determine the effectiveness of change?

3. What generally happens to resistance to change when groups participate in planning for change? Why?

4. What are two major dimensions of change in organizations?

5. When resistance to change is caused by negative attitudes and emotions, how should the group leader deal with these findings?

Participant's Reactions

READINGS AND REFERENCES

Burke, W. Warner, *Organization Development: Principles and Practices* (Boston: Little Brown, 1982).

Coch, L., and French, J. R. P., "Overcoming Resistance to Change," *Human Relations,* 1 (1948), 512–32.

Frost, C., Wakeley, J., and Ruh, R., *The Scanlon Plan for Organization Development: Identity, Participation, and Equity* (East Lansing: Michigan State University Press, 1974).

Marrow, A., Bowers, D., and Seashore, S., *Management by Participation* (New York: Harper & Row, 1967).

Varney, Glenn H., *Organization Development for Managers* (Reading, Mass.: Addison-Wesley, 1977).

44
THE SANITARY COMPANY

PURPOSE:

(1) To develop an understanding of how various theories and change strategies can be used to solve a problem of employee behavior.

(2) To develop an understanding of factors affecting efforts to implement change.

(3) To illustrate the effects of decision making and resistance on planned change programs.

ADVANCE PREPARATION: Read the "Introduction," below, and complete Steps 1 to 3 of Part I in advance.

GROUP SIZE: Any number of small groups. May also be done individually.

TIME REQUIRED Part I: 1 hour (out of class) Part II: 45 minutes (in class)

SPECIAL MATERIALS: None.

SPECIAL PHYSICAL REQUIREMENTS: Movable chairs or separate rooms.

RELATED TOPICS: Applied motivation and job design, Group decision making and problem solving, Managers as leaders.

INTRODUCTION

Changing worker behavior, like skinning cats, may be approached in a variety of ways. How it is approached will depend on the nature of the underlying problem, the theories about behavior we apply in developing a strategy for solving the problem, and how we go about introducing or implementing the strategy. In the first part of this exercise, you will have an opportunity to (1) analyze the problem of absenteeism and turnover in a small company, (2) develop a change strategy, and (3) select a method for implementing your strategy. There are no "right" answers, although some solutions may have more merit than others.

Later, you will be given information and data reported by the consultants who actually intervened in the Sanitary Company situation. At various points in the case you will be asked to predict what you think actually happened. As you will see, the consultants discovered several unforeseen consequences associated with their strategy and method of implementing it.

Developed by Francine S. Hall. Case material adapted from E. E. Lawler, III and J. R. Hackman, "Impact of Employee Participation in the Development of Pay Incentive Plans," *Journal of Applied Psychology* 53 (1969), 467–71; and K. Scheflen, E. E. Lawler, and J. R. Hackman, "Long Term Impact of Employee Participation in Development of Pay Incentive Plans," *Journal of Applied Psychology*, 55 (1971), 182–86.

PART I

PROCEDURE

Step 1

Read the following case description of Sanitary Company.

THE CASE OF THE SANITARY COMPANY

The Sanitary Company is a small company that provides building maintenance services on a contract basis. Employees work part time cleaning buildings and offices during the evening. Most employees work four hours a night, five nights a week. They are paid at an hourly rate.

Employees work in groups ranging in size from 2 to 25 persons. There are about 15 such "work groups" in the company. Each group is responsible for doing all the cleaning in one building. The actual cleaning work is similar for each group.

Employees are expected to report for work each night at the building to be cleaned. The company has managers who are responsible for supervising the cleaning crews, but they are not members of the actual work groups.

Employees tend to have low levels of education. Some of them are illiterate. About half of the employees are women. Many of the women are housewives during the day. For most of the male employees, work with the Sanitary Company is a second job. The employees range in age from 16 to over 70.

Step 2

Assume that you have been hired as consultants to the company that is described in the case. The company President, M. K. Nunes, has told you that he is concerned with the high rate of *turnover and absenteeism* in his company. He has asked you to diagnose his company's problem and to recommend a plan for solving it. Specifically, he wants your answers to the following questions:

1. What do you think the **real** problem is? Why?
2. What solution(s) would you propose? Why?
3. How would you implement your plan? What reasons would you give for doing it this way?

What will you tell the company president?

Step 3

Prepare your plan in three parts:

1. *Diagnosis:* Identify the variables that may be causing the absenteeism and turnover. Remember that behavior such as this is usually a **symptom** of a more serious problem.
2. *Change Recommendation:* Given the factors you identified as possible causes,

outline a plan for changing the situation. In other words, prescribe an appropriate solution or remedy.

3. *Implementation strategy:* Given the change you want to bring about, describe the manner in which you will introduce it in the organization. Consider such factors as your role, the roles of people in the organization, modes of communication, and attitudes of organization members.

In each part, detail your analysis and recommendations, and provide the rationale on which they are based.

Step 4: 1 hour
The total group should convene. Each individual or group presents the plan that he/she/they developed. The group leader will summarize these on the board. After all plans have been presented, discuss the Sanitary Company case in terms of the questions listed below.

DISCUSSION QUESTIONS
1. What are the pros and cons of the different plans?
2. Which would be most feasible? Why?
3. Which would generate the most and least resistance? Why?
4. Which would have the highest likelihood of success? Why?
5. What employee needs does each plan meet or use as motivators?

GENERALIZATIONS AND CONCLUSIONS

Concluding Points
1. What is the best strategy to employ when attempting to change employee behavior?

2. What is the foundation for developing an effective change strategy?

PART II

PROCEDURE

Step 1: 10 Minutes
Your group leader will read an account of how the consultants who actually intervened in the Sanitary Company approached the problem. When the leader has finished, discuss the prediction question which follows.

Prediction Question: What do you think happened to the attendance record for (a) the participative groups? (b) the imposed groups? and (c) the control (no treatment) groups?

Step 2: 10 Minutes

Your group leader will read an account of what actually happened. When the leader has finished, discuss the prediction questions which follow.

Prediction Questions: (1) Why do you think the plan was successful for some groups and not for others? (2) What do you think the long-term effect will be? After one year, what do you predict the attendance record will be? (3) Do you think the company management will continue the plan?

Step 3: 10 Minutes

Your group leader will read an account of what happened. Discuss the prediction questions which follow.

Prediction Questions: (1) Why do you think it took so long before the attendance in the imposed groups improved? (2) Why do you think the managers of the two participative groups took the action they did?

Step 4: 15 Minutes

Your group leader will read a summary account of the Sanitary Company case. Discuss this case as a total group. What conclusions can you draw from it?

GENERALIZATIONS AND CONCLUSIONS

Concluding Points

1. What other considerations are as important as the technical aspects of a change plan?

2. When a plan requires "acceptance" in order to work, what decision-making style is most appropriate?

3. In deciding who to include, what should be considered?

Participant's Reactions

READINGS AND REFERENCES

Coch, L., and French, J. R. P., "Overcoming Resistance to Change," *Human Relations,* 1 (1948), 512–32.

French, Wendell F. and Bell, Cecil H., Jr., *Organization Development: Behavioral Science Interventions for Organizational Improvement,* (3rd Ed.), Englewood-Cliffs, N.J.: Prentice-Hall, 1984.

Scheflen, K., Lawler, E. E., III, and Hackman, J. R., "Long Term Impact of Employee Participation in Development of Pay Incentive Plans," *Journal of Applied Psychology,* 55 (1971), 182–86.

Vroom, V., and Yetton, P., *Leadership and Decision Making* (Pittsburgh: University of Pittsburgh Press, 1973).

SECTION THIRTEEN
LIFE, WORK, AND CAREER ROLES

INTRODUCTION

Before you begin the career planning activities in this section, it would probably be helpful if we explained what we mean by "career," and what we consider to be an effective and comprehensive approach to career planning. For example, many people tend to think of a career as a particular job or occupation and the sequence of promotions they hope to get in that job. Hall (1976), however, suggests that we can understand careers better if we make certain assumptions:

1. *Career per se does not imply success or failure.* The notion that one is a failure if one does not advance and become promoted is an assumption of our culture, but not the best assumption to make if you want to understand how individuals approach their careers. Therefore,
2. *Career success or failure is best assessed by the person whose career is being considered, rather than by other interested parties.* Clearly, any career can be a success if it is a source of deep satisfaction and reward to the person who lives it. The best measure of success may be *psychological success,* the extent to which the person feels he or she is achieving personally valued goals and outcomes in the career. In other words,
3. *The career is made up of both behaviors and attitudes*—what one does and how one feels about it. And, finally,
4. *The career is a process, a sequence of work-related experiences.* Here, Hall suggests that we think of a career as:
   - a life-long sequence;

Prepared by Donald D. Bowen.

- including all work-related experience (whether paid or not) and not strictly limited to a single profession or occupation;
- a major, but not the only, component of one's life—which is not to say that family life, leisure activities, and other aspects of life are not strongly influenced by the satisfactions and frustrations people experience in their careers.

These considerations led Hall (1976, p. 4) to define a career as:

. . . the individually perceived sequence of attitudes and behaviors associated with work-related experiences and activities over the span of the person's life.

Since our concept of career emphasizes the subjective experience, the personal perception and feelings of the person in the career, we believe (as do many authorities on careers) that effective career planning must begin with an assessment in depth of one's own needs, values, motives, strengths, and weaknesses if one is to find a good career-person fit. John Crites[1] suggests that career planning should follow a five-step approach, in the following order:

1. *Self-assessment.* As already suggested, the objective of this phase is to think through and get in touch with your most important needs, values, interests, strengths, and weaknesses. Find out what they are and decide how they need to be dealt with in your career. Self-assessment activities (almost always better if done in a group) and tests (usually available from your college counseling center or placement office at little or no cost) should provide the basic data here. Don't forget to look at how *all* aspects of your life may be affected by your career experiences.
2. *Career opportunity information.* The objective here is to identify vocational and organizational paths that are likely to prove most satisfying to you. Suggested sources of information include your college placement office, interviews with people in the occupations you are interested in, and books—especially *Dictionary of Occupational Titles, Occupational Outlook Handbook, and Occupational Outlook Quarterly.*
3. *Goal setting.* In this phase you should set some overall objectives for your career and also some shorter-term, five-year goals. Remember, a good goal is specific and concrete (measurable) and is stated in terms of a specific time period or deadline.
4. *Planning.* Develop a specific plan for achieving your major goals. What must you do? What must others do? What sequences of events or activities are necessary?

   Both planning and goal-setting should be discussed in great detail with the important support groups in your life—close friends or members of your immediate family to whom you usually look for understanding, support, and advice when you are making major life decisions.
5. *Problem solving.* Problem solving is an activity that goes on throughout the

[1]John O. Crites, *Theory and Research Handbook: Career Maturity Inventory* (Monterey, Calif.: McGraw-Hill, 1973).

process of working toward your goals. It is the dealing with obstacles, blockages, problems, and so on that develop as you pursue your goals. Problem solving requires assessing the situation and oneself, establishing a goal that will solve the problem, and laying a plan to achieve the goal.

In the following pages, as well as in earlier sections of this book, you will find a number of self-assessment activities to get you started in planning your career. There are a number of books of activities that provide complete career planning programs for the individual or the group. Some of the best known include:

Bolles, R. N., *What Color is Your Parachute?* (Berkeley, Calif.: Ten Speed Press, 1972).

Crystal, J. C., and Bolles, R. N., *Where Do I Go From Here With My Life?* (New York: Seabury Press, 1974).

Kotter, J. P., Faux, V. A., and McArthur, C. C., *Self-Assessment and Career Development* (Englewood Cliffs, N.J.: Prentice-Hall, 1978).

Weiler, N. W., *Reality and Career Planning* (Reading, Mass.: Addison Wesley, 1977).

For those interested in what is known about careers and how this knowledge can be used to manage the human resources of the organization more effectively, we suggest:

Bowen, D. D., and Hall, D. T., "Career Planning for Employee Development: A Primer for Managers," *California Management Review,* Winter (1977), 23–35.

Hall, D. T., *Careers in Organizations* (Pacific Palisades, Calif.: Goodyear, 1976).

Hall, D. T., and Hall, F. S., "What's New in Career Management," *Organizational Dynamics,* Summer (1976), 17–33.

Schein, E. H., *Career Dynamics: Matching Individual and Organizational Needs* (Reading, Mass.: Addison-Wesley, 1978).

45
LIFELINES

PURPOSE:
To introduce a typical self-assessment component used as a first step in career planning.

ADVANCE PREPARATION: Read the Introduction to Section 13 and any other readings the instructor may assign before beginning the exercise. The instructor may also ask that the lifelines be prepared before the group meets to discuss them.

GROUP SIZE: Unlimited—small discussion groups of three to five persons are required.

TIME REQUIRED: Depends on number of persons in subgroups and design option specified. Ranges from 40 to 140 minutes, but can be done as an outside assignment (see Instructor's Manual for alternatives and variations).

SPECIAL MATERIALS: None

SPECIAL PHYSICAL REQUIREMENTS: Room large enough to seat small groups comfortably and permit discussions with minimal distraction from others. (Movable chairs will be helpful.) Separate meeting rooms for the small groups are desirable.

RELATED TOPICS: Icebreakers, Planned change, Motivation: basic concepts, Interpersonal communication.

INTRODUCTION

In this exercise, you will work on examining your own values and priorities for your life, and set career goals for yourself in terms of your own needs. You will find it helpful to approach this process by sharing your feelings and attitudes with others in the small group you will work with. In respect to any piece of personal data, however, you should always feel free to withhold that information from others if you would be uncomfortable sharing it.

PROCEDURE

PART I

Step 1: 10 Minutes

Take a piece of notebook paper. At the top, write "Where am I now?—Career." Proceed as follows: Envision a business progress chart as you draw a line that depicts the past,

Adapted from: J. William Pfeiffer and John E. Jones (eds.), "A Handbook of Structured Experiences for Human Relations Training," Vol. II (Revised). San Diego, CA: University Associates, 1974. Used with permission.

present, and future of your *career*. On this line mark an "X" to show where you are now. A business chart looks like this:

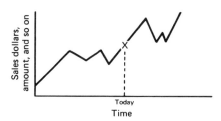

Write a brief explanation of the career line that you have drawn. Pay particular attention to the *peaks* and *valleys* of your lifeline. Peaks indicate that you were satisfying some of your most important needs at that time. Valleys probably mark times when these important needs were frustrated. What can you infer about which needs are most important to you from your lifeline? *Above* your lifeline, write in the most important decisions you have made in your life to date. Indicate where these occurred in relation to the peaks and valleys. Also, indicate the most important decisions you think you might be making at future points in your life. Evaluate for yourself the *outcomes* of those decisions.

Now, below your lifeline, indicate what you think you would have done *if you had not made each of these decisions* (or if you had made a different decision at each of these points). How would your life have turned out differently?[1]

Step 2: 10 Minutes

Take another piece of notebook paper. Label it "Where am I now?—Affiliations." Envision a business progress chart as you draw a line that depicts the past, present, and future of your personal *affiliations* (family and friends). On this line, mark an "X" to show where you are now. Write a brief explanation of the affiliation line that you have drawn. Again, analyze the peaks and valleys for what they can tell you about your most important needs.

Step 3: 10 Minutes

Head up another piece of notebook paper with "Where am I now?—Personal Fulfillment." Envision a business progress chart as you draw a line that depicts the past, present, and future of your *personal fulfillment.* (Consider every level from personal growth to material acquisition.) Write a brief explanation of the personal fulfillment line that you have drawn, paying special attention to the peaks and valleys.

PART II

Step 4: 5 Minutes

If the group has not already been subdivided into smaller groups, break into three-to-five person groups according to the group leader's directions.

---

[1]Suggested by an idea in Bolles (1978).

Step 5: 5 Minutes per Person

Take turns sharing your *career* lifeline with others in your group. Explain your lifeline in detail and discuss what you have inferred about your most important needs from the peaks and valleys of the lifeline.

Note: For the other members of the group, this is a chance to practice your listening and counseling skills. Don't give advice, but do listen carefully and ask any questions you can think of that might help the person presenting her lifeline to develop a better understanding of what the data mean. If you already know the person well, does his explanation make sense in light of how you perceive him? If you do not know the person, here is a chance to get to know her a lot better.

Step 6: 5 Minutes per Person

Take turns sharing each *affiliations* lifeline, proceeding as before in Step 5.

Step 7: 5 Minutes per Person

Take turns sharing each *personal fulfillment* lifeline.

PART III

Step 8: 30 Minutes

Working alone, prepare a brief statement of what you now consider to be *the most important needs to be satisfied in pursuing your career*. You may not feel that all of the needs you identified in your lifelines are still important; list only those that you now feel are most important.

For each need you list, what are the types of work or other situations that seem to provide the most satisfaction of that need? What changes in your career plans do you need in order to provide as much satisfaction of the need as possible?

Rank-order the needs in terms of their *importance* to you in assuring your own happiness. Does this suggest any additional changes you need to make in your career plans?

Now, develop answers to the following questions:

1. What barriers or obstacles to these satisfactions might you encounter from the following sources:
   a. Yourself?
   b. Significant other people in your life?
   c. Your work environment?
2. What *resources* (i.e. help) might you mobilize from the following sources?
   a. Yourself?
   b. Significant other people in your life?
   c. Your work environment?

Include the discussion of your obstacles and resources in your statement.

DISCUSSION QUESTIONS

1. Psychologists often argue that most people have rather fuzzy career plans because their sense of identity (their sense of who they are) is hazy. (For example, see Fromm, 1947, and Erikson, 1968.) From your experience with this exercise, would you agree or disagree? Did the exercise enhance your sense of identity? Did this help you to clarify your career plans?
2. Suggest further steps for continuing your career planning.
3. Do you feel that a person can plan a career without considering the impact of career on affiliations and personal fulfillment (and vice versa)?

GENERALIZATIONS AND CONCLUSIONS

Concluding Points

1. Develop a career strategy statement for yourself that you can use to plan and manage your career. Make your objectives, *specific* and *concrete,* develop *action plans* for achieving these objectives, develop a *timetable* for accomplishment of the major steps, and identify a *support group* of people (friends or family) who will encourage you and counsel you on achieving your goals.

2. For many people, career planning means a process in which they merely collect information on available jobs and employers. In this exercise, you have been collecting information about yourself. What might be the relationship between these two strategies?

Participant's Reactions

READINGS AND REFERENCES

See the readings suggested in the Introduction to Section 13. A number of additional life planning activities are suggested in:

Bolles, R. N., *The Three Boxes of Life* (Berkeley, Calif.: Ten Speed Press, 1978).

The relevance of one's "identity" in career planning is discussed in:

Erikson, E. H., *Identity: Youth and Crisis* (New York: Norton, 1968).
Fromm, E., *Man for Himself* (New York: Fawcett, 1947), pp. 62–113.

46
CAREER PLANNING:
STRENGTHS AND WEAKNESSES INVENTORY

PURPOSE:
(1) To diagnose your occupational strengths and weaknesses.
(2) To develop a career plan based on your strengths and weaknesses.
(3) To introduce you to commonly used career planning techniques.

ADVANCE PREPARATION: This exercise may require substantial advance preparation. Steps 1 to 5 should be completed before the group meets. Participants may need to read or review one of the exercises or readings discussed in the introduction and body of the exercise. Some participants may need to make trips to the library or arrange discussions with persons in the type of work they are thinking about (see Step 3).

GROUP SIZE: Subgroups of two to six may be used; total group may be of any size.

TIME REQUIRED: In-class time depends on size of subgroups; 10 minutes per group member plus setup and discussion time (i.e. for subgroups of five, 65 to 85 minutes).

SPECIAL MATERIALS: None.

SPECIAL PHYSICAL REQUIREMENTS: Room or an area large enough to seat small groups comfortably and permit discussions with minimal distraction from others. (Movable chairs will be helpful.) Separate meeting areas for subgroups are *desirable,* but not essential.

RELATED TOPICS: Planned change, Motivation: basic concepts, Interpersonal communication.

INTRODUCTION

Obviously, different occupations and professions require different strengths (skills, abilities, talents, etc.) of the people who are effective in their work. The skills and abilities required for a particular line of work reflect the activities that are involved in the job, which, in turn, are largely dictated by the "raw materials" involved in the work. Broadly speaking, all jobs require dealing with one or more of four types of raw materials: things, data, ideas, and people. Figure 1 suggests some of the elemental job activities required for each of these raw materials.

Some jobs seem to require the ability to deal with only one type of material: bookkeepers work mostly with data, carpenters with things, philosophers with ideas, and sales clerks with people. Most jobs require the ability to effectively deal with at

Developed by Donald D. Bowen.

FIGURE 1

Four Categories of Job Activities

Things Here are some activities involving *things:* Move, manipulate, machine (saw, drill, finish, etc.), adjust, assemble, design, operate, handle, construct, arrange, inspect, clean, deliver, store, drive, etc.

Data Here are some job activities involving *data:* Compare, collect, copy, analyze, check, compile, organize, summarize, type, collate, store and retrieve, classify, schedule, observe, diagnose, etc.

People Here are some job activities involving *people:* Counsel, assist, coach, teach, manage, persuade, interview, consult, advise, criticize, lead, communicate, request, encourage, sell, recruit, manage, arbitrate or mediate conflict, negotiate, speak in public, supervise, listen, help others to express themselves.

Ideas Here are some job activities involving *ideas:* Create, compare, critique, publish, think about, argue, comprehend, decide, plan, interpret, define, establish goals, imagine, invent, synthesize, etc.

---

least two types of material. For example, *all* managers deal with people, but the Controller also works with data, the Vice President of Engineering is heavily involved with data and things, and the Vice President of Marketing with ideas and data.

Individuals vary in their preferences and abilities for dealing with different types of work. As suggested by Jung (see the reading by Slocum in the Folio of Resources, pp. 285 to 289), these preferences and predispositions may be fundamental characteristics of personality that differentiate how people collect information (sensing versus intuition) and process information (thinking versus feeling). Using the four-celled diagram in Figure 1 of the Slocum reading (p. 286), it seems reasonable to hypothesize that the STs are the individuals primarily oriented toward *things*, since they are drawn to the concrete and impersonal aspects of experience. NTs are clearly those who prefer *ideas* with their "focus on general concepts and issues." NFs value the "personal and social needs of people," while SFs like detail as it applies to a specific, concrete, immediate situation; that is, *data*. (If you have not read the Slocum piece, you will probably want to familiarize yourself with it at this point.)

Exercise 2, ("Learning and Problem Solving: You're Never Too Jung!") provided a format for identifying your basic problem solving style in terms of the Jungian dimensions. The purpose of this exercise is to give you a chance to evaluate your strengths and weaknesses in each of the four work areas. Effective planning of your career requires that you identify your personal strengths and find a line of work that will let you use those skills that you enjoy exercising the most. Once you have identified a particular vocational area that capitalizes on your strengths, it is also important that you identify any remediable deficiencies or weaknesses that may hinder you from achieving your full potential in your field. You will need to develop specific plans for moving into your chosen line of work (if you are not already in it) and for overcoming your weaknesses.

PROCEDURE

Step 1

1. Take four blank sheets of lined 8½ × 11-inch notebook paper. Put a heading on each sheet, one sheet for each of the four basic areas of:

Things	People
Data	Ideas

2. On the first line of each sheet, write "Satisfying Skills," Beginning with *things,* think of and list all of the things you can do really well with physical materials and objects. Think, in particular, of skills that provide you with a deep sense of satisfaction when you exercise them.

    a. Figure 1 may be a helpful guide in suggesting ideas here.
    b. If you have already done "Lifelines" (exercise 45), look at the Lifelines you drew. The *peaks* of those lifelines can suggest ideas. Consider each peak in terms of:

       What particular skills, abilities, and talents was I using to get to this peak? What important satisfactions did I derive from using those skills?

    c. Other exercises or instruments in this volume may suggest areas of strengths (or weaknesses). Your instructor can probably suggest some if you need help.

3. When you have listed as many skills and abilities as you can think of for *things,* move on to the sheets labeled *people, data,* and *ideas.* Repeat the process until you feel you have listed all of your really important skills and abilities in each area.

Step 2

From your lists of "satisfying skills," which are the most important to you? On a fresh sheet of paper, make a list of your *five* most satisfying skills and abilities—those that you enjoy the most (be careful to retain the "things" "people," etc., labels).

Step 3

Do a or b, below.

   a. *For people who are not certain about their career interests:* What types of careers tend to require the exercise of your most important skills and abilities? Identify as many possibilities as you can before you select the alternative that seems to fit you best. (If you are not sure about some of the possibilities here, there are several ways to get more information. Most colleges and universities have place-ment and counseling centers that will be glad to discuss your interests with you. If you think certain vocations might be a good fit for you, talk to some people in these jobs—don't be afraid to call someone you don't even know. You might be surprised at how willing most people are to help. If you are really at a loss to think of anything, look up some jobs in the *Occupational Outlook Handbook* or *Dictionary of Occupational Titles* in the nearest library. Once you have identified some likely possibilities, check the card catalog for anything that may be written about these jobs.)

As you begin to develop some specific feasible alternatives, pick up any information you can about how people get into this line of work. What are the educational, training and experience requirements you are going to have to fulfill? Is there a practical way for you to meet these requirements? How? Prepare notes on your findings and conclusions. You will need them in Step 5.

You are now ready to establish a *tentative* career objective. The objective you set should have the characteristics shown in Figure 2.

When you have stated your career objective, go on to Step 4.

b. *For people who are satisfied with career choices already made:* Where do you want to go in your occupation or profession? What does it mean to you to "advance" in your field? Don't restrict yourself to thinking only in terms of traditional measures such as salary and organizational level. For purposes of this activity, define advancement as *moving into a new position or redesigning your present job so that it requires you to use even more of your most important and satisfying skills and abilities.* Prepare a statement of your career objective that fulfills the criteria in Figure 2.

FIGURE 2
Characteristics of a Good Career Objective

A good career objective is one that is:

Challenging: A good objective is one that you must stretch to achieve.

Realistic: While your objective should be challenging, it should also be one that you can realistically hope to achieve, given your strengths, weaknesses, needs, circumstances, values, problem solving styles, and so on.

Measurable and Concrete: Establish a time target for achieving your objective. Phrase the objective in specific terms; for example:

   Poor   I want to be an executive.
   Better I'd like to be a vice-president of personnel within five years.
   Best   I'd like to be vice-president of manufacturing of a medium sized (200 to 500 employees) storm door company within 12 years. The position must pay at least $50,000 per year, and the company must place emphasis on quality manufacturing. Possibilities include...

Long Term: Your objective should represent a major career goal or milestone for you. You will probably want to think at least 5 to 10 years into the future.

Relevant: Achieving your objective should be deeply satisfying because it fulfills your most central needs and requires the exercise of those talents and abilities you enjoy using most.

What would need to be done to make this possible? How can you initiate the process that will eventually have a high probability of achieving these changes? What additional experiences or training do you need? Are the opportunities available in you present organization? In other organizations? Prepare notes on your analysis for use in Step 5.

Step 4

Take the original four sheets ("Things," "Data," "People," "Ideas"). Turn them over and head up each sheet respectively: weaknesses/deficiencies—things, weaknesses/deficiencies—data, weaknesses/deficiencies—people, weaknesses/deficiencies—ideas. You are to use one heading on each sheet.[1]

Things I do poorly: These are things you don't do well, but for some reason you want to or have to do them. Don't list things you have no interest in doing or don't need to do.

Things I would like to stop doing: We all have things we'd like to stop doing. These may or may not be things you have a reason for doing.

Things I would like to learn to do well: These are things you must do well and/or things you want to do well.

Which of these deficiencies are most important *right now?* Which must you do something about first in order to begin moving toward the objective you set for yourself in Step 3? Select and rank-order the three most important on the piece of paper where you listed your five most satisfying skills and abilities.

Step 5

Prepare a brief written plan showing how you plan to move toward your career objective (from Step 3), and including your plans for dealing with the weaknesses that stand between you and your objective. (Charts and graphs may be the easiest way of capturing the elements of your plan. PERT, "Critical Path Method," Gantt charts, budgets or other planning devices are often useful here for those who are familiar with them. The Problem Analysis Diagram mentioned in Step 3 may be a useful diagnostic tool.)

Step 6

Form groups according to the Instructor's directions (if you are not already in a group).

Step 7: 10 Minutes per Person

Share your most important strengths and weaknesses, your statement of your objective, and your plan for achieving your objective with the other(s) in your group.

---

[1]These categories are from G. A. Ford and Gordon L. Lippitt, *A Life Planning Workbook for Guidance in Planning and Personal Goal Setting* (Fairfax, Va.: NTL Learning Resources Corporation, 1972).

As each person explains his/her inventory and plans, the other members of the group should:

Provide feedback—does the person seem to be aware of his/her most important strengths and weaknesses?

Offer any suggestions that seem warranted for improving his/her plans.

DISCUSSION QUESTIONS

1. How many individuals found their greatest strengths (weaknesses) in the area of Things? People? Data? Ideas?
2. Do your perceptions of your areas of strengths coincide with your perceptions of your problem solving style in terms of the Jungian types? Why?
3. What further steps would be useful in your career planning?

GENERALIZATIONS AND CONCLUSIONS

Concluding Points

1. Which is the better career planning strategy? Developing plans based on your strengths? Or developing plans aimed primarily at eliminating your deficiencies or weaknesses?

2. How frequently should you revise your career plans?

3. Is there any evidence that preparing career plans helps people to achieve their objectives?

4. Why might management want to provide a career planning service for employees?

Participant's Reactions

READINGS AND REFERENCES

See references listed at the end of the Introduction to Section 13.

47
THE AWFUL INTERVIEW

PURPOSE:
(1) To practice interviewing skills, especially in dealing with difficult interview questions frequently asked by interviewers.
(2) To sharpen your awareness of your strengths and weaknesses in interviewing for a job.

ADVANCE PREPARATION:
(1) Read "Improving Your Performance in the Employment Interview" and "Feedback: The Art of Giving and Receiving Help" in the Folio of Resources.
(2) Read the "Introduction," below, and think about some good questions that might be included in the list in Step 1. If you can't think of good, mind-boggling questions, ask friends who have some experience in job interviews.

GROUP SIZE: Trios or quartets.
TIME REQUIRED: $1\frac{1}{4}$ hours (trios), $1\frac{1}{2}$ hours (quartets).
SPECIAL MATERIALS: None.
SPECIAL PHYSICAL REQUIREMENTS: Trios (or quartets) will need small meeting rooms or an area suitable for holding conversations relatively free of distractions.
RELATED TOPICS: Interpersonal communication, Icebreakers.

INTRODUCTION

Employment interviews are frequently traumatic experiences; interviewers know what they are looking for, and you don't. They are prepared, and you are not. They are relaxed, and you are tense. The cards are all stacked in the interviewer's favor, it seems.

Interviewers are also notorious for asking disconcerting questions: "Tell me about your goals in life." Why do you want to work for International Widgets?" If you answered such questions candidly, but right off the top of your head, you might never get a job. ("My only goal is to get a job so I can begin to find out whether I really like it," or "I want to work for International Widgets because I don't have any other likely looking offers right now.") If you have been confronted with questions such as these, you will understand why we have titled this exercise, "The Awful Interview."

You don't have to let interviewers catch you by surprise. This exercise is based on the assumption that practice can help you prepare for interview situations. We will also assume that honesty really is the best policy. The job-hunter who concentrates on giving a prospective employer the impression that she or he is just the person wanted is employing a defensive strategy. You may become so preoccupied with

Developed by Donald D. Bowen.

projecting an "image" that you have little energy left for the real problem of showing the interviewer what careful thought you have given to planning your career.

PROCEDURE

Step 1: 15 Minutes
The entire group will develop a list of the *10 most awful questions* one can be asked in a job interview. An "awful" question is one that you would find threatening or difficult to answer honestly in a job interview. When the list is completed, write down the 10. You will need them in the remainder of the exercise.

List only questions that have actually been asked in all seriousness in job interviews you or somebody else has experienced.

Step 2: 5 Minutes
The group leader will specify whether the total group should break into smaller groups of threes or fours. Choose people with whom you will be comfortable, people who can be most helpful in providing useful feedback on your interviewing style. When the groups are formed, the group leader will tell you where you are to hold your small group meetings.

Step 3: 45 to 60 Minutes
Meet with your trio or quartet. Proceed as follows: One member volunteers to answer the first question; another is chosen to ask the question. Choosing a question from the list of the ten most awful, the interrogator asks the interviewee the first question. The interviewee must try to *answer the question as truthfully and honestly as he or she can.*

After the answer, other members of the group provide feedback to the interviewee on how they experienced the answer just given. (Remember the criteria for effective feedback emphasized in the Mill reading.)

Upon completion of the feedback, the interviewee becomes the interrogator, chooses a question and a new interviewee, and a new round begins. Continue taking turns until each person has answered at least three questions, or until you are instructed by the group leader to stop.

Step 4: 10 Minutes
Take 10 minutes and write a brief note to yourself covering the following (this note is for you—nobody else will see it): What questions did I handle well? What were my strengths? What questions did I handle poorly? What questions asked of others would give me problems? What can I do to deal more effectively with the questions that give me problems?

Step 5:
Reconvene with the entire group for discussion of the exercise.

DISCUSSION QUESTIONS

1. What did you learn during the exercise about how to answer interviewer's questions more effectively?
2. Do you think employment interviewers obtain valid data in the interview? Why?
3. If you were an interviewer, what kinds of questions would you ask?

GENERALIZATIONS AND CONCLUSIONS

Concluding Points

1. What do authorities in the field have to say about the validity of employment interviewing?

2. Why is the interview so widely employed as a selection device?

3. What steps can the interviewee take to ensure a more effective interview?

Participant's Reactions

READINGS AND REFERENCES

Kotter, J. P., Faux, V. A., and McArthur, C. C., *Self-Assessment and Career Development* (Englewood Cliffs, N.J.: Prentice-Hall, 1978), pp. 109–123.

Medley, H. A., *Sweaty Palms: The Neglected Art of Being Interviewed* (Belmont, Calif.: Life-time Learning Press, A Division of Wadsworth Publishing Co., 1978).

Miner, J. B., and Miner, M. G., *Personnel and Industrial Relations: A Managerial Approach,* 2nd ed. (New York: MacMillan, 1973), pp. 259–264, 273–294.

Schmitt, N., "Social and Situational Determinants of Interview Decisions: Implications for the Employment Interview," *Personnel Psychology,* 29 (1976), pp. 79–101.

Also see references to Reading 64, "Improving Your Performance in the Employment Interview."

48
MANAGING ROLE CONFLICT

PURPOSE:
(1) To understand role behavior.
(2) To analyze personal role conflicts.
(3) To diagnose one's personal role management style.
(4) To set objective(s) for improving one's role management style.

ADVANCE PREPARATION: None, unless assigned.
GROUP SIZE: Any number of pairs.
TIME REQUIRED: 50 to 60 minutes.
SPECIAL MATERIALS: None except pen or pencil.
SPECIAL PHYSICAL REQUIREMENTS: None.
RELATED TOPICS: Power, Interpersonal communication.

INTRODUCTION

One of the biggest problems facing working people, especially working couples and parents, is role conflict. As the number of roles we are expected to assume increases, so do the chances of conflict increase. The conflict is often accompanied by stress. In extreme cases, even health problems may occur. It is no wonder that both employers and employees are trying to reduce conflicts on the job and between job and personal demands. One way to reduce these conflicts is through managing our roles.

To understand the role management process (and thus get a handle on how to cope more effectively), we first need to understand how our role behavior is shaped. In other words, why do we behave as we do, giving too much attention to some demands, not enough to others, or exhausting ourselves to be everything to everyone?

A role consists of three parts: (1) the demands, expectations, responsibilities, and pressures that *other* people impose on us in any given role; (2) our own perceptions of what we think we ought to be doing in that role; and (3) our behavior—how we act, consciously or unconsciously. Our behavior is really shaped by the first two role components. We respond to two different sets or expectations–our own and those of others.

Managing role conflict involves managing these competing sets of expectations as well as our own behavior. Thus, there are really three approaches: we can attempt to change the expectations that other people hold for us (redefine our roles); we can

Developed by Francine S. Hall. "Role pie" based on activity originally developed in Barbara L. Forisha, *Sex Roles and Personal Awareness* (Morristown, N.J.: General Learning Press, 1978), pp. 198–199 and adapted by Donald D. Bowen. Parts of this exercise were adapted from Francine S. Hall and Douglas T. Hall, *The Two-Career Couple,* copyright © 1979, Addison-Wesley Publishing Co., Reading, Mass. Adaptation of Chapter 3, pages 75–79 and 104–106. Reprinted with permission.

change our own attitudes or expectations about what we "ought" to be doing (change our own orientation); or we can accept the various demands placed on us and find a way to meet all of them (reactive coping). The first two ways involve managing or redefining one's role. They are *proactive,* in the sense that we are *reshaping* the demands placed on us by others or by ourselves. The third way is really *passive coping*—trying to do or put up with everything.

How do you manage? How could you manage more effectively? The following Role Inventory can help you to evaluate your current strategies.

PROCEDURE

Step 1: 10 Minutes (Do This Working Alone)

On a sheet of paper, draw a large circle. After reflecting how you have spent your time in the preceding week, divide the circle as if it were a pie into sections representing the different roles in which you spend your time (include work, home, family, and all other roles). Each section should be proportionate in size to the amount of energy and time you invest in that particular activity. Labels might read student, employee, friend, husband, and so on.

Now, consider what sections of your role pie are most important to your sense of being "you"—to your identity. Number the sections from most important to the one of least interest. Let 1 be the section of greatest importance to you, 2 the one of next importance, and so on. Note that the numbers frequently do not correspond to the size of the sections.

If your most important roles or activities are not taking most of your time, consider why this is so. Is it owing to temporary conditions? Are you undervaluing some major activities or overvaluing minor ones? Are there any changes you would like to make in the way you spend your time? You can choose to make changes. What would be the consequences of change? Would you willingly accept the consequences?

Which of the sections in your role pie tend to contribute to role conflict or role overload for you? Identify these sections on your diagram.

Step 2: 15 Minutes

Turn to the "Role Management Inventory." Respond to the inventory in light of the conflicts and overloads you have identified (be candid; you are the only person who has anything to lose or gain from this activity). When you have answered all of the questions, score the inventory according to the instructions that follow the questionnaire. Which is your most important coping style(s)? Is this optimal for you?

ROLE MANAGEMENT INVENTORY*

How do you deal with these conflicts or issues? How often do you do each of the following?

	Nearly All the Time 5	Often 4	Some-times 3	Rarely 2	Never 1
1. Decide not to do certain activities that conflict with other activities.	___	___	___	___	___
2. Get help from someone outside the family (e.g., home maintenance help or child care).	___	___	___	___	___
3. Get help from a member of the family	___	___	___	___	___
4. Get help from someone at work.	___	___	___	___	___
5. Engage in problem solving with family members to resolve conflicts.	___	___	___	___	___
6. Engage in problem solving with someone at work.	___	___	___	___	___
7. Get moral support from a member of the family.	___	___	___	___	___
8. Get moral support from someone at work.	___	___	___	___	___
9. Integrate or combine roles (for example, involve family members in work activity or combine work and family in same way).	___	___	___	___	___
10. Attempt to change societal definition of sex roles, work roles, or family roles.	___	___	___	___	___

*Table and interpretation of scores reprinted from Francine S. Hall and Douglas T. Hall, *The Two-Career Couple*, copyright © 1979, Addison-Wesley Publishing Co., Reading, Mass., pages 76–79. Reprinted with permission.

	Nearly All the Time 5	Often 4	Some-times 3	Rarely 2	Never 1
11. Negotiate or plan with someone at work, so their expectations of you are more in line with your own needs or requirements.	____	____	____	____	____
12. Negotiate or plan with members of your family, so their expectations of you are more in line with your own needs or requirements.	____	____	____	____	____
13. Establish priorities among your different roles, so that you are sure the most important activities are done.	____	____	____	____	____
14. Partition and separate your roles. Devote full attention to each role when you are in it.	____	____	____	____	____
15. Overlook or relax certain standards for how you do certain activities. (Let less important things slide a bit sometimes, such as dusting and lawn care.)	____	____	____	____	____
16. Modify your attitudes toward certain roles or activities (e.g., coming to the conclusion that the *quality* of time spent with spouse or children is more important than the *quantity* of time spent).	____	____	____	____	____
17. Eliminate certain roles (e.g., deciding to stop working).	____	____	____	____	____
18. Rotate attention from one role to another. Handle each role in turn as it comes up.	____	____	____	____	____

	Nearly All the Time 5	Often 4	Some-times 3	Rarely 2	Never 1
19. Develop self and own interests (e.g., spend time on leisure or self-development).	____	____	____	____	____
20. Plan, schedule, and organize carefully.	____	____	____	____	____
21. Work hard to meet all role demands. Devote more time and energy, so you can do everything that is expected of you.	____	____	____	____	____
22. Do not attempt to cope with role demands and conflicts. Let role conflicts take care of themselves.	____	____	____	____	____

Scoring

- Add up the values you entered for items 1 to 12. Divide by 12. This is your *role-redefinition score:* ____
- Add up the values you entered for 13 to 17. Divide by 5. This is your *personal-reorientation score:* ____
- Add up the values you entered for 18 to 22. Divide by 5. This is your *reactive coping score:* ____

Interpreting Your Scores

These three scores give you some indication of the extent to which you use each of the three strategies. The scores can range from a *high* of 5 to a *low* of 1. If you *score over 3* on a scale, you score relatively high, meaning that you make frequent use of this coping strategy. A score of *less than 3*, indicates relatively infrequent use of this coping strategy. Here are some problems that may be indicated by your scores on the three scales:

Low Role-Redefinition Scores

You often let others place demands on you, often unrealistic demands. You need to negotiate with these people, your role senders, to make certain that the roles they impose on you are compatible with other responsibilities and interests. Some ways of doing this include:

- Simply agree with role senders that you will not be able to engage in certain activities. (For example, in our community, a hotbed of volunteerism, we are both known as "spot-jobbers." We will accept specific one-shot volunteer jobs, but we will not accept continuing positions.)

- Enlist assistance in role activities from other family members or from people outside the family (for example, cleaning or baby-sitting help).
- Sit down with role senders (boss, spouse, children) and discuss the problem. Together, work out an acceptable solution.
- Integrate conflicting careers by working with your spouse or working in related fields (so that the two careers become more like one). This method of coping has been described as "linking up."

If you can successfully reduce role conflicts by practicing some of these proactive negotiations, you will be stopping them at the source, and chances are you'll be very happy with the results—*you* will be managing the situation.

Low Personal-Reorientation Scores
Your problem is that you don't distinguish between the roles assigned to you: you lack a clear vision of what roles are truly important. You need to reevaluate your attitudes about various roles and take on only those heading the list. Some hints to help you achieve this are:

- Establish priorities. ("A child with a high fever takes precedence over school obligations. A child with sniffles does not. A very important social engagement—especially one that is business related—precedes tennis.")
- Divide and separate roles. Devote full attention to a given role when in it, and don't think about other roles. ("I leave my work at the office. Home is for the family and their needs.")
- Try to ignore or overlook less important role expectations ("The dusting can wait.")
- Rotate attention from one role to another as demands arise. Let one role slide a bit if another needs more attention at the time. ("Susan needs help now. I'll pay those bills later.")
- Remember that self-fulfillment and personal interests are a valid source of role demands. ("Piano and organ playing are a release for me while the children are small and need me at home.")

This style of coping means changing yourself rather than the family or work environment, although personal reorientation may be a necessary step to take before you can accomplish real role redefinition. Before you can change other people's expectations of you, you have to be clear about what you expect of yourself. Personal reorientation alone is not significantly related to satisfaction and happiness.

High Reactive Coping Scores
You try to take on every role that happens your way. You cope with conflict by working harder and sleeping less. Your style of coping includes:

- Planning, scheduling, and organizing better.
- Working harder to meet all role demands. (As one expert on women's roles and role conflict said in frustration, "After years of research, I've concluded that the only answer to a career and a family is to learn to get by on less sleep!")
- Using no conscious strategy. Let problems take care of themselves. This reactive behavior, in contrast to role redefinition, is a passive response to role conflict. Not surprisingly, people who use this style report very low levels of satisfaction and happiness (passive coping).

Reactive coping is not a very effective way of dealing with your roles. Rather than managing *them*, you are letting them manage *you*. If your goal is to eliminate conflict, then you need to reorient your own perceptions as a first step toward negotiating with others to restructure the roles in your life.

Step 3: 5 Minutes (And Do This One Working Alone, Too)

From the data you have developed in Steps 1 and 2, identify three changes you want to make in how you manage your life roles. Make these practical changes that you fully intend to implement in the immediate future. Are they changes to reduce role overload or conflict? Do they represent changes in priorities in your life? Do you need the help of someone else to implement them? Who? How do you plan to get it?

Change	Purpose	Will Seek Help From	Will Get Help By
1.			
2.			
3.			

Step 4: 20 Minutes

Find a partner with whom you would be willing to discuss the data you generated in Steps 1 to 3. Share your role diagrams, scores on the Role Management Inventory, and change plans. Help each other assess whether change roles are realistic, given priorities, past styles for managing roles, and personal styles.

GENERALIZATIONS AND CONCLUSIONS

1. What role management strategy is most effective in reducing stress?

2. What role management style is most commonly found?

3. What role management style is associated with the greatest satisfaction with career and family life?

READINGS AND REFERENCES

Bardwick, J., *The Plateauing Trap* (New York: AMACOM, 1986).

Hall, Douglas T., "A Model of Coping With Role Conflict: The Role Behavior of College Educated Women," *Administrative Science Quarterly*, December (1972), 471–485.

Hall, Francine, and Hall, Douglas T., *The Two Career Couple* (Reading, Mass.: Addison-Wesley, 1979).

FOLIO OF RESOURCES, READINGS, AND ASSESSMENT TECHNIQUES

49
NONDIRECTIVE INTERVIEWING

PURPOSE

Nondirective interviewing is particularly useful when the interviewer seeks to help the interviewee in defining a problem the interviewee faces. Hence, it is a basic counseling skill. Other applications include any situation where the interviewer wishes to gain information about a situation as seen from the interviewee's perspective, such as in diagnosis of subordinate's or of organizational problems.

DEFINITION

In the directive interview, the interview provides advice, facts, and a diagnosis to guide the interviewee. Since people often resist advice and being told what to do, the nondirective interview attempts to avoid placing the interviewer in the role of "expert." Rather, the focus is on conducting the interview so that the interviewer does not advise, counsel, direct, or interpret the interviewee's problem. The emphasis is on stimulating the interviewee to talk about the problem, surfacing the interviewee's feelings about the situation, and providing an environment where the interviewee can explore the problem and come up with his own solution—a solution that will be much more valid for the interviewee and that will have his commitment, simply because the interviewee feels real "ownership" for the solution developed.

Adapted from N. R. F. Maier, *Psychology in Industrial Organizations*, 4th ed. (Boston: Houghton-Mifflin, 1973), pp. 532–45, by Donald D. Bowen.

ASSUMPTIONS

Maier lists six essential attitudes that the nondirective interviewer needs:

1. A belief that the individual is basically responsible for himself, and that the interviewer should not assume this responsibility.
2. A belief that people are capable of solving problems and want to do the right thing.
3. Recognition that solution of a problem must conform to the individual's own values and beliefs, and that the individual knows his own feelings and goals better than anyone else.
4. The belief that people will express their true feelings and attitudes only in an accepting, permissive atmosphere.
5. Acceptance of the person as a worthy individual whose problems deserve attention, and acceptance of what the person says as important and of interest.
6. An appreciation and respect for feelings as essential elements of healthy psychological functioning:

FEATURES OF THE NONDIRECTIVE INTERVIEW

The nondirective interview requires the interviewer to use several specific skills:

1. Active Listening.

We all know that we should listen to the other person, but this is easier known than done. It requires more than merely remaining silent and forcing your mind not to wander. The active listener in the nondirective interview lets the other person know that he is involved and interested, yet refuses to become a supporter (which elicits dependency) or a judge (which generates defensiveness). The active listener adopts a body position and facial expression indicative of attention, accepts pauses in the conversation, and facilitates the interview with statements such as "Uh-huh...," "I see...," "I understand," "Do you want to tell me about that?"

If asked to express an opinion, the interviewer responds with "Why don't you tell me how you feel about that?"

2. Accepting Feelings.

Accepting the interviewee's feelings without either agreeing or disagreeing with them is crucial to the nondirective interview. The interviewee's feelings about the situation are usually the most important "facts" to be obtained in the interview. But the interviewee as well as the interviewer may need an opportunity to discover and sort out the feelings that affect the interviewee's behavior and attitudes. Acceptance of feelings is reflected in statements such as: "You really felt good about that, didn't you?" "It sounds like the conversation really made you mad." "I gather that you really miss the people you used to work with."

3. Reflecting Feelings.

In reflecting feelings, the interviewer contributes three elements to the interview: (1) he becomes a more active listener; (2) the interviewee is encouraged to remain in charge of the interview process; and (3) the interviewee is stimulated to explore the feelings further. Reflecting feelings involves restating the feelings of the interviewee. Restatements should not be in the form of questions that can be answered "yes" or "no." They should not be in the form of questions that probe for "facts" ("Where were you at 3:00 A.M. on the morning of the murder?"), or that question the interviewee's judgment or competence ("Why didn't you tell your boss about that?"). A reflecting statement takes the form of a declarative sentence in which the interviewer simply restates the feelings of the interviewee in the interviewer's own words; for example: "You often feel that your boss doesn't listen to you." "It makes you angry when your subordinates behave irresponsibly." "You are not sure what you want to do."

In reflecting feelings, you should reflect only feelings that have been expressed. If more than one feeling is expressed, reflect only the last one mentioned. Inconsistencies or ambivalences should not be criticized, but accepted, since they probably indicate progress in working through the problem.

50
FEEDBACK: THE ART OF GIVING AND RECEIVING HELP
Cyril R. Mill

Feedback is a way of helping another person to consider changing his behavior. It is communication to a person which gives him information about some aspect of his behavior and its effect on you. As in a guided missile system, feedback helps an individual know whether his behavior is having the effect that he wants; it tells him whether he is "on target" as he strives to achieve his goals.

CRITERIA FOR USEFUL FEEDBACK

The giving and receiving of feedback is a skill that can be acquired. When feedback is attempted at the wrong time or given in the wrong way the results will be, at best useless, and may be disastrous. Therefore, developing feedback skills can be important. Here are some criteria for useful feedback.

It is descriptive rather than evaluative. It is helpful to focus on what the individual *did* rather than to translate his behavior into a statement about what he *is*. "You have interrupted three people in the last half hour" is probably not something that a person really wants to hear, but it is likely to be more helpful than, "You are a bad-mannered oaf."

It focuses on the feelings generated in the person who has experienced the behavior and who is offering the feedback. "When you interrupt me I feel frustrated," gives the individual clear information about the *effect* of his behavior, while at the same time leaving him free to decide what he wants to do about that effect.

It is specific rather than general. For example, it is probably more useful to learn that you "talk too much" than to have someone describe you as "dominating."

It is directed toward behavior which the receiver can do something about. Frustration is increased when a person is reminded of some shortcoming over which he has no control.

It is solicited rather than imposed. Feedback is most useful when the receiver feels that he needs and wants it, when he himself has formulated the kind of question which those observing him can answer.

It is well-timed. In general, feedback is most useful at the earliest opportunity after the given behavior, depending, of course, on the receiver's readiness to hear it, support available from others, and so on.

It is checked to ensure clear communication. One way of doing this is to have the receiver try to rephrase the feedback in question to see whether the receiver's version corresponds with what the sender meant.

When feedback is given in a training group, both giver and receiver have opportunity to check its accuracy with others in the group. Thus the receiver will know whether this is one person's impression or an impression shared by others.

Feedback should not be given primarily to "dump" or "unload" on another. If you feel you *have* to say this to the other person, then ask yourself who it is you are trying to "help."

Feedback does not ask "Why?" It stays within the bounds of behavior and one's reactions to that behavior. To theorize about or ask why a person does a certain thing is to plumb the depths of motivation and, perhaps, of the unconscious. Avoiding the "whys" will help one to avoid the error of amateur psychologizing.

Given the premise that properly given feedback can be a fine way to learn about oneself, what are some reasons that we resist it? For one thing, it is hard to admit our difficulties to ourselves. It is even harder to admit them to someone else. We are not sure that the other person can be trusted or that his observations are valid. We may be afraid of learning what others think of us; we often expect to hear only negative opinions about ourselves, tending to overlook our positive qualities.

We may have struggled so hard to make ourselves independent that the thought of depending on another individual seems to violate something within us. Or we may during all our lives have looked for someone on whom to depend, and we try to repeat this pattern in our relationship with the helping person.

We may be looking for sympathy and support rather than for help in seeing our difficulty more clearly. When the helper tries to point out some of the ways *we* are contributing to the problem, which might suggest that we as well as others will have to change, we may stop listening. Solving a problem may mean uncovering some of the sides of ourselves which we have avoided or wished to avoid thinking about.

We may feel our problem is so unique no one could ever understand it and certainly not an outsider.

On the other side of the interchange, it is not always easy to give feedback to others. Most of us like to give advice. Doing so suggests that we are competent and important. We get caught up in a "telling" role easily enough without testing whether our advice is appropriate to the total issue, or to the abilities, the fears, or powers of the person we are trying to help.

If the person whom we are trying to help becomes defensive, we may try to argue or pressure him. Defensiveness or denial on the part of the receiver is a clear indication that we are going about trying to be helpful in the wrong way. Our timing is off or we may be simply mistaken about his behavior, but in any case, it is best to desist until we can reevaluate the situation. If we respond to the receiver's resistance with more pressure, resistance will only increase.

To be fruitful, the helping situation needs these characteristics:

1. Mutual trust.
2. Perceiving the helping situation as a joint exploration.
3. Careful listening, with the helper listening more than the individual receiving help.

4. Behavior from the helper which will make it easier for the receiver of help to talk.

Feedback takes into account the needs of both the receiver and the giver. Positive feedback is welcomed by the receiver when it is genuine. If feedback is given in a training laboratory under the conditions described here, it can become one of the primary means of learning about self.

51
COGNITIVE STYLE
IN LEARNING AND PROBLEM SOLVING
John W. Slocum, Jr.

Carl Gustav Jung (pronounced "Yoong"), upon whose ideas the following reading is based, was one of Freud's most distinguished pupils. Like most of Freud's protégés, Jung eventually broke with Freud and began developing his own theory of human personality. In one part of his theory, he discusses personality types based upon four bipolar dimensions of personality (i.e., extroversion-introversion, perceiving-judging, sensation-intuition, and thinking-feeling). A number of management writers have found the latter two dimensions highly useful in understanding how people learn, communicate, solve problems, and make decisions in organizations.—Ed.

Our model is based on the dual premise that consistent modes of thought develop through training and experience and that these modes can be classified along two dimensions, information gathering and information evaluation, as shown in Figure 1.

Information gathering essentially relates to the perceptual process by which the mind organizes the diffuse verbal and nonverbal stimuli it encounters. The resultant "information" is the outcome of a complex coding that is heavily dependent on the individual's mental set. Of necessity, information gathering involves rejecting some of the data encountered in the environment and summarizing and categorizing the rest. According to Jung (1953), individuals can take in data from their environment by either sensation or intuition; most individuals tend to have a primary style. Sensing types typically take in information via their senses and are most comfortable when attending to details—the specifics of the situation. These individuals tend to break down the information into small "bits" that contain hard facts pertaining to the situation. In contrast, intuitive types typically take in information by looking at the whole situation. They bring to bear concepts to filter data, focus on relationships between items, and look for deviations from or conformities with their expectations. These types tend to concentrate on hypothetical possibilities of the situation rather than hard facts and details.

Each mode of information gathering has its advantages. The sensing type of change agent may overlook the problems inherent in a failure to shape the client organization's problem into a coherent whole. He or she can develop a procedure that utilizes personal experiences and economizes on effort. The intuitive change agent might ignore the relevant detail that can establish bench marks for the organization. The intuitive person, however, is better able to approach a client system with an ill-structured problem for which the volume of data, the criteria for solution, or the

Excerpted from: John E. Jones and J. William Pfeiffer (Eds.), Group & Organization Studies, Vol. III, No. 2, San Diego, CA: University Associates, June 1978. Used with permission.

FIGURE 1
Model of Personal Style

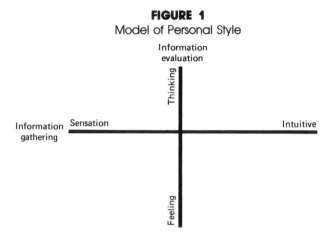

nature of the problem itself does not allow a "scientific" mode of inquiry. Jung maintained that individuals perceive a situation in a set way and, in fact, cannot apply both types of information gathering techniques simultaneously.

Information evaluation refers to processes commonly used in reaching a decision about a problem. Jung (1953) posited that there are two basic ways of reaching a decision: thinking and feeling. Thinking persons tend to approach a problem by structuring it in terms of the scientific method, which leads to a feasible solution. They do not feel comfortable unless a logical or an analytical basis for their decision making can be used. They can take two situations that are inherently different and seek to find ways in which they are similar. Feeling types, on the other hand, make decisions based on extremely personal considerations, for example, how they feel about the situation, the person, the value of the situation, etc. Feeling types want to personalize every situation by stressing individual uniqueness.

The four styles and their characteristics are summarized in Figure 2. Combining these information-gathering modes (sensation and intuition) with the two information-evaluation modes (thinking and feeling) in all possible ways allows us to talk about the following four personal styles: sensation-thinkers (STs); sensation-feelers (SFs); intuitive-thinkers (NTs); and intuitive-feelers (NFs). In each case, the manager was asked to describe his/her ideal organization by writing a story about that organization. According to Mitroff and Kilmann (1975) and Hellriegel and Slocum (1976), this approach is useful because managers are able to share different stories in an atmosphere of trust and freedom without the fear of ridicule.

SENSATION-THINKERS

ST individuals emphasize and concentrate on specifics and factual details. They are sensitive to the physical features of their work environments, e.g., hot or cold, dark or light. The building should be conducive to good work, and the equipment should be maintained. The ideal organization is one in which everybody knows exactly what his or her job requires and the details are set forth in a manual of rules and regulations.

FIGURE 2

Characteristics of Personal Styles

INFORMATION GATHERING[A]

Intuitives	*Sensing Types*
Like solving new problems	Dislike new problems unless there are standard ways to solve them.
Dislike doing the same thing over and over again.	Like an established routine.
Enjoy learning a new skill more than using it.	Enjoy using skills already learned more than learning new ones.
Work in bursts of energy powered by enthusiasm, with slack periods in between.	Work more steadily, with realistic idea of how long it will take.
Jump to conclusions frequently.	Must usually work all the way through to reach a conclusion.
Are patient with complicated situations.	Are impatient when the details are complicated.
Are impatient with routine details.	Are patient with routine details.
Follow inspirations, good or bad.	Rarely trust inspirations, and don't usually feel inspired.
Often tend to make errors of fact.	Seldom make errors of fact.
Dislike taking time for precision.	Tend to be good at precise work.

INFORMATION EVALUATION

Feeling Types	*Thinking Types*
Tend to be very aware of other people and their feelings.	Are relatively unemotional and uninterested in people's feelings.
Enjoy pleasing people, even in unimportant things.	May hurt people's feelings without knowing it.
Like harmony. Efficiency may be badly disturbed by office feuds.	Like analysis and putting things into logical order. Can get along without harmony.
Often let decision be influenced by their own or other peoples' personal likes and wishes.	Tend to decide impersonally, sometimes ignoring people's wishes.
Need occasional praise.	Need to be treated fairly.
Dislike telling people unpleasant things.	Are able to reprimand people or fire them when necessary.
Relate well to most people.	Tend to relate well only to other thinking types.
Tend to be sympathetic.	May seem hard-hearted.

[a]Jung, 1953.

Information flows more readily downward than upward or in lateral directions. Subordinates are judged on the basis of their technical ability to do their job, and if they are not suited for the job, they are urged to transfer to another position in the organization. Each person should receive adequate training for his or her job to ensure uniformity in the application of rules and regulations. The ST individual emphasizes impersonal rather than personal factors, is more authoritarian than democratic, sets realistic as opposed to nebulous goals, and likes a well-defined organizational hierarchy as opposed to a vague and unstructured pattern. In brief, the goals of an ST organization are realistic, down-to-earth, limited, and most often narrowly economic. STs like organizations characterized by high control, certainty, and specificity.

INTUITIVE-THINKERS

NTs are attracted to ill-defined and abstract work situations. They tend to focus on general concepts and issues, as opposed to detailed work rules and hierarchical lines of authority. The goals of the organization should be developed in response to the interrelation between environmental- and member-generated factors such as clean air, water pollution, equal employment, etc. The structure of the organization encourages constant feedback and provides its own goals, controls, divisions of labor, and motivation and reward structures. The NT individual is more idealistic than realistic, more concerned with the intellectual and theoretical concepts of organizations in general than with efficiency, and has a tendency to avoid details of any particular work situation. In brief, NT organizations are impersonally idealistic.

INTUITIVE-FEELERS

NFs usually show an aversion toward paying attention to specifics and usually are preoccupied with broad, global themes and issues such as "making a contribution to mankind." They assert that the organization's main purpose is to serve the personal and social needs of people. The ideal organization for an NF is one that is completely decentralized, with no clear lines of authority, no central leader, and no fixed, prescribed rules of behavior. NFs regularly refer to flexibility and decentralization and are also concerned with the long-term goal orientation of the organization.

SENSATION-FEELERS

SFs are concerned with the detailed human relations in their particular organization and/or department. These individuals are realistic in the design of their organizations, with a major emphasis on the interpersonal environment that is created by the rules and regulations of the organization. The SF designs the organization with its hierarchy and rules for the benefit of the members, e.g., to promote the satisfaction of their needs, to openly communicate with one another, etc.

REFERENCES AND SUGGESTED FURTHER READINGS

Berne, E., *Transactional Analysis in Psychotherapy* (New York: Grove Press, 1961).

Hellriegel, D., and Slocum, J., *Organizational Behavior: Contingency Approaches* (St. Paul, Minn.: West, 1976).

Huse, E., *Organizational Development and Change* (St. Paul, Minn.: West, 1975).

Jung, C., *Collected Works* Vols. 7, 8, 9, Part 1. H. Read, M. Fordham, and G. Adler (Eds.) (Princeton, N.J.: Princeton University Press, 1953).

Kilmann, R., and Taylor, V. A., "Contingency Approach to Laboratory Learning: Psychological Types vs. Learning Norms," *Human Relations,* 27, (1974), 891–909.

Luthans, F., and Kreitner, R., *Behavior Modification* (Glenview, Ill.: Scott Foresman, 1975).

Mitroff, I., and Kilmann, R. "Stories Managers Tell: A New Tool for Organizational Problem-Solving," *Management Review,* 64 (1975), 18–28.

Tichy, N., "Agents of Planned Social Change: Congruence of Values, Cognitions, and Actions," *Administrative Science Quarterly,* 19 (1974), 164–182.

Tichy, N., "How Different Types of Change Agents Diagnose Organizations, *Human Relations,* 28 (1975), 771–799.

Tichy, N., and Nisberg, J., "Change Agent Bias: What They View Determines What They Do," *Group & Organization Studies,* 1(3)(1976), 286–301.

52
OBSERVING AND RATING
GROUP EFFECTIVENESS

The purpose of this activity is to provide a framework for observing and evaluating the effectiveness of decision-making and problem-solving groups. One part provides 11 categories in which observed group-member behavior can be noted and classified. A second part provides a series of rating scales on which the same general categories of group behavior can be evaluated. Examples are given.

Your instructor may ask you to use these observation-and-rating scales to judge your own group or one to which you belong. If you have any questions about the categories or rating scales, please ask your instructor. Once you have completed your observations or ratings, your instructor will tell you how this information will be shared with others.

OBSERVATIONAL CATEGORIES

Criteria	*Behaviors that I observed*

Goals
  Stated?
  Clarified?
  Shared by all?
  Interest?
  Shared commitment?	

Problem Diagnosis
  Systematic diagnosis?
  Symptoms separated from causes?
  Jumping to solutions?	

Decisions
  Decisions made?
  Made by one or two members or
    whole group?
  Level of commitment to solution?	

Participation
  Who talks? How much?
  Participation by all or just a few?
  Who says least?	

OBSERVATIONAL CATEGORIES

Criteria	*Behaviors that I observed*

Listening
  People attentive?
  A lot of competition for "airtime"?
  People often interrupted, cut off?
  People ask for clarification or pursue
    ideas systematically?

Feelings
  Feelings expressed?
  Expression of feelings supported and
    encouraged?
  People considerate of others' feel-
    ings, empathy actively shown?

Influence
  Who influences others most? Least?
    Why?
  How many people have influence?
    When?
  Influence related to the task of the
    group?

Leadership
  Who is the "leader"? Appointed?
    Elected? "Self-chosen"?
  What does leader do to control/
    manage the group?
  Does leader overcontrol or undercon-
    trol the group? How?

Conflict
  Does conflict occur? When?
  Is conflict avoided, minimized or left?
  Is conflict openly expressed and left
    unresolved?
  How do people handle emotions
    (anger, difference of opinion, dis-
    like)?

OBSERVATIONAL CATEGORIES

Criteria	Behaviors that I observed
Trust Do people trust each other? Are people overly polite or "careful" about what they say? Are people defensive? Is criticism of other people or ideas avoided? *Creativity* Are people disinterested in the group and its work? Are new ideas or approaches to problems encouraged and tried? Is there a fixed routine or pattern of work that seems to be inhibiting the group?	

RATING GROUP EFFECTIVENESS

1. *Goals*

1	2	3	4	5	6	7
Poor						Good

Unstated; confused; conflicting; ambiguous; generate little interest

Clear to all; shared by all; all care about goals, committed to them

2. *Diagnosis of Group Problems*

1	2	3	4	5	6	7
Poor						Good

No systematic identification of causes; treat symptoms of problem rather than causes; jump to solutions before adequate diagnosis

Careful and systematic diagnosis; solutions flow directly from diagnosis; remedies attack basic causes

3. *Decisions*

1	2	3	4	5	6	7

Poor   *Good*

Decisions don't get made; decision made by one or two members, or subgroup; low overall commitment to solution

Consensus sought and tested; different ideas integrated into group solution; high overall commitment to solution

4. *Participation*

1	2	3	4	5	6	7

Poor   *Good*

A few carry the discussion; many people passive

All participate; all are involved and actively contribute to group effort

5. *Listening*

1	2	3	4	5	6	7

Poor   *Good*

No listening; a lot of competition to speak; several talk at once or are interrupted; comments and ideas frequently repeated

People are attentive; ask for clarification or elaboration of ideas; communication is effective

6. *Feelings*

1	2	3	4	5	6	7

Poor   *Good*

Unexpressed; expression of feelings discouraged, ignored, or criticized; emotions "bottled up"

Freely expressed; empathy and consideration shown; feelings are considered important "data" for group effectiveness

7. Influence

1	2	3	4	5	6	7
Poor						Good

One or two people dominate; others cut off from influence; means of influence unrelated to group task or goals

Influence shared; many people have input; influence widely distributed; conviction in one's perspective seen as a virtue

8. Leadership

1	2	3	4	5	6	7
Poor						Good

Group needs for a leader not met; either group depends too much on one or two people, or there is a leadership "vacuum"

Leader performs well; leadership role changes in group as different leadership needs become important

9. Conflict

1	2	3	4	5	6	7
Poor						Good

Avoided, minimized, or smoothed over; or open disagreements become angry exchanges that are left unresolved

Differences openly expressed and acknowledged; people willingly confront differences; mutually satisfactory resolution is actively sought

10. Trust

1	2	3	4	5	6	7
Poor						Good

Members distrust one another; are polite, careful, guarded; defensiveness; afraid to criticize others or be criticized themselves

Members trust one another; willing to take risks and reveal sensitive information; candor encouraged; negative reactions can be expressed without fear of reprisal

11. *Creativity and Growth*

1	2	3	4	5	6	7
Poor						*Good*

Members and group in a rut; operate routinely; people and group are rigid in roles, stereotype one another; no progress, new ideas, or new approaches

Group flexible; seeks new and better ways to operate or resolve problems; innovation and experimentation encouraged; new ideas and approaches actively tried

53
ROLES NOMINATION FORM

There are many roles people perform in groups. Some of these relate to helping the group perform its tasks. Others relate to maintaining the group and relationships among members. Finally, there are dysfunctional roles that may hinder the group; behavior is directed toward personal rather than group needs.

Below is a list and a brief description of different roles and functions performed in groups. Read each description and choose one person in the group who fits this description. In other words, based on your perceptions of the group, who performs each function or role? A person may be nominated for more than one role and you may nominate yourself.

At the same time, assess your own behavior in relation to the role description. Use a scale from 1 ("I rarely or never perform this function") to 5 ("I perform this function a great deal or most of the time").

GROUP TASK ROLES   *Nomination*   *Self-Rating*

1. *Initiator/Contributor:* Proposes goals, ideas, solutions; defines problems; suggests procedures.

2. *Information Giver:* Offers facts and relevant information or experience.

3. *Opinion Giver:* States belief about alternatives; focuses on values rather than facts.

4. *Information and Opinion Seeker:* Asks for clarification and suggestions; looks for facts and feelings; solicits ideas and values of other members.

5. *Coordinator/Summarizer:* Pulls ideas, opinions, and suggestions together; summarizes and restates; may try to draw members' activities together; offers conclusions.

6. *Clarifier/Elaborator:* Interprets; gives examples; defines terms; clears up confusion or ambiguity.

7. *Evaluator:* Helps group assess whether it has consensus or is reaching conclusion.

Adapted by Francine S. Hall from K. D. Benne, and P. Sheats, "Functional Roles and Group Members," *Journal of Social Issues* 4 (1948).

GROUP MAINTENANCE ROLES   *Nomination*   *Self-Rating*

8. *Encourager:* Supportive of others; praises efforts and ideas; accepts contributions.
9. *Harmonizer:* Tries to reduce conflict and tension; attempts to reconcile differences.
10. *Gatekeeper/Expediter:* Keeps communication open to all members; opens up opportunities for others to communicate and participate.
11. *Standard Setter:* Expresses standard for group to use; testing procedures; reminds group of its norms.
12. *Follower:* Goes along with group; accepts ideas of others; willing to compromise for the sake of the group.

DYSFUNCTIONAL, SELF-ORIENTED ROLES

13. *Blocker:* Interferes with group progress by getting discussion off on a tangent; focuses on personal concerns rather than group problem; argues too much; resists or disagrees beyond reasonable point.
14. *Recognition Seeker:* Tries to get attention; calls attention to self; boasts; loud or unusual behavior; excessive talker.
15. *Dominator:* Tries to control group at expense of other members.
16. *Avoider:* Acts indifferent; withdraws from discussion; daydreams; wanders off; talks to others; fools around.

OVERALL LEADERSHIP ROLES

17. *Task Leader:* Person whose behavior contributed the most to accomplishing work of the group.
18. *Social (Maintenance) Leader:* Person whose behavior contributed most to building and maintaining group relationships.
19. *Self-Oriented Leader:* Person whose behavior was directed toward meeting his/her own needs; hindered or ignored group needs.

54
SOCIOGRAM

A sociogram is a way to measure patterns of interaction, influence, activity, and so on within a group. The sociogram is based on people's perceptions of each other in terms of such things as productivity, influence, liking, and so on. Each person in the group must make a choice among the other group members in response to key questions. Choices are tallied to determine who is perceived as most and least influential, productive, and the like.

To prepare your group sociogram, first answer questions 1 through 3 below *by yourself.* Then prepare the sociograms *as a group* according to the directions (question 4 below). Finally, compute the choice ratios according to the directions (question 5 below). You will want to take some time to discuss your data after you have completed the choice ratios.

You will need a sheet of paper for each sociogram. Label the first sheet "Influence," the second sheet "Contributions," and the third sheet "Liking." On *each* sheet, draw as many circles as there are group members. Label each circle with the name of one group member. Include yourself.

To develop the "Influence" sociogram, each group member should take a turn reporting the name of the person he selected. As names are reported, draw a line with an arrow (symbols illustrated in question 4 below) to indicate the choices among group members. When everyone has reported his choice, you will have a sociogram. Repeat this process for "Contributions," and "Liking."

The information requested in questions 1 to 3 will be used by you and other group members to study the structure of your group. Only your own group's members and the group leader will see the data.

1. Who is the most influential member of your group? (Do not include yourself.)

2. What group members contribute more than their share to getting the job done? (Do not include yourself. List as many or as few as necessary.)

3. Give the names of the people in your group whose company you most enjoy. (Exclude yourself. List as many or as few as necessary.)

The basic sociogram design for charting group dynamics has been adapted for this exercise by Donald D. Bowen and Francine S. Hall.

FIGURE 1

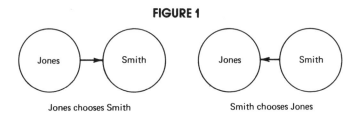

Jones chooses Smith   Smith chooses Jones

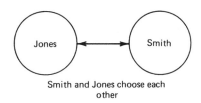

Smith and Jones choose each
other

4. Prepare three group sociograms using this data. The primary symbols to be used are shown in Figure 1.

5. To compute choice ratios for each group member, write the names of your group members under the headings below.

Name   *Influence Ratio*   *Contributions Ratio*   *Liking Ratio*

Using the "Influence sociogram you constructed, compute a choice ratio for each group member as follows:

1. Add the number of times the person was chosen, and divide by the number of possible choices. (Since a person could not choose himself, the number of possible choices should equal one less than the number of group members.)
2. Enter the numerical value for each person's choice ratio next to the person's name above under the "Influence" column.

Repeat the procedure for "Contributions" and "Liking." The larger the choice ratio the more often the person was chosen.

55
HOW CREATIVE ARE YOU?*

By Eugene Raudsepp

President Princeton Creative Research, Inc., Princeton, New Jersey

In recent years, several task-oriented tests have been developed to measure creative abilities and behavior. While certainly useful, they do not adequately lap the complex network of behaviors, the particular personality traits, attitudes, motivations, values, interests and other variables that predispose a person to think creatively.

To arrive at assessment measures that would cover a broader range of creative attributes, our organization developed an inventory type of test. A partial version of this instrument is featured below.

After each statement, indicate with a letter the degree or extent with which you agree or disagree with it: A = strongly agree, B = agree, C = in between or don't know, D = disagree, E = strongly disagree. Mark your answers as accurately and frankly as possible. Try not to "second guess" how a creative person might respond to each statement.

1. I always work with a great deal of certainty that I'm following the correct procedures for solving a particular problem. _____
2. It would be a waste of time for me to ask questions if I had no hope of obtaining answers. _____
3. I feel that a logical step-by-step method is best for solving problems. _____
4. I occasionally voice opinions in groups that seem to turn some people off. _____
5. I spend a great deal of time thinking about what others think of me. _____
6. I feel that I may have a special contribution to give to the world. _____
7. It is more important for me to do what I believe to be right than to try to win the approval of others. _____
8. People who seem unsure and uncertain about things lose my respect. _____
9. I am able to stick with difficult problems over extended periods of time. _____
10. On occasion I get overly enthusiastic about things. _____
11. I often get my best ideas when doing nothing in particular. _____
12. I rely on intuitive hunches and the feeling of "rightness" or "wrongness" when moving toward the solution of a problem. _____
13. When problem solving, I work faster analyzing the problem and slower when synthesizing the information I've gathered. _____
14. I like hobbies which involve collecting things. _____

15. Daydreaming has provided the impetus for many of my more important projects. _____
16. If I had to choose from two occupations other than the one I now have, I would rather be a physician than an explorer. _____
17. I can get along more easily with people if they belong to about the same social and business class as myself. _____
18. I have a high degree of aesthetic sensitivity. _____
19. Intuitive hunches are unreliable guides in problem solving. _____
20. I am much more interested in coming up with new ideas than I am in trying to sell them to others. _____
21. I tend to avoid situations in which I might feel inferior. _____
22. In evaluating information, the source of it is more important to me than the content. _____
23. I like people who follow the rule "business before pleasure." _____
24. One's own self-respect is much more important than the respect of others. _____
25. I feel that people who strive for perfection are unwise. _____
26. I like work in which I must influence others. _____
27. It is important for me to have a place for everything and everything in its place. _____
28. People who are willing to entertain "crackpot" ideas are impractical. _____
29. I rather enjoy fooling around with new ideas, even if there is no practical payoff. _____
30. When a certain approach to a problem doesn't work, I can quickly reorient my thinking. _____
31. I don't like to ask questions that show ignorance. _____
32. I am able to more easily change my interests, to pursue a job or career, than I can change a job to pursue my interests. _____
33. Inability to solve a problem is frequently due to asking the wrong questions. _____
34. I can frequently anticipate the solution to my problems. _____
35. It is a waste of time to analyze one's failures. _____
36. Only fuzzy thinkers resort to metaphors and analogies. _____
37. At times I have so enjoyed the ingenuity of a crook that I hoped he or she would go scotfree. _____
38. I frequently begin work on a problem which I can only dimly sense and not yet express. _____
39. I frequently tend to forget things such as names of people, streets, highways, small towns, etc. _____
40. I feel that hard work is the basic factor in success. _____
41. To be regarded as a good team member is important to me. _____
42. I know how to keep my inner impulses in check. _____
43. I am a thoroughly dependable and responsible person. _____
44. I resent things being uncertain and unpredictable. _____

45. I prefer to work with others in a team effort rather than solo. _____
46. The trouble with many people is that they take things too seriously. _____
47. I am frequently haunted by my problems and cannot let go of them. _____
48. I can easily give up immediate gain or comfort to reach the goals I have set. _____
49. If I were a college professor, I would rather teach factual courses than those involving theory. _____
50. I'm attracted to the mystery of life. _____

Scoring instructions. To compute your percentage score, circle and add up the values assigned to each item:

	Strongly agree	Agree	In-between or don't know	Disagree	Strongly disagree
	A	B	C	D	E
1.	−2	−1	0	+1	+2
2.	−2	−1	0	+1	+2
3.	−2	−1	0	+1	+2
4.	+2	+1	0	−1	−2
5.	−2	−1	0	+1	+2
6.	+2	+1	0	−1	−2
7.	+2	+1	0	−1	−2
8.	−2	−1	0	+1	+2
9.	+2	+1	0	−1	−2
10.	+2	+1	0	−1	−2
11.	+2	+1	0	−1	−2
12.	+2	+1	0	−1	−2
13.	−2	−1	0	+1	+2
14.	−2	−1	0	+1	+2
15.	+2	+1	0	−1	−1
16.	−2	−1	0	+1	+2
17.	−2	−1	0	+1	+2
18.	+2	+1	0	−1	−2
19.	−2	−1	0	+1	+2
20.	+2	+1	0	−1	−2
21.	−2	−1	0	+1	+2
22.	−2	−1	0	+1	+2
23.	−2	−1	0	+1	+2
24.	+2	+1	0	−1	−2
25.	−2	−1	0	+1	+1
26.	−2	−1	0	+1	+2
27.	−2	−1	0	+1	+2
28.	−2	−1	0	+1	+2
29.	+2	+1	0	−1	−2

	Strongly agree	Agree	In-between or don't know	Disagree	Strongly disagree
	A	B	C	D	E
30.	+2	+1	0	−1	−2
31.	−2	−1	0	+1	+2
32.	−2	−1	0	+1	+2
33.	+2	+1	0	−1	−2
34.	+2	+1	0	−1	−2
35.	−2	−1	0	+1	+2
36.	−2	−1	0	+1	+2
37.	+2	+1	0	−1	−2
38.	+2	+1	0	−1	−2
39.	+2	+1	0	−1	−2
40.	+2	+1	0	−1	−2
41.	−2	−1	0	+1	+2
42.	−2	−1	0	+1	+2
43.	−2	−1	0	+1	+2
44.	−2	−1	0	+1	+2
45.	−2	−1	0	+1	+2
46.	+2	+1	0	−1	−2
47.	+2	+1	0	−1	−2
48.	+2	+1	0	−1	−2
49.	−2	−1	0	+1	+2
50.	+2	+1	0	−1	−2
Totals	____	____	____	____	____
Add	____ +	____		+ ____ +	____ =

Total Score _____

80 to 100	Very creative
60 to 79	Above average
40 to 59	Average
20 to 39	Below average
−100 to 19	Noncreative

Further information about the test "How Creative Are You?" is available from Princeton Creative Research, Inc., 10 Nassau St., P.O. Box 122, Princeton, NJ 08540.

56
MANAGEMENT BY OBJECTIVES

PURPOSE:
(1) To understand what "management by objectives" is and how it works in an organization.
(2) To learn to write objectives that are: (a) clear, (b) acceptable to you and to your superior, and (c) useful in a performance appraisal.

ADVANCE PREPARATION: Read "Introduction to Management by Objectives," below. Your instructor will have assigned you a role. After you have read the introduction complete Steps 1 and 2. Step 2 will require you to assume your role (boss/subordinate) as assigned.
GROUP SIZE: Any number of two-person groups.
TIME REQUIRED: 50 to 60 minutes in class, approximately 1 hour preparation.
SPECIAL MATERIALS: Chalk board or newsprint helpful.
SPECIAL PHYSICAL REQUIREMENTS: Movable chairs.
RELATED TOPICS: Managers as leaders, Applied motivation and job design, Life, work and career roles, Motivation: basic concepts, Interpersonal communication.

INTRODUCTION TO MANAGEMENT BY OBJECTIVES

Management by Objective (MBO) is both a management "technique" and process that has become increasingly popular in organizations. The reasons for its popularity are: (1) it is "results"-oriented—designed to produce tangible outcomes; (2) it follows a natural cycle, beginning with planning and following through production and performance evaluation; (3) it can be used at any or all levels in the organization and with all categories of employees; (4) it is relatively simple and inexpensive, depending only on the resources of managers and their employees (once trained).

What is MBO? Very simply, MBO is the use of stated, written performance objectives, developed by involving subordinates to achieve goals of the organization. In theory, MBO helps an organization in at least four ways. First, it *develops commitment* to the goals and objectives of the organization. Second, it helps to *motivate* people to achieve these. Third, it helps to keep people focused on producing results. In this sense it *guides activities* and program development. Finally, MBO *ensures a measure of performance*. Results are evaluated against the outcomes stated in the objective.

How does MBO actually work? It works both from the "top down" and the "bottom

Developed and written by Francine S. Hall, who is grateful to colleagues at Western Michigan University and the U.S. Military Academy, West Point, for materials shared.

up." To be effective, both the superior and the subordinate at each level at which MBO is used must be involved. Typically, the superior will have a set of objectives for the unit under his domain. If the entire organization or several levels are using MBO, then he/she will have set these objectives in accordance with prior negotiation with a superior at the next higher level. Next, the objectives for the unit are shared with subordinates. Each subordinate then drafts a set of objectives for his/her own area of responsibility. Typically, the superior will have certain expectations for each subordinate. At a convenient time, the two meet and discuss the subordinate's objectives until both agree that they are acceptable and can establish a method for measuring performance.

Usually, the superior and subordinate will meet periodically to review progress in achieving objectives. This is essential since conditions may change and objectives may need to be revised or simply rejected as currently inappropriate. At the end of the performance cycle (the deadline for accomplishing the objective), the superior and subordinate will again meet to review performance against the standards established in the objectives. At this point, a new MBO cycle may begin.

Up to this point, we have discussed MBO mainly in terms of performance objectives. In fact, MBO may include a range of objectives and usually does. These may include: (1) innovative objectives—new things you will do; (2) problem solving objectives—problems you will reduce or eliminate; (3) routine objectives—on-going responsibilities; and (4) personal growth objectives—career and development outcomes you wish to achieve.

Regardless of the type of objectives to which you and your boss agree (given the context of your job description and organization's goals), you should also consider the priorities assigned to objectives. Typically, they will fall into one of three categories. *Essential* objectives are those upon which success or failure of an assignment or responsibility rests. They are critical to meeting higher-level objectives in the organization. *Beneficial* objectives are necessary for improved performance in meeting the organization's or unit's goals. Finally, *nice to do* objectives are desirable, but if necessary could be postponed.

Guidelines

Regardless of the types of objectives you may find yourself developing (and their priority), it is important to learn to write meaningful objectives. The following guidelines will help you formulate objectives in your own position. Although every objective may not necessarily conform to all of these criteria, it is recommended that objectives be checked against each criterion. Only when a conscious decision had been made that a specific guideline does not apply should it be bypassed as a factor in validating a particular objective. Guidelines for writing objectives are:

1. *It should start with the word "to" followed by an action verb.* The achievement of a particular objective should come as a result of some sort of action.

Consequently, the commitment to action is basic to the formulation of an objective.

2. *It should specify a single key result to be accomplished.* In order for a particular objective to be effectively measured, each ratee and rater should have a clear picture of when it has or has not been accomplished. Therefore, a single key result should be identified in each performance objective.

3. *It should specify a target date for its accomplishment.* If the objective is the result of normal work output, then the objective would likely be continuing in nature. In this case the target date could be assumed to be the end of the evaluation period. On the other hand, if the objective is a result of improvement analysis, it should generally have a specific target date identified.

4. *It should be as specific and quantitative (and hence measurable and verifiable) as possible.* Probably no area of performance objectives generates a greater degree of skepticism than this criterion. Managers frequently wonder how they can place objective criteria on inherently subjective areas. There is no doubt that this is an extremely difficult challenge, but it can be done. Some progress can be made in resolving this potential dilemma by identifying *specific measurable* activities that, if accomplished, should logically enable achievement of the desired improvement.

5. *It should relate directly to the rated person's role and to the superior's mission and objectives.* Although this guideline is relatively obvious, it is an important criterion to evaluate when testing the validity of a paritcular performance objective.

6. *It should be understandable by those who will be contributing to its attainment.* Performance objectives need only to be understood by the rated and rating person, not to someone who may not be part of the work group. A performance objective that is clearly understood is easier to implement.

7. *It should be realistic and attainable but still represent a significant challenge.* A well-formulated performance objective can and should serve as a motivational tool for the individual. Therefore, it should be one that is within reach, yet not too easy to accomplish.

8. *It should be consistent with the available organizational resources.* A potentially outstanding objective could result in an inefficient use of time and energy if, realistically, the organization is unable or unwilling to devote the required resources necessary to accomplish the objective.

9. *It should be willingly agreed to by the rated person and rater without undue pressure or coercion.* Discussion between the rated person and rater is essential to the success of the program. This guideline does suggest that the actual content of an objective should be the subject of discussion and possibly negotiation between the ratee and rater. Such discussion should result in a mutually understood and agreed-upon objective that reflects the best thinking of each. Generally the motivation of the ratee to effectively achieve the objective will be greater as a result of having reached such an agreement.

In summary, the following key questions can be asked as a final check of each performance objective:

1. Is the performance objective constructed properly? To (*action verb*) (*single key result*) by (*target date*) requiring (*what organizational resources*).
2. Is it measurable and verifiable?
3. Does it relate directly to the unit's objectives and to higher-level mission and objectives?
4. Can it be readily understood by those who must implement it?
5. Is the objective a realistic and attainable one that still represents a significant challenge?
6. Will the result, when achieved, justify the expenditure of time and resources to achieve it?
7. Is the objective consistent with the basic department and organizational policies and practices?

PROCEDURE

Step 1: 10 to 30 Minutes (in Advance)

Below is a worksheet with a list of seven objectives. Critique each objective using the Guidelines (1 to 4) found in the "Introduction to Management by Objectives." If any of the objectives do not meet these criteria, rewrite the objective to conform to the guidelines. Bring your worksheet to class, as assigned.

SETTING OBJECTIVES WORKSHEET

	Action Verb?	Result?	Target Date?	Measurable?
1. To improve the communications and working relations among key employees so that high quality work can be produced.				
2. To develop an improved method to maintain all material-handling equipment. Have in operation by December of this year.				
3. To reduce rejects in electronic component K-234G to 2 percent by August of this year.				

SETTING OBJECTIVES WORKSHEET

	Action Verb?	Result?	Target Date?	Measurable?
4. To continue cost-saving study and implement its recommendations upon completion.				
5. Within 3 months, have all grievances processed, recorded, and answered within 48 hours of receipt.				
6. To increase production per man-hour this year by 2 percent over the last year's average.				
7. To begin a procedure for proper distribution of job description sheets.				

Step 2: 30 Minutes or More (in Advance)

Read the following, then assume the role assigned (Newman or Petricelli) and complete Step 2 as directed.

GENERAL OFFICE: BACKGROUND INFORMATION

General Office serves a faculty of 30 officers in an academic department at one of the nation's service academies. All employees hold temporary or permanent civil service appointments. The office is currently managed by Newman, who is very efficient, outgoing, and interested in encouraging employee development and career advancement.

Four persons report to Newman. Together they are responsible for answering phones, filing, ordering supplies, typing for the faculty, processing of forms and orders, photocopying and duplicating. A separate secretary works for the department administrators.

Typically, three staff members rotate between phones, filing, and typing. The fourth handles all supplies, copying, and duplicating.

Upon assuming the position, Newman found several problems: (1) friction between certain staff members; (2) complaints from officers regarding the turnaround time on class handouts and tests; (3) requests for collating being ignored because of "backlogs and time pressure."

Because of the civil service system and affirmative action policies, Newman cannot fire any of the staff members. Newman has decided that the best chance for eliminating the problems listed above is to use an MBO system with the staff. Newman has shared objectives with the staff and is now preparing to meet with staff members to discuss their objectives.

The first person scheduled for a meeting is Petricelli, a 45-year-old man who has 15 years in the civil service system. Because he doesn't type he has been assigned to be in charge of the supplies, copying, and duplicating functions. Over the years he has come to see this as his "domain," even to the extent of decorating the duplicating room to suit his taste. This has given him a great deal of autonomy in his job compared to the others, who all work in the large outer office. At times he flaunts his role, acting as if his job is higher status. Actually his GS rating is lower than others in the office. Because of this, Petricelli has occasionally had run-ins with the others who *feel* that he is un-cooperative and receiving preferential treatment. He routinely complains of being over-worked but is all too often found in the halls "shooting the breeze." Since the duplicating and copying frequently tie in to typing orders, Petricelli and the others are interdependent when there is a deadline.

Role Assignment: Newman
Develop four objectives you would like to see Petricelli accomplish in the next three months. Write these in the space below. Bring these to class and be prepared to discuss them with him.

1. Innovative objective:

2. Problem solving objective:

3. Routine objective:

4. Personal growth objective:

Role Assignment: Petricelli
Develop four objectives of the type shown below that you would like to accomplish over the next three months. Write these in the space provided and bring to class. Be prepared to discuss these with Newman.

1. Innovative objective:

2. Problem solving objective:

3. Routine objective:

4. Personal growth objective:

Step 3: 10 to 15 Minutes
As a total group, discuss your critiques of the objectives completed in Step 1.

Step 4: 20 to 30 Minutes
Meet in pairs, assuming your role as Newman or Petricelli. The purpose of your meeting is to come to an agreement regarding Petricelli's objectives for the next 3 months. Since these may differ somewhat from what each of you originally wrote (in Step 2), be prepared to present your *final* written objectives to the class. In addition, be prepared to indicate how each objective will be measured in the next quarterly performance evaluation review.

Step 5: 10 Minutes
Your instructor will ask selected pairs to state their objectives. The rest of the class will discuss and critique according to the guidelines presented earlier.

GENERALIZATIONS AND CONCLUSIONS
1. What is the most difficult part of using MBO in an organization? Initially?

Ongoing?

2. What is the most difficult step in formulating objectives?

3. What is most likely to cause a "breakdown" in an MBO system?

4. What are the major benefits of MBO?

Participant's Reactions (Personal Learning Outcomes)

1. Did you find yourself having difficulty either in evaluating, writing objectives, or negotiating objectives?

2. If so, what was the major area of difficulty?

3. What will you do to improve your skills in working with MBO? (State an objective.)

READINGS AND REFERENCES

Carroll, Steven, and Tosi, Henry, *Management By Objectives,* 2nd ed. (New York: Macmillan, 1980.)

French, W. L., and Hollman, R. W., "Management by Objectives: The Team Approach," *California Management Review,* 17, 3 (1975), 13–22.

Jamieson, B., "Behavioral Problems with Management by Objectives," *Academy of Management Journal,* 16 (1973), 496–505.

Morrissey, George L., *Appraisal and Development Through Objectives and Results.* (Reading, Mass.: Addison-Wesley, 1972.)

Odiorne, George, *Management Decisions By Objectives.* (Englewood Cliffs, N.J.: Prentice-Hall, 1968.)

57
TIME MANAGEMENT

After reading much of the popular literature about time management, many people assume it is a quick success gimmick or, at best, a technique for reducing stress. Actually, it is neither of those. What it is is a *basic management skill*. When used properly, time management can help you to be more successful by enabling you to use your time to accomplish important tasks. It can also help to reduce stress by both changing your expectations of yourself and reducing role overload through delegation.

Effective time management involves applying many of the same basic skills required in general management situations. If you are an effective manager of your time now, chances are you have the potential to manage under other conditions or at a different level. Here are some of the reasons.

Basic to effective time management is the ability to set goals and priorities. You have to know what's important, in your life and work, and focus your energies on tasks that lead to accomplishing those outcomes.

People can't manufacture time, they can make better use of the time they have. Managing time does not mean working harder, it just means working smarter—using the time available to accomplish what is truly important.

A second skill involves being able to make decisions. This requires evaluating alternative demands and tasks, choosing the highest payoff alternatives, saying "no" to some requests, and sticking by your decision.

A final skill for managing time—and people—is effective delegation. The only way you can be selective about the use of your time is to delegate responsibility to others. Ironically, effective delegation facilitates both your goals and your subordinates'. They have a chance to learn and develop while you focus on matters that *only* you can take care of.

One of the most useful approaches to effective time management is described by Alan Lakein in *How to Get Control of Your Time and Your Life*. Basic to his system is learning how to *plan* what you want to do and then organizing your use of time to get it done. "Time cannot be altered. We can only manage activities." In other words, managing time, like managing stress, involves learning to manage your own behavior.

In Step 1, identify goals and objectives. What is it you want to accomplish? Think in terms of time frames—long-term objectives as well as short-term, day-to-day objectives. Without planning, long-term objectives may be lost in the rush to carry out day-to-day activities. Or, short-term objectives may not get done because we are allotting too much time to unimportant tasks—things we could forget.

Whether you are planning for today or for next year, the key is learning how to establish priorities. You have to identify and concentrate on those tasks and activities

Developed by Francine S. Hall. Parts of the Introduction from F. S. Hall and D. T. Hall, *The Two Career Couple* (Reading, Mass.: Addison-Wesley, 1979). Used by permission.

that are of highest priority and eliminate those that are low priority. Lakein (1973) suggests using a simple ABC system.

The ABC system works like this: First, list all the goals you want to accomplish. Now ask yourself which ones are really important (will result in the rewards you value) and which are less important. The most important goals are labeled as "A"— top priority. Less important ones are designated as "B," and lower priority goals as "C." Now that you have some sense of what your A goals are, you can begin to plan your time to accomplish these. If you've listed a lot of C goals, you may want to reconsider whether they are worth having as goals at all. Some, however, may be tasks you have to do and cannot ignore forever.

Once you have identified your goals and established priorities, the next step is to think about activities that will help you accomplish them. What will you have to do to achieve your priority goals? Are you building those activities into your schedule or ignoring them? Planning, the key to time management, revolves around consciously allocating and using time for those activities that will help us accomplish our important goals. This doesn't mean that we devote all of our time to them, but only that we ensure that as much time as possible is being used for top-priority items.

Get into the habit of scheduling your day in order to use time efficiently. One of the basic techniques is to make up a daily list of things to do, along with the priorities for those activities. Try the following exercise:

1. List all the things you have to do tomorrow.
2. Now prioritize your list using the ABC system. Which activities are really important for accomplishing priority goals, and which are not?
3. Once you have the activities labeled as A, B, or C, look at the B activities. Which of these could qualify as A's and which are really C's?
4. Now think about scheduling your day to ensure adequate time to get your A activities accomplished.

Lakein offers several important tips for scheduling time and using it more efficiently.

1. Keep a daily "TO DO" list and review it each morning.
2. Block out time for priority activities—either save a time slot in each day or set a day aside each week.
3. Don't let anything interfere with this time.
4. Use your time efficiently. Handle paper only once, don't keep reshuffling it. Don't procrastinate—if something has to be done, do it immediately. Minimize the steps involved in what you do. Delegate as much as possible to others. Unless you absolutely have to do something, assign it to someone else.
5. Learn to know your "prime time." When do you work best? Save it for priority projects.
6. Try to be flexible. Always leave time in your schedule for emergencies or catching up.
7. Plan time to relax. If you are exhausted, you won't be able to work effectively or efficiently.

8. Learn to use transition time to get things done. For example, can you read, catch the news on the radio, or discuss matters with your partner or family while you dress, do your nails, or eat breakfast? How do you use time spent in commuting, coffee breaks, lunch hour, or waiting in offices? Do you carry you list with you so you can save time to plan? Do you carry paper and pencil for writing or have something along to read?

9. Finally, can you turn C activities into things that can be put off indefinitely? How many C activities do you do that, in the end, don't have to be done, or can be done later if they turn out to be important? Learn to discriminate and put them aside.

58
A NOTE ON HOW TO RUN A MEETING
James Ware

Meetings are among the most overused and underutilized of all management tools. One study of managerial behavior found that many executives spent over two-thirds of' their time in scheduled meetings. More significantly, important organizational decisions are almost always reached in management meetings, or as a result of one or more meetings. Given their importance, and the amount of management time they consume, it is indeed a tragedy that so many meetings are so inefficient and, worse, ineffective.

Yet planning and conducting a meeting is not a difficult task. While there are no magic formulas to guarantee success, there are a number of simple procedures that effective managers employ to improve the quality of their meetings.

There are, of course, many different kinds of meetings, ranging from two-person interchanges all the way up to industry-wide conventions with thousands of participants. Most management meetings, however, involve relatively small groups of people in a single organization. This Note will concentrate on a number of techniques for running these kinds of management meetings more effectively. For further simplicity, we will focus primarily on scheduled meetings of managers who are at approximately the same level in the organization, and who have known each other and worked together before.

The suggestions that follow are divided into planning activities to carry out before the meeting, and leadership activities to engage in during the meeting. Both kinds of work are essential: the most thorough preparation in the world will be wasted if you are careless during the meeting, while even outstanding meeting leadership rarely overcomes poor planning.

PREPARING FOR THE MEETING

Perhaps the most useful way to begin is simply to sit down with a blank sheet of paper and think through what the meeting will be like. Write down all the issues that are likely to come up, what decisions need to be made, what you want to happen after the meeting, and what things have to happen before the meeting can take place. Although the circumstances surrounding each meeting are unique, your planning should include the following activities:

Setting Objectives

Most management meetings are called either to exchange information or to solve organizational problems. Generally your reasons for calling the meeting are fairly obvious, especially to you. It is worth being very explicit about your purposes, how-

Reproduced by permission. This case was prepared by James P. Ware (9-478-003). Copyright 1977 by the President and Fellows of Harvard College. Distributed by the Intercollegiate Case Clearing House, Soldiers Field, Boston, Mass. 02163. All rights reserved to contributors. Printed in U.S.A.

ever, because they have major implications for who should attend, which items belong on the agenda, when and where you hold the meeting, and what kinds of decision-making procedures you should use.

An information-exchange meeting can be an efficient mechanism if the information to be shared is complex or controversial, if it has major implications for the meeting participants, or if there is symbolic value in conveying the information personally. If none of these conditions is present, it may be more efficient, and just as effective to write a memo or make several telephone calls.

Problem-solving meetings provide an opportunity to combine the knowledge and skills of several people at once. The ideas that evolve out of an open-ended discussion are usually richer and more creative than what the same people could produce working individually.

These two different objectives call for very different kinds of meetings. Thus, you should be very explicit about what you are trying to accomplish, both to yourself and to the other meeting participants.

Selecting Participants

Invite people to the meeting who will either contribute to, or be affected by, its outcome. Select individuals who have knowledge or skills relevant to the problem, or who command organizational resource (time; budgets; other people; power and influence) that you need access to.

As you build your participant list, you should also give thought to the overall composition of the group. Identify the likely concerns and interests of the individual managers, and the feelings they have about each other. Try to obtain a rough balance of power and status among subgroups or probable coalitions (unless you have clear reasons for wanting one group to be more powerful).

Do everything you can to keep the size of the group appropriate to your objectives. While an information-exchange meeting can be almost any size, a problem-solving group should not exceed 8 to 10 people if at all possible.

Planning the Agenda

Even if you are planning an informal, exploratory meeting, an agenda can be a valuable means of controlling the discussion and of giving the participants a sense of direction. The agenda defines the meeting's purpose for participants and places boundaries between relevant and irrelevant discussion topics. Furthermore, the agenda can serve as an important vehicle for pre-meeting discussions with participants.

Some important principles of building an agenda are listed below:

Sequence items so they build on one another if possible.

Sequence topics from easiest to most difficult and/or controversial.

Keep the number of topics within reasonable limits.

Avoid topics that can be better handled by subgroups or individuals.

Separate information exchange from problem-solving.

Define a finishing time as well as a starting time.

Depending on meeting length, schedule breaks at specific times where they will not disrupt important discussions.

Not every meeting requires a formal, written agenda. Often you simply cannot predict where a discussion will lead, or how long it will take. However, focusing your attention on these issues can help you anticipate controversy and be prepared to influence it in a productive manner. Even if you do not prepare a public, written agenda, you should not begin the meeting without having a tentative, private one.

Doing Your Homework

Your major objective in preparing for the meeting is to collect all the relevant information you can, and to consider its implications. Some of this data may be in written documents, but much of it will probably be in other people's heads. The more important and the more controversial the subject, the more contact you should have with other participants before the actual meeting.

These contacts will help you anticipate issues and disagreements that may arise during the meeting. As you talk with the other participants, try to learn all you can about their personal opinions and objectives concerning the meeting topic. These personal objectives—often called "hidden" agendas—can have as big an impact on what happens during the meeting as your formal, explicit agenda. Thus, the more you can discover about the other participants' goals for the meeting, the better prepared you will be to lead an effective discussion.

These pre-meeting contacts also give you an opportunity to encourage the other participants to do their homework as well. If there is enough time before the meeting to collect and circulate relevant data or background materials, the meeting itself can proceed much more quickly. Few events are as frustrating as a meeting of people who are unprepared to discuss or decide the issues on the agenda.

As part of your preparation you may want to brief your boss and other executives who will not be at the meeting, but who have an interest in its outcomes.

Finally, circulate the agenda and relevant background papers a day or two before the meeting if you can. These documents help to clarify your purposes and expectations, and they further encourage the other participants to come to the meeting well-prepared. Keep your demands on their time reasonable, however. People are more likely to read and think about brief memos than long, comprehensive reports.

Setting a Time and Place

The timing and location of your meeting can have a subtle but significant impact on the quality of the discussion. These choices communicate a surprising number of messages about the meetings importance, style, and possible outcomes.

What time of day is best for your meeting? Often the work flow in the organization will constrain your freedom of choice. For example, you could not meet simultaneously with all of a bank's tellers during the regular business hours, or with all the entry clerks just as the mail arrives. Within these kinds of constraints, however, you often have a wide choice of meeting times. How should you decide?

Early in the day, participants will usually be fresher and will have fewer other problems on their minds. In contrast, late afternoon meetings can be more leisurely, since there will usually be nothing else on anyone's schedule following your meeting. Perhaps the best question to ask is what the participants will be doing after the meeting. Will they be eager to end the meeting so they can proceed to other commitments, or will they be inclined to prolong the discussion? Which attitude best suits your purposes? There is no "best" time for a meeting, but you should consider explicitly what times would be most suitable for your particular objectives.

Two other factors may also influence when you schedule the meeting. First, try to be sure the time is sheltered, so there will be an absolute minimum of interruptions. Second, gear your starting time to the meeting's probable, or desirable, length. For example, if you want the meeting to last only an hour, a good time to schedule it is at 11 A.M.

Try not to plan meetings that last more than 90 minutes. Most people's endurance—or at least their creative capacity—will not last much longer than that. If the subject is so complex or lengthy that it will take longer, be sure to build in coffee and stretching breaks at least every 90 minutes.

Another key decision is where to hold the meeting. The setting in which a discussion takes place can have a marked influence on its tone and content. Just consider the difference between calling three subordinates to your office and meeting them for lunch in a restaurant. Each setting implies a particular level of formality and signals what kind of discussion you expect to have. Similarly, if you are meeting with several peers, a "neutral" conference room creates a very different climate than would any one of your offices. In each case, the appropriate setting depends on your purposes, and you should choose your location accordingly.

The discussion climate will also be affected by the arrangement of the furniture in the meeting room. In your office, you can choose to stay behind your desk and thereby be more authoritative, or to use a chair that puts you on a more equal basis with the other participants. In a conference room, you can choose to sit at the head of the table to symbolize your control, or in the center to be "one of the group."

You should also be certain that you have arranged for any necessary mechanical equipment, such as an overhead or slide projector, an easel, or a blackboard. These vital aids can facilitate both information exchange and problem-solving discussions.

Summary

Each of these suggestions has been intended to help you convene a meeting of people who have a common understanding of why they have come together and are prepared to contribute to the discussion. Of course, this kind of thorough preparation is often simply impossible. Nevertheless, the more preparation you can do, the more smoothly the meeting will go. While you can never anticipate *all* the issues and hidden agendas, you can clearly identify the major sources of potential disagreement. That anticipation enables you to control the meeting, rather than being caught off guard. Even if you have to schedule a meeting only an hour in advance, you can still benefit from systematic attention to these kinds of details.

CONDUCTING THE MEETING

If you have done your homework, you probably have a good idea of where you want the group to be at the end of the meeting. But remember that you called the meeting because you need something from the other participants—either information relevant to the problem, or agreement and commitment to a decision. Your success in achieving those goals now depends not so much on what you know about the problem as on what you and the others can learn during the discussion. Thus, primary concern as you begin the meeting should be with creating a healthy, problem-solving atmosphere in which participants openly confront their differences and work towards a joint solution.

The following suggestions and meeting leadership techniques should help you achieve that goal.

Beginning the Meeting

If you are well-prepared, the chances are that no one else has thought as much about the meeting as you have. Thus, the most productive way to begin is with an explicit review of the agenda and your objectives. This discussion gives everyone an opportunity to ask questions, offer suggestions, and express opinions about why they are there. Beginning with a review of the agenda also signals its importance, and gets the meeting going in a task-oriented direction.

Be careful not to simply impose the agenda on the group; others may have useful suggestions that will speed up the meeting or bring the problem into sharper focus. They may even disagree with some of your plans, but you will not learn about that disagreement unless you clearly signal that you consider the agenda open to revision. The more the others participate in defining the meeting, the more committed they will be to fulfilling that definition.

This initial discussion also permits the meeting participants to work out a shared understanding of the problem that brought them together, and of what topics are and are not appropriate to discuss in this meeting.

Encouraging Problem-Solving

As the formal leader of the meeting, you can employ a wide variety of techniques to keep the group in a problem-solving mode. Your formal authority as chairman gives you a great deal of power to influence the group's actions. Often a simple comment, a pointed look, or even just a lifted eyebrow is all you need to indicate approval or disapproval of someone's behavior.

Perhaps your best weapon is simply your own style of inquiry; if you focus on facts and on understanding points of disagreement, to the exclusion of personalities, others will generally do the same. As the discussion progresses, try to keep differing points of view in rough balance. Do not let a few individuals dominate; when you sense that participation has become unbalanced, openly ask the quieter members for their opinions and ideas. Never assume that silence means agreement; more often it signals some level of difference with the dominant theme of the discussion.

Effective problem-solving meetings generally pass through several phases. Early in the discussion that group will be seeking to understand the nature of the problem. At that point you need to encourage factual, nonevaluative discussion that emphasizes describing symptoms and searching for all possible causes. As understanding is gained, the focus will shift to a search for solutions. Again, you must discourage evaluative comments until all potential alternatives have been thoroughly explored. Only then should the discussion become evaluative, as the group moves toward a decision.

If you can develop a sensitivity to these stages of problem-solving (describing symptoms; searching for alternatives; evaluating alternatives; selecting a solution), you can vary your leadership style to fit the current needs of the group. At all times, however, you want to keep the discussion focused on the problem, not on personalities or on unrelated issues, no matter how important they may be. Make your priorities clear, and hold the group to them. Finally, maintain a climate of honest inquiry in which anyone's assumption (including yours) may be questioned and tested.

Keeping the Discussion on Track

When the meeting topic is controversial, with important consequences for the group members, you will have to work hard to keep the discussion focused on the issues.

Controversy makes most of us uncomfortable, and groups often avoid confronting the main issue by finding less important or irrelevant topics to talk about. If the discussion wanders too far from the agenda, you must be willing to exercise your leadership responsibility to swing the group back to the major topic.

Use your judgment in making these interventions, however. If the group is on the verge of splitting up in anger or frustration, a digression to a "safe" topic may be a highly functional way of reuniting. Generally, such digressions are most beneficial when they follow open controversy, rather than precede it. If you think the group has reached a decision on the main issue, even if it is only an implicit one, then you may want to let the digression go on for a while. On the other hand, if the discussion is clearly delaying a necessary confrontation, then you will have to intervene to get the discussion back on the main issue.

If you began the meeting with an explicit discussion of the agenda, you will find this focusing task easier to carry out. Often a simple reminder to the group, with a glance at the clock, is enough. Another useful technique for marking progress is periodically to summarize where you think the group has been, ask the group to confirm your assessments.

If the discussion seems to bog down, or to wander too far afield, perhaps the group needs to take a short break. Even two minutes of standing and stretching can revitalize people's willingness to concentrate on the problem. And the break also serves to cut off old conversations, making it easier to begin new ones.

Do everything you can to keep the discussion moving on schedule, so you can end on time. The clock can be a very useful taskmaster, and busy managers rarely have the luxury of ignoring it. If you have set a specific ending time, and everyone knows you mean it, there will be far less tendency for the discussion to wander.

Controlling the Discussion

How authoritatively should you exercise control over the discussion? The answer to that question depends so much on specific circumstances that a general response is almost impossible. The level of formality that is appropriate depends on the discussion topic, on which phase of the problem-solving cycle you are in, and on your formal and informal relationships with the other participants. You will normally want to exercise greater control when:

The meeting is oriented more towards information exchange.
The topic generates strong, potentially disruptive feelings.
The group is moving towards a decision.
Time pressures are significant.

There are a whole range of techniques you can use to exert more formal control. For example, if you permit participants to speak only when you call on them, or if you comment on or summarize each statement, there will be very few direct confrontations between other individuals. If you use a flip chart or blackboard to summarize ideas, you will also increase the level of formality and reduce the number of direct exchanges. In some circumstances, you may even want to employ formal parliamentary procedures, such as requiring motions, limiting debate, taking notes, and so on. These procedures might be appropriate, for example, in meetings of a Board of Directors, in union-management contract negotiations, or in policy-setting sessions involving managers from several different parts of the organization.

Many of these techniques are clearly inappropriate for, and rarely used in, smaller management meetings. Although these techniques can give you a high degree of control, they cannot prevent participants from developing strong feelings about the issues—feelings that often become strong precisely because you have not permitted them to be openly expressed.

Thus, it is entirely possible to control a meeting in a fashion that minimizes conflict within the meeting itself. However, one result of that control may be increased tension and even hostility between the participants, leading to more serious future problems. On the other hand, if tension levels are already so high that a rational discussion will not evolve on its own, then some of these controlling techniques may be absolutely essential.

Reaching a Decision

Many management groups will fall into decision-making habits without thinking carefully about the consequences of those habits. The two major approaches to reaching a group decision are voting and reaching a consensus. Each strategy has its advantages and disadvantages.

Voting is often resorted to when the decision is important and the group seems deadlocked. The major benefit of taking a vote is that you are guaranteed of getting a decision. However, voting requires public commitment to a position, and it creates a win-lose situation for the group members. Some individuals will be clearly identified as having favored a minority position. Losers on one issue often try to balance their account on the next decision, or they may withdraw their commitment to the total group. Either way, you may have won the battle but lost the war.

Reaching a group consensus is generally a much more effective decision-making procedure. It is often more difficult, however, and is almost always more time-consuming. Working towards a genuine consensus means hearing all points of view, and usually results in a better decision, a condition that is especially important when the group members will be responsible for implementing the decision. Even when individuals do not fully agree with the group decision, they are more likely to support it (or less likely to sabotage it) When they believe their positions have had a complete hearing.

Ending the Meeting

The most important thing to do at the end of the meeting is to clarify what happens next. If the group has made a major decision, be certain you will agree on who is responsible for its implementation, and on when the work will be completed.

If the group has to meet again, you can save a lot of time by scheduling your next meeting then and there. Having everyone check their calendars and mark down the date and time of the next meeting will save you an unbelievable number of telephone calls.

Depending on the discussion topic and the decisions that have been made, either you or someone else should follow the meeting with a brief memo summarizing the discussion, the decisions, and the follow-up commitments that each participant has made. This kind of document serves not only as a record of the meeting, but as a next-day reminder to the participants of what they decided and what they are committed to doing.

If you can, spend the last 5 minutes or so of the meeting talking about how well the meeting went. Although most managers are not accustomed to self-critiques, this practice is a useful habit that can contribute significantly to improved group problem-solving. The best time to share your reactions to the meeting is right after it has ended. You must evaluate the effectiveness of other management techniques all the time; why not apply the same criteria to your meetings?

SUMMARY

Management meetings occur so frequently that most of us fail to recognize how significant an impact they have on organizational productivity. Improving the effectiveness of your meetings is not a difficult task. Apply these simple techniques carefully, with sensitivity to the combination of people and problems you have brought together, and your meetings should become both more effective and more interesting. The important point, however, is that the techniques *are* simple. They require little more than systematic preparation before the meeting and sensitive observation and intervention while it is in progress.

59
IMPROVING YOUR PERFORMANCE IN THE EMPLOYMENT INTERVIEW.
Donald D. Bowen

When you are granted an employment interview, remember that all you have to sell is yourself and your qualifications (Verderber & Verderber, 1980, p. 312).

Most of us have heard this cliche so often that we never really stop to ask "What does it mean?" A visitor from a less commercially oriented culture in outer space might be more curious and ask what people mean when they talk about "selling yourself" in employment interviews. Looking up the verb "sell" in Webster's, our curious visitors discover it has several meanings

... 1. To deliver or hand over in breach of duty, trust, etc.; to betray. 2. To deliver into bondage, esp. for money. 3. To dispose of or manage for profit instead of in accord with conscience, justice, etc; as in to sell *one's vote. 4.* Slang. *To impose upon; trick. 5. To transfer (property) for a consideration; to give up for a consideration; to convey, ... opposed to* buy. *6. To deal in, as an article for sale; as to sell groceries...* Webster's New Collegiate Dictionary, 1951, p. 768).

At this point, the stranger might legitimately develop some serious doubts about the employment relationships in earth society. Do we really mean to say that we sell ourselves into bondage? Or that we sell out? Or that we sell ourselves like chattel if the price is right? ("Isn't that what you earthlings call 'the oldest profession'?" our visitor might remark).

"No, we don't really mean that. What we are really saying is that the employment interview is an interaction wherein we try to convince a representative of a prospective employer to enter into a contract in which the employee provides work and services in return for wages, salaries, and other monetary and nonmonetary rewards. The hours of work and the duties to be performed are usually prescribed in at least general terms. And the employer (except in the case of professional athletes) cannot sell us to another employer."

"I see," says the spaceperson, raising all seven eyebrows quizzically. "You say you are 'selling yourself' because your objective is to trick and deceive the employer in order to get hired."

You start to deny it, but the words catch in your throat. "Isn't that exactly what many people seem to do?" you muse. Isn't most of the well-meaning advice on how to conduct yourself in an employment interview basically aimed at showing you how to "puff" your assets and conceal your liabilities? Didn't you just read an article on selling yourself in the interview that advised you that if you are asked "what is your greatest weakness?" you should a) try to avoid answering the question, and b) if you can't avoid it, respond by mentioning some trivial, non-job-related characteristic (Gootnick, 1978)?

WHAT NOT TO DO—
INGRATIATION AND IMPRESSION MANAGEMENT

Three questions come immediately to mind when you are advised to employ deceitful tactics in the interview. First, is it ethical (we'll leave this to you to decide)? Second, is it really in my own best interests? Third, will it work?

Let's look at the third question first. There is a great deal of research by social and industrial psychologists on this topic. Social psychologists speak of "impression management" and "ingratiation techniques" to describe situations where a person is trying to get others to see them as more attractive than they feel they really are. Industrial psychologists have conducted research for years to try to learn how to help managers conduct more effective interviews—some of their findings are relevant to our topic.

Table 1 has been developed from a recent review (Wortman and Linsenmeier, 1977) of this research. In the left-hand column, various ingratiation tactics or other factors that applicants might try to use to their advantage are listed. In the right-hand column are problems that may arise or special considerations one must keep in mind in using a particular ingratiation ploy. For example, Tactic 5 entails recognizing that negative information is weighted more heavily than positive information. Therefore, you must not only take into account the considerations already suggested in emphasizing your positive traits (i.e., you must know what this particular employer considers to be positive or negative, and you must maintain a continuous focus on your virtues without appearing immodest or egocentric—a fairly tough act for most of us), but you will have to do this with a degree of subtlety that beguiles the interviewer. Moreover, since most managerial positions require that you be interviewed by several managers (all of whom will compare notes on you, later), the task becomes complicated. Each interviewer is an individual with personal tastes, values, and attitudes that differ from the others to some extent. It is going to require *real* skill to cater to each of these individuals without having them find out that each of them has seen a somewhat different person in their interview.

Cursory assessment of the issues raised in the right-hand column of Table 1 suggests that, unless you can arrange for an interviewer afflicted with terminal stupidity, it is going to take real effort to pull off an act of the type suggested. Compounding the problem is the fact that the employment interview is a stressful situation for most applicants, and the level of stress may become totally debilitating if you must devote most of your energy to guarding against being found out.

Even if you are an accomplished thespian, the question still remains, *is it in your own best interests to practice deceit in the interview?* Schein (1978) points out that, to the extent that applicants can describe themselves fully and accurately to the interviewer, the probability is increased that they will end up well-matched to their jobs. *"There is little to be gained in the long run by falsely selling oneself"* (p. 88— emphasis added).

Wortman and Linsenmeier suggest a number of additional dangers in impression management:

1. The characteristics that were important in getting the job are likely to be required for keeping it. Do you think you can maintain your facade over the long term?

TABLE 1

Ingratiation Tactics and the Employment Interview[a]

Ingratiation Tactic	*Problems and Implications*
1. Emphasize your attractive accomplishments and traits.	a. You must know what the employer considers to be positive or negative traits, etc. (not always obvious).
	b. You must avoid appearing conceited.
2. Avoid appearing conceited or boastful by presenting yourself with some modesty (but don't *brag* about your modesty!).	a. Works best if the interviewer already knows what your good traits are, or when someone else can be relied upon to tell the interviewer (seldom the case in the employment interview).
	b. But, if you think someone else will mention a weakness you have, beat them to the punch (*but* see number 5 below).
	c. Don't emphasize a positive quality if you think it may threaten the interviewer (e.g., don't brag about your degree from Harvard if the interviewer is a college dropout).
3. People like people who are most similar in attitudes, values, and personality to themselves. Try to make it look like you are a lot like the interviewer.	a. But some interviewers will see through obvious attempts to be agreeable, assuming the interviewee is attempting to manipulate them instead (with negative results for you).
	b. It may be better to disagree with the employer on a few points—especially if the points are not pivotal.
	c. Some studies suggest that conformists do not get promoted in management.
4. The interviewer will respond more positively to you if you have at least average characteristics, if the preceeding interviewees have been real *turkeys*.	a. You don't usually have much control over when your appointment is scheduled.
5. Negative information is weighted more heavily in the interview than positive information. Therefore, present only positive information and avoid providing negative data.	a. See number 1, above.
	b. You will have to do this without insulting the intelligence of the interviewer.
	c. How do you deal with a situation where you are interviewed by several managers? How do you avoid telling conflicting stories as you try to tell each manager just what he or she wants to hear?

TABLE 1
Ingratiation Tactics and the Employment Interview[a]

Ingratiation Tactic	Problems and Implications
6. Data presented earlier in the interview make a greater impact. Therefore, make a good first impression.	a. If you have any negative data you will have to reveal, make sure you communicate your positive features first. *But,* don't appear reluctant to talk about your negative points.
	b. Physical appearance is weighted heavily in the interviewer's mind. Attire, makeup, etc., should play up your attractive features and be appropriate for the situation.

[a]Based upon Wortman and Linsenmeier (1977).

2. People who put on a convincing act get feedback on the act, not on the person they really are. Therefore, they never really learn about themselves—just about the fictitious person they have invented. Moreover, they tend to be unaware of their inability to get accurate feedback.
3. Since ingratiators receive only feedback on their phony persona, they come to take it seriously, and eventually *they tend to become the person they have invented.*

EFFECTIVE INTERVIEWING

Are there things you can do to make you more effective in the interview without resorting to artifice or deceit? The answer is clearly affirmative. Here are a number of tips that will help you to prepare for the interview and help you get through it with less nervousness and anxiety (remember, a little stress is good—it will keep you alert and energetic throughout the interview).

1. Always Start at the Beginning
Employers tend to be unimpressed with people who don't know what they want to do (and this is usually easy to spot). Always do your career planning (see Exercises 45 to 48 and the reading introducing the "Life, Work, and Career Roles" section (Section 13 on p. 253).

2. Do Your Homework
Before interviewing with an organization learn all you can about it. A couple of afternoons in the library can pay large dividends, and the recruiter will be impressed. You should arrive at the interview armed with both a basic knowledge of the organization and a couple of intelligent questions about it.

3. Rehearse
"The Awful Interview" (Exercise 48) or a simple role-play of the interview you expect will be immensely helpful in putting you at ease for the actual interview. Repeat treatment several times, if necessary.

4. Go Native

Most organizations have fairly strong norms about appropriate attire, hair styles, facial fur, makeup, and other issues of personal appearance. If you don't know what the standards are likely to be, ask someone in a position to know. The objective here is to look like the folks the recruiter is used to working with.

If you feel that a haircut or wearing a suit is a violation of your integrity, ask yourself whether you really want this job.

5. Playing a Winning Hand

If you have prepared well for the interview, the following tips will help you successfully cope with interview protocol (these suggestions based on Gootnick, 1978):

a. Getting started right:
   (1) *Never* arrive late.
   (2) If the interviewer offers a hand, respond with a firm handshake and a warm smile.
   (3) Do not smoke, even if asked.
   (4) Allow the interviewer to begin the interview.
b. During the interview:
   (1) Early in the interview, make a brief, positive presentation of your abilities, experience, interests, and so on that you feel are of special relevance for the job under consideration.
   (2) Be open and honest; give the recruiter an accurate picture of your needs, talents and interests.
c. Close the interview by:
   (1) Summarizing your credentials
   (2) Expressing enthusiasm for the organization and the job (if you really *are* interested).
   (3) Thanking the interviewer.
   (4) If the interviewer has not already indicated what the next step should be, ask.
d. After the interview:
   (1) Prepare a set of notes for future reference covering all the key points discussed.
   (2) Five to seven days later, send the interviewer a "thank you" letter. In it, express again your interest in the job (if real) and repeat your key credentials.

These guidelines won't guarantee that you get the job, but they should help you to improve your batting average. Good luck in your job hunting!

READINGS AND REFERENCES

Gootnick, D., "Selling Yourself in Interviews." *MBA*, 40 (Nov. 1978), 37–38.

Schein, E. H., *Career Dynamics: Matching Individuals and Organizational Needs*, (Reading, Mass.: Addison-Wesley, 1978).

Verderber, R. F., and Verderber, K. S., *Inter-act: Using Interpersonal Communication Skills*, 2nd ed. (Belmont, Calif.: Wadsworth, 1980).

Webster's New Collegiate Dictionary (Springfield, Mass.: G. & C. Merriam Co., 1951).

Wortman, C. B., and Linsenmeier, J. A. W., "Interpersonal Attraction Techniques of Ingratiation in Organizational Settings," in B. M. Staw and G. R. Salancik (Eds.), *New Directions in Organizational Behavior* (Chicago: St. Clair Press, 1977), pp. 133–178.

60
TOWARD A VIABLE CONCEPT OF ASSERTIVENESS
Donald D. Bowen

In the past 10 years, "pop" psychology has done a booming business. Perhaps the most popular, and often the most controversial strain has been "assertion" and "assertiveness training." Feminists have been particularly avid consumers of assertiveness, since assertiveness training is designed to help people stand up for their rights and achieve their goals. But critics of the "me" generation and its tendency toward self-centered insistence upon immediate gratification of materialistic whims have been suspicious of assertiveness training. In their view, assertiveness encourages satisfaction of the individual's needs—and to hell with everyone else.

We would like to propose a slightly different concept of assertiveness; one we feel makes the notion of assertiveness basically consistent with the notions of interpersonally competent behavior long recognized by students of management and organizational behavior (e.g., Argyris, 1962).

Discussion of assertiveness normally begins with definition of three alternative forms of behavior. *Passive* behavior is inhibited, self-denying, submissive, conflict-avoidant, wherein the person ignores her own needs and feelings in an attempt to satisfy other people. *Aggressive* behavior is the opposite of passiveness: domineering, pushy, self-centered, self-enhancing, and self-expressive without regard for the feelings or rights of others. Both passive and aggressive behavior are varieties of nonassertive behavior.

Some authorities see assertiveness as a midpoint between aggressive and passive behavior (e.g., Bloom, Coburn, and Pearlman, 1975). We believe this is a mistaken view and one that makes understanding assertiveness needlessly difficult. Our definition of *assertiveness* is behavior that involves expressing one's ideas and feelings, and standing up for one's rights, *and doing so in a way that makes it easier for others to do the same.* The assertive person is self-revealing, open and receptive, active, self-respecting, confronting (meaning the person expresses his feelings), and one who communicates directly and honestly to others. The assertive person, being open and receptive to others, also develops a sensitivity to the needs of others and a sense of when it is appropriate to be self-expressive.

By requiring that the assertive person forego pursuing his own ends when doing so inhibits others from expressing themselves or standing up for their own rights, we have posited a more limited notion of assertiveness, but one that avoids the logical traps in questions like the following:

Q: Is it possible to be *too* assertive?

A: No, because the more assertive you are, the more assertive others are encouraged to be.

Q: If I am a little more or less assertive, do I become passive or aggressive?

A: No, because assertiveness is a *different* mode of behavior, not a point somewhere between aggressiveness and passiveness.

Q: Won't I lose my friends and put people off if I am always concerned about my rights and expressing my feelings?

A: Not if you do it assertively, because you must then be concerned with the rights and feelings of others, too. Furthermore, can you ever really be helpful in satisfying the needs of others if you don't devote attention to satisfaction of your own needs, too? (Incidentally, this is a fundamental axiom of mental health.)

Let us now review some basic principles of assertive communication.

ASSERTIVENESS: PRINCIPLES AND EXAMPLES

Assertive communication requires developing specific communication habits and skills. The following are some of the most important:

1. Share Your Feelings In a Statement Beginning with "I"

Example: A colleague has apparently promised to do one thing but has done something quite different.

The assertive statement: "I'm really disturbed about what you did on the GM deal, Dave."

Nonassertive approaches are: "What the hell is the big idea?" or to say nothing while doing a slow burn.

2. Don't Discount Yourself and Don't Discount Others

Example: A colleague asks for your opinion on a decision.

The assertive response is a straightforward "I think. . . "

The nonassertive answers may involve putting down or discounting the other person ("I'm surprised you don't know the answer to that, Sue"), or discounting myself ("Well, I'm only a woman, so I don't know if you will want my opinion", or "Well, I guess I think that. . . ").

3. Don't Be Wishy-Washy and Don't Diffuse Your Message with "Word Whiskers"[1]

The examples of discounting oneself are also problems of being wishy-washy. There are many others, including going on at immense length about all sides of a question. "Word whiskers" are the meaningless speech patterns that many people use ("Um, uh, I guess, uh, I guess that, uh. . . " or "Well, we were just hangin' around, y'know, when this big guy, y'know, about six foot-eight, y'know. . . ").

Whatever your feelings are on a topic, if you are wishy-washy or an accomplished word-whiskerer, no one will listen long enough to find out.

---

[1] Mr. John Gregg suggested this apt term.

4. Be Specific In Feedback and Criticism

This guideline is dealt with in greater detail in Cyril Mill's "Feedback," Reading 54.

Example: You must criticize a report submitted by your subordinate.

The assertive approach: "In this report, Dave, you used LIFO. I want you to use FIFO, because. . ."

The nonassertive responses include, "Mary, this report stinks!" Or, "Lee, how can you be so dense?"

5. Use Neutral, Nonexplosive Language

Some language, as in the case of the defective report, just discussed, stimulates others to be defensive by being accusatory or grossly evaluative. Sarcasm frequently leads to the same result.

6. Be Cooperative, Open and Receptive to Others—They May Know Something You Don't

Example: Suppose a subordinate disobeys your explicit orders.

The nonassertive response is too often second-nature: "What the hell is the big idea, Larry. . . ?"

The assertive boss is aware that the subordinates may know something she does not. "Larry, can you tell me why you did X when I told you Y?"

7. Confront Unpleasant Situations Immediately [or at Least as Soon as Practicable]

And remember, "confront" means share your feelings, *not* dump all over the other person!

8. Make Sure Your Nonverbal Communication Is Congruent with Your Words

Ninety percent of the message we receive from another person is communicated nonverbally (Mehrabian, 1968). Consider the plight of the subordinate whose boss is smiling while she chews him out. Or the person who asks her boss for a raise in an inaudible mumble (reinforced by a nervous shuffling of feet and eyes riveted on the floor).

DEVELOPING ASSERTIVENESS SKILLS

Becoming more assertive is hard work. There are two important lessons one must master. First: you must learn to discriminate between assertive and nonassertive behavior. Second, you must practice your assertiveness *skills* continually until you have developed a repertoire of behavior that is readily available to you in a wide range of situations—even when you are under substantial pressure.

Is it all worth it? Perhaps you really have little choice if you are to work effectively within an organization (or if you are to have satisfactory relationships with people in other aspects of your life, for that matter). The answer might be best summarized in the words of one of our students, a young woman who holds down a job in computer programming during the day while working towards her bachelor's degree at night.

Prof: What do you think? Should we encourage our students to be more assertive?
Student: You bet!
Prof: Why?
Student: Because it feels so *good* when you know you have done it!

READINGS AND REFERENCES

Argyris, C., *Interpersonal Competence and Organizational Effectiveness* (Homewood, Ill.: Irwin, 1962).

Bloom, L. F., Coburn, K. and Pearlman, J., *The New Assertive Woman* (New York: Dell, 1975).

Mehrabian, A., "A Communication Without Words," *Psychology Today,* September (1968), p. 53.

ADDITIONAL READINGS

Alberti, R. E., and Emmons, M. L., *Your Perfect Right,* 2nd ed., (San Luis Obispo, Calif.: Impact Press, 1974).

Fensterheim, H., and Baer, J. *Don't Say Yes When You Want to Say No* (New York: Dell, 1975).

Kelley, C., "Assertion: The Literature Since 1970," in J. E. Jones and J. W. Pfeiffer (Eds.), *The 1977 Annual Handbook for Group Facilitators* (La Jolla, Calif.: University Associates, 1977), pp. 264–265.

Richardson, N., "Assertiveness Training for Men and Women," in A. G. Sargent, *Beyond Sex Roles* (St. Paul: West, 1977), pp. 336–350.

APPENDIX: LIST OF CONTENTS
NOT TO BE CONSULTED UNTIL INSTRUCTED TO DO SO

APPENDIX

EXERCISE 8
GENERAL INSTRUCTIONS*

J. J. Stein is an audit partner with a "Big 8" accounting firm. The work in the office includes large SEC clients, and small business clients.

Eight audit managers report to J. J. Stein. The duties of the audit manager are technical and supervisory. The organizational chart for Stein's office is shown in the diagram.

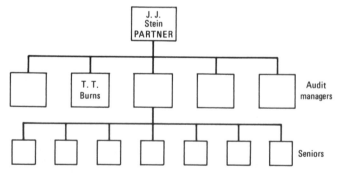

Firm policy requires that all partners periodically interview each of their managers, the purpose being

1. To evaluate the manager's performance.
2. To give recognition for jobs well done.
3. To correct weaknesses.

The firm believes that staff should know how they stand and that everything should be done to develop management personnel. The evaluation interviews were introduced to help serve this purpose.

*These materials are adapted from the famous Burke-Stanley role-play developed by N. R. F. Maier.

T. T. Burns is one of the managers reporting to Stein; today an evaluation interview will be conducted by Stein with T. T. Burns. Note that the interview is devoted to performance evaluation and is not intended to cover "career counseling."

T. T. Burns has a college degree in accounting, and, in addition to his technical duties, he supervises the work of several seniors and staff accountants. Burns has been with the firm for 8 years and has been a manager for 2 years. He is married and has two children. He owns his home and is active in the civic affairs of the community in which he lives.

EXERCISE 30
ROLE FOR "HERB PHILLIPS, M.D., Ph.D."

As head of Booth's research division, you are very aware of the deaths caused by Vanatin. Although it is the best product of its kind that Booth produces, there are products produced by Booth's competitors that are just as effective and have fewer negative after-effects. It is because of Booth's superior marketing, advertising, and drug distribution system that Vanatin has fared so well competitively. Still, it is the profits of drugs like Vanatin that help to finance new drug research, and to maintain your large and highly productive research laboratories.

EXERCISE 43
ROLE FOR "THOMPSON," SUPERVISOR

You are the supervisor in a shop and supervise about 20 workers. Most of the jobs are piece-rate jobs and some of the workers work in teams and are paid on a team piece-rate basis. In one of the teams, Jackson, Walters, and Stevenson work together. Each one of them does one of the operations for an hour and then they exchange, so that all workers perform each of the operations at different times. The workers themselves decided to operate that way and you have never given the plan any thought.

Lately, Clark, the methods expert, has been around and studied conditions in your shop. Clark timed Jackson, Walters and Stevenson on each of the operations and came up with the following facts:

| | *Time per operation* | | | |
	Position 1	*Position 2*	*Position 3*	*Total*
Jackson	3 min.	4 min.	$4\frac{1}{2}$ min.	$11\frac{1}{2}$ min.
Walters	$3\frac{1}{2}$ min.	$3\frac{1}{2}$ min.	3 min.	10 min.
Stevenson	5 min.	$3\frac{1}{2}$ min.	$4\frac{1}{2}$ min.	13 min.
				$34\frac{1}{2}$ min.

Clark observed that with the people rotating, the average time for all three operations would be one-third of the total time or $11\frac{1}{2}$ minutes per complete unit. If, however, Jackson worked in the no. 1 spot, Stevenson in the no. 2 spot, and Walters in the no. 3 spot, the time would be $9\frac{1}{2}$ min., a reduction of more than 17 percent. Such a reduction in time would amount to a saving of more than 80 minutes. In other words, the lost production would be about the same as that which would occur if the workers loafed for 80 minutes in an eight-hour day. If the time were used for productive effort, production would be increased more than 20 percent.

This made pretty good sense to you, so you have decided to take up the problem with the crew. You feel that they should go along with any change in operation that is made.

EXERCISE 9
THE HOVEY AND BEARD COMPANY CASE
PART II

By the second month of the training period, trouble had developed. The employees learned more slowly than had been anticipated, and it began to look as though their production would stabilize far below what was planned for. Many of the hooks were going by empty. The women complained that they were going by too fast, and that the time-study man had set the rates wrong. A few women quit and had to be replaced with new operators, which further aggravated the learning problem. The team spirit that the management had expected to develop automatically through the group bonus was not in evidence except as an expression of what the engineers called "resistance." One woman whom the group regarded as its leader (and the management regarded as the ringleader) was outspoken in making various complaints of the group to the foreman: the job was a messy one, the hooks moved too fast, the incentive pay was not being correctly calculated, and it was too hot working so close to the drying oven.

Discuss: if you were a consultant, what would you recommend?

PART III

A consultant who was brought into this picture worked entirely with and through the foreman. After many conversations with him, the foreman felt that the first step should be to get the employees together for a general discussion of the working conditions. He took this step with some hesitation, but he took it on his own volition.

The first meeting, held immediately after the shift was over at four o'clock in the afternoon, was attended by all eight operators. They voiced the same complaints again: the hooks went by too fast, the job was too dirty, the room was hot and poorly ventilated. For some reason, it was this last item that they complained of most. The foreman promised to discuss the problem of ventilation and temperature with the engineers, and he scheduled a second meeting to report back to the employees. In the next few days the foreman had several talks with the engineers. They and the superintendent felt that this was really a trumped-up complaint, and that the expense of any effective corrective measure would be prohibitively high.

The foreman came to the second meeting with some apprehensions. The operators, however, did not seem to be much put out, perhaps because they had a proposal of their own to make. They felt that if several large fans were set up so as to circulate the air around their feet, they would be much more comfortable. After some discussion, the foreman agreed that the idea might be tried out. The foreman and the consultant discussed the question of the fans with the superintendent, and three large propeller-type fans were purchased.

The fans were brought in. The women were jubilant. For several days the fans were moved about in various positions until they were placed to the satisfaction of the group. The operators seemed completely satisfied with the results, and the relations between them and the foreman improved visibly.

The foreman, after this encouraging episode, decided that further meetings might also be profitable. He asked the operators if they would like to meet and discuss other aspects of the work situation. They were eager to do this. The meeting was held, and the discussion quickly centered on the speed of the hooks. The operators maintained that the time-study man had set them at an unreasonably fast speed and that they would never be able to reach the goal of filling enough of them to make a bonus.

The turning point of the discussion came when the group's leader frankly explained that the point wasn't that they couldn't work fast enough to keep up with the hooks, but that they couldn't work at the pace all day long. The foreman explored the point. The employees were unanimous in their opinion that they could keep up with the belt for short periods if they wanted to. But they didn't want to because if they showed they could do this for short periods they would be expected to do it all day long. The meeting ended with an unprecedented request: "Let us adjust the speed of the belt faster or slower depending on how we feel." The foreman agreed to discuss this with the superintendent and the engineers.

The reaction of the engineers to the suggestion was negative. However, after several meetings it was granted that there was some latitude within which variations in the speed of the hooks would not affect the finished product. After considerable argument with the engineers, it was agreed to try out the operators' idea.

With misgivings, the foreman had a control with a dial marked "low, medium, fast" installed at the booth of the group leader; she could now adjust the speed of the belt anywhere between the lower and upper limits that the engineers had set.

Discuss: What do you think the results of this action will be? Will production go up, down, or stay the same? Will satisfaction go up, down, or stay the same?

PART IV

The operators were delighted, and spent many lunch hours deciding how the speed of the belt should be varied from hour to hour throughout the day. Within a week the pattern had settled down to one in which the first half hour of the shift was run on what the operators called a medium speed (a dial setting slightly above the point marked "medium"). The next two and one-half hours were run at high speed; the half hour before lunch and the half hour after lunch were run at low speed. The rest of the afternoon was run at high speed with the exception of the last 45 minutes of the shift, which was run at medium.

In view of the operators' reports of satisfaction and ease in their work, it is interesting to note that the constant speed at which the engineers had originally set the belt was slightly below medium on the dial of the control that had been given the women. The average speed at which they were running the belt was on the high side of the dial. Few, if any empty hooks entered the oven, and inspection showed no increase of rejects from the paint room.

Production increased, and within 3 weeks (some 2 months before the scheduled ending of the learning bonus) the operators were operating at 30 to 50 percent above the level that had been expected under the original arrangement. Naturally their earnings were correspondingly higher than anticipated. They were collecting their base pay, a considerable piece-rate bonus, and the learning bonus that, it will be remembered, had been set to decrease with time and not as a function of current productivity. The operators were earning more now than many skilled workers in other parts of the plant.

Discuss: What do you think will be the final reaction of plant management? If *you* were part of Hovey and Beard's top management team, what would you recommend?

EXERCISE 36
ROLE OF "FRAN KUROWSKI," SUPERVISOR OF SUBASSEMBLY

Looks like the chickens are finally coming home to roost. This organization has been living on luck for 9 years now, and now they are about to find out what a bunch of amateur managers they really are. Not a one of them knows the first thing about inventory management, so here we are, stuck with a million defective gaskets and nothing we can do but try to rework them to where they will get by.

Donna Kelly made the first mistake in not ordering at the right time; then, when they got past Roy Conti's inspectors, ol' Kelly made it worse by not telling Bob Young what had happened. She asked Mike Cohen and me to rework them and try to slip them through inspection. Fat chance that Roy Conti would give us any help; if Roy wasn't so buddy-buddy with Young, he'd be pushing a broom in the shop instead of running Quality Control. But then Bob Young seems to like to surround himself with mediocrity—look at these other clowns.

One of these days (maybe today!) Donna Kelly or Roy Conti is going to make a mistake so obvious that even Bob Young will know the difference. When that happens, they might be looking for a bright MBA with some new ideas to run this show. Better play it cool and be ready when the time comes. Meanwhile, as long as I am in the clear, it will be fun to watch Donna and Roy try to talk their way out of this one.

motivator; intellectual ability

EXERCISE 14
EPITAPH INSURANCE COMPANY
ROLE FOR VICE-PRESIDENT, MARKETING

S. W. Cartwright founded the Epitaph Insurance Company ten years ago, and it has done well. The company has grown from an office in Cartwright's home to a large, highly efficient firm that underwrites $100 million in life insurance policies annually. Cartwright's secret to success was to provide exceptional service to policy holders while keeping costs to a minimum in order to compete with such firms as Farmers, Allstate, and State Farm. Cartwright is fiercely proud of Epitaph, and maintains tight personal control of those aspects of the business he regards as vital to the success of the firm. One of these is personnel costs. As far as you can tell, no executive has ever been given more than a five percent annual raise in the history of the firm. Your raises in the past averaged 4 1/2 percent per year.

Cartwright has been a good boss to work for: the kind of person who takes a personal if somewhat paternalistic interest in his key employees. He occasionally exhibits a rather spectacular temper, but most of the time he is reasonable, kindly, compassionate, and considerate. His entire life seems to be tied up in Epitaph, and he has no hobbies or outside interests.

You joined Epitaph seven years ago, and you have risen rapidly through the ranks from underwriter to Vice-President of Marketing. You have been responsible for several major accomplishments that have made Epitaph one of the most profitable firms in the industry, including launching a new line of group policies, revamping the sales force, initiating a national advertising campaign, and cutting sales costs by 7%. Although you have received several promotions, you have lately discovered that your salary of $120,000 per year lags, by a good 20%, behind what other Vice-Presidents of major insurance companies make. Moreover, the gap is widening because their annual raises average around 10%.

You could probably move to another company, but that would mean going through the laborious business of job hunting, moving your family to another city (you have strong roots here), and leaving a company you really enjoy working for. You feel a certain loyalty to Epitaph because the company has been good for you, and you believe strongly in the type of policies Epitaph specializes in. On the other hand, you feel strongly that you deserve a raise.

EXERCISE 8
ROLE OF "D. P. JONES," PRESIDENT

You have just asked C. J. Marshall to come to your office for a conference. Marshall is the production manager for the firm. In most respects, you regard Marshall as an ideal executive. C. J. is cost-conscious and efficient, intelligent, and displays great initiative and unquestionable integrity. Under Marshall's guidance, output has increased steadily. Moreover, C. J. is a personal friend.

You have called C. J. to your office to discuss a problem that has been bothering you for the last year and a half. Despite C. J.'s many virtues, there is one major problem: younger executives in the department refuse to work for Marshall. No production department manager will stay with the company more than six months. They complain that C. J. is authoritarian and never allows them to handle any problem on their own. Marshall is constantly looking over their shoulder and tells them exactly how to conduct even the most trivial aspects of their job.

You would like to appoint Marshall to the vacant position of executive vice-president of the company. At the same time, you are afraid that you may have to terminate Marshall for the good of the company. You have spoken to C. J. several times in the past about this problem, and you feel that you have made it clear that the promotion depends upon C. J.'s having trained a successor—someone to take over the production manager's job when C. J. is promoted.

Recently, so many bright young people have left the company, you are determined that C. J. must either reverse this trend or leave the company.

(You are a little behind in your paper work and you are not aware of any memoranda C. J. may have sent you lately. If C. J. mentions a memo, say that you have not had a chance to read it yet.)

At this point, C. J. enters your office in answer to your call.

EXERCISE 30

ROLE OF "JAMES VANCE," CORPORATE LEGAL COUNSEL

You would prefer not to fight the FDA on Vanatin as you are convinced in the long run that Booth will lose. The FDA has respected research data to support its claim. Other legal tactics are necessary.

You have been checking out various ways of handling the problem with friends. One suggestion has been sent to you by another Booth attorney. He has seen the Vanatin issue develop over the past few years, and he thinks that it would be possible legally to delay any action by the FDA. He suggests that Judge Kent of Kalamazoo (a man whom you know personally) would be willing to serve an injunction on the FDA. This would prohibit the FDA from banning Vanatin until such time as a formal hearing can be held. The results of the hearing, if unfavorable, could then be appealed. In effect, the case could be tied up in the courts for three to five years. A similar move in international courts would not be likely to have an impact on Vanatin sales for 5 to 10 years.

EXERCISE 19

MIDWEST AIRLINES

BACKGROUND

Campus Travel Agency is a major suburban travel agency, serving a wide variety of individual and corporate clients in Columbus, Ohio, near a large Midwestern University. Campus Travel offers the traditional range of services to its customers, including booking reservations, selling tickets and standard tour packages, designing vacation packages for individual and corporate customers, and organizing group-travel packages and discounts.

Midwest Airlines is a major U.S. carrier primarily serving the Midwestern United States and the Caribbean region.

PURCHASE OF TICKETS FOR A GROUP TOUR

Campus Travel has recently been contacted by a local company. The company has shown excellent corporate performance during the past year, and top management has decided to reward a number of its key employees with a four-day trip to the Caribbean island of St. Thomas. The local company has a long-standing business relationship with a major national hotel chain; hence, company representatives have already made hotel, meal, and rental car reservations on their own. They have contacted Campus Travel to make arrangements for airline tickets. The trip is scheduled to occur in late Spring, which is generally considered to be "off-season" for travel to St. Thomas.

CONFIDENTIAL ROLE FOR REPRESENTATIVE OF MIDWEST AIRLINES

As an account representative for Midwest Airlines, you are charged with the responsibility for negotiating ticket prices and commission rates with travel agencies and other large customers. Before the government deregulated the air travel industry in the early 1980s, all of these rates used to be fixed, but now they are all negotiable. In this negotiation, your objective is to sell as many seats as possible, while at the same time minimizing the commission paid to the travel agency.

Agencies normally make 7% commission on business travel and 8% on leisure; however, as a result of deregulation, it is not uncommon for airlines to negotiate an "override" commission up to a ceiling of 15% (7% over the regular commission for leisure travel, 8% over for business travel). While your employer has let it be known to travel agents that overrides are "negotiable," naturally you would prefer to minimize the amount of override paid.

You have just received a telephone call from an agent at Campus Travel in Columbus, Ohio. One of their corporate clients is planning a trip to St. Thomas for its employees, and has asked Campus Travel to arrange the airline tickets. The currently listed round-trip coach fare from Columbus to St. Thomas is $670, and the agency's normal commission on this fare would be 8% per ticket. However, the travel agent will most likely want to negotiate an override commission on this sale.

You are now about to negotiate the commission rate with a representative of Campus Travel Agency. On the table below, you will find a chart depicting the various percentage commission rates and the net revenue per ticket to the airline at each of those percentages. Your objective is to book the trip but minimize the commission you will pay, since this affects the airline's profit. Be prepared to have the travel agent push you for the best possible price. At the same time, do not agree to a deal that you find unacceptable. On this type of trip, you have normally not negotiated any override over 5 percent (13 percent total), and that was for a group of 100 passengers. You also sometimes "throw in" additional things to make the deal attractive, which don't cost the airline very much: free luggage tags (cost you about $.50/each), free alcoholic beverage coupons (cost the airlines about $.80/each), a separate room with refreshments for the group to gather at the airport, and, if necessary, one or two free tickets for the tour organizers, which are only given for large groups. You may offer these as you feel it is necessary to get a better deal on paying less commission to the agency. Finally, the Campus Travel agent may hint that a favorable price on this deal could lead to a lot more future business. However, travel agents say this all the time, and you have no real way of knowing whether this is true or not.

MIDWEST AIRLINES: TABLE OF REVENUE
On Each Ticket Sold (Round Trip)

% of Commission	$ Revenue Per Ticket
8%	$616.40
8.5	613.05
9	609.70
9.5	606.35
10	603.00
10.5	599.65
11	596.30
11.5	592.95
12	589.60
12.5	586.25
13	582.90
13.5	579.55
14	576.20
14.5	572.85
15	569.50

EXERCISE 43
ROLE FOR "WALTERS"

You work with Jackson and Stevenson on a job that requires three separate operations. Each of you works on each of the three operations by rotating positions once each hour. This makes the work more interesting, and you can always help out the others by running the job ahead in case one of you doesn't feel so good. It's all right to help out, because you get paid on a team piece-rate basis. You could actually earn more if Stevenson were a faster worker, but Stevenson is a good friend whom you would rather have in the group than someone else who might do a little bit more.

You find all three positions about equally desirable. They are all simple and purely routine. The monotony doesn't bother you much because you can talk, day-dream, and change your pace. By working slowly for a while and then fast, you can sort of set your pace to music you hum to yourself. Jackson and Stevenson like the idea of changing jobs and, even though Stevenson is slow on some positions, the changing around has its good points. You feel you get to a stopping place every time you change positions and this kind of takes the place of a rest pause.

Lately some kind of efficiency expert has been hanging around, standing some distance away with a stop-watch. The company could get more for its money if it put some of these people to work. You say to yourself, "I'd like to see one of them try and tell me how to do this job. I'd sure give them an earful." If Thompson, your supervisor doesn't get that expert out of the shop pretty soon, you're going to tell Thompson what you think of company spies being dragged in.

EXERCISE 20
ROLE FOR DR. JONES

This is a negotiation simulation. In this simulation, you will play the role of Dr. Jones, representing your company in the negotiations. Your opponent will play the role of Dr. Roland, representing his company in the negotiations.

The session leader will play the role of Mr. Cardoza. Once you have read these instructions, he will give you further information.

You are Dr. J. W. Jones, a biological research scientist employed by a pharmaceutical firm. You have recently developed a synthetic chemical useful for curing and pre-venting Rudosen. Rudosen is a disease contracted by pregnant women. If not caught in the first four weeks of pregnancy, the disease causes serious brain, eye, and ear damage to the unborn child. Recently there has been an outbreak of Rudosen in your state, and several thousand women have contracted the disease. You have found, with volunteer patients, that your recently developed synthetic serum cures Rudosen in its early stages. Unfortunately, the serum is made from the Ugli orange, which is a very rare fruit. Only a small quantity (approximately 4,000) of these oranges were produced last season. No additional Ugli oranges will be available until next season, which will be too late to cure the present Rudosen victims.

You've demonstrated that your synthetic serum is in no way harmful to pregnant women. Consequently, there are no side effects. The Food and Drug Administration has approved of the production and distribution of the serum as a cure for Rudosen. Unfortunately, the present outbreak was unexpected, and your firm had not planned on having the compound serum available for six months. Your firm holds the patent on the synthetic serum, and it is expected to be a highly profitable product when it is generally available to the public.

You have recently been informed on good evidence that Mr. R. H. Cardoza, a South American fruit exporter, is in possession of 3,000 Ugli oranges in good condition. If you could obtain the juice of all 3,000, you would be able to both cure present victims and provide sufficient inoculation for the remaining pregnant women in the state. No other state currently has a Rudosen threat.

You have recently been informed that Dr. P. W. Roland is also urgently seeking Ugli oranges and is also aware of Mr. Cardoza's possession of the 3,000 available. Dr. Roland is employed by a competing pharmaceutical firm. He has been working on biological warfare research for the past several years. There is a great deal of industrial espionage in the pharmaceutical industry. Over the past several years, Dr. Roland's firm and yours have sued each other several times for infringement of patent rights and espionage law violations.

You've been authorized by your firm to approach Mr. Cardoza to purchase 3,000 Ugli oranges. You have been told he will sell them to the highest bidder. Your firm has authorized you to bid as high as $250,000 to obtain the 3,000 available oranges.

EXERCISE 21
ROLE FOR BRENDA BENNETT

You are Brenda Bennett, Director of Personnel for the Levver Corporation. You have just taken over the position of Director of Personnel, and have inherited a lot of ill-will and dead weight. Past personnel practices have been less than perfect. However, the people running the summer intern program this year are some of the best that you have.

Several weeks ago, Harold Stokes, Vice-President of the Engineering Department, requested two summer interns. Jim Lexington, your subordinate and head of the intern program, informed Stokes that Engineering would have to wait because the hiring would not begin for at least two weeks. Then, without further consultation, Engineering went and hired two students themselves.

You are concerned for several reasons. First, the intern program comes out of your budget, and you will be damned if you will pay for two students not hired through your staff. Second, both students are white males—sons of friends of Joe Barnes, who is the manager of Electrical Engineering and reports to Stokes. You are concerned about the EEO implications. Third, the intern program involves some general overall orientation and development work before students are assigned to projects, and these students will be out of phase. Fourth, from your view there seem to be better applicants. Finally, you feel it is necessary to begin establishing Personnel's "territorial rights," and this is as good a time as any. You have a good case.

With these thoughts in mind you called Stokes, and he put you off before you had a chance to explain your concerns. Thus, you called your "boss" at this location, Samantha (Sam) Pinder to discuss the problem. You report primarily to the Vice-President of Human Resources of Levver, who works at another location. You have only an indirect ("dotted line") reporting relationship to Pinder. Nevertheless, since Pinder manages the office you work in, he or she has the responsibility to try to handle this problem.

You only had a chance to tell Pinder the basic problem on the telephone, but not any of the details. You know Pinder will expect some compromise from you, and you are willing to seek common ground—provided most of all of your five concerns are somehow alleviated.

EXERCISE 22

SCRIPT FOR SCENE 1 OF "THE STORM WINDOWS" (NOT TO BE READ BY "LEIGH BROWN")

The telephone installers are all seated about the lunch table. They have just finished eating their lunches. Dale Jones is reading a newspaper.

Frenchy: With weather like this, the baseball team will be able to get an early start on their workouts. I wonder what kind of a team we'll have this year?

Chris: I hear they have some pretty good boys coming along. Especially that Thompson kid. He's supposed to be a pretty hot pitcher.

C.J.: Yeah, and with weather like this, Chris ought to be able to get an early start on spring training.

Chris: What are you talking about? Spring training for what?

C.J.: Spring training for taking down storm windows and putting up screens and washing windows!

Frenchy: Good point, C.J., you have to be in pretty good shape to handle that job.

Dale: Don't worry about old Chris. Chris has got just about all the brains anybody needs to go along with the brawn that job takes. Chris is the best screen "putter upper" I've seen in all my years with the company.

Chris: Well, I've got some news for you wise guys. I'm not putting up *any* screens.

Dale: Don't tell me you've lost that old "desire" in there, buddy. We need you.

Frenchy: Good old Chris won't let us down. Who else besides Chris would be smart enough to handle the job?

Chris: Well, I've put those screens and storm windows up for the last time. From now on somebody else is going to put them up or they can stay where they are.

C.J.: You talk big while Brownie is down to the bank, but it wouldn't surprise me if Brownie notices what a nice day it is and, seeing as how we're not too busy, tells you to get going on the storm windows and screens.

Chris: Yeah? And if that happens, you know what I'm going to tell Brownie to do with those storm windows!

Dale: We know what you're going to tell Brownie to do with them. You're going to tell Brownie to have you remove them and cover them up, so you won't have to wash them in the fall.

Chris: I'm not working on those windows. And that's final!

EXERCISE 43
ROLE FOR "JACKSON"

You are one of three people on an assembly operation. Walters and Stevenson are your team-mates and you enjoy working with them. You get paid on a team basis, and you are making wages that are entirely satisfactory. Stevenson isn't quite as fast as Walters and you, but when you feel Stevenson is holding things up too much, each of you helps out.

The work is very monotonous. The saving thing about it is that every hour you all change positions. In this way you get to do all three operations. You are best on the no. 1 position, so when you get in that spot you turn out some extra work and thus make the job easier for Stevenson who follows you in that position.

You have been on this job for two years and have never run out of work. Apparently your group can make pretty good pay without running yourselves out of a job. Lately, however the company has had some of its methods experts hanging around. It looks like the company is trying to work out some speed-up methods. If they make these jobs any more simple, you won't be able to stand the monotony. Thompson, your supervisor, is a decent person and has never criticized your team's work.

EXERCISE 8
ROLE OF "C. J. MARSHALL," PRODUCTION MANAGER

You have just been notified that your boss, D. P. Jones, the president of the company wants to see you. As you walk to Jones' office, you wonder what D. P. wants to see you about. It might be one of two things.

Maybe D. P. is going to promote you to executive vice-president. Several times in the past year D. P. has seemed to be thinking along these lines. As D. P. put it, if you could prove yourself as production manager, the job would be yours. Well, your record certainly indicates you deserve the promotion! Productivity has never been higher, and you have guided the production organization to an effective solution of every problem which has come up. You are damn *proud* of your many accomplishments.

Or D. P. might want to respond to your memorandum of last week on recruitment of supervisors and trainees in production. You have recommended:

1. offering substantially higher salaries in hopes of attracting better quality personnel;
2. instituting a personnel testing program to weed out incompetent and irresponsible applicants.

Although you are very proud of your accomplishments in Production, the one problem that bothers you is the quality of lower and middle managers in your department. You have lost several of these people lately, but you were glad to see most of them go. Most of them were sullen, irresponsible, and not very bright. Most were already in jobs over their heads, and none had potential for promotion.

It has been a constant drain on your energies trying to improve the performance of these subordinates. No matter how much coaching, pleading, encouraging, and threatening you do, it seems as if you have to double check all of their work to be sure it is done correctly. Through your watchfulness you have corrected mistakes that would have cost the company many thousands of dollars.

D. P. Jones is an old personal friend, and you have enjoyed your working relationship.

At this point you enter D. P.'s office.

EXERCISE 30

ROLE OF "CYRUS BOOTH, M.D.," CHAIRMAN OF THE BOARD

As Chairman of the Board, it is your job to have the Board reach a decision on the two issues within the time allowed. You *must* reach a decision by the end of that time, since some of the Board members have to leave to catch a plane.

Your general philosophy about meetings is to try to allow for various sides of the issue to be discussed before a decision is reached. Legally speaking, a majority vote is required to reach a decision. You prefer a consensus decision, but a formal vote may be used at the end of the meeting if necessary. At the end of the meeting, you are to record the decision on the Group Decision Form (page 177) and hand it to the instructor.

Personally, while you are concerned about the effect that a cut in the sale of Vanatin will have on earnings, you are also concerned that this company, which you have led through its period of greatest growth, also maintain its image of honesty and integrity. This is more than just "corporate image." Booth must be devoted to the maintenance of health and prevention of sickness, for in the last analysis that is how you and your family will be judged in history. You will make every effort to ensure that the decision reached today reflects a unified consensus of the Board.

EXERCISE 34
ROLE FOR LEE NOLAN

SETTING
The scene takes place in the office of Jan Summers. Summers is President of the Bloomington Security Bank. A few years ago, Bloomington Security was acquired by the Filmore National Bank, a statewide bank holding company. Bloomington Security employs 67 people organized into four major departments: Operations, Loans, Accounting, and the newest department, Marketing. You (Lee Nolan) are Vice-President of Marketing.

The occasion of the upcoming meeting in Summers' office is to discuss the objectives of your department. Since being acquired by Filmore, Bloomington Security organizes managerial responsibilities according to a management-by-objectives system.

Jan Summers
Jan Summers is President and your immediate boss. Jan reports directly to Bob Evans, Filmore Vice-President for Regional Operations, whose office is located in Metropolis. Jan has a Bachelor's degree in business from the State University, and has attended several banking executive-development programs. After graduation, Jan worked several years for Filmore's major competitor in Metropolis, assuming a variety of responsibilities. Summers moved to Bloomington Security several years ago as Manager of Operations. When Sam Warhorse, the previous President, retired, Summers was promoted to President.

Summers has the reputation of being bright and energetic, and so far your relations have been cordial. However, you have also been told that the main reason Summers got the Presidency was that Jan had a reputation for being very tough and demanding of subordinates, perhaps even leaning on them too much at times. This discussion will be an important one for setting the tone of your relationship for the future.

Since Jan has become President, Bloomington Security has moved from fourth to second place in size among the 11 banks in the 120,000-population metropolitan area. However, the current economic slump is putting severe pressure on profits.

Lee Nolan (Your Role)
You are Vice-President of Marketing for the Bloomington Security Bank. After graduating from Metropolitan University with a degree in marketing, you spent a few years with a Metropolitan advertising agency. You came to Bloomington only six months ago to fill the newly created Marketing Vice-Presidency. This is your first formal evaluation with Summers.

Scenario for Lee Nolan

The date is April 10.

You enter the office of Jan Summers, your boss.

Jan establishes purpose of meeting—to go over objectives for your Marketing Department. These objectives were established late last December for the first quarter of the year.

The objectives are:

I. PERFORM A MARKET RESEARCH ANALYSIS ON THE DRIVE-IN BANK OPERATIONS; SUBMIT REPORT MARCH 10.

The analysis was completed on time. You believe that the quality of the report was good and that the information will be valuable for planning. You had some difficulty in meeting this deadline. Two of your key marketing research staff quit after Christmas. A second major problem was access to the bank's computer. The manager of the computer center did not seem to understand the necessity for the number of runs that you had to make and the importance of relatively quick turnaround, given your deadlines. For the most part, the computer center wanted to be able to do your work only when they had slack time—nights and weekends. You needed to have a much higher priority in getting your analysis done for this report and will have to get better cooperation in the future.

II. OBTAIN A NET INCREASE OF 50 CUSTOMERS PER MONTH IN A NEW LOAN-BY-MAIL SERVICE.

The service is designed to help checking account customers get loans by mail, which would automatically be credited to their checking accounts. You have found that your advertising program attracted an average of 55 customers per month. However, delays in processing loan applications in the loan department caused a number of these customers to overdraw their checking accounts, and many angrily quit doing business with the bank. Other customers were only attracted to the program for a short period of time. As a result, you only show a *net* increase of 34 customers per month over the first quarter.

III. PREPARE AND RELEASE A NEW SET OF RADIO "SPOT" ADVERTISEMENTS BY FEBRUARY 20.

Most of your efforts in the first quarter went toward doing the market research analysis and promoting the Certificate of Deposit program (Objective 4). Given that you were shorthanded, you did not have the staff to work on this as well. As a result, time slipped by and the radio spots did not get released until March 15.

IV. INCREASE CERTIFICATE OF DEPOSIT (CD) SALES BY 10% IN FEBRUARY AND MARCH BY OFFERING SMALL APPLIANCE "GIFTS" TO PURCHASERS.

This special promotion was one of your "pet" ideas. You were confident that it would work, even though your boss was skeptical that it would have an impact. The actual increases of CD purchases was 14% in February and 17% in March.

Summary

The objective of the upcoming meeting is to review and discuss your performance during this past quarter. Although you and Summers have not yet set performance goals for the next quarter, Summers may make general recommendations regarding specific goals to be set or the way in which goals performance will be monitored during the next quarter.

EXERCISE 30

ROLE FOR "ELMER B. PARKER," OMBUDSMAN AND CONSUMER ADVOCATE

You have been hired by the Board to represent the interests of the consumers of Booth's products, which in this case means both the doctors who prescribe the drugs and the patients who ultimately consume them. While you are aware that Vanatin makes life easier for some doctors, you feel that these doctors ought to know better. Any difficulty doctors might have if the drug were removed from the market is far outweighed by the deaths stemming from the use of the drug. Except for your vote, your ultimate weapon is to "blow the whistle" and give the Vanatin story to the newspapers. This would, however, cost you your job so that you could not continue to have the "moderating effect" that you have previously been able to exercise on Board decisions.

EXERCISE 43

ROLE FOR "STEVENSON"

You work with Jackson and Walters on an assembly job and get paid on a team piece-rate basis. The three of you work very well together and make a pretty good wage. Jackson and Walters like to make a little more than you think is necessary, but you go along with them and work as hard as you can so as to keep production up where they want it. They are good people and often help you out if you fall behind, so you feel it is only fair to try and go along with the pace they set.

The three of you exchange positions every hour. In this way you get to work all positions. You like the no. 2 position the best because it is easier. When you get in the no. 3 position you can't keep up and then you feel Thompson, the supervisor watching you. Sometimes Walters and Jackson slow down when you are on the no. 3 spot and then the supervisor seems satisfied.

Lately the methods expert has been hanging around watching the job. You wonder what's up. Can't they leave people alone who are doing all right?

EXERCISE 36
ROLE OF "BOB YOUNG," PRESIDENT

As you enter the meeting, you are thoroughly annoyed that delivery dates are not being met consistently—and that when they are met, there have been increasing customer complaints about defective parts. These problems are relatively new to Young Manufacturing, but you want to resolve them once and for all, today. If the company's reputation begins to slip, it could jeopardize the contracts you are negotiating for the firm.

You have not been able to determine what conditions have led to this problem, or who is responsible. In order to try to find out, you have called this meeting. You are determined to resolve the problem before you leave.

You have some private feelings about each of your subordinates, perceptions you have developed in day-to-day dealings over the years:

Roy Conti, Manager of Quality Control, is an old personal friend as well as a long-time business associate. He has served the firm faithfully since its founding. Lately, however, he seems preoccupied, as though something were bothering him and taking his mind from his work. About three years ago, he was pushing Donna Kelly to hire his son. But Kelly chose Fran Kurowski instead, which was a good move because Fran was obviously better qualified, what with an MBA and all.

Donna and Roy still work well together, so it doesn't appear that there are any lingering hard feelings.

Donna Kelly, Production Manager, is probably your most valuable employee. She deserves the lion's share of credit for Young Manufacturing's success; she knows production, keeps costs down, maintains quality, and trains bright young people. If the company expands, you are planning to make Donna a vice-president and eventually to put her on the Board of Directors.

Mike Cohen, Supervisor of Final Assembly, seems to be slipping lately. In the past, if there were a quality problem, Final Assembly could either rework the parts or at least catch the bad ones before they were shipped. Now, however, bad parts are getting through, and, on top of it all, deliveries are running behind schedule. But Mike's people aren't working overtime, and—when you strolled past the Final Assembly area yesterday—they didn't even look busy. People were horsing around as though they didn't have any work to do. You are wondering how long Kelly will wait before she speaks to Cohen.

Fran Kurowski, Supervisor of Subassembly, looks like a bright young supervisor with a great future at Young Manufacturing. Donna Kelly has brought Fran along well, and, although Fran occasionally makes the mistakes of impetuous youth, you are willing to put up with a few bad decisions if Fran continues to learn from them.

The meeting you are going to hold will last only 20 minutes. Begin by representing the problem to your subordinates. Be sure to get the situation straightened out before you have to leave to catch your plane. Find out what information your subordinates might have that is relevant to solving the problem before making any decisions or issuing any instructions.

EXERCISE 14
EPITAPH INSURANCE COMPANY
ROLE FOR S. W. CARTWRIGHT

You founded the Epitaph Insurance Company ten years ago, and it has done well. The company has grown from an office in your home to a large, highly efficient firm that underwrites $100 million in life insurance policies annually. Your secret to success has been to provide exceptional service to policy holders while keeping costs to a minimum in order to compete with such firms as Farmers, Allstate, and State Farm. You are fiercely proud of Epitaph and maintain tight personal control of those aspects of the business you regard as vital to the success of the firm. One of these is personnel costs. You feel that you more than make up for the fact that executive salary increases at Epitaph are a little below the industry average (5% maximum as compared to 10% or better for the industry) by the personal interest you take in the lives and careers of your key people. You have helped some bright people along the way to very successful careers at Epitaph. While most of them have repaid your kindness with genuine loyalty to the company, a couple of them have taken advantage of you—and that really makes you boil!

The Vice-President of Marketing joined Epitaph seven years ago and has risen rapidly through the ranks from underwriter to Vice-President with a current salary of $120,000 per year. The Vice-President could probably move to another company and improve on that, but what other company would provide the opportunities to advance so quickly? All the Vice-President needs to do to assure a very bright future at Epitaph is to continue to perform as in the past. Substantial contributions by the Vice-President have included launching a new line of group policies, revamping the sales force, initiating a national advertising campaign, and cutting sales costs by 7%.

EXERCISE 8
ROLE FOR "T. T. BURNS," AUDIT MANAGER

You feel that you get along fine with your assigned staff. You have always been pretty much of an idea person and apparently have the knack of passing on your enthusiasm to others assigned to your jobs. There is a lot of "we" feeling on your jobs because it is obvious that your jobs are the most productive, since there has been no significant overtime by your staff.

You believe in developing your staff and always give them strong recommendations. You feel you have gained the reputation of developing your staff because they frequently go out and get much better jobs. Since the attrition rate is high in your profession, you feel that the best way to stimulate morale is to develop new staff and demonstrate that a good person can get somewhere. Recently two of the outstanding audit seniors working for you have turned down outside offers after discussing their career opportunities with you. You are planning to recommend them for manager.

The other managers in your office do not have your enthusiasm. Some of them are dull and unimaginative. During your first year as manager you used to help them a lot, but you soon found that they leaned on you, and before long you were doing their work. There is a lot of pressure. You got your promotion by producing, and you don't intend to let other managers interfere. Since you no longer help the other managers, your production has gone up, but a couple of them seem a bit sore at you. One audit senior is a better person than most of them, and you'd love to see this senior made a manager. Since the firm has some dead wood in it, Stein ought to recognize this fact and assign them the more routine jobs. Then they wouldn't need your help, and you could concentrate your efforts on your jobs. At present, Stein passes out work pretty much as it comes in, in order. Because you are efficient, you get more than your share of these jobs, and you see no reason why the extra work shouldn't be in the form of "plums." You suggested to Stein that the more routine jobs be turned over to other managers.

You did one thing recently that has bothered you. One of your "routine" clients changed the date of an important meeting, and you should have told Stein about it, but it slipped your mind. Stein was out when you had it on your mind, and then you got involved in another client problem and forgot all about the matter. As a result, Stein had to make a special out-of-town trip and was quite sore about it. You told Stein you were sorry.

Today you have a performance appraisal interview with Stein. It shouldn't take very long, but it's nice to have the partner tell you about the job you are doing.

EXERCISE 34
ROLE FOR JAN SUMMERS

SETTING
The scene takes place in your office (Jan Summers). You are President of the Bloomington Security Bank. A few years ago, Bloomington Security was acquired by the Filmore National Bank, a statewide bank holding company. Bloomington Security employs 67 people organized into four major departments: Operations, Loans, Accounting, and the newest department, Marketing.

The occasion of the upcoming meeting in your office is to discuss the objectives of Lee Nolan, Marketing Vice-President. Since being acquired by Filmore, Bloomington Security organizes managerial responsibilities according to a management-by-objectives system.

Jan Summers (Your Role)
You (Jan Summers) are President of the Bloomington Security Bank and report directly to Bob Evans, Filmore Vice-President for Regional Operations, whose office is located in Metropolis. You have a Bachelor's degree in business from the State University,

and have attended several banking executive-development workshops over your career as a manager and executive. After graduation, you worked several years for Filmore's major competitor in Metropolis, holding a variety of responsibilities. You moved to Bloomington Security several years ago as Manager of Operations. When Sam Warhorse (the previous President) retired, you were promoted to President.

Since you have become President, Bloomington Security has moved from fourth to second place in size among the 11 banks in the 120,000-population metropolitan area. However, the current economic slump is putting severe pressure on profits. A key element in dealing with this problem is the performance of the new Marketing Department, headed by Lee Nolan.

Lee Nolan

Lee Nolan is Vice-President of Marketing for the Bloomington Security Bank. After graduating from Metropolitan University with a degree in marketing, Lee spent a few years with a Metropolitan advertising agency. Lee came to Bloomington only six months ago to fill the newly created Marketing Vice-Presidency. Since then, Nolan has developed several new marketing programs and analyses.

Lee Nolan has the reputation of being bright and energetic, and you think Lee can do the job. However, you have also been told that Nolan has the tendency to take the credit when things go right, but to blame others when things go wrong. This discussion will be an important one for setting the tone of your relationship for the future.

Scenario for Jan Summers

The date is April 10.

Lee Nolan, Manager of Marketing, enters your office.

You establish the purpose of the meeting—to go over Nolan's objectives. These objectives were established late last December for the first quarter of the year.

The objectives are:

I. PERFORM A MARKET RESEARCH ANALYSIS ON THE DRIVE-IN BANK OPERATIONS; SUBMIT REPORT MARCH 10.

The analysis was completed on time. The report was written well, and the analysis provided valuable information for planning. You have had some complaints from the manager of the bank's computer center that frequent and irregular requests from Lee for last-minute computer runs have been disruptive to the computer center and has required them to put operators on overtime. Ed Marsh, Computer Center Manager, says that there is plenty of computer time available during slack periods (particularly nights and weekends) if Nolan could schedule the work more efficiently. However, Nolan rushes in "at the last minute" and insists on immediate turnaround for the reports.

II. OBTAIN A NET INCREASE OF 50 CUSTOMERS PER MONTH IN A NEW LOAN-BY-MAIL SERVICE.

For the first three months, the net increase has been an average of 34 customers per month.

III. PREPARE AND RELEASE A NEW SET OF RADIO "SPOT" ADVERTISEMENTS BY FEBRUARY 20.

The spots were actually released on March 15.

IV. INCREASE CERTIFICATE OF DEPOSIT (CD) SALES BY 10% IN FEBRUARY AND MARCH BY OFFERING SMALL APPLIANCE "GIFTS" TO PURCHASERS.

You were skeptical this program would really work. You did not think people could still be lured into making bank deposits by offers of toaster ovens and hair dryers. Nolan fought you hard for it, however, and you agreed. The actual increases of CD purchases was 14% in February and 17% in March.

Summary

The objective of the upcoming meeting is to review and discuss your performance during this past quarter. Although you and Nolan have not yet set performance goals for the next quarter, you may want to make general or specific recommendations to Nolan regarding specific goals for the next quarter or the way Nolan's goals performance will be monitored and evaluated.

EXERCISE 30
ROLE OF "PHILIP BROWN," PRESIDENT, AND VICE CHAIRMAN OF THE BOARD

You were the President of Booth when Vanatin was introduced into the market. Naturally, you feel that Vanatin was, and still is, a good product both for Booth and for the people who have used it. If you didn't feel this way, you wouldn't have put Vanatin on the market in the first place. A cut in the sales of Vanatin would bring about managerial dislocations and threaten to reverse the strong growth of profits under your command. Furthermore, it has become increasingly difficult to develop new products because of extensive testing requirements of the FDA. On the other hand, as the chief executive officer of Booth, you are concerned about the kind of company that you lead.

EXERCISE 19
CAMPUS TRAVEL AGENCY

BACKGROUND

Campus Travel Agency is a major suburban travel agency, serving a wide variety of individual and corporate clients in Columbus, Ohio, near a large midwestern university. Campus Travel offers the traditional range of services to its customers, including booking reservations, selling tickets and standard tour packages, designing vacation packages for individual and corporate customers, and organizing group-travel packages and discounts.

Midwest Airlines is a major U.S. air carrier primarily serving the Midwestern United States and the Caribbean region.

PURCHASE OF TICKETS FOR A GROUP TOUR

Campus Travel has recently been contacted by a local company. The company has shown excellent corporate performance during the past year, and top management has decided to reward a number of its key employees with a four-day trip to the Caribbean island of St. Thomas. The local company has a long-standing business relationship with a major national hotel chain; hence, company representatives have already made hotel, meal, and rental car reservations on their own. They have contacted Campus Travel to make arrangements for airline tickets. The trip is scheduled to occur in late Spring, which is generally considered to be "off-season" for travel to St. Thomas.

CONFIDENTIAL ROLE FOR CAMPUS TRAVEL AGENCY

As a travel agent for Campus Travel Agency, you are charged with the responsibility for negotiating a deal with Midwest Airlines on round-trip tickets for a group charter between Columbus, Ohio, and the island of St. Thomas. In this role play, you will meet with a representative of Midwest Airlines, primarily to negotiate the amount of commission you will receive on these tickets.

You have investigated the published prices of all of the major airlines that fly between Columbus and St. Thomas. Large group bookings are attractive to airlines, particularly in the off-season. (It is now off-season in St. Thomas, which is mostly a winter and spring resort.) There has been little or no price competition on the route (for off-season rates) in several years, nor have there been any announcements that price changes are forthcoming.

The currently listed round-trip coach fare is $670.00. Your normal commission on this fare would be 8%, plus a possible additional supplement of up to 7% from the airlines. (Before the early 1980s, all of these rates were regulated by the government, but now they are highly negotiable.) Thus, for each booking to St. Thomas, you could make up to 15% commission on each ticket (approximately $100). The company has estimated that there will be approximately 50–70 passengers.

You have contacted several of the airlines that fly this route. One of them, Caribbean Airlines, was willing to offer you an additional 2% commission on top of your normal 8% commission if you would book the flight with them. (This discount is for each seat; no other bonuses were included.) After evaluating this rate, you decided to call Midwest Airlines to see if you could get a better price.

You are now about to negotiate the commission rate with a representative of Midwest Airlines. On the table below, you will find a chart depicting the various percentage commission rates, and the per-ticket profit to you at each of those percentages. Your objective is to obtain the tickets at the highest commission rate possible, since that will directly affect your profit from the sale (the tickets will be sold to customers at

$670.00 each regardless of volume). You must also decide whether you want to disclose the offer that you currently have from Caribbean Airlines. Be prepared to have the opposing representative push you for the best possible price for the airline. While the Midwest Airlines representative may hint that a favorable price on this deal could lead to considerations on other future business, airlines say this to you all the time, and you have no real way of knowing whether this is true or not.

CAMPUS TRAVEL AGENCY:
TABLE OF PROFITS
On Each Ticket Purchased from
Midwest Airlines (Round Trip)

% of Commission	$ Profit
8%	$ 53.60
8.5	56.95
9	63.65
9.5	60.30
10	67.00
10.5	70.35
11	73.70
11.5	77.05
12	80.40
12.5	83.75
13	87.10
13.5	90.45
14	93.80
14.5	97.15
15	100.50

EXERCISE 8
ROLE FOR "J. J. STEIN," AUDIT PARTNER

You have evaluated all the managers who report to you and during the next 2 weeks will interview each of them. You hope to use these interviews constructively to develop each person. Today you have arranged to interview T. T. Burns, one of the eight managers who report to you. Here is the information on Burns in your files.

T. T. Burns: 8 years with the firm, 2 years as manager, married, two children. Evaluation: Highly creative and original and exceptionally competent technically. On those audit engagements for which you are the partner in charge and Burns is the manager, T. T. has shown an exceptional ability to communicate client problems to you on a timely basis. Within the past 6 months you have given Burns extra work, which has been completed on schedule. As far as productivity and dependability are concerned, this person is your top manager.

Burns's cooperation with other managers in the office leaves much to be desired. Before being promoted to manager, Burns's originality and technical knowledge were available to your whole office. You are aware that other managers have sought Burns's help with certain client problems, but apparently Burns has offered no suggestions. Burns seems to imply that there is no time to help, or the response might be kidding and sarcasm, depending on that day's mood.

Furthermore, during the past 6 months Burns has questioned two of his assignments, saying they were routine. Burns stated a preference for more interesting work. You feel that you can't give Burns all of the interesting work and that if this continues, there will be trouble. You cannot play favorites and keep up morale in your office.

On one occasion, Burns forgot to inform you of a change in an important meeting date with a client. As a result, you only learned of the date change on the day before the meeting and had to make a special out-of-town trip in order to attend. Burns has expressed regret over this situation.

Burns's failure to cooperate has you worried for another reason. Although Burns's people are highly productive, there is more turnover among the staff of this group as compared to other managers. You have heard no complaints as yet, but you suspect that Burns may be treating staff in an arbitrary manner. Certainly if Burns talks up to you and other managers, what kind of behavior would this manager show toward subordinates? Apparently, the high productivity in this group is not due to high morale, but to Burns's ability to use staff to do the things for which they are best suited. This method will not fully develop the staff person's potential. You hope to discuss these matters with Burke in such a way as to recognize good points and at the same time correct some weaknesses.

EXERCISE 36

ROLE OF: "DONNA KELLY," PRODUCTION MANAGER

What a fix! If Bob Young finds out about that defective gasket material, it will be my head—and probably Mike's and Fran's, too. A million units of the crummy junk got through Receiving Inspection somehow, and 800,000 of them are still in the warehouse. I had a feeling that my changing our ordering procedure was a mistake, but I wanted to reduce our inventory carrying costs. I never should have tried to cover up the situation after we saw what happened.

But what else could we do? Roy has *always* been Bob's buddy. If I blame Roy, it would be like doing in the crown prince. Roy has been with Young since they started the company, and they are thick as thieves on weekends, too.

And I didn't have much choice, anyway. When that shipment came in, we were down to less than two days' supply in Subassembly. Fran Kurowski would have had to shut down completely if the lot had been rejected, and, at first it looked like Fran and Mike could adjust the assembly procedures fairly easily to compensate for the defects. A shutdown would have put Young Manufacturing out of business for good. Customers aren't going to wait for late deliveries anymore.

As it turned out, things were worse than I thought: Subassembly Inspection began to find defects and held up several lots before they could get to Mike Cohen for final rework. Normally, I would work something out with Roy, but I can't do that this time. Roy hates Fran's guts, and he is just waiting for a chance to see Fran hung. This would be the perfect setup to make Fran the scapegoat. Roy never got over Fran's getting the job that Roy's kid wanted.

Well, somehow I'm going to have to keep the plant operating. It would sure help if Bob Young would ease up the pressure for output and learn to rely on me the way he does on Roy Conti.

EXERCISE 20
ROLE FOR DR. ROLAND

This is a negotiation simulation. In this simulation, you will play the role of Dr. Roland, representing your company in the negotiations. Your opponent will play the role of Dr. Jones, representing his company in the negotiations.

The session leader will play the role of Mr. Cardoza. Once you have read these instructions, he will give you further information.

You are Dr. P. W. Roland. You work as a research biologist for a pharmaceutical firm. The firm is under contract with the government to do research on methods to combat enemy uses of biological warfare.

Recently several World War II experimental nerve-gas bombs were moved from the United States to a small island just off the U.S. coast in the Pacific. In the process of transporting them, two of the bombs developed a leak. The leak is presently controlled by government scientists, who believe that the gas will permeate the bomb chambers within two weeks. They know of no method of preventing the gas from getting into the atmosphere and spreading to other islands and very likely to the West Coast as well. If this occurs, it is likely that several thousand prople will incur serious brain damage or die.

You've developed a synthetic vapor that will neutralize the nerve gas it if is injected into the bomb chamber before the gas leaks out. The vapor is made with a chemical taken from the Ugli orange, a very rare fruit. Unfortunately, only 4,000 of these oranges were produced this season.

You've been informed on good evidence that a Mr. R. H. Cardoza, a fruit exporter in South America, is in possession of 3,000 UGLI oranges. The chemicals from the rinds of all 3,000 oranges would be sufficient to neutralize the gas if the vapor is developed and injected efficiently. You have also been informed that these oranges are in good condition.

You have also been informed that Dr. J. W. Jones is also urgently seeking purchase of Ugli oranges, and he is aware of Mr. Cardoza's possession of the 3,000 available. Dr. Jones works for a firm with which your firm is highly competitive. There is a great deal of industrial espionage in the pharmaceutical industry. Over the years, your firm and Dr. Jones's have sued each other several times for violations of industrial espionage laws and infringement of patent rights. Litigation on two suits is still in process.

The federal government has asked your firm for assistance. You've been authorized by your firm to approach Mr. Cardoza to purchase 3,000 Ugli oranges. You have been told he will sell them to the highest bidder. Your firm has authorized you to bid as high as $250,000 to obtain the oranges.

Before approaching Mr. Cardoza, you have decided to talk to Dr. Jones to influence him so that he will not prevent you from purchasing the oranges.

EXERCISE 30
ROLE OF "JACK BOOTH," SON OF CYRUS BOOTH, PRESIDENT, BOOTH ASSOCIATES, CONSULTANTS

You and your two brothers manage a consulting firm that does most of its business with the Booth Company. You and your brothers control approximately 20 percent of Booth stock, and you are concerned with the potential effects of the proposed ban on corporate earnings. You have become increasingly disturbed recently at the responsiveness of management to the demands of labor, community, and governmental groups. You feel that management is hired by the stockholders, and that management through the Board should be primarily responsive to them. In a well-publicized statement to *The Wall Street Journal,* you stated that "management seems to be more concerned with its own comfort and security than with corporate profits."

A suggestion was recently sent to you by the corporate lobbyist in Washington. He suggests that it might be possible to bring political pressure to bear on the FDA by securing the cooperation of the current Secretary of Health and Welfare. The Secretary might be willing to overrule a proposed ban by the FDA, since the ban would represent a major precedent that increases the power of the FDA at the expense of drug companies and their rights to free enterprise. Getting the Secretary to go along might require some major financial contributions to the President's reelection campaign.

EXERCISE 36
ROLE OF "ROY CONTI," MANAGER OF QUALITY CONTROL

That Fran Kurowski is the problem. Smart-alerk young college whiz kid, ambitious as hell, and sneaky to boot. If Bob Young had only listened to me a couple of years ago, he could have hired Al, my son, and had a faithful employee instead of this brash little sneak.

Kelly was leaning toward Al, but she was afraid of what Young would say if she hired Al, instead of Fran, just because Fran had an MBA and Al didn't. Donna Kelly is a good egg, generally able in her work, and thanks to the exceptional quality control process we operate, has earned a reputation for running a high-quality plant. Donna and I have gotten along well for several years, and I would like to maintain our good working relationship. We solve most of our quality problems on our level without involving Bob Young and that makes both of us look good.

But, dammit! Why doesn't Donna wake up to how Fran Kurowski is trying to push all the crappy work through inspection? I'd like to tell her, right now, but that would cause problems, too. It would embarrass Donna in front of Bob Young, and, to make things worse, Donna seems to think that Fran can do no wrong. Every time Fran is criticized, Donna blows her top and defends Fran to the bitter end.

EXERCISE 43

INSTRUCTIONS FOR OBSERVERS

1. Observe the leader's attitude toward change during the discussion in the office.
    a. Was the leader partial to the new method?
    b. Did the leader seem mainly interested in more production or in improving the job for the crew?
    c. To what extent was the leader considerate of the objections raised by crew? How did the leader react to their opposition?
    d. Did the leader defend the new method or argue for its acceptance? What effect did this have on progress in the discussion?
2. Make notes on conflict handling in the discussion.
    a. Did arguments develop?
    b. Was any crew member unusually stubborn?
    c. Did the crew members have their say?
    d. Did the leader really listen?
    e. What were the main points of differences?
3. Observe evidences of problem-solving behavior.
    a. What was agreed upon, if anything?
    b. In what respects was there a willingness to compromise?
    c. What did the group leader do to help or hinder a mutually acceptable work method?

EXERCISE 21

ROLE FOR HAROLD STOKES

You are Harold Stokes, Vice-President of Engineering for the Levver Corporation. Your electrical engineering group is far behind on a major power-station project. Much of the work on this project involves relatively simple drafting; it requires minimal engineering competence if supervised properly. However, it must be started right away. You and your staff decided that a few summer interns would be perfect for the job. Joe Barnes, the manager of Electrical Engineering who reports to you, tried to hire interns through the Personnel Intern program; however, he was told that hiring could not begin for at least another two weeks. Remembering your past skirmishes with the former Director of Personnel (Brenda Bennett's predecessor), you just told Barnes to go and hire two students, friends of Barnes's son in college, to get the job started.

You are aware that this action probably caused some trouble for Brenda Bennett, the new Director of Personnel. As a matter of fact, you are sure of this, because Bennett called Samantha (Sam) Pinder, the Executive Vice-President, to complain about your actions. Bennett is not necessarily like her predecessor and probably deserves a chance to prove herself. However, the two students are here now, and they appear to be working out well. When Bennett called in a real huff, you told her the students were here now and "that's that!" Moreover, some of the interns Personnel has sent in the past have been complete "duds." You feel that the placement officers in Personnel do not consult well enough with the host departments when making placement decisions.

Bennett's call to Pinder has prompted Pinder to get involved to try to resolve this conflict. Your reporting relationship at Levver is directly to the Senior Vice-President for R&D, who works at another location. You don't report directly to Pinder, and Bennett only reports to Pinder indirectly; nevertheless, Pinder has the most direct responsibility for trying to resolve this conflict.

You know that Pinder is going to expect some compromise, and you will accept anything reasonable—provided the two students stay and your department acquires more control over intern-hiring decisions.

EXERCISE 8

INSTRUCTIONS FOR OBSERVERS FOR BOTH ACCOUNTING AND MANUFACTURING ROLES

1. Observe the manner in which the boss begins the interview.
   a. What did the interviewer do, if anything, to create a permissive atmosphere?
   b. Did the interviewer state the purpose of the interview early in the session?
   c. Was the purpose of the interview stated clearly and concisely?
2. Observe how the interview was conducted.
   a. To what extent did the interviewer learn how the subordinate felt about the job in general?
   b. Did the interviewer use broad, general questions at the outset?
   c. Did the boss criticize the subordinate?
   d. Was the interviewer acceptant of the subordinate's feelings and ideas?
   e. Which one talked the most?
   f. What other things did the interviewer learn?
   g. Did the boss praise the subordinate?

3. Observe and evaluate the outcome of the interview.
   a. To what extent did the boss arrive at a fairer and more accurate evaluation of the subordinate as a result of the interview?
   b. What things did the boss do, if any, to motivate the subordinate to improve?
   c. Were relations better or worse after the interview? If worse, why did this occur?
   d. In what ways might the interviewer have done a better job?

EXERCISE 30
ROLE OF "JOHN C. GAUNTLETT, M.D.," BOARD OF DIRECTORS

You have been aware of the bad publicity on Vanatin. As a practicing physician, you have been prescribing Vanatin for years, and you have seen nothing wrong with it. At the last AMA meeting, other doctors to whom you have talked reported similar findings. Your thought is that an appeal should be sent to all doctors to protest the FDA, on the grounds that a ban by the FDA would be violating the physician's right to prescribe the most effective drugs. The fact that some of the doctors you talked to have been using Vanatin for 13 years indicates that it must have some value.

You have been a member of the Board of Directors for 8 years and own 150,000 shares of Booth stock.

EXERCISE 36
ROLE OF "MIKE COHEN," SUPERVISOR OF FINAL ASSEMBLY

Well, loyalty has always been my trademark. Maybe this time I've gone too far, though. Sure, I owe my job to Donna Kelly, and she has always been a good boss. She sure goofed on this one, though. Donna should have reordered the gaskets months and months ago. But no, to keep inventory costs down she waits 'til the last possible minute, orders a million units, and then gets defective material.

The plan to rework the material in Subassembly and Final Assembly seemed like the only sensible solution when Donna first proposed it. The problem turned out to be tougher than anyone had expected, but what the hell, it was better than letting the company go under. Too bad that Donna and Roy Conti were in no position to tell Young what had happened. Guess they want to save their jobs, too, though.

Can't blame them. It would sure be a terrible time for *me* to be out of work. Martha is going back into the hospital for another operation next week (hope they find it this time!), and the college tuition bills for the twins have to be paid by the end of the month. Besides, it isn't easy for a 50-year-old guy to find a job like this one.

Well, guess I'll just have to continue to try to talk Quality Control into releasing the defective lots of rework so that something gets out the door. Hope we can begin to catch up on some of those delivery promises. Bob Young looks mad, and there's no telling what he's likely to do next.

EXERCISE 27
SCORING SHEET FOR LEADERSHIP QUESTIONNAIRE

Transformational *Your Point(s)*	*Transactional* *Your Point(s)*
1. B _____	1. A _____
2. A _____	2. B _____
3. B _____	3. A _____
4. A _____	4. B _____
5. B _____	5. A _____
6. A _____	6. B _____
7. B _____	7. A _____
8. A _____	8. B _____
9. B _____	9. A _____
10. A _____	10. B _____

Column Totals: _____   _____

NOTE: The higher column total indicates that you agree more with, and see yourself as more like, either a transformational leader or a transactional leader.

EXERCISE 21
ROLE FOR SAMANTHA (SAM) PINDER

You are Samantha (Sam) Pinder, Executive Vice-President Finance and head of the main office staff for Levver Corporation. Brenda Bennett (Director of Personnel) and Harold Stokes (Vice-President Engineering) are about to arrive in your office. Brenda phoned you this morning saying that she had to speak with you about Harold's violation of the procedures for hiring summer interns. Apparently, the Engineering Department (at Harold's request) has been hiring interns directly into the Department without going through Personnel. You asked if she had tried to discuss the problem with Stokes and she said that she had.

Neither Bennett nor Stokes works for you directly. Bennett reports to the Vice President for Human Resources (who works in another office); Bennett has an indirect ("dotted line") reporting relationship to you because she works in the main office. Stokes reports to the Senior VP for Research and Development in a different part of the organization. Nevertheless, you are the most logical one to try to solve this problem. Both Stokes and Bennett are tough, but reasonable people. You feel that if you can bring the two of them together the problem can probably be settled. You called Harold to set up this meeting.